AF516622

Southeast Asian Crisis: An Economic Analysis

Southeast Asian Crisis: An Economic Analysis

Radhika Lobo

SERIALS PUBLICATIONS
New Delhi

First Published–2004

ISBN : 81-86771-35-2

Published by

Head Office : **SERIALS PUBLICATIONS**
4, B.S.S. Hall, Khyber Pass Market,
Civil Lines, Delhi–110054 (India)
Fax: 91-11-23272135
Phone: 23245225
e-mail: serials@satyam.net.in

Branch Office : 4830/24, Prahlad Street, Ansari Road,
Darya Ganj, New Delhi-110002 (India)

Dedicated to the memory of my parents

FOREWORD

Economic theory is a subset of political ideology. This belief has been challenged since the mid-eighties wherein international financial institutions – the International Monetary Fund and the World Bank have been the advocates of economic liberalism that has come to be acceptable to all developing countries irrespective of their ideological differences. Never before was an economic policy transplanted with such speed and embraced with such fervour.

As the success of "tiger economies" gained legitimacy, it was but a matter of time that the metaphor and nomenclature would be stretched. So, while Hong Kong, Taiwan, Singapore and South Korea were designated "Tiger economies", the emulators Indonesia, Malaysia and Thailand were christened "cub economies". This study focuses on the latter and their development strategies.

The author using the binoculars of hindsight while standing on the relative safe shores of India peeks across the sea into the life and times of the Southeast Asian Economies. Noting the gains and advantages that these economies initially recorded having the entire world in their thrall, the author also registers the subsequent dismal failures of these economies. The inferences and lessons India must draw are also identified.

The author has discussed this economic phenomenon in eight chapters. Chapter I is an introductory one. Chapter II gives a birds view of the literature available on the subject while indicating the further areas that this study will bring out. Chapter III discusses the development theories associated with the ASEAN 3. Chapter IV is a complete exposition of the policies and achievements of the Southeast Asian countries in their boom period while Chapter V dissects the causes of the subsequent doom. The dissention faced by the IMF in the post crisis period is the subject matter of the Chapter VI and the inferences to be drawn by India from the development experience of Southeast Asia is that of Chapter VII. Chapter VIII comprises of suggestions and conclusions.

In a nutshell, the author has encapsulated the boom and the doom in Southeast Asia and what part of the success or failure can be attributed to the international financial institutions. The study is appropriate in timing to end the debate as to whether India was justified in embracing liberalisation cautiously rather than by a big bang approach. The objective analysis of the role played by the international financial institutions in the policy making of a developing country approaching it for assistance will be of immense use to all students who undertake studies in the subject. This academic work is meritorious and will form a unique niche on the bookshelf of related literature.

Vinayak Deshpande
Reader, Department of Economics, Nagpur University, Nagpur

PREFACE

The fast paced growth of the Southeast Asian economies of Indonesia, Malaysia and Thailand prompted the international community to dub them as miracle economies. These economies performed well on all counts be it the growth of gross domestic product, the saving and investment rate, the exports growth rate or the extent of foreign capital inflows. They had adopted policies of openness in trade and capital inflows to achieve miraculous results. Such policies came to be touted as worthy of emulation and were advocated for adoption in other developing countries too by the bastions of openness – the IMF and the WB.

With the occurrence of the Asian Crisis starting July 1995 the policies that were hitherto branded as the formulae for success suddenly became taboo and were viewed with much scepticism. The IMF came to the rescue of its protégées in the post crisis period with a standard package of financial aid and policy recommendation. The 'cookie cutter' solutions received severe flak and so did the IMF for its role in the pre and post crisis period. Apparently, economic tutelage was far more dangerous to a nation than political enslavement.

The IMF has been rethinking the efficacy of the open economic policies as a panacea for all economic ailments. It has now begun to insist on building of appropriate institutions and prudential norms to support the policies of openness. The developing countries like India have learnt many lessons from the experiences of the Southeast Asian counties especially relating to capital account convertibility, which was halted till the economy was better prepared.

I would like to acknowledge and place on record my gratitude to Dr Vinayak Deshpande for his enormous inputs and suggestions in the preparation of this book. The role of my family, friends and well-wishers in encouraging me to publish this book has also been tremendous and thanks worthy. Finally, I would also like to thank Serials Publications for the printing and publishing of the book.

Radhika Lobo

Contents

Title	Page No.
Foreword	*vii*
Preface	*ix*
List of Tables, Charts and Graphs	*xiii-xix*
Chapter 1: Introduction.	1-18
Background of Southeast Asia	
A Brief History of International Financial Institutions	
Objectives, Hypotheses and Methodology of Study	
Chapter 2: Review of Literature.	19-31
Studies relating to the East Asian region as a whole	
Countrywise studies	
Studies on Financial Crisis in Asia	
Chapter 3: Perspectives of Development in Southeast Asia	32-122
Miracle Theories	
Reasons for Adopting Open Economic Policies	
Open Economic Policies in Southeast Asia.	
Features of Southeast Asian Development Experience	
Responsiveness of GDP to its Determinants	
Chapter 4: Development Experience of Southeast Asia (1986-95).	123-250
Development experience of Indonesia	
Development experience of Malaysia	
Development experience of Thailand	
Chapter 5: The Asian Currency Crisis.	251-305
Types of Economic Crises.	
Chronology of Crisis is Southeast Asia.	
Factors Responsible for the Crisis.	

Chapter 6: Crisis Management and the Call for a NIFO. 306-375
Measures Adopted to Address the Issue of Economic Crisis
Critical Review of the Role of the IMF in Indonesia and Thailand
Call for a New International Financial Order
Present Scenario of the ASEAN 3

Chapter 7: Development Experience of SEA and Lessons for India. 376-393
The Indian Economic Scenario and Why India Escaped the Contagion.
Impact of Crisis on India.
Outlook for the Future.

Chapter 8: Conclusions and Suggestions 394-399

Annexure A 400-408

Annexure B 409-410

Bibliography 411-416

List of Tables, Charts and Graphs

Chapter 3

List of Tables

Table No	Title	Page No
3.1	Total Factor Productivity	77
3.2	Real Interest Rates	78
3.3	Inflation Rates	79
3.4	Inflation and GDP Growth Rates	80
3.5	Overall Budget Deficit / Surplus	81
3.6	Government Expenditure as % of GDP	82
3.7	Government Revenue as % of GDP	83
3.8	EDT / GNP % and EDT / XGS %	84
3.9	Tariff and Non-Tariff Measures in East Asia And Latin America	85
3.10	Growth Rate of Exports	86
3.11	Exports of Goods & Services as % of GDP	87
3.12	Imports of Goods & Services as % of GDP	87
3.13	Forex Reserves	88
3.14	Net FDI Inflows as % of GDP	89
3.15	FDI as Proportion of Investment	90
3.16	Gross Secondary School Enrollment Ratio as % Of Expenditure / Income	91
3.17	Annual Labour Force Employed in Manufacturing Sector	90
3.18	Annual Imports of Machines & Equipments as % Of Total Imports	92
3.19	Annual Increase in MVA as % of GDP	92
3.20a	Ratio of Deposits to Total Money Stock–Indonesia	93
3.20b	Ratio of Deposits to Total Money Stock – Malaysia	94
3.20c	Ratio of Deposits to Total Money Stock – Thailand	95

3.21a	Government Consumption as % of GDP – Indonesia	96
3.21b	Government Consumption as % of GDP – Malaysia	97
3.21c	Government Consumption as % of GDP – Thailand	98
3.22a	GDI & GDS as % of GDP – Indonesia	99
3.22b	GDI & GDS as % of GDP – Malaysia	100
3.22c	GDI & GDS as % of GDP – Thailand	101
3.23	Manufacturing Exports as % of Total Exports	102
3.24	Commodity Structure of Exports	103
3.25	Correlation Coefficients- Indonesia	104
3.26	Correlation Coefficients- Malaysia	105
3.27	Correlation Coefficients- Thailand	106
3.28	Regression Coefficients- Indonesia	107
3.29	Regression Coefficients- Malaysia	108
3.30	Regression Coefficients- Thailand	109

List of Charts

Chart No	Title	Page No
3.1	Functional Growth Framework	111
3.2	Economic System Approach	112
3.3	Trade Regimes	113
3.4	Degree of Financial Integration	113
3.5	Financial Sector Liberalisation	114
3.6	Financial Institutions- Sources and Uses of Funds-Indonesia	117
3.7	Financial Institutions- Sources and Uses of Funds- Malaysia	118
3.8	Financial Institutions- Sources and Uses of Funds- Thailand	119
3.9	Industrial Policy Regimes	119

List of Graphs

Graph No	Title	Page No
3.A	Flying Geese Pattern	110
3.B	Real Interest Rates	78
3.C	Inflation Rates	79
3.D	Inflation and GDP	80
3.E	Budget Deficit / Surplus	81
3.F	Government Expenditure as % of GDP	82
3.G	Government Revenue as % of GDP	83
3.H	Growth Rate of Exports	86
3.I	FDI / GDP %	89
3.J	FDI as proportion of Investment	90
3.K	Manufacturing Exports as % of Total Exports	102

Chapter 4

List of Tables

Table No	Title	Page No
4.I.1	Basic Economic and Social Indicators of Development in Indonesia	151
4.I.2	Indonesia's Central Government Revenue	152
4.I.3	Central government's Receipts and Expenditure, Indonesia	153
4.I.4	Exchange Rates and Interest Rates	154
4.I.5	Changes in Tariff Schedule	155
4.I.6	Changes in NTB Coverage Over the Reform Period	155
4.I.7	Growth of Manufacturing Output	156
4.I.8	Foreign Investments Approvals by Sector	157
4.I.9	Foreign Investments Approvals by Country	158
4.M.1	Basic Economic and Social Indicators of Development in Malaysia	189

4.M.2	Exchange Rates and Interest Rates	190
4.M.3	Structure of Manufactured Exports	191
4.M.4	Foreign Investment in Malaysia by Industry	192
4.M.5	Foreign Investment by Country Source	193
4.M.6	Education Indicators in Malaysia	194
4.T.1	Basic Economic and Social Indicators of Development in Thailand	228
4.T.2	Exchange Rates and Interest Rates	229
4.T.3	Expenditure on Education	229
4.T.4	Import Tariff Protection in Selected Countries	230
4.T.5	Export Performance by SITC	231
4.T.6	Composition of Gross Exports by Factor Intensity	232
4.T.7	Share of FDI in Thailand by Principal Investors	232

List of Charts

Chart No	Title	Page No
4.I.1	Indonesia: Summary of Economic Reforms, 1983-90	159
4.I.2	Chronology of Financial Sector Reforms, 1983-91	161
4.T.1	Actions taken Before Submitting LDP for SAL I	233
4.T.2	Specific Actions for SAL I	236
4.T.3	Specific Actions for SAL II	240
4.T.4	Incentives of the Thai Board of Investments	245

List of Graphs

Graph No	Title	Page No
4.I.A	Increase in Indonesia's Central Government Revenue	152
4.I.B	Selected Non-Oil Exports From Indonesia (1986-97)	162

Chapter 5

List of Tables

Table No	Title	Page No
5.1	Data on Macroeconomic Fundamentals	283
5.2	Incentive for Foreign Borrowing	284
5.3	Credit Money & Foreign Liabilities	285
5.4	Ratio Between Growth Rates of Credit to GDP	286
5.5	Capital Inflows in the Southeast Asian Countries	287
5.6	Selected Indicators of Corporate Financing	288
5.7	Lending to Property Sector	288
5.8	Estimates of Actual and Peak Non-performing Bank Loans in Southeast Asian Economies	289
5.9	Financial Strength Rating	289
5.10	Stock of Debt owed to Foreign Private Creditors Indicating Maturity Mismatch	290
5.11	Currency Mismatches	290
5.12	Asian Exchange Rate Baskets	291
5.13	External Sector Problems	291
5.14	Real Effective Exchange Rates	292
5.15	Exports by Destination and Imports by Origin 1996	292
5.16	Southeast Asian Export Growths	293
5.17	Hourly Labour Costs in Apparel Manufacture	293
5.18	Bilateral Trade Shares with Thailand	294
5.19	Currency Depreciation	295
5.20	Crisis and Economic Indicators, 1996-1997	297

List of Charts

Chart No.	Title	Page No
5.1	Currency Crisis Starting Dates	298
5.2	Process Leading to the Crisis	300
5.3	Contagion Factors	301

List of Graphs

Graph No	Title	Page No
5.A	Weakness in the Financial System	302
5.B	Return on Average Equity for Banks	303
5.C	Currency Depreciation	295-296

Chapter 6

List of Tables

Table No	Title	Page No
6.1	Packages of Official Support for Crisis Countries	360
6.2	Growth Inflation and Current Account Balances	361
6.3	Fiscal Balance and Public Debt	361

List of Charts

Chart No	Title	Page No
6.1	Chronological Highlights of Financial Assistance To Indonesia and Thailand	362
6.2a	Indonesia's Transaction with the Fund	363
6.2b	Indonesia's Position with the Fund	364
6.3a	Malaysia's Transaction with the Fund	365
6.3b	Malaysia's Position with the Fund	366
6.4a	Thailand's Transaction with the Fund	367
6.4b	Thailand's Position with the Fund	368
6.5	Financial Restructuring Measures agreed upon with IMF	369
6.6	Key Variables of East Asian Economies	370
6.7	IMF Prescription- East Asian Dilemma	371

Chapter 7

List of Tables

Table No	Title	Page No
7.1	Key Macro Economic Variables for India	390
7.2	External Sector Indicators for India	391
7.3	Foreign Inflows	391
7.4	Exchange Rate & Stock Market Index	392
7.5	Stock Market Index in US dollars	392
7.6	Direction of Trade	392

Chapter 1

Introduction

The winds of economic change that swept over the three Southeast Asian economies of Indonesia, Malaysia and Thailand is the single most important event of the decade beginning in the mid 1980s and continuing in to the mid 1990s. This was an euphoric decade during which the gross domestic product grew at a fast pace, exports surged, inflation was maintained at moderate/low rates, foreign investment inflows boomed and, in general, the economies were very buoyant. The economic models pursued by these countries were revered and touted as worthy of emulation for the other developing countries. The World Bank (WB), the International Monetary Fund (IMF), the United Nations Development Programme (UNDP) and other related international organizations all praised and promoted the macroeconomic management of these countries and termed them as 'miracle economies'. Their central banks epitomised financial soundness and this too was an example for the rest of the developing world.

The economic policies followed by these countries focussed on macroeconomic stability and liberalisation in trade and investment. The openness in trade and investment gave a fillip to the export sector and encouraged the inflows of foreign direct investment (FDI). These economies became closely integrated due to these policies and their geographical proximity. Consequently there was a contagion wherein each one benefited through the growth of the other.

By 1995 the first signs of trouble could be seen on the export horizon. There was a decline in the growth rate of exports. Suspicions were aired that there had been over-investment in the non-tradable property and financial sector. This led to the creation of a 'bubble economy'. Another area of concern was related to the change in the pattern of capital inflows. The FDI inflows were being replaced by short term banking inflows. Such vulnerability ultimately snowballed into a full-fledged financial crisis.

The IMF, prime endorser of these countries' policies, stepped in to perform a rescue act following the pleas of its protégées. It offered policy advice and financial aid to Indonesia and Thailand. Malaysia however, did not approach the IMF for financial aid but it did receive some policy advice.

Many mainstream economists have ridiculed the IMF's solutions to the crisis. They termed them as 'cookie-cutter' solutions. A more customised one was needed to tackle the current problem. The solutions aggravated the crisis rather than alleviate it.

These events made the world rethink the efficacy of the models of development pursued by the Southeast Asian economies hitherto. The economies were now accused of having pursued excessive liberalization in the trade and financial sector on the recommendation of the IMF and the WB. In other words the crisis was said to have been caused by such policies. Thus, the international financial institutions were the villains of the piece and were crucified for their roles in both, the pre and post crisis periods.

In the light of the above sequence of events a shower of pertinent questions come up.

- What was the nature of development that occurred in these 'miracle economies'?
- What policies did they follow? To what extent were the international financial institutions involved in the policy making process?
- Did they push the openness and liberalization agenda too far and was this the main cause of the crisis?
- How far can the international financial institutions be blamed for it?
- Is there an alternative to the existing financial order?

This study attempts to find answers to these questions and analyse other related aspects.

Background of Southeast Asia

A brief sketch of Southeast Asia is presented below as a prelude to better understanding of the development experience of these countries.

Geographical Features

The emergence of Southeast Asia as a major sub-division of the world economy can be traced to the World War II period. During the World War II, the term Southeast Asia was used to designate the theatre of war commanded by Lord Louis Mountbatten and it again gained wide currency during the Vietnam War of the 1960s and 1970s[1]. The British activity 'East of Suez' centred around Singapore and Malaya. These territories, especially Singapore came to be regarded in economic, strategic and diplomatic terms as the pivot of a 'Southeast Asian region'[2]. Subsequently the raw materials and markets of this region figured in American strategic thinking and policy statements too.

Southeast Asia may be defined as the region south of China and east of India. Prior to World War II, myriad terms were used to describe this area like 'Further India', 'the Far Eastern Tropics', 'Indo-China' and so on. In other words, the region connoted merely an eastward extension of India, or a tropical appendage to the Far East or merely the land between India and China. In geographical terms it is a conglomeration of islands and peninsulas spread over an area approximately half a million square miles housing one-third of a billion people. This region is bordered on the north by China, on the east by the South Pacific Ocean, on the south by the Indian Ocean, and on the west by the Indian Ocean, the Bay of Bengal and the Indian subcontinent. The countries comprising Southeast Asia are Myanmar (Burma), the Kingdom of Thailand, the Lao People's Democratic Republic, the People's Republic of Kampuchea (Cambodia), the Socialist Republic of Vietnam, the Federation of Malaysia, the Sultanate of Brunei and the Republic of Indonesia, Singapore and the Philippines.

The region stretches over more than 35 degrees of latitude and nearly 50 degrees of longitude. The geographical character varies widely. There are deltas, coastal mountain ridges, and river valleys. The river valleys are generally fertile zones of agriculture while mountain ridges are usually political boundaries. Although Southeast Asia lies in the tropical zone, there is no uniformity in vegetation. It extends from the dry zone of Burma to snow-covered mountains of West New Guinea, from the rolling pastoral grasslands of Northwestern Vietnam to the steep terraced lands of the Philippine Island.

Due to differences in geographical structure and climatic conditions, the population of Southeast Asia is not uniformly distributed over the region. Certain areas such as the Red River of Northern Vietnam, the Irrawaddy in Burma, the Menam Chao Phrya in Thailand and the fertile plains of Java are highly populated. On the other hand the island of Borneo is largely under-populated. In modern times, the fast growing cities of Bangkok, Jakarta, and Saigon are magnets for rural inhabitants who migrate here with the hope of personal advancement and therefore these cities are highly populous. Such migration has thrown up the usual problems of unemployment, overcrowding and inadequate civil amenities. Among the Southeast Asian countries Indonesia as a whole is the most populated country.

Language and Religion

The population of all Southeast Asian countries consists of a mixed group and these countries are truly multinational. There are basically three large ethnic groups. The Malayo-Polynesian people make up more than half the region's population. A majority of them are in Indonesia, Philippines and Malaysia. The second largest ethnic group are the Sino-Tibetan people living in Burma, Thailand, Vietnam and Laos. The third largest language group are the Mon-Khmer races of the Indochina peninsula. Most of them are the Khmers who make up the majority of the population in Cambodia.

In all countries of the region some non-indigenous nationalities, primarily, Chinese and Indians exist. It is generally believed that the cultural traditions of this region have been shaped by these nationalities. Barring Vietnam, where the Chinese influence was greater, the Indian cultural influence reigned supreme in all the other Southeast Asian countries. Obviously, Indian culture was more acceptable to them.

The situation has undergone a change in the present day because of the presence of a larger Chinese population, predominantly in Singapore, Malaysia and Thailand. A considerable proportion of them now form the working class, traders, industrialists, bankers and moneylenders. In other words, they make up a large part of the wealthy bourgeoisie.

The ethnic diversity naturally endows the region with a varied religious character. Malaysia and Indonesia have large Islamic populations. Laos, Thailand, Burma and Cambodia are predominantly Buddhist. Christianity is widespread in Philippines due to the Spanish influence. In Vietnam, the Buddhist-Confucianism values are seen due to the Chinese influence.[3] Hinduism is found in Singapore and Thailand. As mentioned earlier, historically there has been a strong Indian influence in Southeast Asia and thus the genesis of Hinduism in this region is not difficult to trace.

Political and Economic History

The peoples of Southeast Asia have a long and eventful history. A brief discussion of the same will bring out the rich cultural heritage of these nations, the impact of colonialism, the nature of international trade they indulged in and the economic development that took place therein

The 'Classical History' of Southeast Asia can be traced to the ninth century AD. The known states during that period were Java, Srivijaya, Cambodia, Vietnam and Burma.

Java was to the west of the Indonesian archipelago. It was well known for its architecturally unique temples and shrines. These are evidence of the abundant artistic ability that existed in those days.

Further west and to the north of the island of Sumatra was the famous maritime trading empire of Srivijaya, strategically placed on the Malacca straits, which was an Indonesian-Malay state. This state rose to prominence due to its close political relations with China and the international trade that existed between China and India (in some cases beyond India, stretching up to Persia). Goods traded included products of medicinal quality, silks, porcelain, lacquers, etc. Srivijaya came to exert control over all significant trade on the seas in the western section of the Indonesian archipelago and between that region of the archipelago and Southern China. Gradually, by the fourteenth century the maritime power passed on to Malacca. With the opening of the Suez Canal in the 19th century Singapore inherited this mantle of prominence.

In the mainland, was the famous state of Cambodia. The kings in this Angkor region (Khmer of Angkor) from the 9th century began to develop techniques for mastering the environment that eventually provided the economic base for military expansion and a programme of great temple building[4]. Angkorian Cambodia, however, was not essentially a trading state but was a notable combination of human genius, religious belief and geographical location. The Cambodian empire extended from its base in Angkor to sections of modern Thailand, Laos and Vietnam. Temples great and small (including the famous Angkor Wat) were built throughout the region. These temples are indicative of the technological capability of those times. As the Angkorian Empire was rich in culture so also was it in wealth.

Thai people brought about the downfall of this empire sometime by the fifteenth century. From then on the Thais made slow progress to take control over much of the region, which now comprises Thailand.

During the ninth century there was no separate Vietnamese state since Imperial China occupied the Red river delta region and administered it as a Chinese province. The state of Vietnam gained independence from China in 939 AD. At that time this independence did not threaten the Angkorian Empire but modern Vietnam includes many areas of the Angkorian Empire suggesting that at a later time such regions were annexed into Vietnam.

In Burma a great city had been built at Pagan between the eleventh and thirteenth centuries. The Mongols who ruled over China invaded it in 1287 AD. Much later Burmese leaders made efforts to found a stable state.

Formation of Contemporary Southeast Asia and its Colonialisation.

By the fifteenth century a new pattern of states emerged in all of Southeast Asia. Many of today's modern states with their present names had been formed (Thailand was then known as Siam). The history of contemporary Southeast Asia begins with the Portuguese storming the trading centre of Malacca in 1511; capturing this strategic, economic and political water route between the Indian Ocean and the Far East. Thus, dawned the European era in Southeast Asia.

Over the next few centuries, all the states, barring Thailand, became colonies ruled by American and European powers. Indonesia was a Dutch colony. The Spaniards first, and later the Americans ruled over the Philippines. While the British were the imperialist powers in Malay and Burma, the French were in occupation of Indochina (Vietnam, Laos & Cambodia taken together).

These Western advances called into question the old values and ways of governance. Political boundaries became more precisely demarcated. In fact, the region now called Laos came into existence only as a result of colonization. Following this, an economic transformation began in the seventeenth century, which was amply evident in the nineteenth and twentieth centuries.

Trade in the Colonial Period

Economic activity that took place in traditional times (in Srivijaya & Angkor) was very different from that during the European period. In the latter period the sole beneficiaries of the economic activity were the imperial powers and whatever benefits accrued to the locals were purely incidental. Though these foreigners came to this region with the sole intention of amassing wealth; by the early 20th century a lot of development occurred in colonial Southeast Asia.

The main attraction of Southeast Asia was its ***spice*** trade. During the sixteenth and seventeenth centuries, the Portuguese and the Dutch acquired a monopoly over the spice trade at the cost of impoverishing the local peasants. They went to the extent of destroying spice trees outside certain regions so that their monopoly and consequent high prices could be maintained. Gradually they began exerting control over production and marketing of agricultural crops; especially coffee. Rice was the main crop grown in this region but only at the subsistence level.

With the beginning of industrialisation during the nineteenth century these colonies were viewed as sources of cheap raw material. These raw materials were exported to the colonizing country and after being processed into finished goods were imported back into the colony. Some of these raw materials exported were tin from Malaysia and Indonesia, needed for tinplate and bearings; rubber from whole of Southeast Asia to meet multiple needs ranging from motor car tyres to surgical equipment, and copra from Malaysia needed for the soap industry.

As mentioned earlier, rice was grown for subsistence purposes only. But in the nineteenth century, with the demand for it increasing in industrial countries (for consumption purposes), it was now grown on a large scale and became an important item of export. In fact, rice exports provided a stimulus to the rapid expansion and development of Southeast Asia. Other items of export included coffee , tobacco and sugar.

With the development of the export sector a certain amount of economic transformation took place in these economies; helped along by other aspects like the development of infrastructure, roads, canals, rail systems and other modern communication systems.

The barter economy gave way to a new cash economy. The state city of Singapore (then part of Malay) became an entrepot for the Southeast Asian region as a whole, especially after the opening of the Suez Canal in 1869.

Struggle for Independence

In the post World War II period almost all the Southeast Asian countries became independent. Though the initial resistance movements against colonial powers had started between 1870-1900, these were speedily crushed. In the ensuing years there was a consolidation of the colonial empires. Western education and ideas were introduced. The basic motive behind this was to have the native elite participate in the government and thereby strengthen it more.

The anti-colonial wave was resurrected during World War II and a few years prior to it. In Burma and Vietnam it was more prominent and evident whereas in the Dutch East Indies it was much more subtle as it was forged through creation of a national language, national literature and local run schools and colleges.

In the autumn of 1940 Japan established a foothold in Indochina and by December 1941 it began a series of assaults on the rest of Southeast Asia-gradually occupying the region. Japan was now the new imperialist power.

The Southeast Asian people guided by progressive forces, among which Communists played an important role, launched a battle against these new imperialist oppressors. A number of liberation armies and patriotic forces were formed. Gradually each nation attained independence from Japanese occupation, leading to the creation of sovereign states with Burma and Philippines in 1943, and later Vietnam, Laos, Cambodia. Indonesia became independent in 1945 towards the end of World War II. Malaya was liberated as late as 1957 and known as the Federation of Malaysia, consisting of Malaya, Singapore and North Kalimantan. Later in 1965 Singapore withdrew from the Federation and became an independent state.

Post-World War II period

Since the 1940s Southeast Asia has been divided along ideological lines and has been part of the Cold War too. There is a pronounced pro and anti western segregation. As mentioned earlier, the pro-capitalist Southeast Asia consists of Indonesia, Malaysia, Thailand, Singapore and Philippines. The countries of Laos, Cambodia and Vietnam adopted a communist ideology. The pro-capitalist Southeast Asian countries formed the Association of the Southeast Asian Nations (ASEAN) in 1967, which only strengthened this divide.

With the thawing of the Cold War and the break up of the erstwhile Soviet Union, this ideological divide altered to some extent with Vietnam now becoming part of the ASEAN. Singapore, which developed at a much faster pace than other countries in the region, is generally included in the group of newly industrialised countries (NICs), the others being Korea, Hong Kong, Taiwan in East Asia.

Post Independence Era

In the post-independence period Indonesia launched an economic policy aiming at direct economic control of production and trade. Dutch enterprises were nationalised, the state took over many activities including import monopolies. Import and investment licences and procedures were complex and anti Chinese.

In 1965, after Suharto took over as president, he adopted a more favourable stance towards foreign capital. The oil boom during the 1970s gave the government an opportunity to intensify its outward oriented export-led growth. But the gradual appreciation of the exchange rate eroded the competitiveness in the non-oil exporting sector. With the end of the oil boom in the mid 1980s, the government instituted import controls and favoured import substitution. By 1986, the government again shifted to export oriented deregulation [5]. (In Chapter 3 it will be seen that such a policy was adopted after the country received a loan from the IMF to make adjustments in its balance of payments). Exports of textiles, plywood, electronics etc. grew at a very rapid pace.

Independent Malaysia followed certain economic policies of its former British colonial government although it protected its import competing industries. Exports accounted for 1/3rd of its GDP in 1950. Important exports were tin and natural rubber. In 1970 it launched the New Economic Policy (NEP), which was a state led industrialisation programme. An entire range of exportable products from rubber, timber, palm oil, petroleum and tin to light manufactures like textiles, garments and footwear were promoted. Finally a crisis in 1986 forced the government to opt for a more selective export promotion programme.

Since Thailand was never a colony there was no major change in its economic policy in the post World War II period. The economic policy consisted of state control, export taxation, import substitution and a multiple exchange rate. But after 1981 its economic policy changed direction to export-led growth while reducing export taxes. The exchange rate was devalued (intervention by the IMF) and foreign investment was encouraged.

In the mid-1980s the ASEAN3 entered a new and critical stage of development, which led to these transforming into one of the most vibrant regions of the world. Consequently, they were also referred to as the Asian cubs, the second generation NICs, or little dragons to emphasise the nature and fast pace of growth experienced by their economies. Their stupendous rates of growth, their export-led development strategies and their acquisition of affluence in a short period of time have been endorsed by the international financial institutions .

After elucidating the historical and cultural backgrounds of the countries, it is now appropriate that the historical backgrounds and geneses of the agents that helped bring about a transformation into the moribund economies be discussed.

A Brief History of International Financial Institutions

The World Bank and International Monetary Fund were created in 1944 as a consequence of the economic problems thrown up by the two world wars and the economic depression of 1930s.The two world wars responsible for changing the political landscape of the world are also equally responsible for changing the economic equations among nations.

Prior to World War I there was a breakdown of the gold standard, which was restored after the war. The exchange rate by then had become unrealistic leading to countries being forced off the gold standard. The Pound Sterling went off the gold standard and devalued; and all other countries scrambled to devalue, leading to competitive devaluations. As a result trade collapsed, with its value falling by more than 60% between 1929-32.

A number of international conferences were held to help revive trade and the world economy. But due to lack of consensus among the participating nations they did not produce any concrete results. Finally in the early 1940s,during the World War II, J.M.Keynes of the U.K. Treasury and Harry Dexter White of the US Treasury came up almost concurrently with proposals for setting up an international monetary institution that would provide financial assistance to countries with balance of payment (BOP) problems and would stabilise exchange rates and promote free trade.

The Keynes and White plans had dissimilarities and what finally emerged was a hybrid of the two. The final negotiations took place at Bretton Woods in the state of New Hampshire in July 1944, and two institutions namely the WB and IMF came into being. Consequently these institutions came to be referred to as Bretton Woods Twins.

IMF

The IMF became functional in May 1946 with thirty-nine member countries initially, which has now increased to one hundred and eighty two members. The principal function of the IMF is to supervise the international monetary system. Several functions are derived from this, such as surveillance over the monetary and exchange rate policies of member countries, issuing policy recommendations to members and granting credit to countries with temporary BOP difficulties.

As mentioned above the Fund's task included managing the exchange rate system. The exchange rate system adopted was an adjustable exchange rate system (later also known as dollar standard). In such an arrangement, exchange rates are fixed by different countries against the U.S. dollar although occasionally they are allowed to alter the rate.

Thus, the currencies were convertible against the dollar. This system was in operation for quarter of a century.

A series of currency crises occurred in the 1960s largely due to the increasing disequilibria in the BOP of the USA. In 1971, the USA decided to abandon this exchange rate system thereby putting an end to the fixed exchange rate regime conceived at Bretton Woods. A managed float was now adopted wherein central banks of individual countries could intervene to smooth out fluctuations in exchange rates.[6] However, the basic idea of mutual interest in exchange rate matters was maintained

Provision of credit for members is not the Fund's primary function but receives most publicity[7]. The IMF grants credit subject to the fulfillment of certain conditionalities. The conditionalities are aimed at restoring domestic and external balance and price stability. The programme design normally involves fiscal and monetary policy measures, exchange rate policy, public sector reform, trade liberalization, financial sector and labour market reforms. Generally, exchange rate devaluation forms part of the programme too. The common concept underlying the programme is opening up of the economy, and allowing free markets to operate. By removing structural rigidities it is believed that the way is paved for sustained economic recovery / growth.

The World Bank

When the IMF was established at Bretton Woods, it was also decided to set up an international bank simultaneously, which would finance the reconstruction of European economies weakened by the world war. Thus was constituted the International Bank for Reconstruction and Development commonly known as the World Bank. The WB group consists of two sister institutions namely, the International Finance Corporation (IFC) and the International Development Association (IDA). Any country wishing to join the WB has to first be a member of the IMF. Infact, all the current 180 member-nations of the IMF are also members of the Bank and a majority of them are also members of the IFC and IDA.

The WB loans are sanctioned to finance high quality projects or programmes directly contributing to economic development of a nation. In the early 1980s as the industrialised nations were battling against severe recession the WB came up with two new lending programmes namely Structural and Sectoral Adjustment loans. Structural Adjustment Loans are granted to improve the economy and strengthen the export sector thereby leading to a sustainable BOP position in the long term.

Conditionalities for Loans

The Structural Adjustment Loan is granted in conjunction with the IMF and the conditionalities that are attached are based on the"Washington Consensus"- a term coined by the British economist, John Williamson.

Washington is in the name in part because it is the headquarters of the IMF and WB (these policies have been conceived jointly by both these institutions) and in part since it emanated from the USA in the 1980s spearheaded by the then US president Ronald Regan.[8]. Originally, the WC comprised a list of ten propositions focussed on macroeconomic stability, domestic financial liberalisation, privatisation and trade liberalisation. In September 1996, the WC was updated and a list of eleven propositions made (See Annexure A for the complete list).

Generally, a detailed macroeconomic adjustment programme with a structural adjustment programme is drawn up. In fact, in practice these programmes form the basis for the provision of financial assistance and development aid[9]. The borrower agrees to make structural adjustments such as fiscal reform and monetary reform, privatisation, and trade liberalisation.[10]

The macroeconomic policies adopted by ASEAN3 since the mid 1980s were very similar in nature and content to the macroeconomic policy changes and structural adjustment programmes insisted upon by the Fund. These policies had two facets. First, the exchange rate regime was directed towards achieving enhanced competitiveness. In the sense the real exchange rate was kept positive to complement the outward oriented policies. Devaluations in the currencies (effected in Indonesia and Thailand) often followed by depreciations were made to achieve the above. Such an exchange rate policy enabled the ASEAN 3 in successfully avoiding currency overvaluation in the decade of mid-1980s to mid-1990s[11].

The second facet was the adoption of a tight fiscal policy. Budgets had either a low deficit or as in most cases a surplus. The primary objective of such a policy was price stability. A tight fiscal policy also enabled the public sector debt to be low. The public sector debt to GDP ratio was substantially low in the economies of the ASEAN3.

There were other important structural adjustments and stabilisation policy measures followed. On the structural side various liberalisation measures including trade and financial sector liberalisation were adopted. On the stabilisation side apart from the above-mentioned tight fiscal policy, monetary policy was also used as a short-run stabilisation instrument. Varying the intensity of sterilised intervention in the foreign exchange market in accordance with domestic macroeconomic needs was the modus operendi of the monetary policy.

In short, the various policies adopted by the three Southeast Asian economies during the mid-eighties to mid-nineties were outward orientated in nature, gave the export sector a fillip, tried to achieve macroeconomic stabilisation, endorsed devaluation when needed, liberalised the financial sector and opened the capital account. These steps were praised and promoted by the international financial institutions like the IMF and the WB[12].

Objectives, Hypotheses and Methodology of Study

Objectives:

Many individual economists and researchers considered the policies adopted by the Southeast Asian economies since the mid 1980s as guarantors of economic success. However, the financial crisis that broke out in July 1997 washed away much of the success achieved by these nations. The policies that were upto now advocated widely suddenly became taboo and suspect. Even the IMFs rescue packages to contain the crisis were severely criticised so much so that the IMF faced the threat of closure.

Considering these aspects, the specific objectives of this study are:

(a)To examine the macroeconomic policies followed by the Southeast Asian economies (Indonesia, Malaysia and Thailand) since the mid eighties and to observe the pattern of development.

(b) To analyse the extent of the role played by international financial institutions like WB and IMF in formulating the macroeconomic policies and also examine their influence on the development experience of these nations

(c) To determine the factors leading to the financial crisis beginning in July 1997 in Southeast Asia.

(d) To enquire into the countrywise experience of policy options for dealing with the crisis and the role of the international financial institutions therein.

(e) To examine changes introduced in the existing financial system.

(f) To ascertain the relevance of the Southeast Asian development experience and draw lessons from the same for India, if any.

Methodology:

This study is mainly based on secondary sources. The following are the major sources:

a) Various issues of World Development Report, published by Oxford University Press for World Bank.
b) Various issues of Industrial Development Global Report published by Oxford University Press for United Nations Industrial Development Organization.
c) Various issues of Industrial Development Report published by Oxford University Press for UNDP.

d) Various issues of Asian Development Outlook published by Oxford University Press for Asian Development Bank.

e) Articles/Press releases from financial newspapers, Economic journals like Financial Express, Economic Times, Economic and Political weekly, Finance and Development (IMF), World Bank Publications, Business Today, Asian Business Week etc.

f) Various issues of International Financial Statistics.

g) Books written by different authors on related areas.

The data so collected has been consolidated and analysed with reference to the present study and accordingly conclusion have been drawn. Wherever necessary pictorials/graphs/charts/statistics have been used to facilitate explanation. Similarly at places, econometric tools have also been used.

The limitations are largely on account of secondary data constraints. Certain data may not be consistently available in the above-mentioned publication. Data at times is found to vary from one source to the other. Moreover, some subjectivity may have entered the study on account of the researchers own perceptions of the issue.

References for Chapter 1

1. Joel, David (1985), '*In Search of Southeast Asia. A Modern History*'. Honolulu, University of Hawaii, Steinberg Press, p 4.
2. Dixon, Chris (1991), '*Southeast Asia in the World Economy. A Regional Geography*', Britain, Cambridge University Press, p 2.
3. Bone, Robert C. (1960), '*Contemporary Southeast Asia*', New York, Random House, p 9.
4. Osborne, Milton (1975), '*Southeast Asia an Introductory History*', p 26-29.
5. Fernandez Jilberto, Alex E. and Andre Mommen (1996), '*Setting the Neoliberal Development Agenda*', in Alex E.Fernandez Jilberto and Andre Mommen (eds), 'Liberalization in the Developing World. Institutional and Economic Changes in Latin America, Africa and Asia', London, Routledge, p 40.
6. Begg, David, Stanley Fischer, and Rudiger Dornbush (1996), '*Economics*', New Delhi, Tata McGraw Publications, p 718.

7. Baker, A.F.P (1996), '*International Financial Institutions*', London, Longman, p 15.
8. Herman, Barry and Barbara Stalling (1999), '*International Finance and the Developing Countries: Liberalization, Crisis and the Reform Agenda*', in Barry Herman (ed), 'Global Financial Turmoil and Reform: A United Nations Perspective', Washington DC, United Nations University Press, p 14.
9. Baker, A.F.P (1996), '*International Financial Institutions*', London, Longman, p 24.
10. Meltzer, Allan (1999) '*What's Wrong With the IMF? What Would be Better*?' in William Hunter, George Kaufman and Thomas Krueger (eds) 'Asian Financial Crisis', p247.
11. Alba, Pedro, Amar Bhattacharya et al (1999), '*Volatility and Contagion in a Financially Integrated World: Lessons from East Asia's Recent Experience*' in Gordan de Brouwer and Wisaran Puppahavesa (eds) 'Asia Pacific Financial Deregulation', New York, Routledge, p 13.
12. Ahmad, Zakaria Hajiand Baldas Ghosal, (1999)' *The Political Future of ASEAN After the Asian Crisis.*

Chapter 2

Review of Literature

Studies Relating to the East Asian Region as a Whole

The most widely known literature on the East Asian success stories is the celebrated **World Bank Report** titled **The East Asian Miracle Growth and Public Policy, 1994**. This report reviews the achievement and seemingly miraculous growth of eight economies Japan, Hong Kong, the Republic of Korea, Singapore and Taiwan, Indonesia, Malaysia and Thailand. The economies were aptly termed High Performing Asian Economies (HPAEs). The growth rates and other economic indicators have been considered for the time period 1965-90 mainly. Various theories of growth and factors responsible for the fast paced development have been discussed. However, the emphasis is definitely more so on the NIEs i.e. Hong Kong, Korea, Singapore and Taiwan.

After the above-mentioned publication a lot many books/articles were published exploring the East Asian models of growth and comparing them with those of other developing countries. Questions were raised regarding the possibility of emulating these models and achieving of similar results. One such book is "**Lessons from East Asia**, edited by **Danny M. Leipziger** published in 1997 by the University of Michigan press. This book is a collection of papers presented by different economists. It leaves out Japan from the East Asian success stories and sketches the growth patterns and searches for county lessons. The paper in the book titled ***An Overview of East Asian Experience*** by ***Danny Leipziger and Vinod Thomas*** concludes that there is no single model of growth. If any developing country wants to imitate these economies, it will have to match the 'most relevant' of these models to suit its own conditions (Common Foundations of East Asian Success, page 562).

Sueo Sekiguchi's paper titled Dynamism ***of East Asian Economies: Retrospect and Prospect*** published in a book titled **APEC**

Challenges and Opportunities, edited by **Chia Siow Yue**, ISEAS 1994 reviews the dynamism in East Asia. East Asia here includes HPAE (as per WB), Philippines, China Vietnam and North Korea. The paper investigates internal/external factors that have supported economic growth. It also discusses the effects of regional groupings outside the region on the East Asian region. If East Asia wants its trade to be unaffected by the other regional groupings, then reducing protectionism barriers within the region is imperative, opines the author. The paper concludes that East Asia must invest more in human capital if it wants to continue at a high level of economic activity.

Economic and Social Development in Pacific Asia" edited by **Chris Dixon** and **David Drakasis Smith** is another collection of papers presented by various economists that assesses the economic and social development of the Asia pacific economies. An article by ***John Wong*** in this book titled ***ASEAN Economies***: ***Continuing Dynamic Growth in 1990's*** finds out how the Southeast Asian economies including Brunei, Indonesia, Malaysia, Philippine, Singapore and Thailand modified their macroeconomic policies in the early 1990s to overcome the recession. Therefore, despite the recession they managed to grow. Thus, the economies were successful in continuing growth in the early 1990s due to the quick policy responses to changing economic situations.

"ASIA PACIFIC ECONOMIES: A Survey by "**Iyanatul Islam** and **Anis Chowdhury**, as the title suggests, surveys the economic performance of the Asia Pacific countries including the three countries chosen for the present study. The authors have briefly sketched out the economic performance and data of Indonesia, Malaysia and Thailand (separate chapters for each of these countries) for the decade of the 1970s and the 1980s. At the end of each chapter, a note is made on the policy developments of the 1990s. Such policy developments include the liberalisation in trade and investment and changes in the monetary and fiscal policies.

Aptly titled **Booming economies of Southeast Asia**, Longman, Singapore 1990, author **Allan Guillonet** highlights of the economic performance of the ASEAN 3 (among others) during the boom period from the mid 1980s to 1989. It may be mentioned her that the boom period extended upto the mid 1990s. He also briefly discusses the policies followed during the same period and subscribes to the view that timely adjustments in macroeconomic policies helped the ASEAN 3 to achieve the high growth rates that they achieved. A similar book with almost identical conclusions is "**Dynamism of Economic Policy Reform in Southeast Asia and Southwest Pacific**", edited by **Andrew J. Macintyre and Kanishka Jayasuriya**, Oxford University Press, 1995.

Although published in the year 2000, the two volume edition of "**The Economies of Asia 1950-98 Critical Perspectives on the World Economy",** edited by **Robert Ash** et al, Routledge, London/NY, does not cover events since 1997 itself. Thus, the Asian financial crisis is conspicuous by its absence. However, certain papers are devoted exclusively to the financial sector reforms of the early 1990s and these provide an insight into the developments therein. In the paper titled ***Financial** Reform in **Malaysia***" by ***Zainal Aznam Yusof***, the economic reforms and particularly the financial sector reforms for the period 1970-90 are discussed. The paper concludes on the note that the liberalization process could not have succeeded without the government commitment and the right economic conditions. The paper titled ***Reforms of the Financial Sector in Indonesia 1983 –91*** by ***Anwar Nasution*** gives details on deregulation and liberalization programmes adopted in Indonesia in the mid 1980s following a financial repression prior to it.

Focussing mainly on the industrial policies that assisted Southeast Asia achieve its 'miracle economies' status is the book edited by **Seiichi Masuyama** et al, "**Industrial Policies in East Asia",** and ISEAS, 1997. The book was compiled before the Asian financial crisis and hence does not mention the same. It highlights the role of the government in the industrial policy and the positive effect of the same on the Southeast Asian economies. The industrial policies were so designed that it attracted both domestic and foreign investment. Such investment aided and assisted the growth of the economy.

Comparative studies have also been an area examined by many economists. One such study is contained in a book titled **Asia and Africa: Legacies and Opportunities in Development**, edited by **David Lindauer and Michael Roemer.** A series of articles review the Asian success and compare the same with developing economies of Africa. It concludes that the three Southeast Asian economies (Indonesia, Malaysia and Thailand) success stories have a lot of lessons to offer to the African countries and that the latter could have done well to have adopted similar policies as that of the former.

The Myth of Asia's Miracle, a study on the sustainability of the Asian miracle by **Paul Krugman** published in Foreign Affairs, 73(6): 62-78 in1994 did not receive as much publicity then as it did in the post-Asian crisis period. Krugman assumed the role of a soothsayer, who, to some extent had warned the Asian countries of the dangers ahead. In this paper Krugman draws a parallel between the erstwhile Soviet Union and the economies of East Asia to indicate that they were using increased inputs to increase their output. He explained with the help of the concept of Total Factor Productivity (TFP) that if output increases as a result of increased inputs the same becomes unsustainable in the long run. Unless there is an increase in TFP, growth rates will start declining. He had therefore said that the high growth rate in East Asia was not the result of any miracle but on account of increased inputs. Unless these economies increase their productivity, the myth of their growth will become obvious to everyone soon.

Countrywise Studies

Most of the country wise studies attempted have been for a much earlier time period than that considered in the present study.

Indonesia

Many researchers have been attracted towards studying economic reforms that took place in the 1980s as these proved to be a milestone in the economic history of Indonesia. ***Veena Mishra's*** paper titled

Indonesia Adjustment in the 1980s in the book **Economic Restructuring in East Asia and India** edited by Pradeep Agarwal, Subhir Gokaran et al, New Delhi, Macmillan (I), has detailed the major economic reforms undertaken by the Government of Indonesia in the 1980s and the effects that they have has on the economy. She concludes that the market opening reforms will become slower since she predicts that the government will give into rent seeking pressures. According to her the pace of opening out of the economy will depend upon the performance of the economy itself.

Indonesia's Struggle for Economic Development. Pragmatism in action authored by Radius Prawino published in 1998 traces Indonesia's transition to a new paradigm in the 1980s.The policy changes that assisted Indonesia in achieving growth were:

- Deregulation and debureaucratization
- Export led growth
- Creation of a regulatory framework conducive to foreign investment.
- Transfer of economic power from the government to the private sector.

The author briefly touches upon the Asian crisis in the epilogue and says that notwithstanding the crisis the struggle for economic development must continue. The government has to make efforts to build the Indonesian community into a well educated and an economically strong one.

Authored by **Hall Hill, Indonesia's Industrial Transformation**, ISEAS, Singapore, 1997, provides an account of how Indonesia has in the last third of the twentieth century become a remarkable success story. The study emphasises the role of industrialization in the transformation of Indonesia into an industrial economy over a short period of time.

One of the few books providing a birds eye view of the experiences of a borrowing country is presented in **Multilateral Development Banks, Volume 2,** Asian Development Bank, authored by **Nikal Kappagoda**, Intermediate Technical Publication, United Kingdom,

1995. The chapter titled *Borrowing Country Experience* is partly devoted to Indonesia and its borrowing from the World Bank between 1970 – 1992. It gives the reader an idea of the direct and indirect influence the WB would have on the country's macroeconomic policies due to the loans Indonesia has undertaken.

A more recent study on Indonesia can be found in **Indonesia. The Challenge of change**, ISEAS, Singapore, 1999, edited by **Richard W Baker** et al. The study attempts to assess the effects of economic growth and the challenge posed by these changes on twelve basic institutions or sectors on Indonesian life and society. These institutes cover a broad range including economic sectors, government structures and bodies and social organizations. Hence, the book does not limit its scope to the economic aspects but extends it to political and social ones too.

David Bevan et al **The Political Economy of Poverty, Equity and Growth,** Oxford University Press, 1999, has attempted a comparative study of Indonesia and Nigeria. The study covers economic policies followed in Indonesia from the colonial period to 1997 with an emphasis on those made by during the eras of Sukarno and Suharto. Being a comparative study the focus is on the similarities and differences in economic policies and their effects on poverty and growth of the two countries.

Malaysia:

Jomo K.S and Chris Edwards have individually and jointly authored several books/papers on issues relating to the Malaysian economy and its development. The book **Industrialising Malaysia. Policy, Performance, Prospects**, edited by **Jomo K.S**, published by Routledge in 1993 covers the process of industrialization in Malaysia from 1957 since it achieved independence to 1989. It traces the various industrial policies adopted by Malaysia during this period and the industrial growth that took place when each of these policies was adopted. It traces the differences in growth during the period of import substitution as well as of export promotion. .

Robert E.B Lucas and Donald Verny have co-authored **Restructuring the Malaysian Economy**. **Development and Human Resources**, Macmillan Press, Great Britain, 1999. This book traces Malaysia's economic development since the commencement of the New Economic Policy in the late 1960s/early 1970s. According to the study Malaysia has had rapid growth combined with equity. The study traces the important strategies underlying the growth and development, human resource development, equity and restructuring. It concludes on the following note. "The NEP specifically sought a balance between three goals: Growth, Equity and Restructuring; high growth alone was never perceived as sufficient. Rapid growth provided the resources for redistribution and rendered the policies to achieve this more palatable and growth was possible by a stability that may not have been achieved without restructuring'.

Yet another study titled **Malaysia Political Economy, Policies, Patronage and Profits** authored by **Edmund Terence Gomez and Jomo K.S,** Press Syndicate of the University of Cambridge, 1997 deals with Malaysia's economic development experience from a political perspective. It discusses the NEP first, then the policies of liberalization and privatisation of the mid 1980s and finally it also mentions the Vision 2020, a plan put forward by Malaysian Prime Minister Mahatir in February 1991. In this book, the entire focus is on how the Government in Malaysia have made initiatives to formulate public policies to shape the destiny of the country and traces the same up to 1995.

The country report, '**UNIDO, Industrial Development Review Series, Malaysia**", published by Basil Blackwell Limited, United Kingdom, 1991, reviews the economic environment in Malaysia for the period 1985-1990. The report emphasises on the role played by the flexible monetary policy, growth oriented fiscal policies, the two tier trade policy and a constructive industrial policy in assisting growth in Malaysia. However, it points out that certain structural weaknesses exist in the economy, namely, a narrow industrial base, problem of unemployment, shortage of skills and oversized public sector. It concludes by saying that the performance of Malaysia in the decade of the 1990s will depend on policies implemented to deal with these structural weaknesses.

The view that the Malaysian Government has been flexible in adapting to changing economic conditions by reformulating the macroeconomic policies has been put forth by more than one author. ***Ismail Mohamed Sabeh*** et al in ***Malaysia Growth, Equity and Structural Transformation*** in the book ***Lesson from East Asia***", edited by Danny Leilpziger (1997) and **M. Zairudin Sabeh** in "**Macroeconomic Perspectives of Malaysian Economy in APEC Challenges and Opportunities** edited by **Chia Sion Yue**, ISEAS, Singapore, 1994 are both of the above opinion.

Thailand

The Fifth Tiger. **A study of Thai Development Policy** authored by **Robert J. Muscat,** 1994, is a comprehensive study on Thailand's political and economic climate until 1992. It likens the economic development of Thailand with that of the Asian Tigers (Hong Kong, Korea and Singapore Taiwan) and therefore refers to Thailand as the Fifth Tiger.

Peter G. Warr and Bhanupong Nidhiprabha are firm believers that a miracle of sorts did not occur in Thailand. They consider that the economic policies of Thailand assisted it in achieving high rates of growth. No wonder in their book titled **Thailand's Macroeconomic Miracle Stable Adjustment and Sustained Growth** they conclude, "A miracle is something that is unusual, beneficial and inexplicable Thailand's experience of stable growth has been miraculous in the first two senses, but not the third. There was nothing particularly brilliant, farsighted, or mysterious about the way. Thailand adjusted to its changing environment: it was nothing that other developing nations could not emulate or even improve upon if they chose to do so."

Even the paper presented by **Scott R. Christensen** in **Lessons from East Asia** suggests that macroeconomic management and provision of a stable monetary environment is what helped Thailand succeed.

Very similar are conclusions provided by **Kunal Sen** in his paper titled **Thailand: Stabilization With Growth**, which appears in the book

Economic restructuring in East Asia and India. Perspectives on Policy Reforms. Sen opines that the stabilization programme undertaken by Thailand in the 1980s has been crucial to Thailand's growth. He particularly points to the conservative fiscal policy and realistic exchange rate policy (ironic in today's situation) in helping Thailand attain the miraculous growth.

Another noteworthy contribution on Thailand is a book edited by **Medhi Krongkaen** titled **Thailand's Industrialization and its Consequences**. It traces the development of modern Thailand from the early 1960s to early 1990s. The book identifies the various characteristics and nature of Thailand's industrialization. Causes of Thailand's rapid economic growth and development are put down as export growth, growth in FDI and growth in service activity especially tourism.

Well-known author on Southeast Asian studies, **Chris Dixon's** book **The Thai Economy: Uneven Development and Internationalisation**, Routledge, New York, 1999 looks at the Thai economy from a slightly different perspective. He points out to the enigma of uneven development within Thailand despite the miracle economy status accorded to it by the WB. The book traces Thailand's economic history and its internationalisation since 1850 to 1997 and thereby brings out the inequality seen in this country. He further opines that in the general euphoria of Thailand's the other aspects of poverty and inequality has been sidetracked.

Literature linking Thailand's economic policies to international financial institutions are hard to find. However, one such study is **Aid and Power. The WB and Policy based Lending** Volume 2, case studies", Routledge, 1991, edited by **Paul Morley** et al in which a chapter is devoted to it. The main objective of the chapter on Thailand is to evaluate the WB's first and second Structural Adjustment Loans (SAL's) made to this country in 1982 and 1983 respectively. It seeks to answer two questions – why were some conditionalities attached to the loan and were these implemented in practice? The study concludes that the only solution for Thailand was to make the structural adjustments as suggested by WB and that the country did make these adjustments in its policy measures among others.

Studies on Financial Crisis in Asia

In the aftermath of the crisis many articles/books have been published on various aspects of it – causes, consequences, solutions, criticism to solutions and so on. Some of them have been hurriedly compiled and a few of them have been written after a researched study. In the years 1998 and 1999 most of the studies analysed the nature and causes of the crisis for East Asia as a whole, but by the year 2000 the analysis started to narrow down to each crisis-affected country individually. Noteworthy among them are reviewed below.

Edited by **Ross H. Mclead** et al "**East Asia in Crisis. From Being a Miracle to Needing One**", Routledge, London/New York, 1998 is a collection of articles on the East Asian crisis. This book though published in 1998 has separate chapters devoted to the lead up to the crisis, impact of the same, the policy responses undertaken in each of the affected economies, the IMF package (for Indonesia and Thailand) and also a note on the economic responses to policy development. However, each of these aspects is dealt with very briefly. Additionally, the year 1998 was too close to assess the full impact of the crisis.

Just as the title suggests **"Asian Contagion. The Causes and Consequences of a Financial Crisis**" edited by **Karl D. Jackson**, ISEAS, Singapore 1999, enlists the causes and consequences of the Asian crisis. According to the book the crisis was sparked off by a loss of confidence on the part of economic entities that suddenly came to realise the extent to which they were exposed to various kinds of risk. In short it pins the blame on both panic/speculative attack and poor economic fundamentals as causes of the crisis.

A number of articles/books suggest that excessive financial liberalisation/reforms that were effected in the ASEAN 3 were the fundamental cause of the crisis. One such book is "**Asia Pacific Financial Deregulation**", edited by **Gordon de Brouwer** et al, Routledge, New York, 1999. It details the financial reforms undertaken in the ASEAN 3 since the early 1990s and shows how certain liberalization measures put pressure on the current account causing a deficit which in turn lead to the crisis.

Similar conclusions have been drawn by **Mohamed Arif** et al in **"Liberalisation, Growth and the ASEAN Financial Crisis Lessons for Developing and Transitional** **Economies of Asia**", Edward Elgar Publication Incorporation, USA, 2000. The book enumerates the economic and financial reforms in the ASEAN 3 in chronological sequence for the time period 1958 – 1998. The liberal policies have been at times excessive and that according to the study led to the crisis. Since 1997, following the crisis the process of liberalisation has been stopped in its tracks claims the study.

A more comprehensive book on the Asian Crisis is "**The Asian Crisis. The Cures, their Effectiveness and the Prospects After**", Macmillan Press, Great Britain, 2000, edited by Tran Van Hoa. The book looks at the economic performance of the ASEAN 3 (each country dealt with separately) for the period 1992 – 1997 and traces the steady decline in the same. It also discusses the macroeconomic development during 1998 and the policy framework adopted in the post crisis period.

Crisis related literature also extends to the critical appraisal of the IMF package provided as a solution to the crisis devastated economic. Some of them have questioned the existing financial architecture and have made suggestions for a new one.

Barry Herman and Krishnan Sharma editors of "**International Finance and Developing Countries in a year of Crisis**", United Nations University 1998 have brought out a collection of papers presented at the 1997 Discussion at the United Nation. In the paper by Michel Camdessus (the Managing Director, IMF), the IMF's four fold response to the crisis has been discussed – detect financial tensions, help market function more smoothly, strengthen the resource base of the fund and reduce the risk of marginalisation for the poorest member country. In the paper by the editors themselves, they have been kind to the IMF suggesting that the Fund operates with a small staff compared to the number of countries it has to provide support to and therefore in 1997 the staff were very stretched. The world as per them had unrealistic expectations about how much the IMF could deliver.

"Asia in Crisis. The Imposition of the Banking and Financial Systems", Routledge, 1999, by **Philippe F. Delhaise** has a chapter devoted to the cure presented by the IMF. The quotation at the beginning of the chapter is a bit misleading "I fear the Greeks, even where they bring gifts" (reference to the' Trojan horse'). This would suggest that countries should be cautions while accepting IMF loans as conditionalities are attached to it. Ironically, the discussion justifies the IMF conditionalities and also mentions that Thailand was cautioned by the IMF to reduce its short term loans which the former did not pay heed to. The IMFs only fault is that it did not insist or did not play the 'watchdog'.

Martin Khor in his article in the **Far Eastern Economic Review** has not been kind to the Fund at all. He squarely puts the blame on the Fund/World Bank policies or conditionalities for bailing out Foreign Banks in the crisis stricken countries. The article is titled **IMF Bailing out Countries or Foreign Banks** and raises the issue that these banks do not have to undertake the risk element that regular banks have to bear on account of the protection provided to them by the IMF conditionalities.

Sunanda Sen in "**Economic Turmoil in Asia",** EPW July 24, 1999, echoes similar views. She says that "Corrective measures by monetary authorities have failed in deregulated financial markets."

The Asian Financial Crisis: Origins, Implications and Solutions, edited by **William C. Hunter** et al, 1999 comprises an article titled **'What's Wrong With the IMF' by Allan Meltzer.** The opinion of Allan Meltzer is that though the IMF cannot be held responsible for all the errors that Governments make, yet the IMF by minimizing the moral hazard problem avoids recognizing that it is part of the problem. The rescue packages of the IMF tends to encourages risky lending by financial institutions. The paper concludes with about seven suggestions for reform of the current financial architecture. The last one is a bold measure suggesting that international financial institutions are no longer needed for development lending and this should be handled through capital markets.

A full-fledged book on suggestions for reforming the international financial structure is a report titled "**Safeguarding Prosperity in a Global Financial System**. **The future International Financial Architecture**", published by Institute for International Economics, 1998. The book provides for measures to prevent crisis and crisis management. It also warns the emerging countries and their private creditors to be more prudent and careful in the future.

Given these books/ articles there is still a need for a comprehensive study of the development experience of the Southeast Asian countries in the pre and post crisis periods and the role of the international financial institutions therein. Such a study has been undertaken in the present research.

Chapter 3

Perspectives of Development in Southeast Asia

The previous chapter indicates that the Southeast Asian Economies attracted the attention of many economists and researchers. It was the World Bank which first accorded the 'miracle economies'[1] title to the countries of Indonesia, Malaysia and Thailand among others. The countries of South East Asia had consistently outperformed the countries of other developing regions over the last thirty years and more so since the mid-1980s. It is this basic observation that has been crucial in the shaping or formation of an economic miracle thesis.

Gunnar Myrdal in his famous treatise "The Asian Drama", Allen Lane The Penguin, 1968, had observed that in the South and Southeast Asian economies the growth rates were stagnating. He further observed that although there existed an aspiration to achieve high rates of growth the realisation of such aspirations was difficult.

The Southeast Asian countries have subsequently been able to break away from the stagnation. They have been able to achieve high rates of growth, which seems miraculous considering their situation in the 1960s. Infact the date of publication of Myrdal's work marked the end of stagnation in Southeast Asia and the beginning of growth[2].

Miracle Theories

An array of academicians and development planners, apart from a tribe of national, regional and international development agencies have been attracted to the development experience of Southeast Asian countries. They have suggested various theories explaining this miracle. It would be pertinent to examine these miracle theories briefly and enquire into which of these best explain the growth pattern in Southeast Asia. They are:

(i) Neo-Classical approach
(ii) Structuralist approach/Revisionist approach/New Institutional Approach

(iii) Market-friendly Strategy and Functional Growth Framework
(iv) Pluralist and Market-derived Approach/Culturalist explanation
(v) Contagion Approach/Flying Geese Approach
(vi) Economic System Approach

i) Neo-Classical Approach: In the Neo-Classical view it is the individual pursuit of self interest that results in the most efficient allocation of resources and, in the long run, the greatest wealth for society as a whole[3]. Hence, social welfare and wealth are best achieved by allowing the free operation of the market as a natural and neutral, self-correcting and regulating mechanism. The dynamics of social and political power should not be intertwined with it. Neo-Classical economists urge the withdrawal of the State from economic activity. In other words, the formula for successful economic development lies in sound principles of competition, decontrol of prices, and restructuring of resources to produce goods and services that markets demand.

The adherents of this approach emphasise that the High Performing Asian Economies (HPAEs) -including Southeast Asia, have been successful as they have been 'getting their basics right' [4]. These economies have provided a stable macroeconomic climate and reliable legal framework to promote domestic and international competition. There has been an orientation towards international trade and the absence of price controls and other distortionary policies. On account of such liberal policies Southeast Asia has had a 'miraculous growth', opine neo-classicists.

ii) Revisionist View: A variety of nomenclature has been used by different studies, namely – the revisionist view[5], the structuralist view[6] and the new institutionalist approach[7] – to indicate that the governments of Southeast Asian economies played an important and positive role in the development process. According to this view, economic expansion depends on state intervention to create price distortions that direct economic activity towards particular investment areas. Markets left on their own fail to guide investment to industries that would generate the highest growth for the overall economy. Hence, state intervention is essential.

In the Institutional Approach variation of this view, it is argued that unconstrained markets could lead to chaos, collusion, and widespread market failure. Efficient operation of markets require a highly developed institutional framework to regulate economic activity, rules for common property usage and private property ownership; banking and exchange regulations, an effective tax collection mechanism and for the operation of welfare programs. In fact, Masahi Ro Aoki who terms this approach as the 'Market Enhancing View' has pointed out that Governments play a critical role by providing such institutions and formulating policies to enhance economic activity of private economic agents.

In Southeast Asia, Governments deliberately distorted prices by providing an incentive structure to boost certain industries that would not have thrived otherwise. These moves were considered necessary to develop infant industries and strengthen their industrial structure. Policies were so framed and incentives so designed that they targeted certain sectors offering strong opportunities. The incentives offered comprised preferential access to credit, selective trade restrictions and government investments. However, the duration of governmental support to such industries was restricted.

iii) Market-Friendly Strategy and Functional Growth Framework: The market- friendly strategy occupies the middle ground between neo-classical and revisionist views. The appropriate role of governments in a market-friendly strategy is to ensure adequate investments in people, provide a competitive climate for enterprise, welcome international trade and stable macroeconomic management (World Bank, 1993, Page 84). The same report states that 'beyond these goals the government is likely to do more harm than good (Ibid Page 84). This interpretation put forward by the World Bank accedes that governments have a definite role to play in the economy, but it remains largely within the parameters of the neo-classical view.

The 'The East Asian Miracle' presented the Functional Growth Framework, which can be termed as an extension of the market-friendly approach. This approach offered a choice of two policies (fundamental and selective intervention), two methods of competitive discipline (market- based and contest-based), and three central economic management functions (accumulation, allocation and productivity change)[8]. These are indicated in Chart 3.1.

Among the fundamental policies the most important ones followed by the Southeast Asian countries were maintenance of macroeconomic stability and openness to foreign technology. Comparatively, the investment in human capital and in effective and secure financial systems took place more in the Northeast Asian countries. Selective interventions like export push, mild financial repression (keeping interest rates positive but low) were followed with much fervour in Southeast Asia.

'The East Asian Miracle' argues that generally most countries follow only market-based competitive discipline while the HPAEs have gone a step further by creating contests that encourage competition with the benefits of cooperation among firms and between the government and the private sector. Such contests include credit rationing for exports and coordination of private investments in government-business deliberation councils (Malaysia). The important element of each contest is that the government distributes rewards, i.e., access to credit or forex, based on performance of these firms, and to monitor the performance of these firms a high quality civil service is required which was also available in the HPAEs.

With the help of these policy choices and competitive disciplines, and by making pragmatic adjustments in them as and when required, they achieved the growth functions of accumulations and productivity changes. These, in turn, helped rapid and sustained growth and speedy industrialization. However, equal income distribution and alleviation of poverty could not be achieved to the extent as had been in the Northeast Asian economies.

<u>iv) Culturalist Explanation</u>: This approach emphasises that the Confucian tradition historically present in the Southeast Asian culture helped it achieve its miraculous growth. The Confucian traditions emphasise on group over individual values, development of meritocratic institutions and legitimising authoritarian rules. Some researchers/studies have labelled this as the Pluralist and Marxist- derived Political Economy Approach. They opine that the focus in these economies is on social groups, civil societies and political cultures.

The link between the theory stated above and what was actually practised in Southeast Asia is easy to establish. Emphasis on group behaviour is manifest in the cohesive forms of political and business organizations. Similarly, meritocratic institutions have been created by providing incentives for learning and education and ensuring high quality policy making.[9] Two of the ASEAN3 (Indonesia's Suharto and Malaysia's Mahatir) have had long authoritarian regimes. Thus the Southeast Asian experience indicates that Confucian principles have been adapted to the needs of an industrial society.

The Culturalists have also emphasised on two other elements that affect management methods. The first is a belief in the ethical foundations of hard work, loyalty and unquestioning obedience. Such characteristics make for a perfect workplace enabling the smooth conduct of business. The second is the concern for posterity. Such an attitude results in high savings rates and long-term views on investment returns.

The financial crisis that occurred in July 1997 has come to question the culturalist approach. This is because the lifetime loyalty aspect was all forgotten when the market called for lay offs and cost reductions.[10] Workers responses too were 'normal' – protesting and striking, which reflected an employee-employer relationship based on market dynamics, and not the Confucian family type tie.

v) Flying Geese Approach [11] / Contagion Approach:
This approach subscribes to the theory that the development process in the entire East Asian region was like a contagion starting with the leader of the team, Japan in the 1960s, followed by the NIEs in the 1970s, followed by the ASEAN3 in 1980s.

The Flying Geese theory of development pattern suggests that FDI has played an important role in the development process in Southeast Asia. According to this theory, FDI leads to a gradual transfer of production and export of labour intensive products from high wage source countries to lower wage host countries. The pattern of the FDI movement resembles the pattern formed by flying geese.

There is a reallocation of industry (production) and FDI from countries at a higher level of economic development to those at a lower level[12]. In the bargain there is more efficient use of factors of production and hence a higher level of industrialization for both groups. Recipient countries utilise their surplus labour and accumulated capital, technology and management skills, advancing their industrialization. The investing countries at the same time redirect excessive labour from sunset industries to sunrise industries thereby moving to an even higher level of industrialisation.

Low wages and openness are the essential dynamic factors in the Flying Geese theory of FDI. Beginning in the 1970s, low wages and openness in the Asian NIEs of Hong Kong, Taipei and Singapore attracted a large amount of FDI in labour-intensive industries. Transfer of technology from countries of the OECD, especially Japan, was substantial. Subsequently, increasing levels of labour skills and higher wages in the NIEs resulted in flows of FDI in labour intensive industries to Southeast Asia as these economies opened up. Still later, the FDI moved to China and Vietnam.

The same is illustrated in Graph 3.A where after peaking at 80% in 1986 in the NIEs as a destination of FDI; outflows from OECD declined steadily in favour of the ASEAN4. The importance of these countries as a destination for OECD FDI diminished, as China - with its abundance of labour- moved towards greater openness in the 1990s.

The NIEs themselves have metamorphosed into FDI sources, with their outflows resembling the Flying Geese formation. For instance, Taiwan became a major source of FDI for Thailand, followed by Malaysia, followed by Indonesia. Later by the 1990s, FDI flows were directed towards China and more recently to Vietnam.

Given the emphasis on differences in wage levels between Asian countries and the creation of overseas export platforms by multinational firms, the Flying Geese theory of FDI helps explain the remarkable performance of East and Southeast Asian exports[13]. In fact the theory also brings to the fore the challenge that higher income countries face from lower income countries as the latter open up and the FDI flows help them develop. The former have to develop new technologies and launch new/more products in order to remain at a higher economic level. In other words, the challenge to higher income countries is to develop new comparative advantages.

The Interaction Effects Approach or the Contagion Approach offers a similar explanation. It suggests that the Southeast Asian economic growth has been shaped by regional contacts – including flows of goods, investments, technology, aspirations and ideas about governance. The geographical proximity, the ethnic and cultural ties due to a history of migration enabled and facilitated the invitation of policies, technologies, business strategies and direct investment in these economies.

vi) <u>Economic Systems Approach</u>:

Many Japanese academicians seemed dissatisfied with the functional approach to growth presented by the World Bank in explaining the trajectory of East Asian economic development. Hence, a new approach known as the Economic Systems Approach (ESA) evolved. Originally developed by Prof. Shigteru Ishikama, the Dean of the Institute of Development Economics, Japan, it was refined and re-presented by Toru Yanagihara.[14]

ESA places the main emphasis on strengthening of organizational capabilities of economic agents in the process of economic development. The economic agents are households, firms, financial institutions and other infrastructure. The interaction among these economic agents, leads to enhancement of productive capacity, innovation of organizations and a change in resource allocation at the firm/industry i.e., micro level. At the macro level, it leads to enhancement of productive capacity of the whole economy, enhancement of the economic system and a change in the industrial structure. Facilitating and managing this entire process is the role of the government and thereby promoting economic development. This has been summarised in Chart 3.2.

This approach is different from the Functional Approach presented by the World Bank. According to the Functional Approach the market mechanism is a passive response of individual and economic agents to the prevailing incentive structure. In the ESA markets are formed and shaped due to interaction among economic agents. Moreover, these agents undergo an evolution in the development process.

Relevant Approach to Analyse Growth of Southeast Asian Economies:

In all the three Southeast Asian economies, there has been a continuous opening to the world economy since the early 1980s. Privatisation has been accompanied by market deregulation and domestic capital became internationalised entering international financial markets, investing overseas and extending links with foreign corporate groups. At the same time, capital inflows have also been encouraged through various policies. Private banking systems and capital markets have developed significantly. This is an essential pre-requisite to a policy of openness. Yet, a laissez faire policy was not adopted as these governments played an active role in assisting the economic agents.

The functional approach assigns an important role to the government, developing and implementing strategic industrial policies and undertaking public sector investment. All the three Southeast Asian economies permitted some element of government intervention both in the real and financial sector. All of them shared the common characteristic of openness to the rest of the world to allow export-led growth as a feature of their development strategy. Following such a strategy they were able to secure a high degree of exposure to trade and capital flows leading to growth, as is now well-documented economic history.

A range of international institutions including World Bank, International Monetary Fund, Asian Development Bank, APEC, and GATT/World Trade Organization have encouraged these moves. As a matter of fact, since the early 1980s the development discourse has largely been dominated by the policy and research agenda of the World Bank and International Monetary Fund.

The introduction of the Structural Adjustment Lending (SAL) enshrining the neo-classical paradigm as the official and authoritative doctrine of the international development community has exerted strong influence in thinking and practice of economic policies in these countries[15]. Since Indonesia and Thailand received assistance from the World Bank/ International Monetary Fund in the early 1980s, they were under obligation to adopt the package of policy and institutional reforms prescribed and endorsed by the International Monetary Fund/World Bank. Consequently, the development strategy adopted by the Southeast Asian countries is essentially the Functional Approach, whatever variation is seen in practice is that which happened during the implementation or to the extent to which the governments have not adhered to the conditionalities.

It may be noted here that the Culturalist explanations and the Flying Geese Approach also explain the growth and achievements of Southeast Asia. However, these are not adequate and all encompassing. They explain only certain aspects of the growth miracle.

Hence, it can be concluded that the development strategy followed by the ASEAN3 is largely modelled on the neo-classical framework with a little extra role given to the governments than normally permissible. Such a model was termed as the Functional Approach by the World Bank.

Was There a Miracle?

While there are theories explaining the miraculous growth and statistics endorsing the same, there are academicians who have questioned this success and even claimed that the 'development' was, in fact, a maldevelopment. They are not too convinced with the miracle theories, nor with the statistics indicating high levels of growth. Such statistics and growth rates are mere window dressing and a veneer covering the real situation, is what they opine.

Maldevelopment

According to Chris Dixon[16], in the general euphoria that has accompanied recent developments in Southeast Asia the extremely uneven pattern of development within the region have been largely neglected. He opines that unevenness is evident in the distribution of income, skewed pattern of development, the lack of congruity in the structures of employment, export earnings, level of urbanization, access to education, division on basis of gender and ethnicity and the limited access to political power.

The term "development" when applied to the economic growth of Thailand has also been questioned. He considers it a violation of important values like equity, economic democracy, ecological balance and human decency. He further points out that rather than being exemplars to the rest of the developing world, they are warnings of the danger of rapid export-led capitalist growth. He uses the term 'maldevelopment' to describe the Thai experience and defines it as 'a pattern of development with strongly negative socio-economic consequences in terms of inequality, unevenness, cultural fragmentation and a negative impact on women and the environment.

Excessive Dependence on the Global Economy

Another criticism against the Southeast Asian development is that there is excessive dependence on foreign investment and the global economy. The Southeast Asian development has revolved around foreign investment led export-driven industrialization. It is, therefore, dependent and subordinate to such foreign investment and export performance. If any of the following occur, the situation in these economies becomes uncertain:

(a) Perturbations in the global economy

(b) Increase in protection globally will adversely affect exports

(c) Foreign investors are known to move to low wage areas and do not have commitment to the countries they invest in. This has been seen in the movement of garment and footwear industries from Taiwan, South Korea and Hong Kong to Malaysia, from Malaysia to Thailand, from Thailand to Indonesia, from Indonesia to Vietnam and China. For these reasons scepticism has been expressed over the existence of a miraculous growth.

Growth not Sustainable

Another well-known sceptic of the Southeast Asian growth experience is Paul Krugman who had first expressed it in his now famous paper 'The Myth of Asia's Miracle', Foreign Affairs, 1994. He put forth his fears of the sustenance of the high growth rates experienced by the ASEAN3.

According to Krugman, the primary impetus behind growth in Southeast Asia has been on account of an increase in inputs. He cautions that such growth is not sustainable in the long run.

Krugman places a great deal of emphasis on Total Factor Productivity (TFP) for sustained long term growth. In the past the relationship between inputs and outputs was explained using production functions. It is now popular to use TFP. The relationship between input and output depends not only on the amount of input used but also on the technology available in the economy. The addition to output that results from technological progress, rather than an increase in the factors of production, is TFP. This residual is also known as the Solow Residual after Robert Solow of Massachusetts Institute of Technology, who first showed how to calculate TFP.

Given the spectacular economic performance of the Southeast Asian countries, it would be expected that TFP growth should be as spectacular. But surprisingly this is not so[17]. Table 3.1 gives an estimate of TFP for the ASEAN3.

Hence, Krugman opines that mere increase in inputs – investing in more machinery and infrastructure without an increase in the efficiency with which those inputs are used (TFP growth) must run into diminishing returns, input driven growth is inevitably limited. Krugman hence undermines the notion that the experience of these countries is in any sense miraculous and terms them as 'paper tigers'

The journal, The Economist (1995) framed the same argument more bluntly describing it as a "Myth of the Sausage Makers: If you invest in more sausage machines and employ more sausage makers, of course you will make more sausages. Where is the miracle? Growth will slow down when you run out of extra sausage makers".

Miracle Thesis- a Political Document

Lastly, Amsden, Kwon, Lall, Pukins and Yanagihara have all criticised the World Bank study 'The East Asian Miracle'. As mentioned earlier, this study has been very influential in promoting the Asian Miracle thesis. According to the critics, the study is a political document and was written to reflect the beliefs and predictions of the World Bank's upper management. They also alleged that the World Bank has played down the role of the government in its enthusiasm to promote the market-friendly ethos. Again, the study only emphasizes economic measures of success and ignores failures in the social and environmental fields. Hence, the study has falsely promoted a miracle thesis, is what they conclude.

Notwithstanding the above critique to the Southeast Asian success story, it cannot be denied that these economies did perform exceptionally well especially in the decade from the mid-1980s to the mid-1990s. There was an unprecedented increase in the GDP. A structural change took place whereby these economies were transformed into industrialised economies with a high rate of export growth. The high growth rate of exports was one of the reasons for a high level of inward investment in the region. Such inflows further propelled the economies on the path of economic affluence.

Reasons for Adopting Open Economic Policies

It would be pertinent to understand the reasons why the Southeast Asian countries adopted open policies. Certain historical events influenced the course of economic policies in Southeast Asia and the same are discussed below.

Role of the US and Japan:

The first event revolves around the ***US influence*** in the post World War II period. In Southeast Asia economic and security reasons led the US to create global economic and strategic environments favourable to the success of open development policies.[18]

The decision-makers in East Asia were taken in by the economic ideas of liberalism propagated by the US. The US provided access to its markets, provided capital, technology and managerial skills to support the ideas it was advocating.[19] Thus the US influenced the economic policy choices in Southeast Asia in the following three ways.

Firstly, the US, seen as a dominant economic power, provided capital and technology to stimulate economic activity in these countries. Moreover, through institutional innovation like provision of public goods, access to the US market, availability of stable currency to facilitate international transaction; the US managed to lower down transaction costs. Lowering of such costs further stimulated economic activity (read export – import trade). This dispelled any scepticism that remained in the minds of those adopting open policies and reassured them of the likely benefits when executed.

Secondly, certain policies that were considered by the US as growth yielding were pushed through political pressure or with carrots like procurement policies, outright grants, concessional loans etc.

Thirdly, the most dominant and long lasting influence on the economic choices of Southeast Asia has been the creation of global economic institutions like IMF (1944), IBRD (1945) and GATT (1947). Of these, the first two are financial institutions and have a greater bearing on the economic policies due to the financial power they wield. It is the US leadership that provided the impetus for creating these institutions. The US provided global liquidity and encouraged the use of its dollar as a stable currency internationally. Later the same was extended through the IMF/WB that fostered international capital mobility, balance of payment financing, and international economic stability. These institutions made out autarky to be a less viable proposition and instead promoted/advocated a system of international trade with minimum barriers.

Japan too played an important role in shaping economic opportunities for the ASEAN3; mainly at the behest of the US, to keep communism away from the region in the post-war period. In return Japan hoped to gain US support in the form of a massive $4 billion regional economic assistance programme and the creation of an Asian Payments Union. In the 1950s and 1960s Japan made an effort to develop new institutions to promote and foster regional economic cooperation and enhance economic capabilities in the region. It played the role of a well-settled elder brother. Regional institutions like the Southeast Asian Treaty Organization (SEATO), ECAFE, ADB, ASEAN and APEC were established.

Participants at the 1963 meeting of ECAFE discussed the possibility of beginning an Asian Development Bank. In 1960, the Asian Development Bank (ADB) was started with Japan subscribing to 1/5th of the total capital. The US provided an equal share. Today this is an important organization aiding and assisting the Asian region as a whole and Southeast Asia in particular.

The most important multilateral institution in Southeast Asia is the ASEAN. Japan, initially had reservations against its formation, but later on whole-heartedly endorsed it by providing a $1 billion loan to each of the ASEAN5 (ASEAN3, Philippines and Singapore) in 1977 for regional projects.

With the end of the Cold War broader regional institutions like Pacific Economic Co-operation Council (PECC) and Asia Pacific Economic Co-operation were formed. The former was established by a joint Australian-Japanese initiative in 1980 to bring together academicians, business leaders and government officials (in their unofficial capacity) representing 22 nations. The latter i.e., APEC emerged in 1989 in which Asia Pacific heads of government from all major trading entities in North America, Southeast Asia and the Pacific conferred on issues of regional concern. The APEC participants worked towards developing operational mechanisms to increase economic openness by expanding markets and lowering trade barriers.

First Oil Shock:

The second event is the First Oil Shock of 1973. The OPEC countries announced an embargo on supply of crude oil to countries supporting Israel. Subsequently, this led to an increase in the prices by about 125 percent. As such in the early 1970s there was a general rise in prices and the rise in oil prices only propelled it further.

Indonesia and Malaysia were net energy exporters but Thailand being a net importer (upto 90% of its energy needs) was severely affected. About 1/7th of its merchandise exports were used to pay for energy imports. Further, since high prices existed globally, production levels the world over reduced, resulting in a slow down in the pace of development of the ASEAN3.

In the case of Indonesia (a part of the OPEC group) the effect of increase in oil prices was positive. It gained, though not too significantly. In comparison to Saudi Arabia and Iran that produced 8.4m and 6.1m barrels per day respectively, Indonesia produced only 1.4m. Again, the large population in the country diluted any gains that accrued from the oil price hike.

The first oil crisis had a major effect on decision-makers in Malaysia and Thailand also because international investors shied away from these economies (details discussed in Chapter 4). While the flow of FDI had doubled in the early 1970s, it stagnated between 1973-79. To make up for these losses, loans were availed of. Loans had now become easily available from the International Banks that were flush with petro dollars coming from OPEC countries. Such flows (loans) clubbed with remittances from nationals working in the OPEC countries helped overcome the problem to a large extent.

Overall, the first oil shock resulted in a lot of borrowing on the part of these economies from international banks. The high indebtedness was sustainable as the money was being used for investment rather than consumption. However, such loans definitely had a bearing on the policy measures implemented in these economies in later years. This statement will be better understood after the discussion on the Second Oil Shock.

The Second Oil Shock:

The Third event is the Second Oil Shock. After the First Oil Shock the prices stabilised and with the high investment financed from international borrowing, there was a spur in growth. Most countries had not adjusted to the shock but had learned to live with a current account deficit. But the Second Oil Shock occurred and oil prices increased from $12 in 1979 a barrel to $32 in 1981. The resulting debt crisis (including the one in Mexico) demonstrated the flaw in the above strategy. The Second Oil Shock increased the cost of imports, reduced economic growth rates, slowed the expansion of world trade especially between 1980 and 1982. By 1983 current account deficits in the ASEAN3 were as follows: - 7.5% of GDP in Indonesia, 11.5% of GDP in Malaysia and 7.5% of GDP in Thailand.

The situation put pressure on the policy makers to adopt a new line of thinking and make efforts to correct the BOP situation.

Slump in World Commodity prices:

The next event is the slump in world commodity prices between 1984 and 1986 and the oil price plunge in 1986. The former affected Southeast Asia as a whole while the latter, Indonesia. Prices of agricultural raw materials fell from 100 (index) in 1984 to 76 in 1986. The terms of trade of the ASEAN3 were adversely affected as the prices of rubber, tin, palm oil and other major exports declined internationally.

Reduction in private inflows:

The final event that affected policy-making in Southeast Asia is the reduction in the transfer of resources from developed countries to developing countries. This was the fallout of a loss of confidence of private lenders in the developing countries. International banks reduced their foreign lending. At this time, bilateral and multilateral sources like IMF and the WB became an important source of aid. With the loan commitment made by IMF/WB, investor confidence returned in developing economies in general; and Southeast Asia in particular. IMF/ WB loans, of course, came with conditionalities (See AnnexureA). The origin of a number of economic policies implemented in Indonesia and Thailand can be seen in these conditionalities.

Thus *to **sum up,*** the First and Second Oil Shocks (which made the Southeast Asian economies vulnerable) and the indebtedness to international banks left the Southeast Asian economies with little choice but to borrow from international financial institutions like the IMF and the WB. These institutions, therefore, had a bearing on the economic policies followed by these countries. Added to these was the influence of US and Japan. In other words, these countries were left with a Hobson's choice – either liberalize, privatise and globalize and hope to achieve high growth or else continue on the path of low growth. The choice was obvious.

The rest of the developing world kept away from open policies initially but most of them succumbed to the lure of these policies by the end of 1980s/early 1990s.

Features of Southeast Asian Development Experience

Each of the approaches discussed above is derived from or linked to certain features of Southeast Asian development experience. This Section examines such features observed in the ASEAN3 since the mid-1980s. There is considerable similarity in form and timing throughout the region. Hence, it is possible to generalize and collectivise.

These economic policies of the Southeast Asian nations reflect the openness in these economies, their high degree of inter-relationship with the global economy, their receptivity to the changes in the macroeconomic conditions and the influence exerted by the WB/IMF in their formulation and character.

The objective of this section is to examine how each feature (listed below from 1-6) influenced the development of the ASEAN3 and to what extent it was beneficial for growth or otherwise.

1) Macroeconomic Stability:

Macroeconomic stability is generally considered a key factor stimulating economic growth. There are various ways in which macroeconomic stability can be maintained and the Southeast Asian economies seem to have dabbled with all of them:

a) Keeping inflation under control: A strong case exists in favour of the co-relation between price stability and growth. In other words, there are many ***ill effects*** of inflation. High inflation often ***reduces returns to savers*** thus acting as a disincentive to save and invest. This can be explained as follows:

The real interest rate is the difference between the nominal interest rate and the inflation rate i.e.

Real Interest Rate = Nominal Interest Rate – Inflation rate [20]

So higher the inflation rate, lower the real interest rate and smaller the returns to the saver.

Real interest rates averaged 5.88% during 1986-95 in Southeast Asia as a whole as is evident from Table 3.2. It was the highest in Indonesia followed by Thailand and Malaysia. Graph 3.B clearly shows the same. The real interest rates were negative for most other developing countries. The positive real interest rates resulted in high savings rates as can be seen in Tables 3.22a, 3.22b and 3.22c.

High inflation often ***distorts the investment pattern*** by channelising investment to real estate or other such forms of property that are considered as a hedge against inflation for the investors. However, such investment being unproductive creates further inflationary pressure.

Other adverse effects of high inflation include ***low profitability*** resulting in dampening entrepreneurial initiative and formulation of long-term investment plans. It also causes *capital flight* from the host country reducing the investment in the domestic economy. Finally, it results in ***higher real tax collection***, as governments do not respond to inflation by altering tax rates immediately and thereby reducing private savings.

Apart from the above considerations for keeping inflation low, the past experiences of these countries have also prompted them to keep inflation under control.

For instance, in Indonesia aversion to inflation grew out of traumatic inflationary spirals that accompanied economic and political crises. In Malaysia, the success of the fiscal conservatism of the colonial era seems to have shaped post-colonial policies. In Thailand, the tradition of responsible fiscal policies dates back to the 19th century, when a strong currency helped the Kingdom retain its independence.[21]

Table 3.3 shows the inflation rates for Southeast Asia for the period 1986-95. The average rate of inflation for the whole period was 5.13%, which is quite low. Individually it is highest in Indonesia at 8.86%, lowest in Malaysia at 3.98% and moderate in Thailand at 4.84%. The adjoining graphical illustration (Graph 3.C) makes it clearer.

Measures to contain inflation

It is pertinent to enquire into how the inflation rates were kept at low levels in these countries. In **Indonesia**, inflation was quite high in the early 1980s. Responding to the IMF/WB conditionalities, a number of steps were taken in the mid-1980s to control the same through monetary and fiscal policy adjustments. On the monetary side (financial actually), capital markets were deregulated. Interest rate controls and sectorial credit ceilings were removed and subsidised credit was done away with. On the fiscal side, government expenditure was curtailed, tariff rates were lowered and foreign investment encouraged. These policies were directed at increasing production and lowering inflation.[22]

Malaysia presents a totally different case of macroeconomic management where inflation was always low from the 1970s through the 1980s upto the mid-1990s. High economic growth, rapid export growth and prudent fiscal and monetary management were the key elements in keeping inflation at bay.

During the 1970s, **Thailand**, like other oil importing primary producers, experienced recurrent economic crisis and high inflation. In the mid 1980s Thailand's economic policy was closely supervised by the IMF/WB. They recommended (details in Chapter 4) a 5-year programme of structural adjustment including adoption of a strong deflationary monetary and fiscal policy[23]. Hence by the mid 1980s inflation was brought under control. It may be mentioned here that unlike in Indonesia, in Thailand inflation was never a serious problem.

Nexus Between Inflation and GDP

Is there a causal relationship between inflation and GDP? A cursory glance at Table 3.4 and Graph 3.D would make it adequately clear that low rates of inflation in the ASEAN3 has helped in achieving a high GDP rate. The table shows growth rates for Indonesia, Malaysia and Thailand for the time period 1986-95. In fact, even among these three countries, the growth rate has been higher where the inflation rates have been lower. In Malaysia and Thailand GDP growth rate was 8.6% and 9.6% respectively and inflation rates were 2.89% and 4.38% respectively for the time period 1986-95. For Indonesia, GDP growth rate was 7.6% while inflation rate was 8.13%. Taking the ASEAN3 together the average GDP growth rate for 1986-95 was an impressive 8.62% and the inflation rate was a moderate 5.13%.

***b*) Low Budgetary Deficit**: The relationship between budget deficit and macroeconomic stability cannot be ascertained unless one knows how the deficit is financed. If a deficit is financed by excessive monetary financing, it will lead to inflation. However, if the deficit is financed through the government's domestic borrowing, interest rates will go up and crowd out private borrowing. Finally, if the deficit is financed through external borrowing, it can lead to a debt crisis.

In **Indonesia**, the budget deficit was about -5.6% of GDP in 1986 as seen in Table 3.5. The decline in oil prices and the consequent deterioration in the terms of trade were responsible for this[24].

At the behest of the IMF/WB, a structural adjustment and stabilisation (SSA) programme was effected (details in Chapter 4) and sharp cuts were made in government's expenditure. As a result, the deficit reduced to 1.4% of GDP by 1989. Table 3.6 shows that, government expenditure as a percentage of GDP decreased from 21.3% to 15% from 1986 to 1995. On the revenue front, efforts were made to increase receipts. Government revenue as a percentage of GDP increased from 15.7% in 1986 to 18.8% in 1990 after which there was a fall to 14.8% in 1995 as can be seen in Table 3.7.

As far as **Malaysia** is concerned, in the early 1980s budget deficits were high. In 1981-82 it reached about 20% of GDP and came down to 14.1% in 1986. However, by the end of the decade it came down further to 3.0% as is evident from Table 3.5. Malaysia was able to finance its budgetary deficits without much difficulty. Firstly, Malaysia's financial savings levels were quite high and much of these savings went into the domestic financial system[25] (as opposed to real assets or capital flight as in the case of Latin America). The government's provident fund mobilized domestic savings in large measures to finance the budget in a non-inflationary manner. Secondly, since the growth rate of GDP was quite high in Malaysia, much of the monetary financing could be absorbed without resulting in inflation.

In the early 1980s in **Thailand**, the government deficit was 8% of GDP. However, by 1986, as is evident from Table 3.5, it was brought down to – 3.1 in 1986 and further to – 0.7 in 1987. From 1988 onwards, Thailand experienced a budgetary surplus this was maintained upto 1995. Such changes were brought about through steep reduction in Central Government expenditure on one hand and a hike in tax rates on the other.

A graphical representation of the budgetary deficit/ surplus for the period 1986-95 is presented in Graph 3.E. This gives a clear picture of the fiscal austerity followed by these economies during this period.

c) **External Debt under control**: Although Thailand and Indonesia had faced some debt problems and Indonesia had to reschedule some of its debts in the early 1980s, timely assistance from the IMF helped them tide over this problem. Over the period 1986-95, they did not face any serious debt problem.

A high debt/GNP ratio becomes a problem or is harmful to the economy when export growth is not high enough to earn adequate forex to service foreign debt.

Table 3.8 shows the EDT/GNP ratio and EDT/XGS for Indonesia, Malaysia and Thailand for 1980, 1982 and 1985-94. Since the EDT/ XGS ratio was high enough there was no major debt problems in the

ASEAN3 economies. In fact even during the peak periods, i.e., 1987 in Indonesia, 1985 in Malaysia and Thailand when the EDT/GNP ratio was 69%, 86.5% and 47.8% respectively, the EDT/XGS ratio were high at 263.5, 138.4 and 171.7 respectively, and helped sustain the indebtedness.

d) **Relatively stable exchange rate:** With a view to maintain macroeconomic stability Indonesia and Thailand engineered major depreciations in their currencies from the early 1980s to the mid 1980s after which it remained relatively stable. It may be noted here that after 1994-95 until 1997 these currencies started appreciating.

Indonesia's rupiah was pegged to the US$ during 1971-78. But, due to higher inflation in Indonesia as against the US, the Rupiah appreciated vis-à-vis the dollar necessitating major devaluations in 1978 (51%), 1983 (38%) and 1986 (45%). As part of the SSA it rescheduled some capital-intensive projects to conserve forex.

Malaysia's currency was pegged to the British pound sterling during the Bretton Woods period but later in 1974 it was floated. Malaysia's economy enjoyed a healthy growth till the early 1980s due to strong international markets for its raw materials. However, since the mid 1980s these markets shrunk and a reform programme was introduced to encourage foreign and domestic investment and export-oriented industrialization. The stable exchange rate of Malaysia's ringgit helped in achieving this end.

Until 1984, the exchange rate of the **Thai** baht was pegged to the US dollar since 1954. There were two devaluations one in 1981 and the other in 1984. In 1984, the baht was floated against a basket of currencies as part of the Structural Adjustment Programme (SAP) under the IMF. Ever since the exchange rate has remained relatively stable.

In all the ASEAN3 countries, the stability in exchange rates helped increase exports, create a FDI boom and thereby propel the GDP growth rate. Adequate proof of the same is also evident in the subsequent discussion on outward orientation.

e) Quickly Responding to Macroeconomic Shocks:

Each of the ASEAN3 went through a lean phase in the early 1980s and immediately started taking corrective steps to salvage their economies from slipping any further.

In **Indonesia**, the collapse of oil and other commodity prices in the early 1980s, combined with the deep worldwide recession brought about a major deterioration in the terms of trade and a significant fall in exports[26]. By 1982, the current account deficit had grown to $7.2 billion. On the advice of the World Bank, the Indonesian government undertook an SSA programme encompassing exchange rate adjustment, fiscal and tax policy changes, reforms in the monetary, trade and industrial sectors. Currency was devalued, tax laws were simplified and their coverage extended, controls on interest rates were abandoned, capital markets were liberalised, trade and tariff laws were rationalized and restriction on forex reduced.

The benefits of these were as follows:

- Inflation rate dropped from 13% to 7.5% between 1982-89
- Mix of exports changed- non-oil exports took the place of oil exports
- FDI increased

As noted earlier, **Malaysia** enjoyed excellent economic growth during the 1970s. However, in the early 1980s changes in the international economic environment in the form of lower demand for its raw materials created turbulence in the economy. A decline in the terms of trade and an increase in government expenditure lead to a BOP deficit and a fiscal deficit. The government therefore undertook a series of reforms to rescue the economy. They were mainly aimed at promoting investment (both domestic and foreign) in the Malaysian economy and at privatisation. They included –

- Reduction in interest rates
- Monetary policy relaxation
- New Investment Fund (NIF) set up to encourage investment

As a result of the reforms the economic health of the country improved. There was a restructuring in the composition of exports – raw material component was reduced, while manufactured exports were given a boost. It may be mentioned here that the reform process in Malaysia was independent of any major involvement of multilateral organizations. In this, it is different from Indonesia and Thailand that have always approached the IMF/WB.

In the early 1980s, the sharp oil price rise resulted in an increase in the money value of Thailand's imports. The current account deficit was 7% of GDP. However, since the foreign borrowing was moderate, external debt to GDP ratio was 35% in 1982; there was no debt crisis. However, the fiscal deficit was 7% of GDP. Therefore, the Thailand government instituted a macroeconomic adjustment programme in collusion with the IMF/WB. The Thai Baht was devalued, export-promotion schemes introduced, tax collection mechanism was spruced up and reduction of government expenditure was effected. In line with such policy changes, measures to increase FDI were also implemented.

All these had very positive effects. Exports increased, FDI boomed, fiscal deficit turned into a surplus and GDP grew at a miraculous rate.

Hence, macroeconomic stability was effected through low inflation rates, low budget deficit, manageable external debt/GNP, maintaining exchange rate stability and responding quickly to the macroeconomic environment.

2) <u>Openness/Outward orientation:</u>

The Southeast Asian Economies made a decisive switch towards outward oriented strategies. These countries actively encouraged exports, reduced import tariffs and removed quantitative restrictions. Over time they dismantled barriers to capital inflows and outflows.[27]

Before attempting to find out what was the nature of openness or outward oriented policies the Southeast Asian Countries followed and what was the benefit they secured from the same, it would be worth the while to understand the definition of these terms and other related terms.

Some Definitions:

Tariq Banuri[28], has distinguished between these terms. According to him:

a. Openness is a description of the economy indication, its degree of integration with global economy forces. It can be divided into 2 categories:

i) *Trade Openness* – which refers to the exposure of the goods market to the international economy and is measured by the ratio of exports to GDP

ii) *Financial Openness*, which indicates the exposure of the domestic financial system to world capital markets and is measure by the volume, nature and regulation of international capital flows, including the size of the foreign debt, or the existence of capital controls.

b) Outward Orientation: is a description of government policies – trade Liberalisation, devaluation, exchange rate unification, removal of capital controls, financial liberalization – all of which create openness.

c) The liberal economy is a description of an economy with minimal government restrictions, not only on international trade in goods or assets, but also in domestic financial, commodities and labour markets.

d) Economic liberalization is a strategy of policy reforms intended to take the economy from state of illiberalism to liberalism or in more hackneyed terms towards laissez faire.

In this sub-section the outward oriented policies adopted by the three Southeast Asian countries that created trade openness and how they helped in the miraculous growth will be discussed.

The principal mechanism through which trade promotes growth is follows:

- The growth of exports permits economies of scale, a degree of specialization and a level of production that cannot be sustained by domestic dd.

- The growth of imports alleviates growth retarding as shortages especially of goods and services used in production and leads to a slower increase in the costs of wage, goods, raw materials, capital required, technical and services
- Participation in international trade generates positive externalities, particularly with regard to learning that can expand the production frontier[29]

Trade Regimes

In the Southeast Asian economies, various measures were undertaken to increase exports, including devaluation (discussed in previous section), trade liberalisation, removal of capital controls and financial liberalisation. Chart 3.3 summarises the time period at which the trade liberalisation regimes were undertaken in the ASEAN3

In **Indonesia,** the structural reforms undertaken to push exports and create openness included devaluation, rationalisation of trade and tariff laws and less restriction on foreign investment.

The first step towards trade reform was taken in 1985 with steep cuts effected in tariffs as can be seen in Table 3.9. Between May and October 1986, government announced a package of exports incentives, major devaluation and the first of several programmes to simplify import and export procedures. Major exporters were given unrestricted duty free access to import. In 1986, various reforms to reduce inefficiencies in shipping, port handling and customs procedures were introduced. Also to promote non-oil exporters "producer exporters" were allowed the option of importing their inputs free without import duties. Non-tariff barriers (NTBs) such as import licensing were done away with for many products and a shift was made towards tariffs (but were not increased) as an instrument of import policy.

As can be seen from Chart 3.3 on Trade Regimes, **Malaysia** followed a policy of exports promotion right from the 1970s. However, at that time the major component of the exports were raw materials. After 1980-82, Malaysia experienced a decline in the terms of trade due to decline in the world demand for its exports. Therefore, Malaysia made policy adjustments in its trade policy in 1985-86 and managed to reverse the situation. Since then for a period of 8-10 years there was an export boom.

The reforms included reducing the restrictions on foreign ownership and liberalizing the same by tying them to exports and employment requirements. Tariffs were revised to support a shift from import substitution to export oriented investment. Table 3.9 shows that average tariffs declined to 15% by 1996 from 20% in the earlier period. Various measures were undertaken to stimulate manufactured exports. Exchange control measures like repatriation of export proceeds in any foreign currency were also introduced. Tax incentives for exports were increased and imports were liberalised.

To promote exports in **Thailand** devaluation was effected (discussed earlier). A market determined exchange rate was adopted with minimal exchange controls; low and uniform tariff and non-tariff barriers (as compared to other developing countries) were used as policy options. Local content regulation was done away with. Export taxes were reduced. In general, Thailand's economy shifted explicitly towards export promotion.

Growth of Exports and Forex Reserves

What was the outcome of such open policies towards trade? It may be judged by observing Table 3.10 and Graph 3.H It can be seen that the average annual growth rate of per capita GDP was highest for Thailand at 7.7% and so was the average annual growth rate of exports at 23.08 during 1986-95. For Malaysia the same was 5.1% and 16.78% respectively. Only for Indonesia it has been relatively lower at 5.3% and 9.3% respectively.

Export growth induced by open trade policies and financial openness (discussed in next sub-section) brought about an increase in forex reserves as can be seen from Table 3.13. For Indonesia, forex reserves increased from $3.9 billion to $17.8 billion between 1986-96. Similarly for Malaysia for the same time period increase in forex reserves was from $5.6 Billion to $26.1 billion. Thailand too experienced a phenomenal increase in forex during 1986-96 periods from $2.7 billion to $37.1 billion.

Extent of Trade Openness

The extent of openness of the policies and their results can also be observed from Tables 3.11 and 3.12 that show the exports of goods and services as a percent of GDP and imports of goods and services as a percent of GDP respectively. For Malaysia exports of goods and services as a percent of GDP has steadily increased from 55.0% in 1985 to 95.4% in 1995. For Thailand too there is a rise from 22.8% to 42.2% between 1985-95. Finally, for Indonesia, it has increased marginally from 21.9% to 26.2% between 1985-95

A similar story is seen in case of imports of goods and services as a percent of GDP. It has risen from 50% in 1985 to 99.2% in 1995 for Malaysia. For Thailand in the same period the rise is from 25.6% to 49.3% while for Indonesia, the rise is marginal from 20.1% to 29.9% during 1985-95.

Going by the definition of openness to trade with respect to the quantity of exports, Malaysia is the most open followed by Thailand, followed by Indonesia. Thus, the open trade policies have propelled exports and imports and, of course, the GDP.

If trade openness is measured by the extent of reduction in tariff and NTB it can be said that these economies are not very open. Yet, when compared to other developing countries they are more open. This aspect of openness has been considered under the sub-section of trade policy in Chapter 4 for each country separately, as the policies have not been uniform in the ASEAN3.

3. Financial openness and creation of a favourable environment for foreign direct investment (FDI):

Foreign capital was welcomed in the ASEAN3 whatever form it took – short term and long term borrowing, or FDI or portfolio investment. Of these, FDI played a very important role in the economic development of these countries and hence this section deals with the same. FDI is said to be the most stable of capital flows since others tend to reverse during times of political and economic difficulty.

Theoretically speaking FDI brings the following advantages to the host country[30]:

(a) It is an additional source of capital. Therefore, it can be added to the domestic savings and helps increase the rate of growth of output.

(b) FDI helps in overcoming forex shortages.

(c) If the return to capital is higher in the host country, FDI will improve the international allocation of resources (this was explained through flying geese model in Section I of this Chapter).

(d) FDI can serve as a vehicle of technology transfer. Multinational companies bring new production techniques that generate benefits for both the host and source country.

(e) FDI also helps in the expansion of international trade. Infact there exists a close nexus between increase in FDI and increase in exports and imports. In addition, in areas of services such as banking, insurance and telecom, FDI is considered the most important instrument promoting trade.

(f) Another positive spill over effect of FDI is the qualitative improvement in the Human resources. Firms established by FDI tend to train workers more efficiently than local firms, with well-trained managers from the parent firms passing on their management and other skills. This in turn increases awareness towards better and higher education and the need for it.

(g) Finally, FDI tends to enhance competition in the domestic market, especially where previously monopoly/oligopoly situations existed. Therefore, it tends to bring about increased efficiency and also increased economic growth.

Policies to attract FDI

Given the above-mentioned benefits it is worth the while examining in brief, policies that were adopted in Indonesia, Malaysia and Thailand to attract FDI.

In **Indonesia**, since the mid 1980s many efforts were made to make the climate conducive to foreign investment in general and FDI in particular. In 1985, the investment co-ordinating board, BKPM simplified the application procedures for foreign investment documents to be submitted by potential investors were cut to half, waiting period for application reduced from 6 to 2 months and charges to process investment applications were waived. In 1986, further restrictions were eased – all new investment projects were granted a one-year tax exemption on imported equipment and raw material. BKPM lifted visa requirements on businessmen from 29 countries. Foreign companies were granted the same privileges enjoyed by local companies e.g. access to local currency from state owned commercial banks, right to distribute their goods without Indonesian intermediaries etc. In the following years, foreign investors were granted access to the stock exchange and in the number of areas open to foreign investment, pcrtfolio investors could purchase upto 49% of shares and so on.

Malaysia too undertook measures in the mid 1980s to make the climate conducive for foreign investment in general, and FDI in particular. Foreign ownership restrictions were liberalised by tying them to exports and employment requirements. The proportion of foreign ownership could be 100% if the companies increased 50% or more of output or employed 350 full time Malaysian workers. Later this was reduced to 20% of exports and applied to hotel and tourist projects. In Malaysia FDI helped build the electronics and semiconductors sector and expand the existing textiles and apparel industry.

In **Thailand**, foreign investment was strongly encouraged with major concessions allowing ownership of land, repatriation of capital, waiving of duties on imported capital goods and tax holidays. In 1986 the Thai Fund was established in New York and London to interest foreign investors in portfolio investment in Thailand. In 1989, Bank of Thailand relaxed forex controls to permit freer inflows and outflows of funds. There was a continued large influx of foreign investment as a result. The government even played an important role in encouraging the foreign commercial banks to start branches in Thailand.

Gauging the extent of financial openness and FDI trends

As mentioned in the earlier section on trade openness, financial openness implies exposure of the domestic financial system to the world capital markets and may be measured by the volume, nature and regulation of international capital flows, including the size of the foreign debt or the existence of capital controls.

A World Bank study of 1997 provides a comparison of a sufficiently related variable: the degree to which an economy is financially integrated internationally. The index takes into account the country's access to international financial markets, its ability to attract private capital from abroad and its level of diversification of financing. Chart 3.4 shows the overall index of financial integration across two periods 1985-87 and 1992-94.

As can be seen, Southeast Asian economies have moved from medium to high degree of financial integration from time period 1985-87 to 1992-94.

A much more simplified degree of financial openness can be judged from the FDI/GDP percentage. An increase in this would indicate that the policies have been fairly open and that they have been effective in increasing GDP growth. Table 3.14 and the graphical illustration of it shown in Graph 3.I indicate the same. The advantage of taking this indicator is that it removes the effect of market size, inflation and currency movements.

The early and leading role of **Malaysia** is clearly apparent. Since Malaysia is a smaller country, it was one of the first to reach saturation as far as import substitution industrialisation (ISI) policies are concerned and moved to export oriented industrialisation (EOI). In addition, its proximity to Singapore helped to attract labour intensive manufacturing in which Singapore was rapidly losing its competitiveness. There is a dramatic increase in FDI inflows as a percentage of GDP from 1987 onwards upto 1995, peaking in 1992. This trend indicates that the policy measures adopted in the mid 1980s to attract FDI were successful.

Insofar as **Indonesia** is concerned, there are two clear periods when FDI inflow was high. The first was during the mid 1970s when Indonesia had undertaken a SSA programme at the behest of World Bank (details are given in Chapter 4, Section I). The second period when FDI flows increased was from 1987-88 to 1996, peaking in 1996. Indonesia was ranked as the 17th greatest recipient of inward investment in the 1990s. This period co-incided with the improvement in the investment climate after another SSA programme was undertaken. In addition, due to a shift in competitiveness of the NIEs, Indonesia became a preferred FDI destination.

Until the mid 1980s in **Thailand**, the FDI received was far less than its neighbour Malaysia. The situation improved dramatically between 1988-94 with FDI peaking in 1990. During 1990s, Thailand was the 8th largest recipient of FDI. The FDI policies and massive relocation of production away from Japan and NIEs was responsible for this. However, since the 1990s there is a reversal in the trend. The same could be attributed to the bloodless military coup, shortage of infrastructure especially port facilities and availability of skilled workers as the nature of investment projects became more skill intensive.

Table 3.15, which shows FDI as a proportion of investment, corroborates the same story. FDI as a proposition of investment was 10.5% in 1981-85 increased to 16.3% in 1994 in Malaysia. In Indonesia for the same time periods, it increased from 1.0% to 4.2%. In Thailand, it increased from 3.2% to 5.9% between 1981-85 and 1986-90. But in 1994, it fell to 1.2% (the reasons for this reversal are mentioned above). Graph 3.J provides a graphical representation of this and the comparisons in the three time periods is clearer.

Hence from the above discussion it can be concluded that FDI policies coupled with the advantage of the relocation of production that took place from Japan and NIEs to Indonesia, Malaysia and Thailand were effective and they helped increase the GDP growth. The economies had fairly open FDI policies and FDI/GDP grew between 1985-96.

There were other benefits that FDI inflows bestowed on these economies. They were as follows:

a) There was an increased awareness in these economies to improve human skills. One can judge the same by the percentage of secondary school enrolment increase. This is shown in Table3.16. As is evident the GSE ratio has increased more in Malaysia over the period 1980-96 than in Indonesia and Thailand. This can be put down to the fact that Malaysia received much more FDI than Indonesia and Thailand. However, in Indonesia and Thailand, with the increase in

FDI being more during early 1990s, the GSE ratio shows a more dramatic change from the time period 1990 to 1996.

b) FDI has also lead to an increase in employment. The increase is employment is mainly in the manufacturing sector since FDI was directed towards this sector. In the initial boom period, FDI was directed towards labour intensive manufacturing. Table3.17 provides ample proof of how employment has increased between 1986-93 in all three Southeast Asian economies. It increased two fold in Indonesia and Thailand and three fold in Malaysia. After 1993, the labour force employment remained fairly stable since there was a shift towards capital-intensive projects/skill intensive projects. Here Malaysia did not face too much of a problem since by this period it was better prepared for the change but in Indonesia and Thailand, the shortage of such workers caused some difficulty.

c) FDI has brought about an increase in technology transfer the same can be assessed by the increase in annual import of machinery and equipment. Table 3.18provides ample evidence for this.

d) Finally, FDI growth has added to an increase in manufacturing. The sub-section relating to industrial policy gives details of the same.

4. Resource mobilization:

During the 1980s, considerable deregulation of financial institutions and financial markets took place in the DMCs. The importance of the financial sector in the functioning of a market economy and its growth and development is indeed a well-established fact and need not be overemphasized. The financial sector acts as an intermediary between savers and investors in mobilizing funds both domestic and foreign that determines the level of investment and thus economic growth. In general there is said to exist a strong positive correlation between various measures of financial system sophistication and the of the level of economic development as measured by the real GNP.[31] This is because there is an increase in mobilization of domestic saving and this in turn has a favourable effect on the extent and productivity of investment.

Southeast Asian financial sector liberalization reforms started in the second half of the 1980s as seen in Chart 3.5. In Indonesia and Thailand it was part of the broader programme aimed at introducing market mechanization as suggested by the IMF/WB.

In 1988, **Indonesia** adopted a wide-ranging programme of financial deregulation and liberalization following an initial phase of bank deregulation that occurred in 1983. The financial sector was open to private sector participation for establishment of new banks and financial companies. Foreign interests were also welcome. As a result, number of banks increased by about 60 in domestic and joint venture and by 1000 in terms of branches of these banks. Along with opening of banks to private sector interest rates were deregulated. Both these measures together caused an increase in economic growth and rapid expansion of banks. Other liberalization measures included, abandoning of controls on interest rates, lifting of ceilings on sectoral credit and abolishing of subsidized liquidity credit. Discussion in Chapter 4 will clearly show that such measures were advocated by the IMF/World Bank and later made part of the five- year plans.

In Indonesia, the reforms provide evidence that differential taxation of financial instruments can make an important impact on the method of financing private corporate investment. Before 1983, the tax system strongly favoured bank credit over venture capital because withholding tax on bank deposit interest was suspended while equity dividends and bond interests were subject to income tax. However, in 1988, 15% withholding tax on deposit interest rates were introduced to level the playing field vis-à-vis stock market dividends.

Again, in 1989 (October), the government announced several other refinements to 1988 financial sector deregulation packages in the areas of taxation, the stock market and foreign banks

Malaysia's financial sector is relatively well developed. In the mid-1980s financial instability developed to some extent because of a combination of low commodity prices, poor financial market regulations and malpractices in trading. Since then, a prudential regulatory framework has been developed and tightened to prevent abuses.

However, at the same time, restrictive regulations and bureaucratic controls have been sharply reduced.

There were about 38 licensed commercial banks in Malaysia in 1992, 16 of which were foreign owned. As per the Banking and Financial Institutions Act of 1989, foreign banks were required to divest upto 51% of their capital to Malaysian interests but even this did not discourage any of them to leave. Other financial institutions including – Merchant Banks, Islamic Banks (which operate on a profit/loss basis and not on interest rate basis) were established. Numerous Financial and Leasing companies too exist in Malaysia. In 1991, the Base Lending Rate was freed from administrative controls and banks were allowed to set their own rates subject to certain guidelines. Domestic interbank money market borrowing was also completely deregulated.

As far as the capital market is concerned, the Kuala Lumpur Stock Exchange was delinked from Singapore Stock Exchange. Malaysian stocks could no longer be listed on the Singapore exchange. This delinking was accompanied by strong measures to privatise major public enterprises ranging from airline and shipping firms to utility and telecom companies. This programme was aptly titled The Privatisation Master Plan where 69 state enterprises of 246 were to be privatised during 1991-95. Privatisation is seen as a major method to boost the development of the capital market and incoming participation by lower income citizens in the ownership of corporate assets.

In **Thailand**, the financial system remained rather closed and highly regulated during most of the 1980s. Controls were maintained on foreign exchange transactions, interest rates were regulated and strict licensing procedures for banks enforced. The rate at which the economy was growing, the large inflows of FDI and rapid growth of manufacture required that the development of financial institutions be undertaken at a fast pace too.

Hence, in the second half of the 1980s, the Bank of Thailand and the Ministry of Finance undertook financial sector liberalization reforms. Regulation of the banking system, capital markets and conduct of the monetary policy was the focus of these reforms. The interest rates were liberalized and some barriers between bank and nonbank financial institutions were eliminated. Forex controls were reduced. Ceilings on depreciation, interest rates have been lifted and those on lending rates were eliminated by 1992.

The Bank of Thailand was now to play a more active supervisory role focussing on bank capacity adequacy and quality of assets. The bank capitalization guidelines were revised and brought in line with the standards set by the Bank for International settlements (BIS).

Measures were also adopted in order to eliminate differential tax treatment of financial instruments in Thailand in 1991. Financial transactions were exempted from VAT while for the other transactions, tax rate was reduced and harmonised. In addition, the Public Company Act was amended to eliminate discrimination between listed and non-listed firms. This was done in order to develop the debenture and bond market.

The financial sector liberalization helped to increase savings and investment. However, it would be meaningful even to discuss what other factors lead to a rise in savings rate and investment rates.

Other Measures to increase savings rate:

Effect of policy fundamentals on savings rates: Two policy fundamentals that have affected the savings rate in a positive manner are the macroeconomic stability and budgetary choices.

As explained in the sub-section on macroeconomic stability, efforts were made to keep inflation rates at moderate/low levels. Hence, the real interest rates were positive and consequently there was low risk associated with holding financial assets (forms of savings). In other words, low inflation encouraged saving. Table 3.2 shows the real interest rates that were positive for the entire period 1986-95.

However, the real test is to see if such positive real interest rates resulted in increased deposits. Table 3.20a shows the ratio of Time and Savings Deposits to total money stock (M2) for Indonesia. It is very clear that the ratio has increased from 41% to 58% from 1986 to 1995. Thus, it can safely be said that positive real interest rates did increase savings. A similar picture is seen in the case of Thailand where the ratio of Time and Savings deposits to total money stock increased from 87 to92 and between 1986 and 1995 (See Table3.20b).

The other measure adopted to increase public savings was through the budgetary policy. There was an increase in taxation revenues and reduction in government expenditure. More emphasis was placed on the latter than the former. Tables 3.21a, 3.21b and 3.21c show government consumption as a percentage of GDP for Indonesia, Malaysia and Thailand respectively. It can be seen that in Indonesia it came down from 11.0% in 1986 to 7.8%in 1995; in Malaysia from 16.9% in 1986 to 12.6% in 1995 and; from 12.7% to 9.8% in Thailand for the same period.

Creation of Postal Savings institutions: In Malaysia specifically, to encourage savings and savers confidence, government run postal savings systems were established to attract small savers. This method is generally an effective method of mobilizing household savings. General Postal Savings Systems (like in India) piggy back on the mail delivery infrastructure and therefore minimize overhead and fixed cost. Postal Savings System offer small savers greater security and lower transaction costs than the private sector and are therefore considered more attractive to the low income and rural households. Malaysia also has a well-developed mandatory pension scheme.

Measures to promote investment

In order to promote investment, the bond and equity markets were developed. In the early 1980s the ***bond market*** was relatively small and enjoyed a government protected monopoly. For instance, the Thailand government had created a monopoly for its private long-term credit banks. However, in the post 1985 period, these economies realised the value of healthy bond markets. They eased laws that discriminated against corporate bonds. Thailand and Indonesia took the first step towards this by strengthening their rating and regulatory agencies. Later Malaysia too introduced a corporate bond-rating agency.

The ASEAN3 undertook to develop an ***equity market*** as well. The local private banks had underwriting privileges for the issue of stocks and bonds in Indonesia. Capitalization and size requirements for new issues were revised to introduce new uniform minimum requirement of Rp 200 million. In 1987 to further strengthen the capital market, a secondary 'OTC' market was established.

Another measure aimed at promoting investment by the ASEAN3 was through the ***creation of a wide range of financial institution*** to address the problem of long-term credit for industry and to fill the gap in the type of credit provided by private entities. Charts 3.6, 3.7 and 3.8 summarise the same.

Taxation policy to encourage investment

Like other developing economies the ASEAN3 too have employed a wide variety of tax policies to increase/encourage investment. These policies cover the entire gambit of reduced tax rates, tax holidays, investment credits, accelerated depreciation allowances and generous tax deductions.

In **Indonesia** the process of rationalization of the tax structure started much earlier. Here in 1985 itself the Sales Tax was replaced by VAT, levied at a rate of 10% on manufacturing and construction sectors and fuel oils. Simplified guidelines for tax obligations were made out and relief was granted through allowing for self-assessment and eliminating "tax bargaining" between taxpayers and tax officers.

In **Malaysia,** the government realised that high corporate taxes and highly variable incentives were doing more harm than good and therefore, began simplifying the tax system since 1989. The 1989 budget reduced corporate taxes from 40% to 35% and began phasing out the 5% development tax over a five- year period. In addition, sales tax exemption was removed from additional high value food products. Again in 1990 budget, 142 items obtained reductions in import duty, sales tax, and surtax and excise duties.

In **Thailand,** too the tax systems were very complex. Business and taxes were high and consisted of a bewildering array of rates. The government hence, since 1989 began to remedy the situation. The personal tax structure was partly simplified. The original tax rate was reduced. A 10% VAT was introduced to replace complex business taxes. In fact, this served two purposes, investment was also encouraged and tax addition and revenue collection too improved.

Increase in Investment Rates

The benefits that accrued with the adoption of such measures to increase investment can be gauged by seeing Tables 3.22 a, 3.22b and 3.22c.

In Indonesia GDI as a percentage of GDP increased from 28% in 1986 to 36% in 1990 and remained at an average of 31% thereafter until 1996. In Malaysia, GDI increased from 26.0% to 41% over the time period 1986-96. Similarly in Thailand GDI increased from 21.8% to 41.7% for the same time period.

The virtuous circle of investment, saving and GDP growth seems to have worked in Indonesia, Malaysia and Thailand.

5) Industrial Policy (IP):

Essentially, there are two ways of looking at an industrial policy [32]. The *first*, is a narrow view where IP used as an interventionist instrument in the allocation of resources and industrial organizations. The policy instruments normally used are import protection, direct subsidies, subsidized low interest rate loans and administrative interference in resource allocation and in industrial organizations. The *second*, broader point of view includes other indirect measures that governments take to improve the environment for industrial development. In Southeast Asia over a period of time, there has been a shift from interventionist policies to more indirect measures. In Indonesia and Thailand a reciprocal system known as 'clientelism' had been adopted. In this system, the industrial regime derives support, policies and finance from private firms, families and individuals who in turn receive low interest, protection, monopoly licenses and other such economy favours[33]. Such kind of intervention tends to lead to protected positions and rent seeking.

Chart 3.9 shows that the industrial policy regimes followed a distinct pattern. Initially they were all ISI in nature, later they all moved to export oriented policies. Booms favoured greater state intervention while foreign exchange constraints led to more liberal policy stance[34]. In the early 1980s industrial entry was directly controlled, there were limits on capacity, rules were enforced on the content of indigenous inputs and in general, foreign investment was not much encouraged. However, since the mid 1980s there was a change wherein trade was liberalised and foreign investment was encouraged.

The Southeast Asian industrial policy in the post reform era emphasised on development of export industries. The industrialization pattern was therefore an export led one. The selection of industries was guided by the principle of comparative advantage determined by existing and evolving factor endowments. Hence, initially production in resource-based industries dominated. This gradually shifted to labour intensive and finally to skill based industries. The policy was open to utilization of foreign human resources. It heavily relied on industrial linkage with the East Asian subregion as a whole and emphasized a great deal on FDI and capital markets. Chapter 4 gives the details of the industrial policies followed in these countries.

Efficacy of the IP

There were many ways of assessing the efficacy of the liberal export led industrial policies adopted by these economies:

Firstly, it can be assessed through the favourable effect that the industrial policy had on the ***manufacturing value added***. (MVA). Table3.19 indicates that over the time period (1986-95), MVA as a percentage of GDP in Indonesia has increased from 6.6 to 10.6. The change has been more dramatic in Malaysia where the increase is from 4.6% in 1986 to 13.1% in 1985. Similarly, in Thailand it increased from 7.9% in 1986 to 11.9% in 1995.

An observation to be made here is that in all three economies the MVA as a percent of GDP increased between 1986 – 90/91, after which it dropped marginally until 1992 and after that it started rising again. Such a wave-like pattern is seen because initially all the economies had resource based or labour intensive manufacturing. Gradually they started shifting to skill based manufacturing. During this transition period there was a drop in the value added, but it rose again once the structural adjustments were made. The value addition to industry has been one of the most important factors contributing to the growth in GDP. The next section providing quantitative evidence will prove the same.

A second indicator of the success of the industrial policy is the increase in the share of ***manufactured exports*** as a percentage of total exports. Table 3.23 shows that for 1980-95, in Indonesia the manufactured exports as a percent of total exports was 2.3% and it increased to 61.2%; in Malaysia it increased form 22% to 79% and in Thailand it increased from 29.6% to 83.5%. Indonesia had initially relied on oil exports (mineral exports) and after the oil price crash, it changed its export structure to replace it with non-oil goods and other manufactures. Hence, it was a late starter. This is clearer from the adjoining Graph 3.K.

Yet another way of assessing the efficacy of the industrial policy would be to see the changing structure of ***exports mix*** (Refer Table3.24). Broadly speaking, it can be said that all three economies initially relied on Group I commodities, which are basically primary goods, but between 1967-94, the same reduced. The drop in exports of this category is more obvious in case of Malaysia and Thailand than in the case of Indonesia. There is a rise observed in Group II (labour- intensive and resource based goods) and here the rise is more evident in Indonesia than in Malaysia or Thailand. The growth has been quite high in recent years in Group IV and V, which are skill intensive and this, is observed more for Malaysia and Thailand. Indonesia has not been able to keep pace with skill intensive exports to the extent that the other two countries in the region have.

Thus, the industrial policy along with the trade and foreign investment policies has helped in boosting GDP growth, through an increase in value added to industry and through an increase in manufactured exports. Within the manufactured exports sector there is observed an increase in the skill based exports and this is more evident in Malaysia and Thailand as compared to Indonesia.

6) Labour Inputs:

According to growth accounting concepts of development economics, a country's economic growth can be divided into three contributory parts: growth of ***labour input, growth of capital input and growth of total factor productivity (TFP)***[35]**.** The fact that capital inputs like increased domestic and foreign investment have resulted in a high GDP growth is already established in points 4 and 3 respectively. This leads to the next question that whether growth in the Southeast Asian economies has been propelled by technological innovation/TFP or by increased labour inputs.

TFP is the residual element after eliminating the contribution of labour and capital to growth. Notable economist Paul Krugman is of the opinion that it is not TFP but increased labour and capital inputs that has propelled growth in Southeast Asia. Krugman has equated the mechanism of East Asian growth (note that though this includes Southeast Asia, but Krugman's emphasis was more on Northeast Asia) to that of the former Soviet Union that relied on massive capital inputs. According to him, in East Asia too growth has been propelled by increased labour inputs and through increased capital inputs i.e., increased domestic and foreign investment.

As already noted earlier the TFP for Indonesia, Thailand and Malaysia have been low. Sarel's estimation for the time period 1979-96 would become more relevant for the present study. It shows that TFP was 0.9, 2.0 and 2.0 for Indonesia, Malaysia and Thailand respectively. In fact, it is lower than that in Taiwan – 2.5 (which in itself is low). The highest in East Asia is that of Hong Kong at 3.8.

Thus, it is clear that the growth in Southeast Asia that TFP has not really contributed to economic growth.

The question whether ***labour inputs*** have or not helped growth can easily be confirmed seeing the growth of labour employed in manufacture. There has been a definite increase in the number of labour employed in manufacture. Table 3.17 shows the same for the ASEAN3 countries. Note that the labour employed in manufacture has increased: in Indonesia from 5606 thousand to 10773 thousand indicating a 52% rise; in Malaysia from 861thousand to 2178 thousand indicating a 39% rise; and in Thailand from 2089 thousand to 4334 thousand indicating a 52% rise for the time period 1985-96.

Thus, the important factors responsible for the high growth rate of the ASEAN3 in the decade of 1986-95 are largely the *macroeconomic stability* that they maintained, their *outward orientation in trade* (export push), their *financial openness* towards *FDI*, their ability to *mobilise resources* and increase investment, their *liberal industrial policy* and the *increased labour inputs*.

Through a theoretical discussion, it is only possible to enumerate the various factors responsible for the growth of the ASEAN3 economies during the decade of 1985-95. In order to substantiate the results, econometric evidence is also presented here to indicate how much each factor contributed to GDP growth.

Econometric Model - GDPs responsiveness to its Determinants

This section deals with the responsiveness of the Gross Domestic Product to its various determinants. The response of the GDP (the dependent variable) to the factors (independent variables) affecting it is studied with the help of the technique of regression. The regression analysis is carried out for all the countries selected for this study.
An attempt has been made to establish the interrelationship between the growth rate of GDP and different macroeconomic variables for the decade 1986-95 for Indonesia, Malaysia and Thailand.

Dependent Variable: GDP growth rate (Y)

Independent Variables:	**Proxy Variables**
1) Macroeconomic Stability (Ms)	Budget deficit/ surplus
2) Outward Orientation in Trade (Ot)	Exports of Goods and services
3) Outward orientation in Investment (FDI)	Foreign Direct Investment
4) Savings (S)	Gross Domestic Saving
5) Industrial Policy (Ip)	Manufacturing Value Added
6) Labour inputs (L)	Employment in manufacturing

Thus,

Y = f {Ms, Ot, FDI, S, Ip, L}

In equation form

$$\mathbf{Y = \propto_0 + \propto_1 Ms + \propto_2 Ot + \propto_3 FDI + \propto_4 S + \propto_5 Ip + \propto_6 L}$$

The following results were obtained from the time series data collected for the selected countries for the time period 1986-97.

Correlation Coefficients:

The correlation matrix for all the three countries is presented in Tables 3.25, 3.26 and 3.27 for Indonesia, Malaysia and Thailand respectively. As expected, the value of correlation between the variables was quite high. Notwithstanding this general observation, a few exceptions are observed. For instance, in the case on Indonesia the correlation between budget deficit and other macro variables is in the range of 0.581 to 0.653.

Regression Coefficient

The enter method was used to obtain regression coefficients. The regression coefficients in the case of **Indonesia** are shown in Table 3.28 . The same indicates that the *regression coefficients* for Manufacturing Value Added (MVA) in industry works out to 0.841 and is higher than the corresponding regression co-efficient for other variables. In other words, MVA is the most significant variable affecting GDP. The *elasticity* of GDP with respect to MVA works out to 0.1639. Thus, a 1% increase in average MVA raised the GDP by 0.1639. The higher value of R^2 of the multiple regression indicates that the six independent variables considered together explain 99% of the total variation in the GDP.

For **Malaysia,** too similar results are obtained and the same is presented in Table 3.29. The most significant variable affecting GDP is MVA. The *beta coefficient* is 1.003. Here the *elasticity* of GDP with respect to MVA is 0.247. Thus, a 1% rise in average MVA raised the GDP by 0.247.

The results are consistent even in the case of **Thailand** (Table 3.30). Here too MVA is the most significant factor affecting GDP. The *regression coefficient* for the same is 0.912. The *elasticity* of GDP with respect to MVA is 0.2491. In other words, a 1% rise in average value addition to industry increases the GDP by 0.2491. R^2 shows that all the six variables taken together account for 99% of the total variation in GDP.

The values of elasticities indicate that change in GDP cannot occur independently with one single variable. The effect on GDP becomes significant when all the variables act together.

Therefore, the results of the regression analysis confirm that the independent variables Ms, Ot, FDI, S, Ip, and L have a positive effect on GDP. In other words, GDP responds positively to a low budget deficit, higher growth of exports, larger inflow of FDI, higher savings, increased value addition to industry and increased labour inputs.

Table 3.1

Total Factor Productivity

Country	(Bosworth & Collins)		Sarel
	1960-94	1984-94	(1979-96)
Indonesia	0.8	0.9	0.9
Malaysia	0.9	1.4	2.0
Thailand	1.8	3.3	2.0

Source: ADO 1999

Table 3.2

Real Interest Rates

Country	Average real interest rates
Southeast Asia (A-3)	5.88
Indonesia	9.14
Malaysia	2.8
Thailand	5.7

Source: Basic data from Key Indicators of Developing Asian and Pacific
Countries (various issues) and ADO (various issues)

Note: Calculated by subtracting inflation rate from interest rates on deposits
(sav & time) for each country and their average was taken

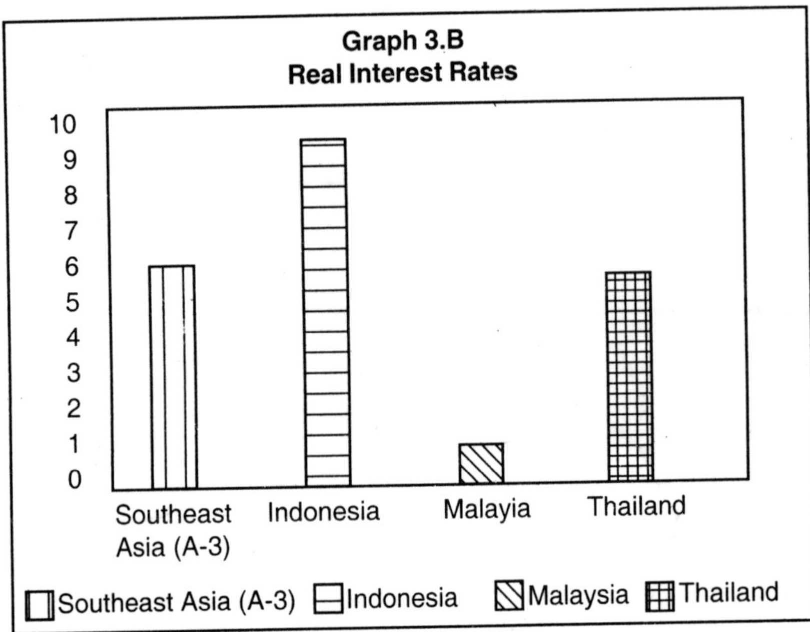

Table 3.3

Inflation Rate

Year	Indonesia	Malaysia	Thailand
1986	5.9	0.7	1.8
1987	9.2	0.9	2.6
1988	8	2	3.8
1989	6.5	2.8	5.4
1990	7.4	2.6	6
1991	9.2	4.5	5.8
1992	7.6	4.7	4.1
1993	9.6	3.6	3.4
1994	8.5	3.7	5.1
1995	9.4	3.4	5.8
Average	8.13	2.89	4.38

SEA Avg. 5.13

Source: Various issues of ADO

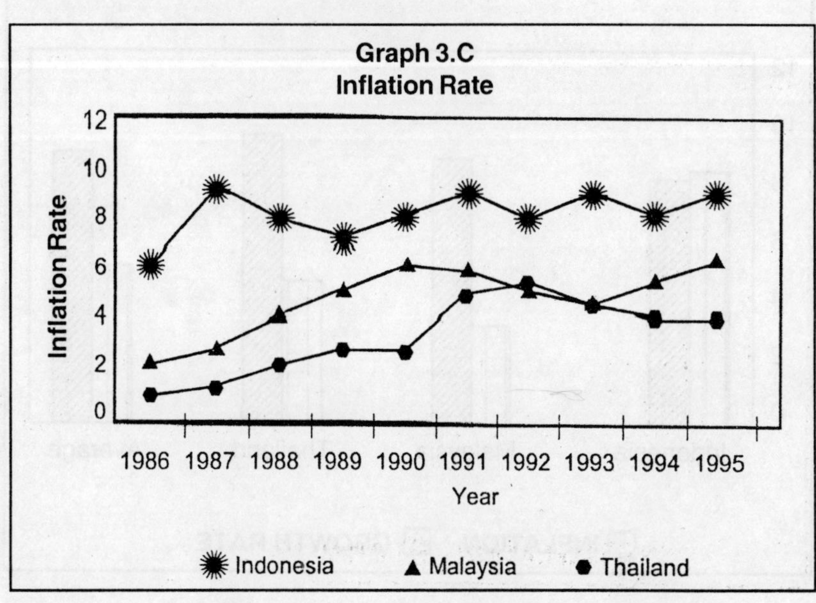

Table 3.4
Inflation and GDP Growth Rates

Inflation Rate				
Year	**Indonesia**	**Malaysia**	**Thailand**	**Average**
1986-90	7.40	1.80	3.92	4.37
1991-95	8.86	3.98	4.84	5.89
1986-95	8.13	2.89	4.38	5.13

Growth Rate of GDP				
Year	**Indonesia**	**Malaysia**	**Thailand**	**Average**
1986-90	6.30	6.80	9.92	7.40
1991-95	8.92	10.40	9.44	9.58
1986-95	7.60	8.60	9.68	8.62

Source: Various issues of ADO

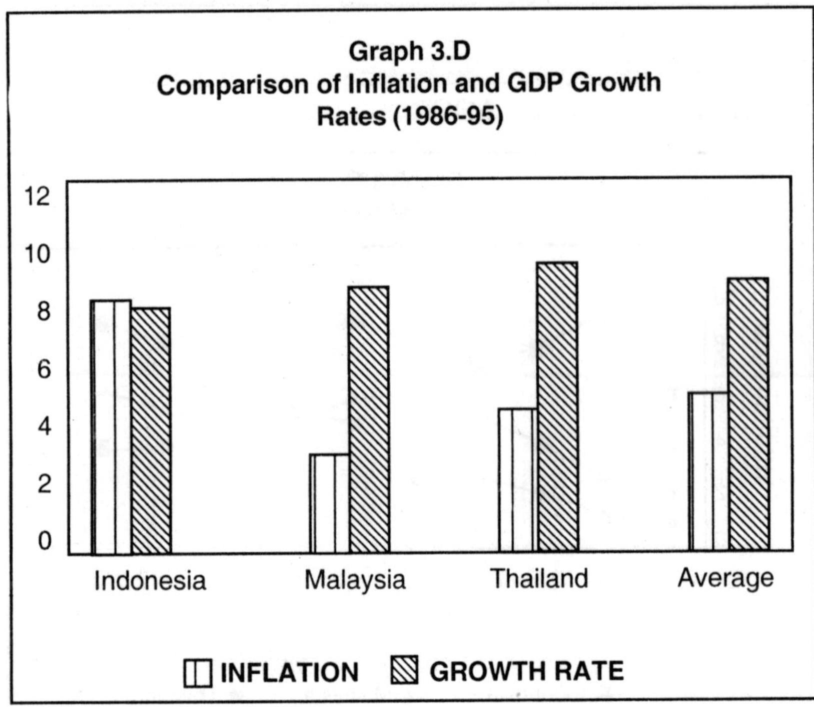

Table 3.5

Overall Budget Deficit/Surplus

Year	Indonesia	Malaysia	Thailand
1986	-5.60	-14.10	-3.10
1987	-4.90	-8.90	-0.70
1988	-4.00	-4.30	2.40
1989	-1.40	-3.30	3.50
1990	-1.80	-3.00	4.90
1991	-0.70	-2.00	4.00
1992	-0.40	-0.80	2.60
1993	-0.40	0.20	1.90
1994	0.20	2.40	2.70
1995	-0.20	0.30	2.80

Source: Various issues of Asian Development Outlook

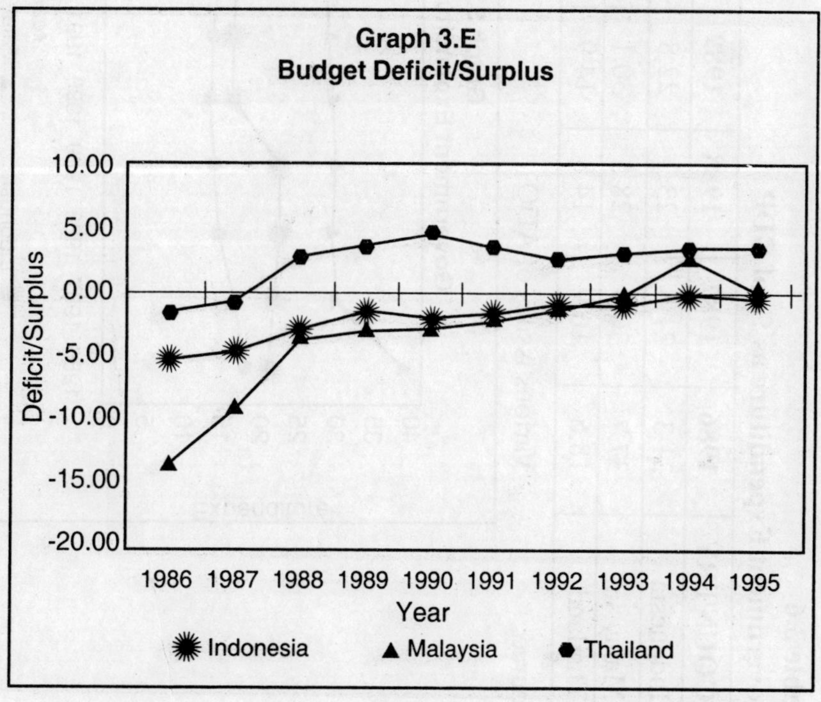

Table 3.6
Government Expenditure as % of GDP

COUNTRY	1986	1987	1988	1989	1990	1991	1992	1993	1994	1995
Indonesia	21.3	21.6	23.2	22.8	16.9	17.3	17.2	16.3	16.1	15.0
Malaysia	37.7	30.5	28.5	30.1	29.5	28.5	27.7	25.5	24.2	23.1
Thailand	18.6	16.9	14.8	14.9	13.9	14.4	15.7	16.5	16.1	15.6

Source: Various issues of ADO

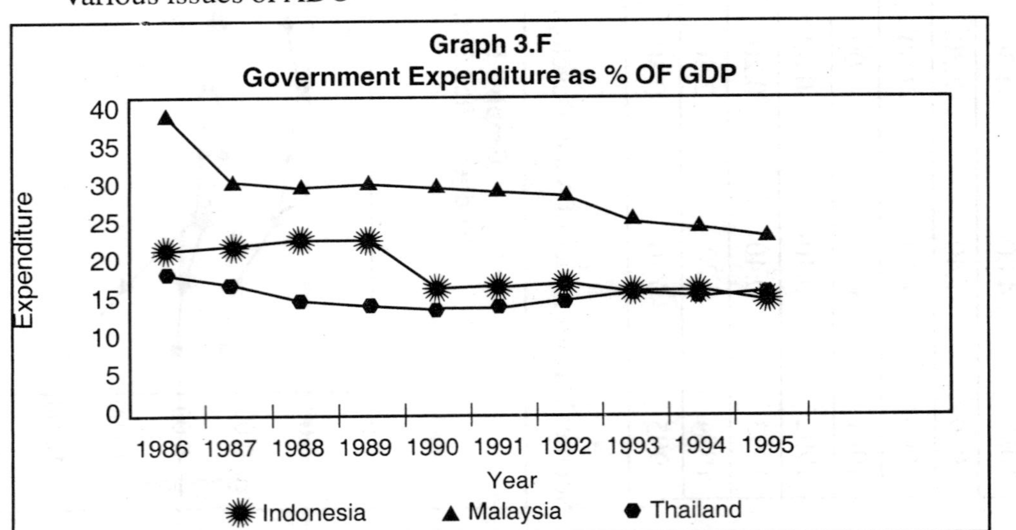

Table 3.7
Total Revenue as % of GDP

Country	1986	1987	1988	1989	1990	1991	1992	1993	1994	1995
Indonesia	15.70	16.70	16.20	17.20	10.00	6.60	16.80	15.90	16.30	14.80
Malaysia	27.30	22.80	24.20	24.90	25.80	26.20	26.70	31.30	32.00	28.80
Thailand	15.50	16.10	17.10	18.40	18.80	18.50	18.10	18.20	18.90	18.40

Source: Various issues of ADO

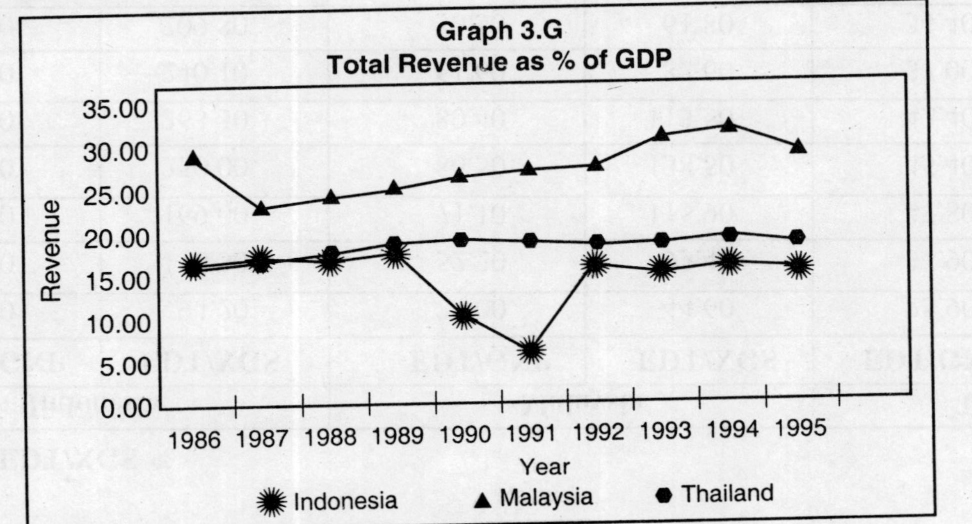

Table 3.8
EDT/GNP % & EDT/XGS %

Year	Indonesia		Malaysia		Thailand	
	EDT/GNP	EDT/XGS	EDT/GNP	EDT/XGS	EDT/GNP	EDT/XGS
1980	28.00	94.20	28.00	44.60	25.90	96.80
1982	27.40	116.30	52.20	93.40	34.90	130.00
1985	41.00	169.00	71.10	115.90	47.80	171.70
1986	52.20	250.00	86.50	138.50	45.40	152.50
1987	69.00	263.50	80.40	113.50	42.40	128.80
1988	64.30	240.10	61.60	82.60	37.00	99.70
1989	59.70	209.80	50.50	61.80	34.40	87.20
1990	66.10	225.10	44.60	52.10	35.00	90.20
1991	66.40	226.60	47.60	54.20	39.00	94.80
1992	66.40	221.80	36.40	42.70	36.20	91.80
1993	58.90	211.90	38.70	41.50	37.10	93.00
1994	57.40	195.80	36.90	37.70	43.10	103.10

EDT: External Debt XGS: Exports of Goods and Services
Source: Key Indicators of Developing Asian and Pacific Countries (various issues)

Table 3.9

Tariffs and Non-Tariffs Measures in East Asia and Latin America

Region/Country	Average Tariffs		Core Non Tariff frequency ratio	
	1984-88	1994-98	1989-94	1995-98
East Asia	19.40	10.40	26.50	14.20
Hongkong,China	0.00	0.00	2.10	2.10
Indonesia	28.40	13.20	53.60	31.30
Korea, Republic of	21.00	8.50	50.00	25.00
Phillippines	28.00	16.80	11.50	-
Taiwan, China	22.40	11.20	1.00	2.10
Singapore	0.30	0.40	1.00	2.10
Thailand	41.20	23.20	36.50	17.50
Latin America	29.50	11.40	20.00	8.80
Argentina	28.10	11.60	3.10	2.10
Bolivia	17.80	9.70	0.00	-
Chili	22.00	11.00	5.20	5.20
Columbia	37.80	11.60	55.20	10.30
Mexico	18.70	12.90	27.80	13.40
Uruguary	33.70	11.20	32.30	0.00

Source : OECD proceedings, "FDI and Recovery in Southeast Asia"; OECD, France, 1999

Table 3.10

Growth Rate of Exports

Country	Average annual growth rate of percapita GDP (1986-95)	Average annual growth rate of Exports (1986-95)
INDONESIA	5.3	9.3
MALAYSIA	5.1	16.78
THAILAND	7.7	23.08

Source: IMF Data

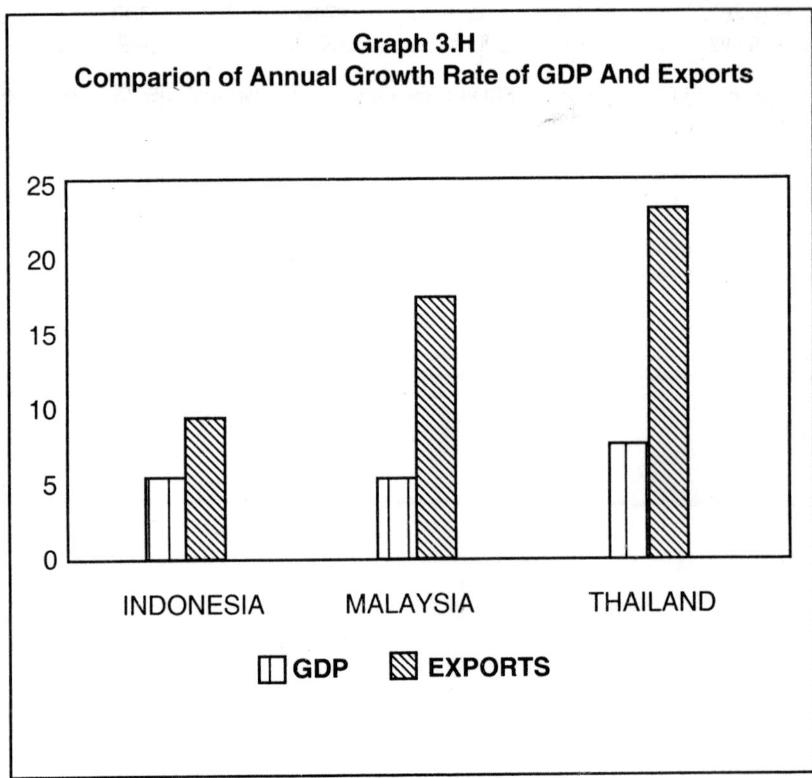

Table 3.11

Exports of Goods & Services as % of GDP

Year	Indonesia	Malaysia	Thailand
1985	21.9	55.00	22.80
1986	17.70	56.40	25.70
1987	23.30	63.80	28.80
1988	23.60	67.30	33.00
1989	24.50	73.10	35.20
1990	25.60	76.40	33.60
1991	25.30	79.10	36.10
1992	26.70	77.20	37.10
1993	25.70	82.00	38.00
1994	25.50	91.30	38.70
1995	26.20	95.40	42.20
1996	25.00	88.17	39.60
1997	29.00		61.20

Table 3.12

Imports of Goods & Services as % of GDP

Year	Indonesia	Malaysia	Thailand
1985	20.10	50.00	25.60
1986	18.80	50.50	23.70
1987	21.70	19.60	28.30
1988	20.80	56.90	34.60
1989	21.40	66.90	37.90
1990	24.00	74.30	41.30
1991	24.50	82.90	42.90
1992	25.10	75.90	41.80
1993	24.20	82.10	42.50
1994	24.70	92.90	43.80
1995	29.90	99.20	49.30

Table 3.13

Forex Reserves in Billion $

Country	1983	1984	1985	1986	1987	1988	1989	1990	1991	1992	1993	1994	1995	1996	1997
Indonesia	3.60	4.70	4.80	3.90	5.40	4.90	5.30	7.30	9.10	10.10	10.90	11.80	13.30	17.80	16.08
Malaysia	3.50	3.40	4.60	5.60	7.00	6.10	7.30	9.30	10.40	16.70	26.80	24.80	22.90	26.10	20.00
Thailand	1.50	1.80	2.10	2.70	3.90	5.90	9.40	13.20	17.20	20.01	24.07	28.80	35.40	37.10	25.60

Source: Various issues of ADO

Table 3.14

Net FDI Inflows as a % of GDP (1970-97)

Country	1970	1971	1972	1973	1974	1975	1976	1977	1978	1979	1980	1981	1982	1983
Indonesia	0.80	1.40	1.80	0.10	-0.20	1.50	0.70	0.50	0.40	0.30	0.20	0.10	0.20	0.40
Malaysia	2.20	2.20	2.10	2.10	6.20	3.80	3.60	3.20	3.20	2.80	3.80	5.30	5.60	4.40
Thailand	0.60	0.50	0.80	0.70	1.30	0.20	0.40	0.50	0.30	0.20	0.60	0.80	0.50	0.80

Country	1984	1985	1986	1987	1988	1989	1990	1991	1992	1993	1994	1995	1996	1997
Indonesia	0.30	0.40	0.30	0.40	0.70	0.80	1.00	1.20	1.30	1.30	1.20	2.30	2.70	2.10
Malaysia	2.30	2.20	1.80	1.50	2.20	4.70	5.80	8.30	9.00	7.80	5.80	4.80	5.20	5.30
Thailand	0.90	0.40	0.60	0.60	1.70	2.50	2.90	2.10	1.90	1.00	0.60	1.20	1.30	

Source: OECD Proceedings, "FDI & Recovery in Asia", OECD, France, 1999

Graph 3.I

Net FDI Inflows as a % of GDP (1970-97)

FDI Inflow

Year

Indonesia — Malaysia — Thailand

Table 3.15
FDI as a Proportion of Investment

Country	1981-85	1986-90	1994
	Pre-reform	Post Reform	
Indonesia	1.0	2.0	4.2
Malaysia	10.8	10.5	16.3
Thailand	3.2	5.9	1.2

Source: OECD Proceedings, FDI & Recovery in Asia, OECD, France, 1999

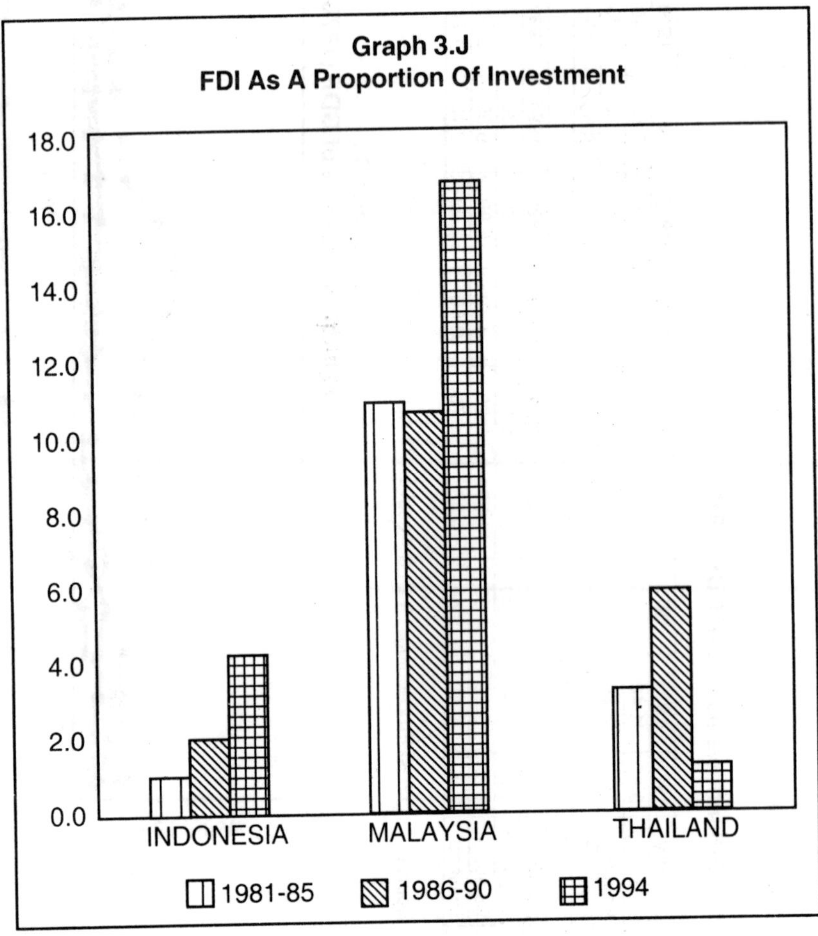

Table 3.16

Gross Secondary School Enrolment Ratio (GSE Ratio)
(as a percentage of Expenditure/Income)

Country	1980		1990		1996	
	Female	Male	Female	Male	Female	Male
Indonesia	23.3	34.7	39.7	48.2	47.6	55.8
Malaysia	45.7	49.7	60.0	55.6	66.1	57.5
Thailand	27.9	29.6	29.5	30.5	56.5	57.5

Source: Key Indicators of Developing Asian and Pacific Countries (various issues)

Table 3.17

Annual Labour Force Employed in Manufacturing Sector in Thousands

Country	1986	1987	1988	1989	1990	1991	1992	1993	1994	1995	1996
Indonesia	5606	5818	5997	7335	7693	7946	8255	8784	10841	10127	10773
Malaysia	861	929	961	1171	1333	1470	1639	1742	1892	2052	2178
Thailand	2069	2438	2461	2770	3133	3465	3600	3961	3851	4377	4334

Source: International Trade Statistics Year Book 1996, UN, New York, 1997

Table 3.18

Annual Imports of Machinery and Equipment as % of Total Imports

Country	1985	1986	1990	1991	1992	1993	1994	1995	1996
Indonesia	28.7	27.0	32.5	36.0	36.6	35.1	30.8	29.6	32.0
Malaysia	35.4	37.3	42.0	45.8	45.4	47.3	50.3	51.6	52.9
Thailand	20.8	24.4	29.4	31.9	31.1	33.5	36.0	36.6	NA

Source : **International Trade Statistics Year books 1996**
Pub: UN, New York, 1997

Table 3.19

Annual Increase in Value Added in Industry as a % of GDP (1986-95)

Country	1986	1987	1988	1989	1990	1991	1992	1993	1994	1995
Indonesia	6.6	5.2	5.2	8.2	11.5	11.7	8.2	9.8	11.2	10.6
Malaysia	4.6	6.7	12.7	11.0	13.2	11.2	8.9	10.1	12.4	13.1
Thailand	7.9	12.8	17.4	16.2	16.1	12.1	9.9	10.6	9.9	11.9

Source: Industrial Trade Statistics Year Book 1996, UN, New York, 1997

Table 3.20 (a)

Ratio of Deposits to Money Stock
Country - Indonesia

YEAR	Savings and Time Deposits (St) (bn Rp)	Total Money Stock (M2) (bn Rp)	Ratio of St/M2% St/M2%
1986	11355	27661	41%
1987	16230	33885	47%
1988	20939	41998	49%
1989	30518	58704	51%
1990	46150	84630	54%
1991	52632	99058	53%
1992	67560	119053	56%
1993	82953	145202	57%
1994	98372	174512	56%
1995	130891	222638	58%

For tables 20 & 21 (a) to (c)

Source : Basic data from "Key Indicators of Developing Asian and Pacific Countries (various issues). Ratios are the researcher's calculations.

Table 3.20 (b)

Ratio of Deposits to Money Stock
Country - Malaysia

YEAR	Savings and Time Deposits (St) (mn Ringgit)	Money Stock (M2) (mn Ringgit)	Ratio of St/M2% St/M2%
1986	40879	56098	72%
1987	42653	59771	71%
1988	42635	64072	66%
1989	47123	74392	63%
1990	47234	83902	56%
1991	59591	96092	62%
1992	73588	114480	64%
1993	89803	139800	64%
1994	99435	160365	62%
1995	125691	198873	63%

Table 3.20 (c)

Ratio of Deposits to Money Stock
Country - Thailand

YEAR	Savings and Time Deposits (St) (bn baht)	Total Money St/M2% (bn baht)	Ratio of Stock (M2)
1986	590	672	87%
1987	698	808	86%
1988	835	956	87%
1989	1067	1207	88%
1990	1373	1529	89%
1991	1606	1832	87%
1992	1949	2117	92%
1993	2321	2507	92%
1994	2618	2829	92%
1995	3065	3310	92%

Table 3.21 (a)

Government consumption as % of GDP

Country - Indonesia

YEAR (1)	GDP (2)	Government Consumption (in bn. Rp.) (3)	Government consumption as % of GDP (in bn. Rp.) (4) = 3/2 x 100
1986	102683	11329	11.0
1987	124817	11764	9.4
1988	149669	12756	8.5
1989	179582	15698	8.7
1990	210866	18649	8.8
1991	242969	20785	8.5
1992	282395	24731	8.7
1993	329776	29751	9.0
1994	382220	31014	8.1
1995	454514	35584	7.8

Avg. = 7.1

Table 3.21 (b)
Government Consumption as % of GDP

Country - <u>Malaysia</u>

YEAR (1)	GDP (in mn. RM) (2)	Government Consumption (in mn. RM) (3)	Government consumption as % of GDP (4) = 3/2 x 100
1986	71594	12127	16.9
1987	79625	12239	15.3
1988	90841	13015	14.3
1989	102451	14808	14.4
1990	115701	16209	14.0
1991	132381	18412	13.9
1992	142381	19340	13.0
1993	165206	21606	13.0
1994	190274	23936	12.5
1995	218671	27636	12.6

Avg. = 13.9

Table 3.21 (c)
Government Consumption as % of GDP
Country - Thailand

Year (1)	**GDP** (in mn. Baht) (2)	**Government consumption** (in mn. Baht) (3)	**Government Consumption as % of GDP** (4) = 3/2 x 100
1986	1133397	144564	12.7
1987	1299913	147224	11.3
1988	1559804	156710	10.0
1989	1856992	176798	9.5
1990	2183545	205354	9.4
1991	2506635	231127	9.2
1992	2830914	280203	9.8
1993	3170258	315982	9.9
1994	3630805	354387	9.7
1995	4188929	413018	9.8

Avg. = 10.1

Table 3.22 (a)

GDI and GDS as Percentage of GDP

Country - Indonesia

YEAR	Growth rate of real GDP %	GDI (% of GDP)	GDS (% of GDP)
1986	5.90	28.30	27.30
1987	4.90	31.40	32.90
1988	5.80	31.50	34.00
1989	7.50	35.20	37.60
1990	7.40	36.90	39.20
1991	6.40	35.00	37.00
1992	7.20	32.40	35.30
1993	7.30	29.50	32.50
1994	7.50	32.50	32.20
1995	8.20	31.90	30.60
1996	8.00	30.80	30.20

For Tables 22(a) to (c)
GDI - Gross Domestic Investment
GDS- Gross Domestic Saving
GDP- Gross Domestic Product

Source: Various issues of ADO

Table 3.22 (b)

GDI and GDS as Percentage of GDP

Country - Malaysia

Year	Growth rate of real GDP %	GDI (% of GDP)	GDS (% of GDP)
1986	1.20	26.00	32.10
1987	5.40	23.20	37.30
1988	8.90	26.00	36.30
1989	8.70	28.80	33.90
1990	9.80	32.30	32.30
1991	8.60	35.70	30.20
1992	7.80	35.10	36.50
1993	8.30	37.80	37.70
1994	9.20	40.40	38.80
1995	9.50	43.50	39.50
1996	8.60	41.50	42.60

Table 3.22 (c)

GDI and GDS as Percentage of GDP

Country - <u>Thailand</u>

Year	Growth rate of real GDP %	GDI (% of GDP)	GDS (% of GDP)
1986	4.90	21.80	22.40
1987	9.50	23.90	24.80
1988	13.20	28.80	29.80
1989	12.00	31.50	31.10
1990	10.00	36.80	31.00
1991	7.50	35.70	33.30
1992	8.10	40.00	35.20
1993	8.70	39.90	35.60
1994	8.60	40.30	36.00
1995	8.80	41.60	33.60
1996	5.50	41.70	33.70

Table 3.23

Manufacturing Exports as % of Total Exports

Year	Indonesia	Malaysia	Thailand
1980	2.3	22	29.6
1981	3.0	23	29.4
1982	3.6	25	29.6
1983	6.6	29	32.7
1984	10.2	32	35.4
1985	18.1	32	39.9
1986	19.3	42	44.8
1987	25.0	44	52.6
1988	29.8	47	51.5
1989	32.0	51	57.3
1990	35.4	56	64.3
1991	40.8	61	66.8
1992	47.5	66	62.8
1993	48.5	71	80.4
1994	50.6	76	82.0
1995	60.3	79	83.0
1996	61.2	79	83.5

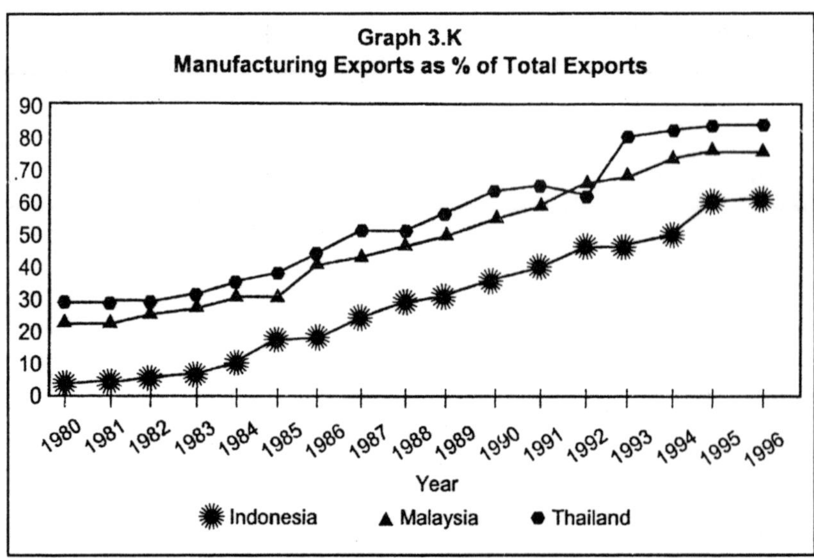

Table 3.24

Commodity Structure of Exports 1965-94

Commodity Gp	Indonesia				Malaysia				Thailand			
	1967	1975	1985	1994	1965	1975	1985	1994	1965	1975	1985	1994
Gp I	96.7	95.8	75.9	42.0	94.8	81.0	63.6	23.6	98.0	85.7	63.3	28.7
Gp II	0.2	0.4	16.4	43.6	1.5	5.6	7.0	12.0	1.6	11.1	22.5	27.1
Gp III	0.1	0.3	0.4	3.0	0.3	0.8	2.2	3.0	0.1	0.8	1.7	3.3
Gp IV	2.5	1.4	1.0	3.9	2.3	5.7	20.7	29.8	0.1	1.6	9.6	20.7
Gp V	0.5	2.1	6.3	7.5	1.2	6.9	6.5	31.6	0.1	0.9	3.0	20.2

Gp I Food; other primary commodities

Gp II Wood and paper products; Textiles; clothing and footwear; non-metallic mineral products; Toys and sports equipment

Gp III Iron & Steel; Farbricated metal products; Ships and boats; Others

Gp IV Rubber and plastic products; Non-electrical machines; electrical machinery; Road motor vehicles

Gp V Chemicals and pharmaceuticals; Computer; office equipment; communication equipment; Others

Source: OECD Proceedings, FDI & Recovery in Asia, OECD, France, 1999.

Chart 3.25

Correlation Matrix - Indonesia

		GDP	BD	EX	FDI	GDS	MVA	EMP
GDP	Pearson Correlation	1.000	0.583	0.998**	0.279	0.999**	1.000**	0.978**
	Sig. (2-tailed)	-	0.077	0.000	0.435	0.000	0.000	0.000
	N	10	10	10	10	10	10	10
BD	Pearson Correlation	0.583	1.000	0.581	0.590	0.609	0.591	0.653*
	Sig. (2-tailed)	0.077	-	0.078	0.073	0.061	0.072	0.041
	N	10	10	10	10	10	10	10
EX	Pearson Correlation	0.998**	0.581	1.000	0.264	0.997**	0.997**	0.971**
	Sig. (2-tailed)	0.000	0.078	-	0.461	0.000	0.000	0.000
	N	10	10	10	10	10	10	10
FDI	Pearson Correlation	0.279	0.590	0.264	1.000	0.305	0.296	0.372
	Sig. (2-tailed)	0.435	0.073	0.461	-	0.392	0.407	0.290
	N	10	10	10	10	10	10	10
GDS	Pearson Correlation	0.999**	0.609	0.997**	0.305	1.000	0.999**	0.979**
	Sig. (2-tailed)	0.000	0.061	0.000	0.392	-	0.000	0.000
	N	10	10	10	10	10	10	10
MVA	Pearson Correlation	1.000**	0.591	0.997**	0.296	0.999**	1.000	0.982**
	Sig. (2-tailed)	0.000	0.072	0.000	0.407	0.000	-	0.000
	N	10	10	10	10	10	10	10
EMP	Pearson Correlation	0.978**	0.653*	0.971**	0.372	0.979**	0.982**	1.000
	Sig. (2-tailed)	0.000	0.041	0.000	0.290	0.000	0.000	-
	N	10	10	10	10	10	10	10

**Corelation is significant at the 0.01 level (2 - tailed)

*Corelation is significant at the 0.05 level (2 - tailed)

Chart 3.26

Correlation Matrix - Malaysia

		GDP	BD	EX	FDI	GDS	MVA	EMP
GDP	Pearson Correlation	1.000	0.930**	0.996**	0.908**	0.995**	0.999**	0.989**
	Sig. (2-tailed)	-	0.000	0.000	0.000	0.000	0.000	0.000
	N	10	10	10	10	10	10	10
BD	Pearson Correlation	0.930**	1.000	0.924**	0.892**	0.931**	0.925**	0.922**
	Sig. (2-tailed)	0.000	-	0.000	0.003	0.000	0.000	0.000
	N	10	10	10	10	10	10	10
EX	Pearson Correlation	0.996**	0.924**	1.000	0.893**	0.994**	0.998**	0.974**
	Sig. (2-tailed)	0.000	0.000	-	0.000	0.000	0.000	0.000
	N	10	10	10	10	10	10	10
FDI	Pearson Correlation	0.908**	0.829	0.893**	1.000	0.918**	0.906**	0.901**
	Sig. (2-tailed)	0.000	0.003	0.000	-	0.000	0.000	0.000
	N	10	10	10	10	10	10	10
GDS	Pearson Correlation	0.995**	0.931**	0.994**	0.918**	1.000	0.996**	0.971**
	Sig. (2-tailed)	0.000	0.000	0.000	0.000	-	0.000	0.000
	N	10	10	10	10	10	10	10
MVA	Pearson Correlation	0.999**	0.925**	0.998**	0.906**	0.996**	1.000	0.983**
	Sig. (2-tailed)	0.000	0.000	0.000	0.000	0.000	-	0.000
	N	10	10	10	10	10	10	10
EMP	Pearson Correlation	0.989**	0.922**	0.974**	0.901**	0.971**	0.983**	1.000
	Sig. (2-tailed)	0.000	0.000	0.000	0.000	0.000	0.000	-
	N	10	10	10	10	10	10	10

**Corelation is significant at the 0.01 level (2 - tailed)

Chart 3.27

Correlation Matrix - Thailand

		GDP	BD	EX	FDI	GDS	MVA	EMP
GDP	Pearson Correlation	1.000	0.847**	0.998**	0.924**	0.992**	.999**	0.958**
	Sig. (2-tailed)	-	0.002	0.000	0.000	0.000	0.000	0.000
	N	10	10	10	10	10	10	10
BD	Pearson Correlation	0.847**	1.000	0.814**	0.857**	0.788**	0.863**	0.784**
	Sig. (2-tailed)	0.002	-	0.004	0.002	0.007	0.001	0.007
	N	10	10	10	10	10	10	10
EX	Pearson Correlation	0.998**	0.814**	1.000	0.997**	0.997**	0.995**	0.957**
	Sig. (2-tailed)	0.000	0.004	-	0.000	0.000	0.000	0.000
	N	10	10	10	10	10	10	10
FDI	Pearson Correlation	0.924**	0.857**	0.917**	1.000	0.899**	0.928**	0.789**
	Sig. (2-tailed)	0.000	0.002	0.000	-	0.000	0.000	0.000
	N	10	10	10	10	10	10	10
GDS	Pearson Correlation	0.992**	0.788**	0.997**	0.899**	1.000	0.988**	0.964**
	Sig. (2-tailed)	0.000	0.007	0.000	0.000	-		0.000
	N	10	10	10	10	10	10	10
MVA	Pearson Correlation	0.999**	0.863**	0.995**	0.928**	0.988**	1.000**	0.954**
	Sig. (2-tailed)	0.000	0.001	0.000	0.000	0.000	0.000	0.000
	N	10	10	10	10	10	10	10
EMP	Pearson Correlation	0.958**	00.784**	0.957**	0.789**	0.964**	0.954**	1.000
	Sig. (2-tailed)	0.000	0.007	0.000	0.007	0.000	0.000	-
	N	10	10	10	10	10	10	10

**Corelation is significant at the 0.01 level (2 - tailed)

Chart 3.28

Regression Results for Indonesia

Independent Variables Entered	**Method**
Budget Deficit/Surplus	Enter
Exports of Goods and Services	
Foreign Direct Investment	
Gross Domestic Savings	
Manufacturing Value Added	
Employment in Manufacturing	

DependentVariable: GDP

Model Summary

R	R Square	Adjusted R Square	Std Error of the Estimate
1*	1	0.999	2963.3476

* Independent Variable

ANOVA

	Sum of Squares	df	Mean Square	F	Sig
Regression	1.21E+11	6	2.01E+10	2287.264	0
Residual	26344287.1	3	8781429.04		
Total	1.21E+11	9			

Coefficients

		Beta Coefficient	t	Significance
Constant	2029.318		0.09	0.934
Budget Deficit/Surplus		-0.057	-1.101	0.351
Exports of Goods and Services		0.068	0.222	0.839
Foreign Direct Investment		0.07	1.229	0.307
Gross Domestic Savings		-0.025	-0.151	0.89
Manufacturing Value Added		0.841	3.145	0.051
Employment in Manufacturing		0.104	1.335	0.274

Chart 3.29

Regression Results for Malaysia

Independent Variables Entered	**Method**
Budget Deficit/Surplus	Enter
Exports of Goods and Services	
Foreign Direct Investment	
Gross Domestic Savings	
Manufacturing Value Added	
Employment in Manufacturing	

DependentVariable: GDP

Model Summary

R	R Square	Adjusted R Square	Std Error of the Estimate
1*	1	1	371.7852

* Independent Variables

ANOVA

	Sum of Squares	df	Mean Square	F	Sig
Regression	2.15E+10	6	3.58E+09	25921.769	0
Residual	414672.639	3	138224.213		
Total	2.15E+10	9			

Coefficients

		Beta Coefficient	t	Significance
Constant	26198.481		7.38	0.005
Budget Deficit/Surplus		0.021	2.429	0.093
Exports of Goods and Services		-0.172	-2.515	0.087
Foreign Direct Investment		-0.005	-0.617	0.581
Gross Domestic Savings		0.007	0.123	0.91
Manufacturing Value Added		1.003	7.999	0.004
Employment in Manufacturing		0.148	5.017	0.015

Chart 3.30
Regression Results for Thailand

Independent Variables Entered	**Method**
Budget Deficit/Surplus	Enter
Exports of Goods and Services	
Foreign Direct Investment	
Gross Domestic Savings	
Manufacturing Value Added	
Employment in Manufacturing	

Dependent Variable: GDP

Model Summary

R	R Square	Adjusted R Square	Std Error of the Estimate
1*	1	0.999	35858.7993

* Independent Variables

ANOVA

	Sum of Squares	df	Mean Square	F	Sig
Regression	**9.35E+12**	6	1.56E+15	1211.998	0
Residual	**3.86E+09**	3	1.29E+09		
Total	**9.36E+12**	9			

Coefficients

		Beta Coefficient	t	Significance
Constant	338025.25		1.682	0.191
Budget Deficit/Surplus		0.001	0.047	0.966
Exports of Goods and Services		0.217	1.125	0.342
Foreign Direct Investment		-0.007	-0.456	0.68
Gross Domestic Savings		-0.096	-0.188	0.863
Manufacturing Value Added		0.912	1.675	0.192
Employment in Manufacturing		-0.031	-0.305	0.781

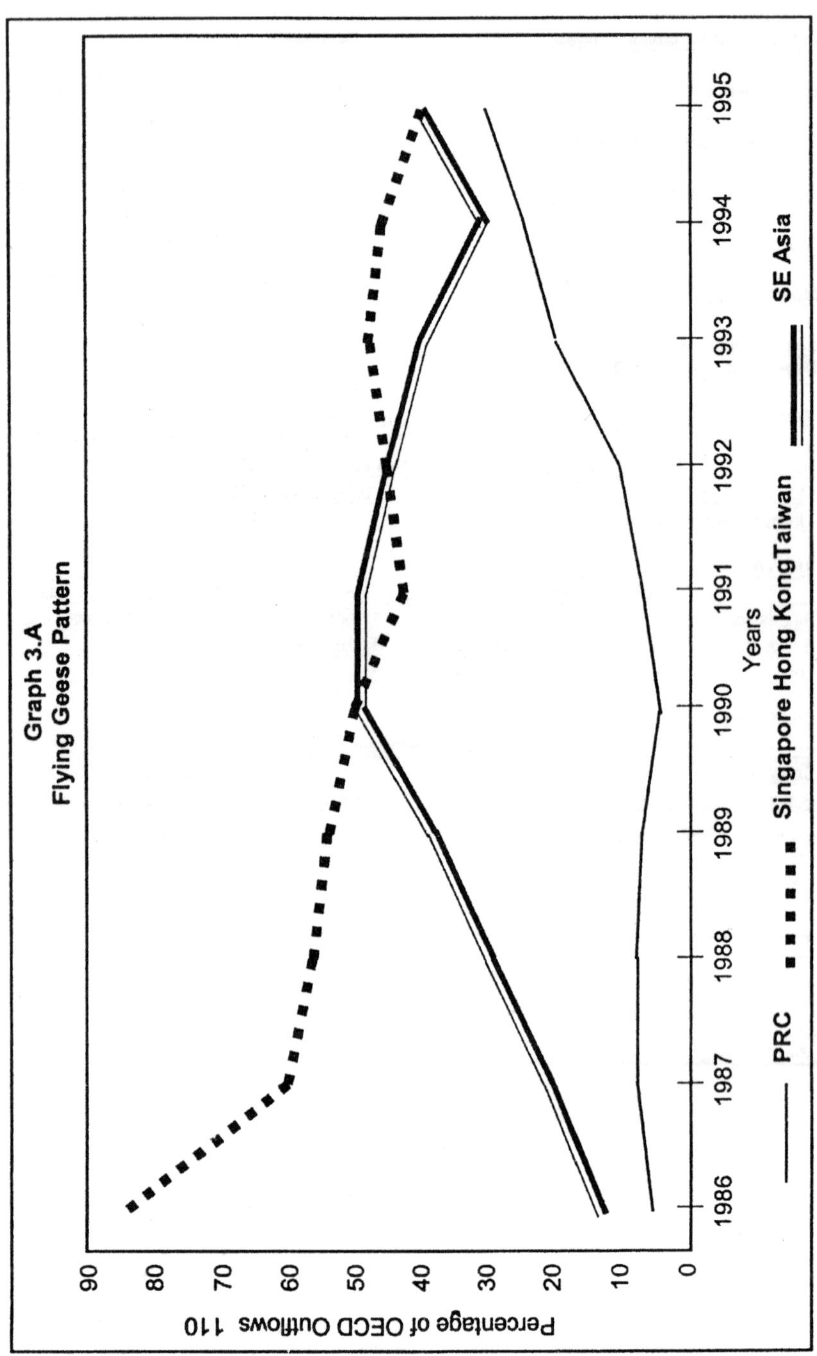
Graph 3.A
Flying Geese Pattern
Percentage of OECD Outflows
0
10
20
30
40
50
60
70
80
90
1986
1987
1988
1989
1990
1991
1992
1993
1994
1995
Years
PRC
Singapore Hong KongTaiwan
SE Asia

Chart 3.1

FUNCTIONAL APPROACH TO GROWTH

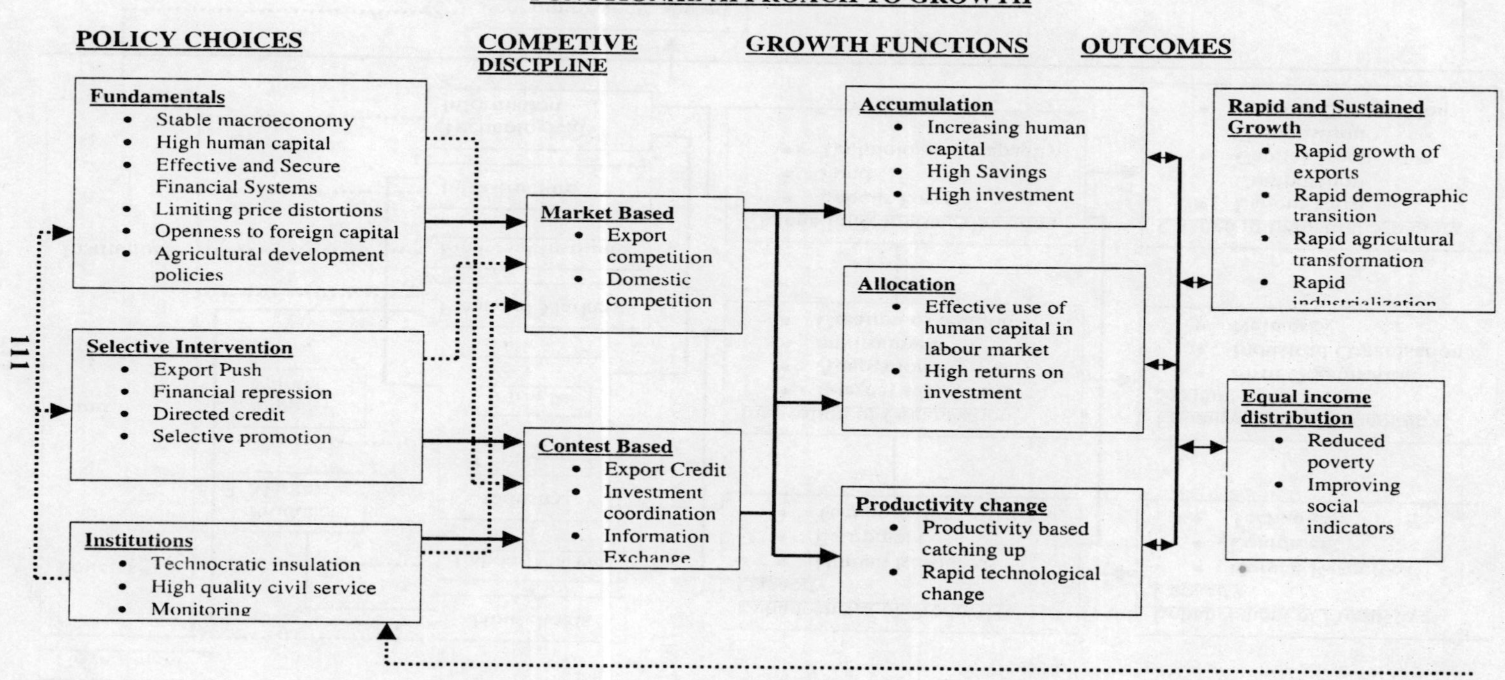

Source: Yanagihara, Toru (1997), 'East Asian Development Experience. Economic Systems Approach and Applications

Chart 3.2

Economic System Approach to Economic Development

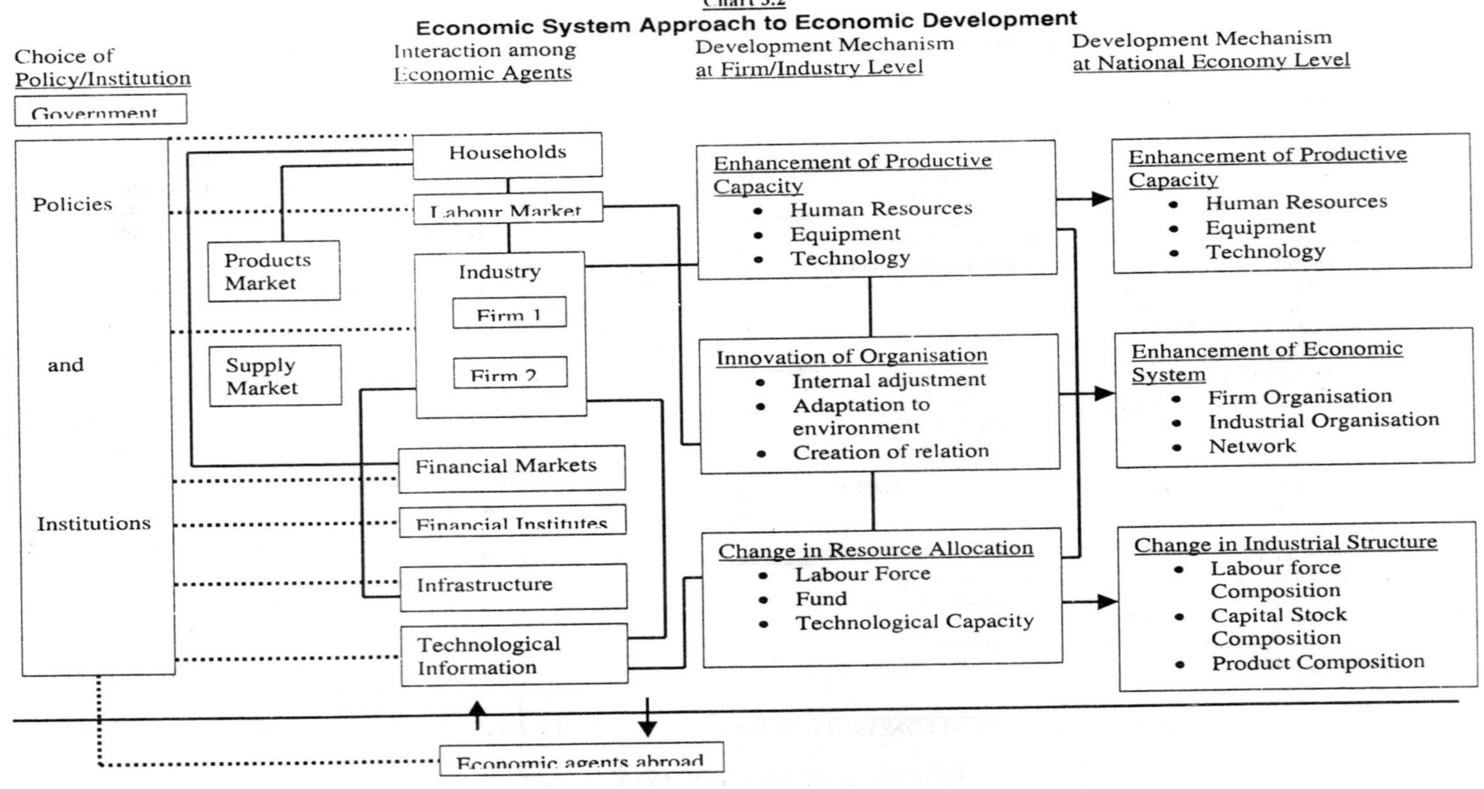

Source: Yanagihara, Toru (1997), 'East Asian Development Experience. Economic Systems Approach and Applications

Chart 3.3

Trade Regimes

Indonesia	Malaysia	Thailand
Nationalism & guided development (1948-66)	Market led development (1950-70)	Natural Resource based exports (1950-70)
Outward oriented new order government (1969-73)		
Oil and commodity boom (1974-81)	Export promotion and Import substitution. (1971-85)	Favouring Import Substitution (1971-80)
Adjustments to external shocks (1980-85) Deregulation (1986-onwards)	Adjustments and liberalization (1986-90)	Reform and Export incentives (1981-onwards)

Source: World Bank (1993), *East Asian Miracle*, Washington DC, OUP

Chart 3. 4

Degree Of Financial Integration

Country	1985-87	Country	1992-94
Korea	High	Thailand	High
Malaysia	High	Korea	High
Thailand	Medium+	Indonesia	High
India	Medium+	Malaysia	High
Indonesia	Medium+	Pakistan	High
Sri Lanka	Medium-	Philippines	High
Philippines	Medium-	India	Medium+
Pakistan	Medium-	P.R. China	Medium+
Myanmar	Low	Sri Lanka	Medium-
P.R. China	Low	Myanmar	Low
Banglades h	Low	Banglades h	Low

urce: World Bank Study 1997

Chart 3.5
Financial Liberalization in South Asia

Economy	Deregulation of interest rates	Stimulation of competition	Development of financial markets	Reform of regulatory and supervisory systems
Indonesia	1983: Interest rate restrictions on most deposit categories of state banks eliminated. Interest rates of private banks were deregulated. Credit ceilings abolished. Central bank discount window policies were revised. Some priority lending maintained. 5 1990: Drastically reduced Central Bank refinanced facilities and revised interest rates under the program to approach market rates	1986-88: Eased restrictions on scope of financial institutions activities. Banks were allowed to own multiservices financial companies (leasing, venture capital, consumer finance) 1988: Relaxed licensing/ branching restrictions and lifted bans on entry of new private domestic and foreign banks. NBFIs allowed to issue Certificates of deposit (CDs)	1984: Central Bank Certificates issued' through auctions to stimulate money markets. 1985: Security houses established to serve as market makers in money market instruments. Bankers acceptances (BAs) introduced 1988: Established over the counter (OTC) market to encourage firms to go public. Licensed new private stock exchanges. Equalised tax treatment of time deposits, CDs and equity. Permitted banks and NBFIs to raise capital from the securities mark et.	1988: Set lending limits for single borrowers/companies. Reorganised supervisory and monitoring system, hired more staff, implemented an offsite monitoring program. Supervision of rural banks shifted to Central Bank. 1991-92: Instituted strict loan loss provisioning guidelines and Bank for International Settlements (BIS) minimum capital adequacy standards. Required publication of bank financial statements. Increased powers of Bank of Indonesia with regard to seeking more documentation, undertaking examinations, replacing management, as well as revoking a banks license. Formed the Securities and Exchange Commission to monitor, regulate and establish rules for operation of capital markets.

Chart 3.5 Contd.

Economy	Deregulation of interest rates	Stimulation of competition	Development of financial markets	Reform of regulatory and supervisory systems
Malaysia	1983: Central Bank administered Base Lending Rate introduced as floor. 1991: Interest rate liberalization completed. Base Lending Rate freed from administrative control. Some priority sector lending guidelines still remain.	1974: Maintains ban against foreign banks branches. However domestic banks face increased competition as they have been encouraged to expand branching networks in smaller towns and rural areas. 1974-76: New financial instruments such as Negotiable, CDs and bankers' acceptances introduced.	1976: Kuala Lumpur stock exchange established. 1987: Malaysian government securities with market based coupon rates introduced. 1988: Foreign securities houses permitted to hold upto a 40% stake (increased from 30%) in local securities houses. 1989-90: Established an off-shore banking market. Central Bank issued guidelines on the issue of private debenture securities. 1991: Established a Co-operative Credit Rating Agency.	1983-86: Operations of Islamic Bank and DTC (5) brought under Central Bank supervision. 1988: Issue of Code ethics with guidelines on minimum standards of conduct for bankers. Included specific guidelines for share trading activities also. 1989: Banking and Financial Institutions Act – conjugated the Banking Act of 1969. Stricter single borrower lending guidelines and credit worthiness standards enforced. Instituted a standardized format of financial reporting to increase transparency.

Chart 3.5 Contd.

Economy	Deregulation of interest rates	Stimulation of competition	Development of financial markets	Reform of regulatory and supervisory systems
Thailand	1980: Interest rate ceilings for financial institutions freed from 15% limit imposed by Usury law. 1984: General Credit restrictions abolished but restrictions on bank lending rates re-imposed. Ceilings for loans to priority sectors lowered. 1989: Abolished deposit rate ceilings on commercial bank time deposits greater than one year. Overdraft ceilings from 50 million Baht to 30 million Baht.	Ceiling on lending rates still regulated 1988: Revoked 1962 Banking Law that prohibited new domestic or foreign bank branches. 1989: Introduced new financial products like long term loans with a three, five or seven-year maturity.	1984: Established transferable CDs market. 1985: Introduced Bangkok Inter Bank Offered Rate	1985: Additional supervision enactments instituted on site monitoring and off-site surveillance, regular periodic submission of income and expense accounts, balance sheets etc. Introduced punitive measures and sanctions for illegal activities , defined minimum–capital adequacy standards, single borrower exposure limits and an asset portfolio classification System. 1989: Securities and Exchange Commission created with responsibilities to supervise and regulate the securities industry.

Chart 3.6
Country-Indonesia
Financial Institutions-Sources And Uses Of Funds

Sr. No.	Name of the institution	Total assets	Market share (Ownership)	Source of Funds	Use of Funds
1)	State Development Banks (BAPINDO)	4,903 bn. Rupiah (US$ 2.673 mn.) (1989)	7.5% (govt.)	Borrowing from Central Bank, corporate bonds	Finance for priority areas consistent with development plans
2)	Regional Development Bank	7,767 bn. Rupiah (US$ 4.322 mn.) (1989)	27 States	Mainly deposits	Finance for regional development
3)	Private Development Banks	NA	NA	Deposits, medium and long term securities	
4)	Development Bank type Financial Companies	479 bn. Rupiah (US$ 290 mn) (1989)	NA	Partially financed by the government and cooperative banks	

Source : World Bank Data.

Chart 3. 7

Country-Malaysia

Financial Institutions- Sources And Uses Of Funds

Sr. No.	Name of the Institution	Total assets	Market share (Ownership)	Source of Funds	Use of Funds
1)	Malaysia Industrial Development Financial Corporation (MIDF)	553 mn ringgit 1988	Half Govt. Half Pvt.	Borrowing from the Government and Central Bank	Finance for Industry, in part. Small and medium size enterprises in food, metals, lumber and rubber industries
2)	Development Bank of Malaysia	821 mn ringgit 1987	2.6% Govt.	Borrowing from the Govt.	Medium to long term finance and guarantees for bhoomiputera enterprises
3)	Industrial Bank of Malaysia	241 mn ringgit 1987	Govt.	Borrowing from the Government and Central Bank	Finance for Ship building and Shipping Industry
4)	Sabah Development Bank	1069 mn ringgit 1987	Govt.	Govt. subscription and foreign banks	Medium to Long term finance for agriculture Industry, Electric power and Real Estate
5)	Agricultural Bank of Malaysia	1725 mn ringgit 1987	Govt.	Govt. subscription and borrowing from Govt. Institutions	Finance for promotion of commerce and industry in Sabah and Sarawak

Source : World Bank Data

Chart 3. 8

Country –Thailand

Financial Institutions Sources And Uses Of Funds

Sr. No.	Name of the Institution	Total assets	Market share (Ownership)	Source of Funds	Use of Funds
1)	Industrial Finance Corporation of Thailand	29,598 mn Baht US$ 1,152 mn (1989)			
2)	Bank of Agriculture (BAAC)	45,004 mn Baht US$ 1,752 mn (1989)			
3)	Government Housing Bank	27,811 mn Baht			

Chart 3.9

Evolution Of Industrial Policies In Southeast Asia

Country	1950-70	1961-71	1971-85	1986
Thailand	-	Import substitution	1981 capital goods	Export orientation
			Export Industries	Technology intensive industries
Malaysia	Import substitution (moderate)	-	Added export orientation	Liberalization
				Export orientation
Indonesia	-	New order (Liberalization)	Import Substitution	Export orientation Liberalization

References of Chapter 3

1. World Bank (1993), '*The East Asian Miracle*', Washington, Oxford University Press.
2. Rigg, Jonathan (1991), '*Southeast Asia the Human Landscape of Modernization and Development*', London, Routledge.
3. Rodan, Garry et al (eds) (1993), '*The Political Economy of Southeast Asia*'.
4. World Bank (1993), '*The East Asian Miracle*', Washington, Oxford University Press, p 9.
5. Ibid.
6. Leipziger, Danny (ed) (1997), '*Lessons From East Asia*', USA, The University of Michigan Press, p 546.
7. Rodan, Garry et al (eds) (1993), '*The Political Economy of Southeast Asia*'.
8. Hosono, Akio (1998), "*The Roles of State and Market in the Development Process, With Special Reference to the East Asian Miracle*' in Akio Hosono et al (eds), 'Development Strategies in East Asia and Latin America' Great Britain, Macmillan, p 30.
9. Leipziger, Danny (ed) (1997), '*Lessons From East Asia*', USA, The University of Michigan Press, p 547.
10. Flyn, Norman (1999), '*Miracle to Meltdown in Asia: Business, Government and Society*' London, Oxford University Press.
11. Akamatsu, Kaname (1956), '*Flying Geese Pattern of Industrial Development of Japan: Machine Tool Industries*', Japan, Hitoshuti University.
12. Bende Nabende, Anthony (1999), '*FDI, Regionalism, Government Policy and Endogenous Growth*', England, Ashgate Publishing House.
13. Asian Development Bank (1999), '*Asian Development Outlook 1999*', New York, Oxford University Press.
14. Yangihara, Toru (1997), '*East Asian Development Experience: Economic System Approach and Application*', Tokyo, Institute of Development Economics.
15. Ibid.
16. Dixon, Chris and David Drakakis-Smith (1997), '*Contemporary and Historical Perspectives on Uneven Development in Southeast* Asia', in Chris Dixon (ed),

'Uneven Development in Southeast Asia' USA, Ashgate, p 1.

17. Asian Development Bank (1999), '*Asian Development Outlook 1999*', New York, Oxford University Press.
18. Bowie, Alasdain and Danny Unger (1997), '*The Politics of Open economies: Indonesia, Malaysia, the Philippines, and Thailand*', London, Cambridge University Press, p 27.
19. Ibid.
20. Begg, David, Stanley Fisher and Rudiger Dornbush (1996), '*Economics*', New Delhi, Tata Mc Graw, p 593.
21. World Bank (1993), '*The East Asian Miracle*', Washington, Oxford University Press, p 111.
22. Dasgupta, Biplab (1998), '*Structural Adjustment, Global Trade and the New Political Economy*', New Delhi, Vistar Publication,p 333.
23. Dixon, Chris (1991), '*Southeast Asia in the World Economy*', Britain, Cambridge University Press, p 179.
24. Leipziger, Danny (ed) (1997), '*Lessons From East Asia*', USA, The University of Michigan Press, p 9.
25. World Bank (1993), '*The East Asian Miracle*', Washington, Oxford University Press, p 109.
26. Centre For International Private Enterprise, '*Market Based Structural Economic Reform. An International Survey*', Connecticut.
27. Asian Development Bank (1999), '*Asian Development Outlook 1999*', New York, Oxford University Press.
28. Banuri, Tariq (1991), '*Economic Liberalization: No Panacea*', New York, Oxford University Press, p 10.
29. Islam, Azizul (1995), '*Asian Policy Experiences- a Comparative Analysis*' in V.R.Panchamukhi and Rehman Shobham (eds), 'Towards an Asian Economic Area', India, Macmillan, p 30-31.
30. Bende-Nabende, Anthony (1999), '*FDI, Regionalism, Government Policy and Endogenous Growth*', England, Ashgate Publishing House.
31. Asian Development Bank (1992), '*Asian Development Outlook 1992*', Manila, Oxford University Press.
32. Masuyama, Seiichi (1997), '*The Evolving Nature of Industrial Policy in East Asia. Liberalising, Upgrading*

and Integration', in Seiichi Masuyama et al (eds) 'Industrial Policies in East Asia' Singapore, ISEAS, p 5.

33. Roemer, Michael (1994), '*Industrial Strategies Outward Bound'*, in David Lindauer and Michael Roemer, 'Asia and Africa: Legacies and Opportunities in Development', Institute for Contemporary Studies, p 251.
34. Rowen, Henry (1998), '*Behind East Asian Growth: The Political Foundations of Prosperity'*, New York, Routledge, p 97.
35. Masuyama, Seiichi (1997), '*The Evolving Nature of Industrial Policy in East Asia. Liberalising, Upgrading and Integration'*, in Seiichi Masuyama et al (eds) 'Industrial Policies in East Asia' Singapore, ISEAS, p 3.

Chapter 4

Development Experience of Southeast Asia (1985-96)

The previous chapter has thrown light on the macroeconomic policies pursued by the Southeast Asian economies. However it only gives a brief description of the same in a generalised manner. Hence it is purported to discuss the development experiences of the ASEAN3 individually and in detail in this chapter.

The ASEAN3 had experimented in export-oriented industrialisation (EOI) even prior to the mid 1980s, but it is only since the mid 1980s that the same was flagged off with fervour. In Indonesia and Thailand the role of IMF and WB has been pivotal in shaping these policies. In Malaysia similar policies were followed as a panacea to the recession that had set in the early 1980s.

Development Experience of Indonesia

Profile

Indonesia is an archipelago of more than 17,000 islands and lies along the equator between northern Australia and the south-eastern tip of the Asian mainland. The south and west coats of Indonesia face the Indian Ocean and to the north lie the straits of Malacca and the South China Sea. The Pacific Ocean lashes the remote northern coast of Irian Jaya. It has an area of more than 2 million sq. kms. Its islands differ in size and geographical characteristics and only 6000 of them are inhabited. It has a population of 204.39 million and is the fifth most populous country in the world. The five big islands-Java, Sumatra, Sulawesi, Kalimantan and Irian Jaya account for 92 percent of the area and 94 percent of the population. Infact two thirds of the population live in Java and this has one of the highest population densities in the world.

Indonesia came into contact with the broader world of civilization by participating in the spice, resins and fragrant woods trade along Asia's great maritime trade route linking China, India and Southeast Asia in about 100AD[1]. Quite naturally it's rich natural endowments and geographical location attracted many traders from Arabia, India, China and Europe. These traders brought with them their ***culture and religion***, which has left long lasting, effects on Indonesia. The same is evident from the fact that Indonesia has a diversity of cultures and religions. The dominant religion in Indonesia is **Islam**, which was introduced by Arabic traders in the 15th century. There are a significant number of Hindus centered around Bali, whereas in the eastern parts of the country, Christianity is the main religion.

The official national *languag*e of Indonesia is **Bahasa Indonesia**, but there are about 25 languages and 250 dialects in Indonesia. Bahasa Indonesia is a modernised version of what was 'Market Malay'- the language of traders during the colonial era. The largest Chinese communities in Southeast Asia are in Indonesia. Therefore the Chinese language is also spoken here.

Colonisation and Trade

Indonesia has had a long colonial rule. The Portuguese arrived in 1511, and then the Dutch in 1596. The Dutch rule lasted over 150 years and was the most long lasting. There were two brief interludes during the Dutch regime- the English between 1811-16 and the Japanese between 1942-45.

Until 1799, the Dutch carried out activities under the flag of the United East India Company (VOC). The VOC was mainly concerned with the spice cultivation and trade and the ensuing profits. Since the profits were quite enormous (the VOC paid 3 stuivers- a Dutch coin for cloves and resold it for 75 stuivers in Europe in the second half of the seventeenth century). They tried to create a monopoly by restricting production. The local rulers were paid highly to declare clove production as illegal in their territories.

Indonesia became a formal Dutch colony by 1799. The Dutch rule of Indonesia was interrupted by the British rule in 1811-16 under Sir Stanford Raffles. After 1817 the Dutch once again ruled over Indonesia. The Dutch had set up a cultivation system known as cultuurstelsel. This was a system wherein a land rent was payable in kind and coffee, sugar, indigo were to be planted compulsorily for export purposes. In 1870, this system was abolished and replaced by one where the government gave out land on long term leases to non-Indonesians. Traditional exports like coffee, sugar, tea and tobacco gave way to rubber, copra, tin and oil.

By 1901, the Dutch decided to bring a new ethical policy of ensuing justice, protecting the Javanese peasants and improving rural living standards of education. Inspite of this policy, there was a high degree of illiteracy even in 1930.

Struggle for Freedom

By 1914, nationalist movements began and the foundation for the freedom struggle was laid. Till then there were two competing parties namely, Sarekat Islam and Communist Party of Indonesia. They were now unified and renamed PNI (Nationalist Party of Indonesia) Its leader was Sukarno and the party had only the goal of achieving independence. His rival in the party was Hatta who was a western educated Indonesian.

The freedom struggle became stronger when the two buried their differences during the Japanese occupation (1942-45). After the Japanese surrender in 1945, Sukarno declared independence and established the Republic of Indonesia with himself as the President. This led to a protracted Guerrilla war with the Dutch and they eventually gave way to International pressure especially that from the USA and the **Republic of Indonesia was formally born on August 24,1950.**

The Sukarno Era (1949-1965)

This period was characterised by an ***inward oriented and interventionist approach*** of the government. It was the fall out of the anti-colonial and anti-Chinese attitude in the post independence era. A system of imports and investment licenses was established to promote domestic (read Indonesian only) importers and traders. But this system misfired on account of massive corruption and rent seeking. Hence a new policy of **Guided Democracy and Guided Economy** was introduced. This was based on state control of production and trade. Dutch enterprises were nationalised and state enterprises took over all aspects of the economy including the monopolies established in the earlier period. Foreign investments too were discouraged. Prices were strictly controlled for a number of essential commodities. Also as taxes were considered a painful relic associated with colonial rulers, recourse was frequently made to the printing press to finance the Government's huge expenditure[2]

These policies were disastrous for the economy. The economic indicators confirmed the same. The GDP growth rate, which was about 4.1%p.a. between 1951-59, fell to only 2.0% p.a. during 1960-66. Infact it was less than the annual rate of population growth. The standard of living fell and per capita real income was 3.6% in 1966 lower than that in 1958 . Inflation soared to 1000% p.a. Forex reserves were negative and service on debt exceeded forex revenue. To add to all this there existed rampant corruption, rent seeking, black-marketing and smuggling. This economic turmoil discredited the government and in a violent political coup that followed Sukarno's government was swept way.

The New Order (1966-1972)

Sukarno's Successor was **Kemure A Suharto** who became the newly elected President of Indonesia. The immediate task of the Government was to put the house in order and the period 1967-72 was accordingly devoted to economic stabilization and rehabilitation. One of the first changes announced by the new Government was a reversal of Sukarno's policy of hostility towards private enterprise and financial institution and introduced a ***relatively liberal policy***.

IMF Package

Within a few days of announcement of the liberal policies, credit poured in from the US, followed by UK and Japan. Then in the summer of 1966, an ***IMF mission*** arrived in Indonesia to work out a new stabilization program that became an inherent part of the new Government's policies. These were incorporated in the Repelita I 1969-70 to 1973-74 (five-year plan). It may be noted here that in August 1964, Sukarno had announced Indonesia's withdrawal from the IMF and World Bank and declared that the coming year would be 'A year of self-reliance'. However in February 1967, Indonesia formally rejoined the Fund. This was the beginning of long-term relationships with the Bretton Woods institutions.

A small group of young Indonesian economists were trained in the US and at the IMF and it was this joint effort that culminated in the stabilization and rehabilitation program[3]. A familiar package of anti-inflationary measures to compliment the decontrol of foreign exchange was drawn up including a balanced budget, reduction in government's expenditure, improvement in tax collection system, a realistic exchange rate through a devaluation, an end to subsidies, a review of pricing policy of the state enterprises, reduction in the number of Government employees, and severe limitation on the creation of bank credit[4].

A more favourable climate for financial institution was created by announcing the intention to restore foreign owned companies earlier nationalized. A new Financial Institution Bill was approved wherein foreign companies were guaranteed against nationalization for a period of atleast 20 years. Many generous tax concessions were also made.

The IMF, as a gesture to such liberalization granted $174 million in adhoc to tide over the crisis and arranged for rescheduling of debts through the 'Paris Club' members (US, Britain, Japan, Australia, France, w. Germany, Italy, Netherlands, World Bank, OECD & IMF).

Other Source of Aid

The other source of aid came from the Inter- Governmental Group of Indonesia (IGGI). The IGGI was formed in 1967, favoured by the US to persuade capitalist nations to share the aid burden. The aid burden was proportionate to the benefits in investment and trade that these countries would derive from the host country (Indonesia). The IGGI credits financed hundreds of millions of dollars of imports each year, which Indonesia would not have been able to pay for with its foreign earnings. The country's foreign payments were thus balanced by foreign loans.

Changes in economic situation

The macroeconomic adjustments described above brought about some respite. Output in agriculture and manufacturing sector increased and GDP growth reached 9.2 % in 1970 and 14% by 1973. Inflation came down to 112% in 1967, abated further to a double digit
of 19% by 1969 and by 1970, it was a controllable 8.8%. Due to extensive tax collection mainly from imports and the oil boom (discussed in the next sub-section) and the exports, Government revenue increased. However, the annual rate of new credits expanded from $175 million in 1966 to $876.60 million in 1973-74 resulting in high indebtedness of Indonesia. In addition, unemployment increased due to mass dismissal of employees in Government and private firms because of the IMF austerity program. Even the inflation rose back to double digits by 1973.

The Oil Boom (1973-81)

The oil boom had varied effects on the economy of Indonesia. Initially it proved to be a boon. The Arab countries had imposed an oil embargo in October 1972. This the led to an increase in the world oil prices by four times. Indonesia, a net oil exporting country, benefited considerably from the rapid increase in world oil prices. Most of the oil windfalls accrued to the government and its revenue increased. The percentage of non-mining GDP rose from 15.6% in

1970-72 to 30.9% in 1979-81. Net oil and Liquified Natural Gas earnings increased from US $6 billion to US $19.0 billion between 1973 and 82. As compared to oil revenues earned by some other OPEC countries this was very small.

With ample resources made available by the oil boom, Indonesia once again embarked in an Import Substituting Industrialization Strategy (ISI) aided by large government investments in upstream mega projects[5]. Economic reforms during Repelita II and III (the 5 years plan) became more protective. Tariff and non-tariff barriers escalated while restrictions and controls on financial institution became stringent.

The oil revenues as mentioned earlier were used to complete certain Government projects, commitments to which were made in the previous period. It was also spent on rural development, agricultural sector, education and health and family planning. The country even tried to avoid the 'Dutch disease'* by making investments in the non-oil sector, placing quantitative restrictions and regulatory controls and also devaluing the currency twice, once in 1971 and again in 1978 by 10% and 50 % respectively. The devaluation became essential as the appreciation in the real exchange rate was eroding the competitiveness of the non-oil economy.

On the down side, the economy was hit by inflation again with it reaching about 30 % by 1973 and further 40% by 1974. This was quickly brought down to 6.72 % by 1979 through a change in the targeted credit policy wherein a ceiling was imposed on domestic borrowings. The economy became progressively inward oriented creating a bias against exports in favour of rent seeking. Even the devaluation was to some extent nullified due to the domestic inflation and this further affected exports adversely. Public sector once again became dominant and heavily dependent on the oil revenues.

The most serious problem was that pertaining to the national oil company called Pertamina that had borrowed heavily from international markets including in the form of short-term loans. Such loans were taken, firstly, because cheap international credit was available to Islamic countries through the recycling of petro dollars by the low absorbing Gulf States and secondly, because Petamina had made heavy investment in the non-oil economy. The central bank i.e. the Bank of Indonesia had to take over these debts and at that time foreign reserves amounted to $10.5 billion only [6]. After this, the official borrowing proceeded very cautiously.

Post Oil Boom Adjustment (1982-88)

The oil boom had given Indonesia a brief respite. As has been earlier noted, foreign exchange earnings from oil and gas between 1978-79 and 1981-82 increased from $74 billion to $190 billion indicating a 157% rise and constituting 81% of forex.

* Erosion of competitiveness in the non-oil sector due to windfall gains from the oil sector.
The revenue of the Government derived from taxes on the oil and gas sector increased from Rp 2309 billion in 1978-79 to Rp 8575 billion in 1981-82 indicating a rise of 271% and constituting 70% of government revenue[7].
However the breathing period from the oil boom did not last long. By 1982 the economy faced two external shocks.
Firstly, the economy experienced a sharp deterioration in the external terms of trade largely due to the fall in oil prices and to some extent due to the fall in commodity prices. Secondly, the depreciation of US dollar vis-à-vis major currencies during 1985-88 (following the Plaza accord of 1985) added substantially to Indonesia's external debt burden.

Due to a global economic recession the oil prices fell from US $ 35 a barrel in January 1981 to US $25 a barrel in January 1986 to US $ 9.86 a barrel in August 1986. Indonesia's external terms of trade declined over 30% and its current account deficit rose from 3% of GNP in 1981-82 to about 8% in 1982-83 and was as high as 6% in 1986-87. Oil and gas export earnings originally estimated at $21.4 billion in 1982-83 were revised to $17.2 billion in October the same year. The value of non-oil exports declined by 9.5% in 1979, 25% in 1980 and 12% in 1981. This decline was due to a fall in commodity prices on account of the worldwide recession, increased domestic constructions and a fall in exports of log due to the Government's attempt to replace the same with exports of processed wood.

Quite naturally, such declines were reflected in the government budget. The domestic revenue from oil and gas dropped from Rp 8575 billion in 1981-82 to Rp 7000 billion in 1982-83, indicating an 18% fall. Non-oil revenue too declined from Rp 3699 billion to about Rp 3000 billion i.e. an 11% decline.

The Role of WB and IMF

The WB Report of 1981 had predicted a bleak future for Indonesia's balance of payments in 1980's. This report presented a comprehensive critique of Indonesia's development strategy at a time when the fiscal difficulties flowing from the oil market crisis were first becoming apparent. According to the report the structural approach to development planning together with the accompanying state regulation of investment and intervention in the economy, produced distortions which inhibited not only economic growth but also adversely affected the equitable distribution of wealth. It claimed that the import substitution industrial sector has benefited a relatively small and well-connected group of industrialists for whom mobilization of political resources had constituted a more important skill than expertise in investment and production. Restrictions on trade, investment and credit operated in favour of the owners of capital stock. The consumers and workers bore the burden of an inefficient and protected economy in the form of lower wages, higher prices and inefficient allocation of investment funds.

The following specific recommendations were made by the ***Bank***:

1) A movement away from reliance upon oil taxes through a more effective mobilisation of domestic resources including:
   (i) A sustained programme of developing non-oil taxation.
   (ii) Improved efficiency in the domestic capital market and the removal of fixed ceilings and preferences in credit policy.

(iii) Phasing out of budget subsidies which was about 15% of the budget and 4.2% of the GDP, redirecting these funds to areas of productive investment.

2) The dismantling of restriction on investments inorder to allow the market to determine allocative efficiency. This would involve a shift from Import substitution manufacturing into sectors which could be internationally competitive and the removal of restrictions on investment based on ownership. A crucial consequence of such a change in policy would be the removal of existing structural constraints on foreign and domestic Chinese investment in favour of investment by state and indigenous private investment.

3) Improvement of the legal and administration infrastructure for economic activity to provide efficient, predictable and rational procedures to replace the present capricious and cumbersome system.

4) Deregulation of the economy to eliminate the complex and costly procedures, which deter investment, consume inordinate time and energy and breed corruption.

Indonesia's reliance on loans made it increasingly susceptible to pressures from the World Bank for structural adjustment.

The IMF too had warned that oil prices was about to fall when the head of the IMF mission had visited Indonesia in July 1981. By September the same year, the Government was preparing a policy response to a prospective decline in revenue [8].

As mentioned above one of the problems associated with the oil slump was the balance of payments. The easiest option was to avoid adjustment by using the reserves and by borrowing at this stage from the IMF commodity buffer stocks scheme and a $1 billion was from Morgan Guaranty. However, this did not help much and the current account deficit declined further. This necessitated two devaluations- 28% in March 1983 and 31% in September 1986. On account of this non-oil exports tripped from $5 billion in 1983 to $14.4 billion in 1990 and their share of total exports rose from 25%

to 56%. Negotiations between the western creditors, principal aid donors, the IMF and the IBRD resulted in the formation of Inter Government Group on Indonesia (IGGI) .The IGGI was to co-ordinate and channelise Indonesian loans on increasingly easy terms.

Indonesia had also borrowed from the IGGI and by the fiscal year1983/84 the same had touched a record $2.2 billion. Infact another WB report of 1983 predicted that Indonesia would need to borrow $4.5 billion per year between 1984-85 and 1986-87 of which $3.4 billion would come from IGGI, to cover forex needs[9]. Infant, by the early 1990s annual lending through the IGGI was in the neighbourhood of $4 billion.

The ADB is yet another source of borrowing for Indonesia. Indonesia is by far the ADB's largest borrower, accounting for 21.5% of total lending during 1970-92[10]. The country borrowed in the phase 1970-74 for initial adjustment, it also borrowed when Government investment increased on account of oil revenues and yet gain to tide over the lower oil revenues problem. By ADB's own admission, this lending program complemented the macro economic policy reforms financed by trade policy and private sector development loans that were provided by the WB. The ADB support covered sector loans for power, irrigation, roads, urban development, water supply and a program lending for development of non-oil exports and cash and food crops section. However, policy conditionalities in financial sector loans by the WB covered relevant macro economic policies such as exchange and investment rate policies while the ADB loans dealt with reforms of the capital market and financial institutions covered by these loans. In addition, the WB assists the Government in setting its macro economic policy agenda and formulating policies. The ADB takes note of these policies but undertakes no active dialogue on them. Even on sectoral policies, it appears that the WB conducts a more active policy dialogue in comparison with he ADB in ensuring performance on conditionalities[11] .

Between mid 1983-84, total international banks subscription exceeded $750 million. Donors were also supportive during 1983-

84 there was such a marked increase in government receipts that total receipts were roughly the same % of GDP as t the height of the second oil boom.

There have been some indigenous reform ideas but these have been not totally dissociated from those of international agencies. Apparently the policy direction proposed in the 1982's were recommended by a group of people that have been effective in the policy arena, namely the economic technocrats headed by Widjojo Nitisasatro. It was widely believed in Indonesia that the idea of market reform might have been in place even before donor agencies like the IMF/WB prescriptions came up. But it cannot be said with conviction that if such reform ideas were radically different from those of the IMF/WB, there would have been as strong support from these agencies to Indonesia and it's stabilization and structural program that it embarked upon since the 1980's.

Interestingly the foreign observers have often supported the independence of Indonesia's policy reforms while it is the domestic critics who have commented that the country's economic policy makers simply follow meekly whatever these international agencies prescribe. The truth most likely lies somewhere in between these extreme positions as can be seen in the discussion on reforms in the following section.

Reforms During the 1980s and Beyond

As aforementioned the WB had become increasingly critical of Indonesia's ISI strategy and instead was advocating the opening of the economy to international capital flows, and removal of distortions in the form of subsidies. The crisis of the 1980's propelled by the worldwide recession and plunge in oil prices brought the Indonesian economy on the brink. Hence the government responded immediately and fairly forcefully to the same through a Stabilization and Structural Adjustment program (SSA) with some spectacular results. It is from this period onwards that Indonesia "took off" and went on later to be known as one of the miracle economies or HPAE in the WB lexicon.

The essential characteristics of the SSA approach were:

- Deregulation and debureaucratisation.
- Export led growth without dependency on oil.
- The creation of a regulatory climate conducive to foreign investment.
- Transfer of power from the government to the private sector.

In general the entire approach was outward oriented.

Reforms were undertaken in the field of **exchange rate**, **fiscal policy**, **monetary and financial policy**, **trade and industrial policy** and **foreign investment policies** as a response to the crisis and pressure from international financial agencies. A summary of economic reforms in Indonesia is provided in Chart 4.I.1.

Exchange rate management:

Like other countries during the Bretton Woods period, Indonesia too had a fixed exchange regime. In 1971 it switched to pegging against the US dollar. Again after 1978, ***a basket peg*** was put in the place of the same ***with a heavy weightage on the US dollar.***

Indonesia effected four devaluations between 1971-86; in 1971 (10%); in 1978 (50%); in 1983 (28%); and in 1986 (31.6%). Indonesia has used devaluation as an instrument to manage external balances (current account), debt problems, propel exports and to suppress imports.

The 1971 devaluation was effected to correct a current account deficit. But in 1978, both the balance of payments and international reserves were strong, yet devaluation was necessary as the exchange rate had appreciated too much and was adversely affecting the non-oil exports. This devaluation helped to increase non-oil exports and restrain imports.

Again in 1982, price of oil began to fall and the same coincided with an international decrease in prices of other export commodities. The balance of payments deteriorated sharply, reaching a record of

7.7 % of GNP by 1982. In early Aug 1982, the Asian Wall Street Journal voiced the widely held belief that Indonesia would soon be forced to devalue the currency[12]. Contrary to this, a week later on August 16 1982, President Suharto ruled out a devaluation of the rupiah.

But in the months to follow the situation became worse. Imports grew without an export recovery. Capital flight accelerated and forex reserves fell to $3.3 billion. In the same month OPEC cut oil prices by $5 a barrel. Indonesia was faced with three choices- launch a program of massive deficit spending, increasing the offshore borrowing or devalue the currency. The third seemed the best way out and in 1983, the rupiah was devalued by 28% against the US $, from Rp 703 per US $ to Rp 707 per US $ Thus this devaluation too was made to correct the adverse balance of payments. The 1986 devaluation of 31% from Rp 1134 to Rp 1644/$, however, was made for maintaining export competitiveness.

Both these devaluations were effected in combination with prudent fiscal and monetary measures that kept inflation under control (see Table 4.I.1). The basic objective of these devaluations, as mentioned earlier, were to achieve and maintain reasonable real effective exchange rates in order to ensure the profitability and international competitiveness of imports and exports. Also the devaluations purported to make imports expensive and ease the balance of payments situation. Finally the devaluation also aimed at promoting non-oil exports. All three objectives were achieved.

The devaluation stimulated exports till the mid 1990s (See Table 3.11) and increased capital inflows (See section on FD1 policies) .The forex reserves stood at $4.8 billion by March 1986 and increased to $13.3 billion by 1995 (See Table 3.13).

The stimulation of exports reduced the transitional costs of adjustment and facilitated trade liberalization without much pain. There was however one problem. Since the exchange rate was pegged to the US$ and since the country maintained open current and capital accounts firms borrowed directly from overseas. These loans were in foreign currencies. The Central Bank did nothing to stop such inflows and this undermined the confidence of the local currency. The exchange rate which was Rp 1641 per US$ in 1986, gradually depreciated to Rp 2383 per US$ in 1996 as can be seen from Table 4.I.4. This decline occurred in order to realign the economy to maintain export competitiveness.

Fiscal Policy:

During the 1970s, the oil reserves generously filled the government coffers. Oil reserves as a share of Central Government revenue increased from 26% in 1969-70 to 71% in 1981-82. With the drastic fall in oil prices coupled with the existing narrow tax base, a change in the fiscal policy became absolutely essential. Also the fiscal deficit had reached nearly 5% of GDP in 1982-83 compared to 1.3% in the previous year.

The new policy called for correcting the imbalance through ***cutting government expenditure*** and ***mobilising domestic resources*** by way of widening the tax base and sprucing up the tax mechanism.

To reduce expenditure, the Governments routine operating budget was downsized. Many large capital-intensive projects were postponed or fully abandoned. Some of the specific projects selected for rephasing were a $1.6 billion Olefin Plant, a $1.5 billion aromatic plant, a $1.35 billion oil refinery and a $600 million lumina plant. The projects selected for suspension or cancellation were highly capital intensive and were to be financed with loans from abroad that had to be matched by exports from the Indonesian Government[13]. There was strong criticism from the groups who were involved in the projects and from those who felt that this would slow down the country's economic development

The other efforts made by the government to reduce the expenditure were cut in subsidies, restraints on civil services employment and salaries, and reduction in the share of expenditure allocated to social programs including health and education. All these measures helped in bringing down real public expenditure by 19%between 1982-83 and 1986-87.

On the ***revenue front*** also efforts were being made to reduce the fiscal deficit by introducing tax reforms to boost non-oil tax revenues and improve the tax system. It was realised that over the longer term Indonesia could not remain dependent on oil and gas as a source of government revenue[14]. The reform introduced a thoroughly modern tax system, which recognised that a complex system with high marginal rates was not only difficult to implement but also adversely affected economic efficiency.

The new tax system simplified the Income Tax law and introduced a new schedule based on relatively low tax rates. The new tax code reduced tax rates in the range of 15% to 35 % and moved to a self-reporting Income Tax system. The cut off point for taxable income was doubled, reducing the proportion of the population paying Income Tax from 15% to10%. In general the tax system was restructured in such a manner that it simplified the procedure of tax administration.

Changes were introduced in the indirect tax structure too. The sales tax was replaced with a value added tax (VAT) in April 1985 the rate of which was 10 %. Hence Indonesia was a pioneer insomuch as it was the first among the developing countries to introduce a VAT. The VAT rate of 10% was applied to manufacturing and construction sectors and for fuel oils. An additional tax of 10-20% was levied on luxury goods sold in domestic markets. The VAT was introduced with the aim of avoiding taxation on full value at each stage in the production chain.

As a result of these measures, there was an ***increase in non-oil revenue*** from 5.5 % of GDP in 1982-83 to 11.2% of GDP in 1993-94 as is evident from Table 4.I.2. The adjoining Graph 4.I.A shows the comparative picture more clearly. At the same time, dependence on oil and gas revenue was reduced and the revenue collection came down from 11.9 % to 4.3 % for the same time period. The number of ***registered taxpayers*** more than ***doubled*** and the share of Income

Tax in total revenue increased from approximately 2% in 1980-85 to 14% by 1989-90 as can be seen from Table 4.I.3. The ***share of VAT collection*** for the same time period rose from 3% to 15% while the share of corporate oil taxes decreased from 54% to 29 %. Table 4.I.1 indicates that the overall budget deficit which was 5.0% of GDP in 1982-83 was scaled to 3.0 % of GDP in 1988-89 and further to 0.4% of GDP by 1993.

Budget austerity measures combined with appropriate monetary management, contributed to a ***reduction in the rate of inflation***. Inflation came down from a whopping 15.8% in 1973-81 to 9.71 % in 1981-85, it further declined to 7.2 % in 1990. However went up marginally to 9.43 % in 1995(See Table 4. I.1). However since GDP growth during 1985-95 was about 7-8 % p.a on an average, the inflation could be sustained.

Monetary and Financial Policy:

Following the oil market crash, Indonesia's programme of financial sector reforms moved into high gear[15]. Reforms encompassed the ***banking sector***, the ***stock market*** and exchange rate management (already discussed separately) All the reforms aimed at making the system simpler and more market oriented. A summary of the financial sector reforms undertaken in Indonesia are presented in Chart 4.I.2.

During the oil boom monetary policy instruments were ceiling on credit disbursement and interest rate controls. Subsidized interest rates existed for the identified priority sectors. This policy was effective in limiting credit expansions in certain sectors. The effect of the tight money policy was nullified due to excess liquidity originating from the augmented net foreign assets prompted by two oil booms and the uncontrolled liquidity credits to the priority sectors.

With the plunge in oil prices and the consequent reduction in government revenue and the rising balance of payment deficit, it became necessary to initiate monetary and financial reforms in June 1983.

Monetary Policy and Banking reforms: - The banking system mainly consists of the Central Bank (Bank Indonesia), the commercial and development banks of which 7 are sate owned banks. They constituted about 90 % of the gross assets of the financial system in 1991. Non-banking financial institutions (NBFI's), which are largely owned by domestic and foreign banks jointly, accounted for only 2% of the gross assets. Other financial institutions such as savings banks, leasing companies, securities companies and retirement funds were a fast growing segment of the financial system but these firms as a group were relatively small.

The first round of reforms initiated included the following: -

Government owned banks were allowed to set interest rates freely on deposits and loans. This reduced the volume of subsidized central bank credit.

The administratively determined credit ceilings were lifted.

New market oriented instruments - Bank Interest Certificates (SBI), Certificate of Deposits issued by commercial banks (SBPU)- were developed by the monetary authorities.

The immediate effects of the financial reforms were a rapid increase in interest rates on bank deposits and a sharp increase in time and savings deposits. This was a positive change especially considering that real interest rates were negative during the oil boom. It was a move to link domestic interest rates to international interest rates in order to avoid capital flight.

The next packages of reforms were announced in October 1988 and March 1989, known as Packet October or ***Pakto***. These were designed to stimulate growth and innovation among government, private and foreign banks operating in Indonesia. They included

- Restrictions on new entry into the banking sector were removed.
- All restrictions on expansion of domestic branch banking were lifted.
- Foreign banks were permitted in any one of the six major cities of Samrabaya, Semarang, Medan, Bandung, Ujung Pantang and Denpasar. Also foreign banks were permitted to open joint ventures with Indonesian banks.

The reserve requisite was reduced from 15% to 2 % enabling the banks to make more lending.

State owned enterprises (SOEs) were freed of the obligation to deposit all their funds with government banks. Instead they were required to keep only 50 % of these funds, and, the rest of 50 % could be kept outside the government banks. This regulation was intended to create a competitive environment and thereby improving their efficiency.

A 15 % withholding tax was applied to interest on savings and time deposits. This step was taken to give an impetus to the country's stock exchange. Before Pakto, interest on bank accounts was tax exempt, whereas dividend incomes and capital gains from stocks were taxed. Because interest rates on bank deposits were so attractive, there was no incentive to invest in stocks. By taxing interest from bank deposits the tax bias in favour of bank deposits was removed and this led to a significant increase in investment in stocks.

Capital Market Reforms

Indonesia had a stock exchange since 1912. The original equities market was established under the Dutch rule in Jakarta when the city was still known as Balavia. Later a second exchange was established in Surabaya. Trading stopped on the exchange in 1956 after Sukarno's government had began nationalizing foreign firms. Although the New Order Government under Suharto realised the importance of a stock exchange as a vehicle for mobilising capital and fostering growth of the private sector, it could do so only in 1977. On August 10,1977, the present Jakarta Stock (JSE) was established[16].

The Ministry of Financial and the Capital Market Policy Council (BAPEPAM) work towards drawing up policies and regulation of the operation of the stock exchange. They also evaluate applicants for listing and monitor the progress of listed companies[17]. A middleman agency- PT Danareksa was established in 1976 to buy and sell shares of listed the companies.

After Pakato measures, another set of deregulation measures was introduced on December 22,1988 known as Paket December (***Pakdes***). These included

- Regulations limiting daily price swings to 4% of price of stocks were removed
- Insider trading was prohibited and the board on any exchange could not hold more than 10 .5 % of that exchange's total shares.
- Foreign shareholders were allowed to buy shares upto 49% of shares listed on any company except of commercial banks.
- Foreign securities houses were allowed to form joint ventures with local partners.
- Guidelines for advanced financial services such as factoring, leasing, securities trading and credit cards were made.
- An Over the Counter (OTC) market was established.

In the second phase of reforms the stock exchange was privatised and separated from the BAPEPAM.

All these reforms helped in increasing the number of companies listed on the stock exchange from 57 in 1989 to 255 by 1997[18] The capitalization value of the exchange rose from $ 249 million to 75$ billion for the same period[19]. Hence foreign capital inflows shot up. Prices of stocks surged and this resulted into listing of more companies in the market.

In 1992 the trading system was automated and this was one of the most significant reforms in the JSE. The listing in 1998 was 283, a further increase of 30 odd companies in one year only. Just before the currency crisis took place in July 1997, the market capitalization was about 45 % of the GDP compared to only 3% in 1970

Other benefits of financial sector reforms:

The financial sector reforms created a bigger and deeper financial sector. Money market depth is generally measured by the ratio of ***M2/GDP.*** Table 4.I.1 shows that this ratio increased from 19.9 in 1981-85 to 52.5 in 1996. The table also shows that ***Gross fixed capital formation*** improved from 28.0% in 1981-85 to 36.1% in 1996. The growth in

GFCF always has close connection with growth in GDP. The number of banks exploded breaking the monopoly of the state banks over the years.

Trade and Industrial Policy:

During the early 1980's Indonesia's trade regime was very inward oriented and had highly protective trade barriers. It protected domestic production and discouraged imports. Supported by the oil boom, the government's industrial policy was geared towards encouraging upstream industries like cement, fertilizers, synthetic fibres and iron/ steel. In the late 1982 and early 1983 decrees were made increasing the number of products for which 'approved import license' was needed. As the phrase suggests the right to import certain goods was restricted to only those with an approved license. In fact by the mid 1980's over 1700 items were covered by some form of restrictive license or the other20.

The private sector was in general subjected to a multitude of controls- a restrictive investment and production capital licensing system, limiting entry and extensive control of financial institution, cumbersome land and labour laws. These high NTB and high tariff barriers coupled with the restrictive regime of controls and regulations fostered the development of high cost and inefficient industries[21].

With the loss of income due to decline in oil related export earnings and a sharp deterioration in the terms of trade, the Government (read under pressure from the IMF/ WB) reversed the development strategy. Beginning in 1985 the government started implementing far reaching reforms in the trade regime and industrial policy.

Trade regime

In March-April 1985 the tariff system was rationalised. The tariff ceiling was lowered from 225% to 60%. Most tariff rates ranged between 5% and 35%. The number of tariff levels was also reduced from 25 to 11. Further tariff reductions were made in October 1986 and May 1990 wherein tariff ceiling became 40%.

In April 1985, inorder to reduce costs and speed up customs clearance, the inefficient customs department was replaced by a private Swiss surveillance company (Société Generale de Surveillance- SGS) which was given the job of certifying imports and clearing them[22]. This was an immediate success. The average time spent on customs procedures was cut by several weeks and the cost of freight forwarding for exports and imports fell substantially.

In May 1986-87, 'producer exporters' were allowed to import their inputs bypassing 'approved importers' that too duty free. A duty drawback facility was created to enable exporters to reclaim import duties when they paid it. This reduced the costs of production of exports. The Government announced a further trade reform package focussing on the removal of import licensing restrictions and reducing the anti- export bias. The basic idea was to move away from a trade regime dependent on NTB to one based on tariffs.

The information relating to changes in tariff and NTB rates is presented in Table 4.I.6. The share of imports subjected to NTBs fell from 43% in 1986 to 13% in June 1991. The proportion of domestic production protected by NTB too fell from 41% to 22%. Although there was a shift from NTB to tariffs, the tariff rates did not rise. Only the number of goods now subjected to tariffs increased. The average level of tariffs (unweighted) fell from 37 in the pre 1985 period to 20% by 1991. Also the average tariff, rates fell from 22% to 10% when weighted by import value and from 29% to 15% weighted by domestic production for the same time period as shown in Table 4.I.5.

In order to provide a boost to exporters, duty exempt and duty drawback schemes were introduced. Initially there were some doubts whether the complex regulations and the new government board BAPEKSTA, operating within the Ministry of finance, would function effectively. But such doubts were immediately put to rest. Between 1986 and 1989, the number of firms registered under the scheme increased from 247 to 1950. The time taken to process application was cut down from 24 to 10 days in case of drawbacks and from 12 to 9 in case of exemptions. By December 1989, 38% of non-oil imports and 24% total manufacturing exports were registered under this scheme.

Other regulatory reforms included liberalizing the investment licensing system. The licensing and approval procedures were streamlined. By 1989 the complex and large list of activities closed for private investment were reduced. This provided more scope for private investors. Virtually all areas of manufacturing which were open to domestic investors were also opened to foreign investors. Hence investment licensing was no longer a significant barrier to entry of firms in the tradable goods sector. The deregulation also led to a much greater competition from foreign firms. These measures were supplemented by reducing impediments to financial institutions[23] (Details relating to this is provided in the sub-section on FDI)

Out come of the trade and industrial policy reforms:-

The export promotion measures helped ***non-oil exports*** to grow by 13% between 1983-84 and 1988-89. Also non-oil manufactured goods exports increased at a spectacular rate of 26% during the same period as is evident from Table 4.I.7. Graph 4.I.B shows the selected non oil exports for the time period 1986-97. Significant gains were seen particularly in exports of processed wood, textiles, garments and rubber products. This remarkable export performance reflected the increasing competitiveness of the Indonesian economy. Over time new export capacities were created across a wide range of manufacturing items which enabled the sustenance of the export momentum till about 1995.

Table 3.25 shows the changing ***composition of exports*** and Table3.24 shows the increasing percentage of manufactured exports. Both these adequately prove that the trade and industrial policy reforms were directed towards increasing manufactured exports and a shift away from oil exports. Also Table 3.11 shows the EGS/GDP has increased indicating that Indonesia has over the years become increasingly export oriented. In comparison to Malaysia and Thailand it is definitely less outward oriented.

Even the process of streamlining investment approvals bore fruit. These measures along with the other reforms created an environment conducive to business transactions including a sharp increase in both domestic and foreign investments. ***Domestic approvals*** by BKPM doubled in value during 1989-.90 and 1990-91. Between 1986 and 1990, the number of domestic projects approved by BKPM rose sharply from 350 to 1329 with their Rupiah value increasing from Rp 4441.0 billion to Rp 57878.0 billion. Therefore although a number of upstream government investment projects were cancelled, it was more than compensated by a rise in FDI.

As compared to the 1970s and early 1980s when much of the private investment was directed towards import substitution, the bulk of new investment approvals were directed towards export activities. There was also an increase in manufacturing output and non-oil manufacturing. A cursory glance at Table 4.I.7 will make this clear. The decline in the oil prices during 1982 and 1985 explains the extremely large increase in manufacturing output by 22%. After this, over the period 1985-92 both manufacturing output and the non-oil manufacturing output grew on an average by more than 11% p.a.

Thus it can be said that the trade and industrial policy reforms had the desired positive effects on the economy.

Foreign Investment Policy

Just as in the case of the trade and industrial policy reforms, with the declining oil revenues in the mid 1980s., Indonesia came to appreciate to a greater extent the potential role of FDI in economic development. Starting in 1986, Indonesian authorities launched a new investment promotion drive by relaxing limits on foreign ownership for export oriented investments and facilitating investment licensing procedures. Firms exporting 80% of production (later modified to 60%) could have upto 95% foreign equity. The BKPM also simplified its application forms and promised a reduction of the delays in making decisions. This first package was followed by almost annual reforms, resulting in considerable relaxation of the terms of governing foreign investment[24].

The 1987 package opened more sectors to foreign investors and the promotion of private over public investment. The minimum initial capitalization requirements for foreign investment projects were reduced. The strictures on expatriate employment and the use of imported inputs were eased.

In 1989, the BKPM scrapped a cumbersome positive list of areas open to foreign investors and replaced it with a short Negative List defining only areas closed to domestic and foreign investment and those closed only to foreign investment. The List also mentioned those areas where 100% foreign investment was permitted and those where restrictions and limitations existed. The list opened more than 300 sectors to foreign investors with just 6 being completely closed to foreigners. Wholly owned foreign firms were allowed to establish export houses and import firms solely importing goods for further processing and re-export.

The rule which permitted upto 95% foreign ownership was changed in 1993. Now, 51% of a company's equity had to be handed over to local interest within 15 years. (This clause was withdrawn in the post crisis period)

In 1994 the Government of Indonesia undertook ***further reforms***. The package

i) permitted 100 % foreign ownership throughout Indonesia, although priority was to be given to projects in export promotion zones or industrial estates wherever feasible;
ii) lifted the previous requirement for wholly foreign owned companies to have a minimum paid up capital of $50 million and permitted investors to determine capital outlays based on the commercial viability of the project;
iii) significantly relaxed the domestic partnership and divestment requirements introduced in 1974. The obligation for foreign investors to establish joint ventures with local partners and to

prepare for the transfer of at least 51% of the company's equity to Indonesian ownership was abolished. A token divestment of as little as 5 % was required after 15 years.

iv) reduced the minimum equity holding for Indonesian partners in joint ventures from 20% to 5% and required no further divestment in this case. This increased equity limit also applied to joint ventures in deregulated strategic industries.

v) allowed foreign and Indonesian partners to determine changes in the composition of share ownership;

vi) set a 30-year validity for foreign investment licenses with a possible 30-year extension.

Many incentives were provided and export promotion measures were undertaken to facilitate the export oriented FDI financed projects. Incentives included exemption or relief from import duties, tax holidays (restored only in 1996 after being withdrawn in 84), tax incentive for industry/project considered to be a natural priority in terms of exports or for the development of remote area. There were exemption for VAT and sales tax on luxury goods and materials purchased domestically for use in export manufacturing. Many of these reliefs were later (1996) available even to those industries not located in the EPZ.

The policy reforms co-incided with a period of sharp shifts in competitive positions of firms in Japan and the NIEs. Hence Japan and NIEs started to relocate industries in Indonesia since this provided cheaper labour resources and land costs. Liberalization in Indonesia helped such relocation to take place more smoothly and on a large scale.

Policy outcome

Indonesia experienced a boom in inward direct investment from the mid 1980s until the crisis. In the 1990s Indonesia was ranked 6th among non-OECD countries and 17th in the world for FDI inflows. ***FDI inflows*** as a percentage of GDP grew steadily from 0.13% in 1981 to peak at 2.4% in 1996 (See Table 3.14). Compared to that in Thailand and Malaysia, it is nevertheless small especially considering the size of Indonesia and it's natural resources.

The sectoral distribution of FDI flows is shown in Table 4.I.8. Only 7.8% was directed towards primary sector while 64.3% was directed towards secondary sector and 27 % was directed towards tertiary sector. The tertiary sector investment had started increasing in the post 1993 period. Since investment here is mainly in non-tradables, the costs here were rising to unrealistic levels before the crisis and when the crisis took place, this bubble burst.

Information relating to sources of FDI are presented in Table 4.I.9. The ***sources of FDI*** were mainly from Japan and the NIES. In 1985, fifty percent of Japan's outflows was to Indonesia alone, mostly in resource based and labour intensive manufacturing. By 1996, Indonesia still held Japan's FDI more than any other Asian developing country.

Singapore too has been increasing its investment in Indonesia. This has been encouraged by increasing cost of labour in Malaysia where Singapore had initially located it's labour intensive units.

US and European countries have preferred to Investment in Indonesia's oil and gas sector while the NIEs have been targeting the tertiary sector off late.

Other benefits: -
The improved investment climate led by a surge in FDI caused a high growth in non-oil exports. Non-oil exports as a percentage of GDP doubled in the late 1980s. As far as export orientation is concerned some sectors (within the non-oil export sector) are more export oriented than others. For eg. Sectors such as wood, tint are more export oriented. Electrical and electronic goods sector has emerged as a leading export sector accounting for 10% of industrial output in 1995 as compared to about 4% in 1991. Exports of electrical appliances grew from $1 billion in 1992 to $3 billion in 1996.

Electrical and electronic appliances were the 3rd largest source of export earnings in 1995 after plywood and garments but ahead of footwear and processed rubber. In the electronic sector 80% of exports are from foreign producers (foreign firms and joint ventures) However it may be noted here that these firms source about 60% of the components they need for production. This is because the relatively high level of technology necessary for production was not available in Indonesia. It was only around 1996 that very preliminary efforts were being made by some Korean and Japanese firms to source them locally.

Faced with increased competition from other developing countries and stagnant slow growth in overseas markets exports of garments and plywood have suffered in the past few years. But footwear, processed rubber and electronic goods have increased their shares of earnings. This trend was ofcourse interrupted by the currency crisis. Graph 4.I.B shows the performance of non-oil exports for the period 1986-97.

Overall Indonesia's exports are bunched in such a way that they are either at the upper end or lower end of skill and technology range. Table 3.25 shows that since the structure of exports is such that there is a dominance of plywood, textiles and garments, it reflects the country's low position in technical skill. At the same time in recent years exports of electronic goods are increasing. But as mentioned earlier their parts are not produced indigenously but sourced.

Table 4.I.1

Basic Economic and Social Indicators of Development in Indonesia

Year	1981-85	1986	1987	1988	1989	1990	1991	1992	1993	1994	1995	1996	1997
Indicators													
National A/cs													
GDP Growth %	4.74	5.9	4.9	5.8	7.5	7.4	6.4	7.2	7.3	7.5	8.2	8.0	4.6
Per Capita GDP		3.7	2.8	3.6	5.2	5.3	4.3	5.4	5.5	5.8	6.5	6.2	2.9
M1/GDP %	10.4	10.3	10.3	10.1	12.0	12.0	11.7	11.1	10.2	10.9	10.6	9.8	11.0
M2/GDP %	19.9	22.1	23.6	29.0	35.0	42.5	43.7	45.8	43.4	45.3	49.0	52.5	55.6
Trade Deficit % of GDP	5.0	6.0	5.7	5.9	4.9	5.5	4.2	5.6	5.3	4.6	3.0	0.9	7.9
Budget Deficit % of GDP	-1.0	-5.6	-4.9	-4.0	-1.4	-1.8	-0.7	-0.4	-0.4	-0.2	-0.2	-0.5	-1.0
Current A/c Deficit % of GDP	0.6	-4.9	-2.8	-1.7	-1.2	-2.2	-3.7	-2.2	-1.3	-1.6	-3.6	-3.4	-3.9
Private Consumption Deficit % of GDP	59.3	58.4	57.3	56.2	55.4	55.0	55.0	55.2	55.7	57.9	58.7	55.4	62.1
Govt. consumption deficit % of GDP	10.8	10.6	10.3	9.4	9.3	9.5	9.1	9.5	9.0	8.2	8.2	7.6	6.8
GFCF Deficit % of GDP	28.0	30.2	31.3	33.3	33.5	34.4	35.5	35.9	33.2	34.3	33.8	36.1	31.5
Govt. expenditure deficit % of GDP	21.2	21.3	21.6	23.2	22.8	16.9	17.3	17.2	16.3	16.1	15.0	16.3	17.3
Inflation	9.71	5.8	9.3	8.0	6.5	7.2	9.41	7.53	9.69	8.52	9.43	7.93	11.6

Table 4.I.2

Indonesia's Central Government Revenues 1982-83 to 1993-94

	1982-83	1985-86	1986-87	1989-90	1990-91	1991-92	1992-93	1993-94
Revenue (including external grants)	18.2	19.7	15.1	16.1	20.2	17.9	17.1	17.8
Oil & Gas	11.9	11.3	5.9	6.4	8.6	6.6	5.8	4.3
Non-oil & gas	5.5	6.7	7.1	8.8	10.2	10	10.3	11.2

Source : Central Bureau of Statistics (BPS), & World Bank Staff estimates

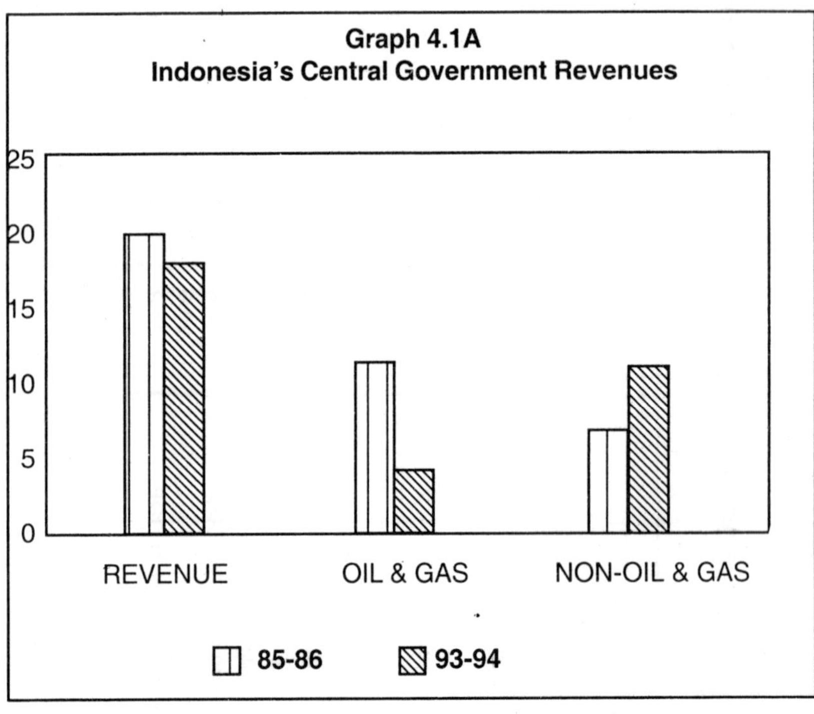

Table 4.I.3

Central government Receipts and Expenditures, Indonesia 1984-85 to 1989-90

	1984-85	1989-90
Share in Total Revenue (%)	2.33	14.38
Income Tax	3.29	15.29
VAT		
Oil and Gas	53.83	29.48
Share in GDP (%)		
Non oil taxes	5.55	9.4
Government expenditure	21.2	18.7

Source : Central Bureau of Statistics (BPS), & World Bank Staff estimates.

Table 4.I.4

Exchange Rates and Interest Rates

	1981-85	1986	1987	1988	1989	1990	1991	1992	1993	1994	1995	1996	1997
Exchange rate Rp/$	906	1641	1650	1731	1797	1901	1992	2062	2110	2200	2308	2383	4650
Interest rates %													
Deposit rate	10.10	15.39	16.78	17.72	18.63	17.53	23.32	19.6	14.55	12.5	16.72	17.3	20.01
Lending rate		21.49	21.67	22.1	21.7	20.83	25.53	24.03	20.59	17.8	18.05	19.2	21.82

Source : IMF, International Financial Statistics (various issues)

Table 4.I.5

Changes in Tariff Schedule (including surcharges)

%	Pre-1985	1989	1991
Average tariff rates (%)			
Unweighted	37	27	20
Weighted			
By import value	22	12	10
By domestic production	29	19	15
Index of dispersion*	62	93	83

Source : World Bank staff estimates
*Measured by the co-efficient of variation

Table 4.I.6

<u>Change in NTB Coverage over the reform period</u>

NTB Coverage as	Mid-1986	End of 1986	June 1991
% of import value	43	21	13
% of domestic production	41	29	22

Table 4.I.7

Growth of Manufacturing Output

Year	Growth of total manufacturing output (%)	Growth of non-oil manufacturing (%)
1981	23	19
1982	2	2
1984	3	3
1985	22	13
1986	10	12
1987	11	13
1988	12	13
1989	10	12
1990	11	13
1991	11	11

Table 4.I.8

Foreign Investment Approvals by Sector ($ million)

	1996	1997	1998	1967-98	
Primary	**3218**	**465**	**998**	**16900**	**7.80%**
Agriculture	1306	437	965	6092	2.80%
Fisheries	80	27	33	639	0.30%
Forestry	135	-	0	637	0.30%
Mining	1697	2	0	9532	4.40%
Secondary	**16075**	**23017**	**8389**	**139241**	**64.30%**
Food	691	573	342	5663	2.60%
Textiles	514	373	217	7197	3.30%
Wood	101	70	71	1475	0.70%
Paper	2907	5353	41	25925	12.00%
Chemicals	7362	12376	6179	65055	30.00%
Non-metal minerals	793	1457	237	7116	3.30%
Basic metals	651	357	394	8447	3.90%
Metal goods	2938	2322	891	17727	8.20%
Other	74	126	17	636	0.30%
Tertiary	**10638**	**10350**	**4177**	**60354**	**27.90%**
Construction	297	307	198	1787	0.80%
Hotels	1716	463	451	11200	5.20%
Housing/office building	3000	1398	1271	12411	5.70%
Transport	695	5900	79	14495	6.70%
Utilities/trading/other	4933	2283	2178	20461	9.50%
Total	**29931**	**33832**	**13563**	**216494**	

Source: BKPM , as reported to Bank Indonesia

Table 4.I.9

Sources of FDI

Foreign investment approvals by country	**1996**	**1997**	**1998**	**1967-98**	**shares***
Japan	7655	5421	1331	34778	21.60%
U.K.	3391	5474	4745	24353	15.10%
Singapore	3130	2299	1267	18360	11.40%
Hong Kong, China	1106	251	549	14411	8.90%
US	642	1018	568	10219	6.30%
Chinese Taipei	535	3415	165	12795	7.90%
S. Korea	1231	1410	202	8976	5.60%
Malaysia	1393	2289	1060	6629	4.10%
Australia	450	187	85	6547	4.10%
Germany	165	4468	71	6309	3.90%
Netherlands	1330	319	412	5651	3.50%
Thailand	1611	19	3	1769	1.10%
France	71	457	8	1465	0.90%
Joint projects among two or more investing countries	5051	5529	2718	55225	
Others	10233	7600	3520	9007	5.60%
*excludes joint projects					
Total	**29931**	**33832**	**13563**	**216494**	

Source: BKPM , as reported to Bank Indonesia

Chart 4.I.1

Indonesia: Summary of Economic Reforms 1983-90

Reforms	Contents	Repercussions
July 1987	Still further reduction in import licensing with no tariff increase	Same as in October 1986
	System of textile quota allocation improved	
November 1988	Inter-island shipping deregulated	Increased competition
	Removal of monopolies in imports of steel and plastic	Increased confidence in government efforts to deregulate the economy
May 1990	Deregulation in pharmaceuticals and animal husbandry	Increased competition
	Adjustment in tariffs	Improved investment climate
	Reduction in number of surcharges	
	Further removal of non tariff barriers	
Investment		
1985	Simplification of application procedures for foreign investment	Reduction in waiting period and number of documents
May 1986	Allowance of 95 percent foreign ownership in export-oriented investments	Increased exports and further increased investment
	Local distribution opened to export-oriented firms	Japanese department store "SOGO" opened
	Export credit scheme opened for participation by joint ventures	Increased confidence in the economy
	Retail trade opened to foreign firms	
1986	One-year tax exemption on imported equipment	Enthusiastic response from foreign investors
	Visa requirements from 29 countries lifted	
	Investment from Eastern European countries no longer needs intelligence approval	
September 1986	Maxi devaluation (More than 30 percent)	Increased export competitiveness
July 1987	Deregulation of investment and capacity licensing	Improved investment climate
	Stock exchange opened to foreign investors	
November 1988	Further deregulation in shipping industry	Increased competition
	Joint ventures allowed to distribute their own products domestically	
May 1989	Replacement of priority list with negative list	Improved investment climate further

Reforms	Contents	Repercussions
June 1989	Attempts to improve efficiency of state enterprises Encourage privatisation	Some state enterprises showed improved efficiency Increased signs of more "going public"
1989	Foreign portfolio investors allowed to purchase 49 percent of nonbank companies listed on stock exchanges	Improved foreign confidence in the economy
November 1989	Steps to improve performance of state enterprises Specific steps to improve efficiency in 75 enterprises	186 out of 210 state enterprises affected Sales of equity in 52 state enterprises Mergers of joint ventures in 59 state enterprises
1990	Up to 30 percent of shares of three large scale cement enterprises offered to public	Increased expectations of further privatisation

Chart 4.I.2

The Chronology of financial sector reforms in Indonesia, 1983-1991

June 1983	Elimination of credit ceilings and ending of control on interest rates for time deposits and credits; reduction in the types of priority/programme credits which are eligible for Bank Indonesia liquidity credits.
February 1984	Reintroduction of Bank Indonesia certificates (SBI) to support open market operations and introduction of rediscount windows.
January 1985	Introduction of money market instruments (SBPU) consisting of promissory notes of bank customers, of banks, NBFIs and trade bills. Rediscount facilities to banks were also set up by Bank Indonesia to the day-to-day reserve management as well as maturity management.
May 1987	With the objective of improving fund management, Bank Indonesia raised the interest of SBPUs, SBIs, discount facilities, and the swap premium.
July 1987	Introduction of auction system for the trade of SBIs and SBPUs.
October 1988	Introduction of measures to foster competition, i.e.: (1) lessening the restrictions on entry and branching for foreign/domestic banks; (2) allowing NBFIs to issue Certificate of Deposits (CDs); (3) permitting banks and NBFIs to raise capital in the stock market; (4) easing entry to leasing, insurance, venture capital, consumer finance and securities activities; (5) reducing reserve requirements from 15 to 12 per cent; and (6) improvements to other aspects of protective and preventive measures.
March 1989	Introduction of decrees clarifying matters with regard to NBFI's, legal lending limits, joint venture capital ownership and bank mergers, the definition of bank capital, reserve requirements, bank investment in stocks, and bank exposure to foreign exchange fluctuations.
January 1990	Reduction in the scope of credit programmes which are eligible for Bank Indonesia, i.e. liquidity credit,. Introduction of legal lending limits requirements. A regulation was stipulated to require all domestic banks to lend 20 percent of their portfolio to small firms and cooperatives, and foreign and joint venture banks to extend at least 50 per cent of their credit for export-oriented activities.
February 1991	Various measures were stipulated to improve banking management and supervision by, amongst other things, requiring banks to step up capital base according to BIS regulations.
November 1991	Reimposition of ceilings on offshore borrowing for the public sector (including state banks), improvements in swap mechanism, and elimination of swap premia.

Source : Anwar Nasution "Reforms of the Financial Sector in Indoensia, 1983-91", Routhedge, London 2000

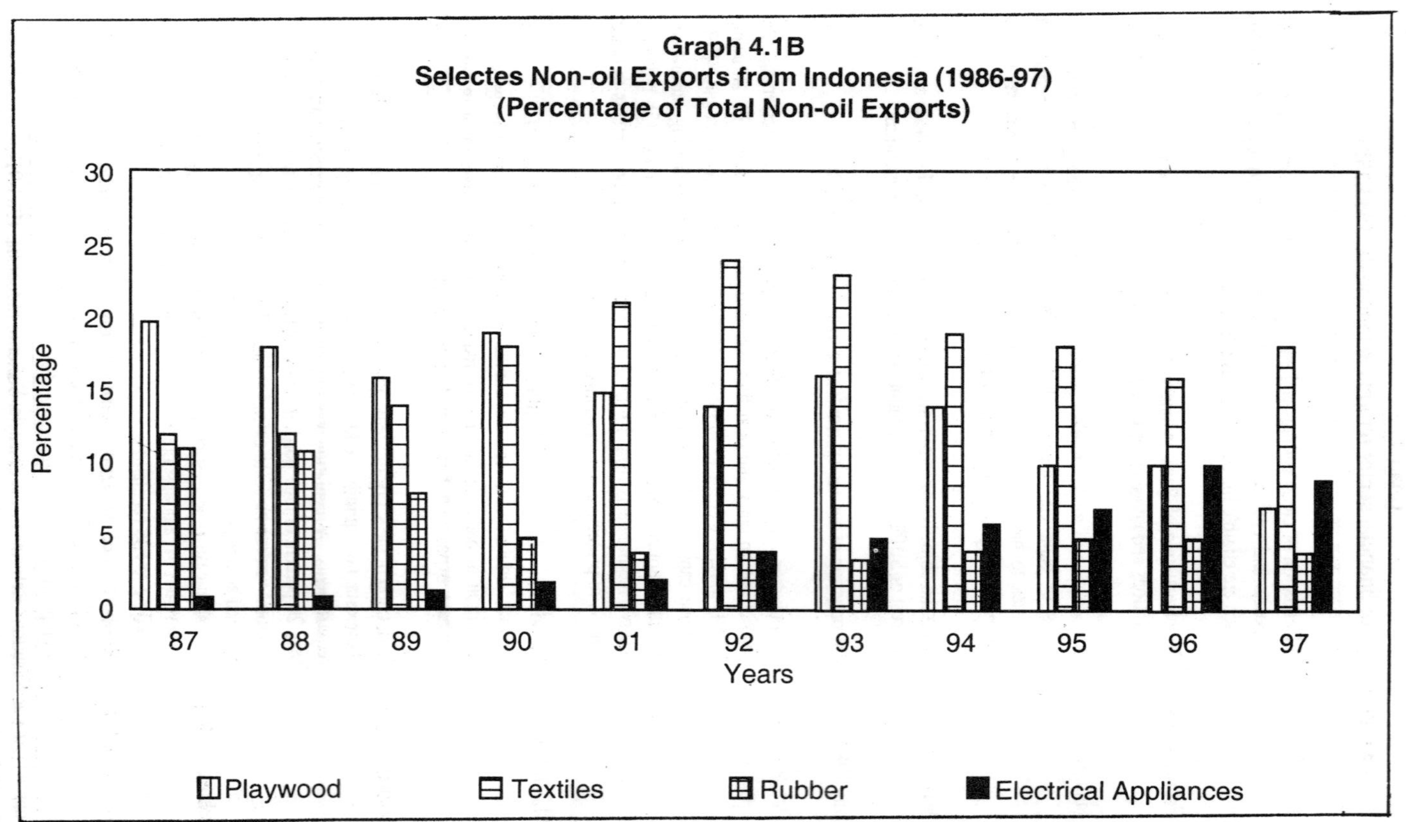
Graph 4.1B
Selectes Non-oil Exports from Indonesia (1986-97)
(Percentage of Total Non-oil Exports)
Percentage
30
25
20
15
10
5
0
87
88
89
90
91
92
93
94
95
96
97
Years
Playwood
Textiles
Rubber
Electrical Appliances

Development Experience of Malaysia

Profile

Federation of Malaysia consists of two parts, West and East Malaysia. West and East Malaysia are separated by the South China Sea, which stretches to about 700 Kilometres. West Malaysia covers the greater part of the Malay Peninsula and borders on Thailand in the North and Singapore in the South. East Malaysia occupies the Northern part of Kalimantan. In the East it borders on Indonesia and in the West on Brunei. It consists of eleven states in Peninsular Malaya and two states on the Island of Borneo. Of these the eleven important ones are Pahang, Perak, Johore, Kelantan, Trengganu, Kedah, Sembilan, Pertro, Penang and Malacca Melaka. The Federation spans an area of 50,700 square miles and has a population of 9006 million (July 1, 1998)

Islam is the dominant **religion** in Malaysia. Other ethnic groups are the Buddhist Chinese and the Hindu Indians. Christians form a small minority in Saban and Sarawak.

The official language in **Malaysia** is **Malay**. Other principal languages spoken are English, Chinese and Tamil.

Historical Perspective

The historical roots of Malaysia can be traced back to eighth century when it was part of the Sumatran Empire of Srivajaya. Its strategic location at the intersection of the sea trade routes from India to China made it an important region. In the fifteenth century Parameswara, the Sumatran Prince, founded the Malacca Kingdom in Malaya. Malacca became an influential trading and cultural centre and this had an important bearing on the future political, religious and cultural aspects of Malaysia.

Around the end of the fifteenth century and the beginning of the sixteenth century, the Prince Parameswara adopted Islam and the name Sultan Iskandar Shah. He changed the course of indigenous cultural development in the entire region. His conversion established

Islam as the religion of those living on the Peninsula[25] (which holds good even today).

Colonisation

Malacca was captured by the **Portuguese** in 1511 and subsequently, by the **Dutch** in 1641. During this period the country was split up into a number of principalities. Between 1786 and 1819, the **British** colonial powers captured Penang, Malacca, and Singapore and they came to be jointly termed as the Straits Settlement. This region was very important, as it was the crucial trade route to China. By the mid seventeenth century the current geopolitical pattern of the Malay States was broadly established.

Over the period 1874-88, the British made agreements with Malay rulers of Perak, Selangor, Negri Sembilan and Panang (these came to be referred to as the federated states). As per these agreements the Sultans had to take the advice of the British on all state matters except those concerning religion and custom. By 1914 the other States of Kedah, Pertis, Kelantan and Trengganu (unfederated states) too accepted the British supremacy.

The Federated Malay States and the Unfederated Malay States combined with the Strait Settlements (except Singapore) later formed the Federation of Malaysia in February 1948.

Independence Struggle

The British Rule was interrupted by the **Japanese occupation** during 1942-1945. After this a new political force by the Malaya rulers known as the United Malaysian National Organization was formed and the same marked the beginning of the freedom struggle in Malaysia. They protested against the granting of citizenship to both the Malay and to the Non Malay people, and other such practices. In other words, they were against the granting of equal rights to all residents. Various other revolutionary groups emerged namely the Communist Party, the All Malayan Council of Joint Action and the Pan Malayan Federation of Trade Unions. The first and two merged later to form the People's United Front.

Unable to crush the nationalist struggle, the British finally gave in and **independence** was proclaimed on **August 31, 1957**. The United Malaysian National Organization President Tunku Abdul Rahman became the first Prime Minister.

Singapore joined the Federation of Malaya in 1963 when it gained independence. But, in order to prevent the Chinese becoming a numerical majority Sarawak and Saban were also taken into the Federation to form the Federation of Malaysia [26]. However in 1965 Singapore broke away from the same.

Economic Development in the Post-independence Period

Right from the colonial period Malaysia was well integrated into the world economy through international trade in rubber and tin. The British controlled most of the plantations and mines, so much so that by 1938 almost 93 percent of British capital in Malaysia was in plantations and mines. The European companies controlled 65-70 percent of export trade.

Production of food and consumer goods was limited. Imports of the same therefore became necessary. Prior to independence, European companies controlled 60-70 percent of import trade.

At the time of independence Malaysia's standard of living was quite high. On account of the export earnings from tin and rubber, the average annual GDP in Malaysia between 1957-1970 was 6.4 percent per annum [27].

Up to the late 1960s there wasn't much structural change in the economy, but gradually diversification took place in the economy. Palm oil and cocoa were also produced. Today Malaysia is one of the world's largest producers and exporters of palm oil.

Malaysian had an ISI strategy up to the late 1960s. The *First Malaya* Plan (1955-60) and *Second Malaya* Plan (1961-650 as well as the First Malaysian Plan (1966-1970) bears witness to the same.

Under this plan almost half of the total public development expenditure was invested in developing infrastructure particularly in transport, power and communication. Also tariff protection was offered to import substitute manufacturing. It may be noted here that the capital intensive industries were not totally substitutes for imports. For instance many of them were subsidiaries for assembling, finishing and packaging goods produced with imported materials. Similarly, in the motorcar assembly industry, completely built up units was replaced by knock down packs to be assembled locally.

Despite fairly high rate of economic growth in Malaysia, problems such as inequalities of income, poverty, inter ethnic strives were very rampant during the period 1959-1970.

New Economic Policy (1970-90)

During the federal elections in May 1969, communal strives came into the forefront. Several riots and other forms of protests forced the suspension of the Parliament and the declaration of a state of emergency. By February 1971, the Parliamentary Government was restored.

Around this time, there were some constitutional amendments made relating to language, citizenship and the special position of Malaysians. Also economic planning was now based on social criteria rather than on financial and administrative aspects as in the case of the First Malaysian Plan.

In the Second Malaysian Plan for 1971-1975, the ***New Economic Policy*** 1970-1990 was incorporated. The main ***aim*** of this policy was to promote national unity by pursuing the twin objectives of ***eradication of poverty*** and the restructuring of society with a view to disassociate racial aspects with economic function and ***to improve the Bumiputera*** (indigenous Malaysian) position. To realise the first objective, long term targets were set. It was hoped that by 1990, the incidence of poverty should be reduced to 19 percent of the population from the estimated 50 percent in 1970.

To realise the second objective Malaysian ownership of share capital in limited companies was introduced. The proportion of this share capital was allotted to Malaysians – (a) employed in manufacture, (b) students enrolled in institutions of higher learning, and, (c) for those placed in managerial positions. It was targeted that at least thirty percent of the total commercial and industrial activities should be managed and owned by the Bumiputera.

The desire to improve the position of the indigenous community led to an increase in the state's direct economic role. The Government began a policy of nationalization. It used to buy, then restructure the equity of the foreign held companies through trustee companies. It then operated the productive enterprises and simultaneously trained the individual Bumiputra who would eventually take it over. A number of specialist agencies were established to assist in the training of the Bumiputera. These agencies used public funds to invest in Malaysian agencies and provided a range of technical and consultancy services.

The Government also made efforts to diversify agricultural production and use material resources more intensively. It established regional development authorities to integrate agriculture and rural development. Due to decline in rubber and cocoa, palm oil production was encouraged. Also since petroleum and natural gas reserves were found in Saban and Sarawar, Malaysia became a net exporter of oil with a surplus that grew from RM 607million in 1976 to RM 3.4 billions in 1980 [28].

The launch of the NEP co-incided with a shift in the direction of the industrial policy from ***ISI to EOI***. Various incentives were provided to encourage the export sector. Tax holidays were given to approved firms for a period of eight years, company income tax exemptions were made to encourage employment, exemption from import duty for capital equipment and raw materials for export oriented production was permitted and accelerated depreciation allowances were made. Under the Free Trade Zone Act of 1971, new industrial estates or Export Processing Zones (EPZ) were established to encourage investments in export manufacture.

Two types of export-oriented industries developed, the resource-based industries and labour-intensive manufacturers. By the early 1980s firms located in the EPZs zoomed ahead of the industries located elsewhere. This was a change from the situation in the early 1970s when rubber and tin had accounted for about eighty percent of Malaysia's export earnings. But by the mid 1980s, there was a further change when skill based manufacturers like electrical and electronic components grew dramatically and accounted for slightly more than half of total manufacturing exports.

Shortcomings of the EOI phase

There were some shortcomings of the EOI phase and the NEP policy between 1972-1982.

(a) Foreign exchange earnings were low in the ISI phase. The EOI strategy did little to change the situation. Although the total sales amounted to $ 6853 mn, the material inputs constituted 70% of gross sales. In other words net foreign exchange earnings were only $2,489 mn [29].

(b) Employment in manufacturing sector increased but the average real wage in 1978 was below that in 1968 [30]. As the State Owned Enterprises (SOEs), had to cater to social objectives of employment creation and regional development they ran into losses. The enterprises had to follow the dictates of the Industrial Co-ordination Act (ICA) whose pivotal objective was to induce Bumiputera participation in the industrial development of the country[31].

(c) The extent of technology transfer was very insignificant. Manufacturing exports had increased ten-fold, yet there was no increase in locally manufactured inputs and therefore limited opportunity existed for industrial learning and technology transfer. In other words most of the value added was through increased employment rather than increased technology.

(d) Scarce national savings were allocated in line with NEPs restructuring priorities rather than investment needs. The returns on concessionary loans to Bumiputera enterprises were low and frequently negative.

(e) All the above problems created an uncertain investment climate thereby discouraging private investment. There was a fall in investment in both real and nominal terms. Foreign capital too was not forthcoming since the Government was making an attempt to nationalise Foreign Owned Enterprises (FOE).

Look East Policy (1981-1986)

The economic problems discussed above and the change in Malaysia's political leadership (Prime Minister Mahathir Mohamed took over) led to a shift in development policy. While not abandoning the objectives of the NEP for political reasons (which in any case had a long term perspective till 1990), a Look East Policy was adopted. This policy was modelled around the import substituting industrialization policy of South Korea. Thus, a ***second round of ISI*** was now adopted in Malaysia. But the ***results of the same were not too encouraging***.

Prior to the Second Oil Shock an accelerated external demand led to an increase in prices and production of major export commodities. But at the same time imports too had become expensive leading to an inflationary situation. Hence a tight monetary policy was adopted to contain the ***inflation*** that stood at 4.5 percent. Yet, by 1980 the inflation ***rose*** to 9 percent.

Moreover, the commodity boom resulted in an appreciation of the Malaysian ringgit. Following the Second Oil Crisis in 1979, there was a worldwide recession especially in the OECD countries. This appreciated exchange rate along with the worldwide recession caused a reduction in Malaysia's exports. The export earnings, which had grown at 6% in the second half of the 1970s, fell by 4% in 1981.

There ensued a ***deterioration in the terms of trade*** resulting into a current account deficit of 14.1 % of GDP in 1982.

As mentioned in the earlier sub-section, private investment had started to fall. The fall became steeper in the early 1980s. Between 1980-1985 private investment expanded at an average annual rate of only 1.8 percent as compared to 10.6 percent in the 1970s. In 1982 alone ***private investment fell*** by 2.3 percent.

Further Push to ISI

Such economic malaise should logically have discouraged the continuance of an ISI approach. Surprisingly, it reinforced the conviction of the Mahathir Government to follow the heavy industrialization ISI Look East Policy. Accordingly, a public sector agency known as Heavy Industries Corporation of Malaysia (HICOM) was set up. A number of industries such as iron and steel billet plant, an additional cement plant, the national car project, small engines plant, shipbuilding and repairs and a petrochemical plant were all started. The main objective of the heavy industrialization programme was to create opportunities for Malaysian industrial entrepreneurs through the development of intermediate industries, to encourage capital deepening and expansion of domestic industrial base.

Unfortunately many of these enterprises did not have a good start in the face of excessive global production capacity and competition. Some of the enterprises had to be provided heavy protection to be able to survive. But, since they required large imports, production costs went up. Moreover, since most of these projects had long gestation period they became economically unviable and unprofitable.

To support the heavy industrialization programme, the annual public sector investment in commerce and industry increased from $0.3 billion in 1978-1980 to $0.9 billions in 1982 to $1.5 billions in 1984. The massive investments also meant that the public development expenditure was very high. Public development expenditure as a share of GNP almost doubled from 14.3 percent in 1976-1980 to over 27 percent in 1981-1982. Hence the ***budget deficit*** was about ***20 percent of GDP in 1982***.

The investment was funded extensively through foreign borrowings. The net foreign borrowing by the Federal Government increased from 10 percent in 1980, to 20 percent in 1982, and further to 38 percent by 1986. The WB report on Malaysia of 1989 pointed out that the enterprises where investments were made, were neither frugal nor efficient in cost administration. Possibly, if the borrowing had been from internal sources more surveillance could have been exercised.

There was only one encouraging factor. The net foreign inflows were positive and hence the currency did not depreciate. In fact, Malaysia's real effective exchange rose in real terms due to the foreign financing. It may be noted here that the rise in real exchange rate was definitely not on account of improved export performance as the terms of trade shows deterioration during the time period 1981-1986 from 101 to 88. Manufactured exports had stood virtually still if not decreasing while manufactured imports had started to increase on account of the heavy industrialization programme.

Thus the big push given to heavy industrialization was not showing good results. Infact it brought Malaysia to a crisis situation by the mid 1980s. The real GDP in 1985 contracted. Many Malaysians returned from Singapore (60,000) after losing their jobs. The overall unemployment rate was about 8.5 percent[32]. Real manufacturing output dropped by 3 percent in 1985 and ***manufacturing exports were lower in 1985 than in 1984***. Part of the reduction in export demand was on account of recession in the global semiconductor industry.

Putting the house in order

The fiscal deficit and the trade deficit resulted in a severe recession in 1985-1986. This recession acted as a catalyst for a rethink of the Malaysian industrialization and trade strategies. To revive the economy, the Government decided to reduce the role and size of the public sector and promote exports.Malaysian industrialization and trade strategies.

To revive the economy, the Government decided to reduce the role and size of the public sector and promote exports.Malaysian industrialization and trade strategies. To revive the economy, the Government decided to reduce the role and size of the public sector and promote exports.

Quite naturally the recession caused an outflow of capital. Rather than protect the exchange rate Malaysia it fall. It allowed the exchange rate to decline by a little over 7 percent vis-à-vis the US dollar. In terms of the IMF's SDR (a basket of currencies), the ringgit fell by about 20 percent. The real exchange rate too fell by about the same rate.

The depreciation helped lower production costs. Also due to increased unemployment (as mentioned above many Malaysians had returned jobless from Singapore) the real wages too declined. With such changes taking place the economic situation improved. Hence, the depreciation of the RM contributed to the recovery of the economy.

Liberalisation Since the Mid 1980s

The 1985-1986 recession triggered off a second round of ***market liberalization*** and a more active promotion of private sector growth [33]. In addition, with the NEP ending in 1990 the Government got the opportunity to re-establish its priorities for the long-term development of the country. A new strategy document known as the National Development Policy (NDP) was released in 1991 with a "Vision 2020" wherein it aimed at Malaysia becoming a developed nation by that year. Malaysia required a growth rate of 7 percent per annum to achieve the same. The National Development Policy also contained a 10 year Second Outline Perspective Plan (OPP2) for 1991-2000 and the Sixth Malaysian Plan (6MP) for 1991-1995. Hence while the OPP2 and 6MP were providing medium term economic policy perspectives, the Vision 2020 provided the long-term objectives.

The liberalization measures undertaken by the Malaysian Government since 1986 in the ***fiscal policy, monetary and financial policy,*** and the ***trade and industrial sector*** as well as in ***policy towards FDI.*** The same are discussed below.

Fiscal Policy

The major ***objectives*** of the fiscal policy were strengthening ***the Government's financial position*** and downsizing ***of the public sector.*** These objectives were reflected in the formulation of national plans prepared during the period of liberalisation.

The ***Fifth Malaysian Plan*** (1986-1990) was committed to a stable course of macroeconomic management. The plan recognised the need to maintain a stable economic environment so as to make it conducive to private investment. Accordingly, both the fiscal and monetary policies were directed towards maintaining stable prices, favourable exchange rates and a healthy BOP position.

In 1988, measures were introduced to widen the tax base including a broadening of the sales tax through a reduction in exemptions and restrictions on tax-free inputs and the redefinition of allowable deductions on life insurance companies[34]. The 1988 budget also included a two year extension of the life of the reinvestment allowance due to expire in 1988 and an increase in the rate of allowance from 25% to 40 %.

In subsequent budgets, there was a revamping of the tax system, streamlining of tax incentives and developing the capital market. Tax measures included:

- a 5 percent reduction in the company and non-resident income tax rates from 40 to 35 percent;
- a gradual abolition of the development tax starting with a 1 percent reduction from 1990;
- imposition of a 5 percent withholding tax on interest derived from long term fixed deposits;

- reimposition of a 5 percent sales tax on certain foodstuffs and building material;
- a streamlining of allowances granted under the Promotion of Investment Act of 1986, and some amendments to the Petroleum Income Tax Act.

To speed up the rate of growth in the private sector, the Government introduced a number of additional tax deductions and exemptions related to agricultural and overseas construction projects as well as to private property. Small-scale industries were granted a number of tax incentives including pioneer status to those firms, which met specific criteria. Tax incentives were also provided to multinational companies to set up operational headquarters in Malaysia.

Short-term measures to increase revenue of the government were sale of government holdings in the national airline (MAS) and the national shipping company (MISC) to Bank Negara (Central Bank of Malaysia). Privatisation was identified as one of the solutions to resolve the problems of the Non Financial Public Enterprises (NFPEs). This was because the NFPEs were absorbing a large proportion of Federal Allocations to fund operating expenses, especially to service their large debt burden.

With the introduction of the Privatisation Master Plan (PMP) in 1991, under NDP, privatisation became the main tool for achieving certain economic objectives. Under this new strategy, the States direct role was to be reduced and the activities of the state were restricted to investment in infrastructure, promoting human capital development and encouraging technological progress.

The ***Sixth Malaysian Plan (1991-1995)*** emphasised the need for an expansion of physical and social infrastructures to support the growth process and to enable the economy to absorb rapid increases in private investment. The high priority projects were expansion of the transport and communication systems, the upgrading of human resources and the development of science and technology.

From 1991-1995, RM 55 billion was allocated to the Federal Government's development expenditure. Out of this 19.7 percent was allocated to transport and communication (expanding and upgrading roads, railways, airports and ports). Commerce and Industry was to account for about 10.5 percent of development expenditure including expenditure on industrial estates. Malaysia has also spent a sizable amount on HRD as part of the industrial development strategy (details relating to this are presented in the section on Industrial Policy.)

The ***fiscal deficit came down from 18.9 percent of GDP in 1982 to 4.8 percent in 1988 and to -0.8% in 1992 and further to 0.3% in 1995*** as is evident in Table 3.5. Thus, the fiscal deficit was curbed through both reduction in government's expenditure and through increased revenue.

Monetary and Financial Sector Policies:

The financial sector in Malaysia consists of the ***Banking Institutions***, ***the non-banking financial intermediaries*** and the financial markets including ***capital markets*** for direct financing[35]. The financial system is supervised by the Central Bank – the Bank Negara Malaysia (BNM) and the Securities Commission (SC) (Established in 1959).

The Central Bank and the commercial banks (36) essentially constitute the monetary institutions, but the *banking system* also includes financial companies (40) and Merchant Banks (12), Discount Houses (6), Money and Foreign Exchange Brokers (30) and the Credit Guarantee Corporation. The Banking and Financial Institutions Act (1989) (BAFIA) that was enacted in response to the 1986 collapse of Deposit Taking Co-operatives (DTCs) enabled the Central Bank to regulate both banking and licensed financial institutions.

The *non-bank financial intermediaries* can be divided into five groups – the development financial institutions, the savings institution, provident and pension funds, insurance companies, and others, which include the building societies and unit trusts.

The *Capital Market* comprises of a primary securities market, in which issues of government and corporate securities are offered for sale, and the secondary market, in which such securities are traded. The important Stock Exchanges are the Kuala Lumpur Stock Exchange and the Bumiputera Stock Exchange.

Financial liberalization started in Malaysia since 1978, but received an impetus since the late 1980s. The real sector liberalization and reform took priority over financial sector liberalization in Malaysia. Infact there was a greater control and supervision of the financial system as difficulties arose during the recession in the form of mismanagement, overexposure to some sectors and bad debts. The Government was concerned with bank failures and erosion of public confidence and brought in the concept of Lead Banks. It was only since 1987 after the economic recovery that steps towards financial liberalization in the actual sense got underway.

The thrust of the ***Monetary Policy*** was to maintain domestic price stability and external competitiveness of the exports while ensuring adequate bank liquidity to fund productive private sector activity at reasonable costs. Towards this end expansion of money supply was kept in line with GDP growth; ***interest rates*** were reduced; and the ***Exchange Rate Policy*** was kept in line with market forces allowing the ringgit to find its realistic par value with key currencies.

Interest Rate Reforms: In October 1978, the Central Bank freed interest rates of Commercial Banks and allowed them to be market determined. However, in November 1983 a Base Lending Rate (BLR) was introduced so that banks would not lower lending rates below this.

Between 1985 and 1987 due to a tight position of liquidity, interest rate controls of a different kind were instituted. Here the Commercial Banks and Financial Companies had to peg their interest rates to the deposit rate of two leading banks and this differential could be 0.5 percentage points for the former and 1.5 percentage points for the latter. By February 1987 the pegging arrangement was called off. By February 1991 the Base Lending Rate was totally freed from administrative controls except for certain priority sector lending. Interest rates were maintained at low levels except during 1980-1985. Borrowing cost to firms was the lowest in the 1990s, with the lending rate being as low as 8.3 percent on an average in 1990s as presented in Table 4.M.2.

It may be mentioned here that in the latter half of the 1990s the low lending rate became a bane for the economy. The low lending rate encouraged the firms to make long term investments with low profits especially at a time when exports were declining. The declining exports led to further borrowing. Hence in effect there was a situation of excessive borrowing, declining exports and non-performing loans, which led to a crisis eventually.

***Exchange Control Liberalisation and Exchange Rate Reform*:**
In May 1973, Exchange Control Regulations were eased. Prior to 1973, a discriminatory policy was followed between countries in and outside the sterling area. Such discrimination was removed and hence there was free flow of funds in and out of Malaysia. Further liberalization in *Exchange Control* was effected in January 1987. A number of measures were announced which reduced the formalities that businessman had to comply with when exporting their goods. Also investors were provided with greater access to credit to expand productive capacity. The public were allowed to trade freely in gold. The only exchange controls that were still in place were the ones needed to monitor the prompt settlement of exchange receipts.

As far as the *exchange rate* is concerned, Malaysia's ringgit was linked to the Pound Sterling until 1972. In June 1972, this link was broken and the US Dollar was made the intervention currency. In the next year the RM was allowed to float meaning that the US Dollar was no longer the interventionist currency. Every currency had its own exchange rate against the RM. Finally in 1975 the value of RM was determined against a basket of major currencies (weights being proportionate to the respective country's trading share) and this till 1998 remained the Exchange Rate Policy. The changes in the Exchange Rate Policy since 1998 are discussed in Chapter Six.

Capital Market Developments

Development of the capital market was a priority for the Central Bank of Malaysia. A number of steps were initiated to modernise the capital market as a new source of funds for business and industrial activity.

The Malaysian Government Securities (MGS) value was lower than other financial assets. In addition, most of the MGS were held by only certain institutions hampering the Central Bank from indulging in open market operations. Accordingly, in 1987 measures were taken to make MGS more liquid and market based. Adjustments were made in SLR. Well-capitalized financial companies were allowed to participate in the interbank money market. For this an Interbank Funds Transfer System, the Scriptless Securities Trading System, the Kuala Lumpur Automated Clearing House and the Day-one Settlement System were established.

Other reforms in January 1989 were as follows [36]:

- Appointment of principal dealers: Certain Commercial Banks, Merchant Bank and Discount House were appointed to underwrite new issues of MGS and to make a secondary market in them.
- MGS with a maturity of ten years were auctioned through the principal dealers.
- In addition, open market operations of the Central Bank were now to be conducted through these dealers.
- Restrictions on investments (portfolio structure) of Discount Houses were removed. They could restructure their portfolio (JUNE 1990).
- To develop the Corporate Bonds new guidelines were issued and a private credit rating agency was set up in November 1990.

Effect of financial liberalization:

The effect of financial liberalization on the economy can be seen from in Table 4.M.1. The GDP growth rate was about 7 percent in the 1980s (despite the 1985-1986 recession) and about 7.8 percent during 1991-

1997. In 1998, however, the GDP registered a re-growth of – 5.2 percent.

The monetary policy objective of maintaining stable prices and exchange rates was achieved. *Inflation* was highest at 4.65 percent during 1981-1985, but came down to 1.79 percent in 1986-1990. It remained in the manageable range of 3-5 percent during the 1990s.

Exchange rate stability has also been maintained. Table 4.M.2 shows that the exchange rate of the ringgit vis-à-vis the dollar was fairly stable in the 1990s. The average exchange rate between 1986-90 was 2.64 and the same increased marginally to 2.91(average) between 1991-97. In fact even this slight rise can be attributed to the sudden change in 1997-98.

Since the Central Bank was concerned about containing inflation, monetary growth was discouraged. The ***M2/GDP*** ratio was 0.59 for 1981-1985 and went up to 0.991 in 1996 as can be seen from Table 4.M.1. However, in 1988 and 1989, there was a monetary expansion on account of the strong demand for credit by the private sector. Infact total lending to private sector increased by 9.9 percent in 1988. However, in the 1990s money growth was restricted to to check excessive credit demands of the private sector.

Industrial and Trade Policy:

Industrial policy

Malaysia's Industrial Policy experience has been a zigzag policy where there have been phases of ISI and EOI. In the colonial era imports and exports of food and simple consumer items took place. In the post independence period till the late 1960s, an ISI strategy was adopted. Since the late 1960s to early 1980 an EOI Policy was pursued. In the next phase that is since the early 1980s the Government did not altogether abandon the EOI but pursued the

ISI more vigorously as it promoted select heavy industries. The final phase of the industrial policy, i.e. since 1987, has again been EOI in nature.

The basis of the industrial policy strategy since the mid 1980s has been the ***Industrial Master Plan*** (1985 – 1995). Basic strategies and direction for industrial development set by the IMP (which had identified 12* industrial groups) were as follows:

- Accelerating outward – oriented industrialization with a focus on large-scale expansion of manufacturing exports and widening their range.
- Developing resources based industry for exports
- Diversifying and upgrading non-resource-based industry for exports
- Selectively promoting strategies heavy industry to support export industry.
- Making and re-adjusting in the industrial structure, modernization and nationalization.

*The 12 industrial groups were, 7 resource base industries including, wood based, chemical and petrochemical, rubber, palm oil products, food processing, non-ferrous metal production and non-metallic mineral production; and 5 non-resource based industries including, electronic, electrical and transport equipment, machinery and engineering products, ferrous metal and textiles and clothing.

- Developing technology and manpower
- Taking into consideration existing infrastructure when planning the physical location for new Industry.
- Moving away from assembly type to producing components indigenously.
- Enhancing participation of small and medium firms.
- Creating conducive environment for private sector involvement in Research and Development activities.
- Developing a technically competent human resource for Malaysia's Industrial Development.

The incentive measures instituted for industrial development in 1987-1988 were – the Excess Profits Tax of three percent were abolished, the maximum corporate tax rate was reduced to 35 percent, reinvestment allowance was raised from 25 percent to 40 percent for a period of two years, and a number of additional steps were taken to reduce administrative delays at the federal and state levels in processing applications for licensing and tax exemptions.

To ***promote exports*** specifically, certain industrial estates were designated as Free Trade Zones. Here duty free raw materials and capital equipment could be imported, customs formalities were streamlined to enable smooth trade, various infrastructure facilities were provided in the Free Trade Zone and finally Income Tax exemptions were provided for firms in Free Trade Zones.

Improvements in the quality of ***education and training*** formed an important part of Malaysia's industrial strategy. Malaysia's educational standard is quite impressive even though it is below the level of Taiwan and Korea. Enrolment standards in Malaysia are presented in Table.3.16. The Gross Secondary School Enrolment ratio for Females and Males was 45.7 percent and 49.7 percent respectively in 1980 and this has increased to 66.1 percent and 57.5 percent respectively in 1996.

Also the Government recognised the need to increase vocational training policies. The World Bank Report of 1989 indicated that Malaysia was low on TFP. Hence the Sixth Plan allocated RM 8.5 Billion for educational and training. Also in 1989 an amount of only 0.8 percent of the GNP was allocated to Research and Development Activity. In later years Research and Development Activity was linked to incentives. Those private firms that undertook Research and Development were offered tax exemptions and government grants.

Other important aspects of the industrial policy since the mid 1980s included liberalization of licensing requirements under the Industrial Co-ordination Act (ICA), the relaxation of guidelines governing foreign equity participation and increasing the availability of funds, including the establishment of the New Investment Fund (NIF) and the

ASEAN-Japan Development Fund to provide funding for priority projects and small and medium enterprises. A new Promotion of Investment Act was introduced in 1986 to replace the administratively cumbersome Investment Incentives Act of 1968. This Act was again revised in 1988 and provided attractive tax incentives for the manufacturing and agricultural sectors.

Trade Policy:

Till the mid 1980s the overall trade policy worked with a strong bias against exports outside the Free Trade Zone [37]. The tariff system consisted of widely varying effective rates of protection to import substitution activities. These were not even offset by the incentives for exports. Since the mid 1980s, the authorities undertook to reduce this bias in trade policy by reviewing the tariff structure, exchange rate policy and rationalizing fiscal and financial incentives. The last three aspects have been discussed under the respective heads and so here the discussion is limited to the change in tariff structure.

The ***tariff liberalization*** measure was an important factor in creating a more export-conducive environment. The average unweighted tariff rate decreased from 13.6 percent in 1984 – 1987 to 12.8 percent in 1991 – 1993 as indicated in Table 3.9. The import-weighted average tariff rate was reduced from 14.7 percent to 11.2 percent for the same time period. The tariff liberalization measures have increased in recent years in Malaysia, as part of its commitments to multilateral and regional trading arrangement namely the WTO and ASEAN free Trade Area (AFTA). Hence in the post Uruguay round trade-weighted average nominal tariff rate was only 9 percent compared to 11.2 percent previously. Since 1993, Malaysia has reduced or abolished import duties on about 4,000 items.

***Effects of Industrial and Trade Policy Reforms*:**

The depreciation of the RM in 1986, the relaxation of ICA, and PIA, the liberalization measures effected through the IMP and the rationalization of the tariff structures made Malaysia a very attractive place for investment. These factors combined with favourable external market conditions have resulted in Malaysia being transformed into a manufactured export oriented economy.

Table 4.M.1 indicates the growth rates in terms of ***real GDP***. The economy grew at an average rate of 8.3 percent between 1987-1994. In 1994, the growth rate was 9.2 percent and that in 1995 it was 9.5 percent.

Exports as a percentage of GDP too has grown significantly. From Table 3.11 it can be seen that EGS/GDP % has increased from 55 in 1985 to 95.4 in 1995.The industrial and trade policies helped to increase the growth rate of manufactured exports and the same is presented in Table 4.M.3. ***Manufactured Exports*** grew from 22 percent of total exports in 1981 to 66 percent in 1992. By 1994 share of manufacturing exports in total export was about 76 percent by 1995 the same was 79.0 percent.

There is a change in the ***composition of manufactured exports*** and data pertaining to the same is also shown in Table 4.M.3. In 1981 nearly half (52 percent) of total manufacturing exports consisted of electrical and electronic products and machinery, textiles, apparel and footwear constituted 13%, and food, beverages and tobacco constituted 11 percent. By 1996 there was a change in the export mix. The proportion of the above mentioned commodities in total manufacturing amounted to 69%, 5% and 3% respectively..

Quite naturally ***manufacturing employment*** too has grown rapidly in Malaysia. Table 3.17provides data relating to it. The labour force employment in manufacturing has increased from 861 thousand in 1986 to 2052 thousand in 1995.

The liberal trade and industry policy has also brought benefits in the form of increased FDI flows. This, however, is discussed in the next section.

FDI Policy

Fundamental to the growth of exports and the Malaysian economy is the role-played by FDI [38]. Since 1990 Malaysia has been the fifteenth largest recipient of FDI inflows worldwide and fourth among non-OECD countries after China, Brazil and Singapore.

Foreign firms have played a vital role in the process of growth and diversification of Malaysia and foreign investment has been key to the outward oriented development strategies adopted at various times. Long before it was fashionable to attract foreign investors, Malaysia had been doing it. In the 1960s the ***Pioneer Industries Ordinance*** and the ***Investment Incentives Act*** was established to attract and develop export oriented industries. Tax holidays, investment tax credit, accelerated depreciation allowances, exemption from import duties and surtax were some of the incentives given. However, the authorities were not really targeting export oriented firms, they were merely favouring specific industry over others.

In the mid 1980s due to the chaotic economic situation, FDI flows became slower and were not forthcoming. Hence an effort was made to revive inflows of FDI into Malaysia.

Measure undertaken to attract FDI

The Malaysian authorities offered generous incentives and more liberal conditions under the 1986 ***Promotion of Investment Act.*** Companies undertaking activities in manufacture, agriculture, tourism, research and development and technology and vocational training became eligible for incentives.

Pioneer Status or an investment tax allowance (ITA) were given to companies undertaking the production of goods or the following activities (a) 'promoted products' or activities, (b) high technology products (c) strategic products of natural importance (d) research and development (e) technology or vocational training and (f) SSI (pioneer status only) [39].

A company given a pioneer status is exempted from taxation on part (normally 70 percent) of its statutory income for five years and in some cases for ten years. A company eligible for an ITA could enjoy allowance of a given percentage for qualifying capital expenditure within five years from date it was first incurred. This allowance could be set off against part of the statutory income in the year of the assignment.

Other incentives offered are export credit refinancing facilities; export credit insurance and guarantee schemes etc.

However, it may be mentioned that Malaysia has two distinct policies towards inward investments. Any firm which exports a high percentage of its output, contributes significantly to technology transfer or offers some other clear benefit to Malaysia faces relatively few restrictions, on the contrary it receives a host of fiscal and other incentives. On the other extreme foreign companies interested in the local markets are discouraged and face numerous restrictions. This step was initiated in order to encourage the Bumiputeras.

The restrictions on inward investments are discussed here. The screening of both Greenfield investment and takeovers were undertaken by the Malaysian authorities. Foreign investment required the approval of either the Malaysian Industrial Development Authorities (MIDA) or the Foreign Investment Committee (FIC) or both. The Ministry of International Trade and Industry (MITI) which include the MIDA places restrictions on foreign investment through licensing, location, equity structure, distribution pattern, pricing use of local professional services, construction date, quality standards, use of local raw material and technical requirement

Unlike most Asian countries Malaysia does not have a negative list in which foreign investment is prohibited. Infact the constitution also guarantees against nationalisation. Profits, dividends, interests, royalties and fees, as well as capital repatriation are freely allowed after the withholding tax is paid and ofcourse subject to nominal permission of the Central Bank.

Hence in general the FDI policy in Malaysia was very conducive to investment till 1998 when many of the policies were reversed following the experience of the crisis. The same is discussed in Chapter 5.

Results of Liberal FDI Policy:

What was the nature of FDI flows, its quantum, source and into which channels were they directed. It would be worthwhile to examine the same.

The percent of the ***ratio of foreign investment to domestic investment*** was 8.8 percent in1984-89 and this increased to 22 percent in 1990-95. This is a definite indication of a surge in FDI in the early 1990s. The ***rise in FDI inflows*** is indicated in Table 3.14. The FDI inflows as a percentage of GDP have increased from 1.5 percent in 1987 to 8.3 percent in 1990. It peaked to 9 percent in 1991 and then came down to about 5 percent in 1996.

Viewing at ***foreign investment*** in Malaysia ***by industry***; electrical and electronic products sector ranks first in Malaysia with 30% percent of total foreign paid up capital and 34 percent of total fixed assets as can be seen from Table 4.M.4. Unlike Indonesia and Thailand, Malaysia did not move from textiles to electronics. It went directly from being a raw material producer to a manufacturer of electrical products.
As far as ***sources of FDI*** are concerned Singapore (32 percent) and United Kingdom (18 percent) were the most important investors in Malaysia's manufacturing sector in 1983 as is evident from Table 4.M.5). By 1996 Japan (33) and Taiwan (15) have usurped this position, although Singapore (18) still has a sizable investment.

Economic policy option of Malaysia and Role of IMF/WB

Malaysia's approach to development has been similar to that in Indonesia and Thailand since 1986. Malaysia had a liberal policy prior to 1981, but the same was reversed in 1981 with the look east policy of Mahatir. This policy, which promoted ISI, proved a failure resulting in a recession in 1985-86 and Malaysia then reverted to liberalization. The difference between Malaysia and the other two countries viz; Indonesia and Thailand is that, Malaysia never underwent a structural adjustment programme. There are several reasons for the same.

1) Although it has borrowed from the IMF and WB these loans have been inconsequential. Malaysia took a loan from World Bank for certain projects, for eg. The Bank Pembangunan Malaysia Berhad, a development bank was involved in implementing a World Bank assisted programme for the development of small sized enterprises.

2) The strong leadership and conviction of Mahatir that the country can come out of its economic difficulties without the IMF bail out is instrumental in Malaysia staying away from these international institutions.
3) Malaysia's debt problem was smaller as against that experienced by Indonesia and Thailand during the mid 1980s.
4) Since Malaysia had not availed of IMF/WB loans in the period prior to the oil shock (as Indonesia and Thailand had) it was easier for Malaysia to stay away. Generally it is observed that those countries that avail of it once, do so again and again.
5) Malaysia mobilized resources internally to cover its fiscal deficit. To cover the external deficit Malaysia depreciated its ringgit and as a result its exports increased. Also in the next few years as the economy grew, export earnings were adequate to repay old debts. In addition the need for foreign borrowing was replaced by FDI and hence external dependence came down.

6) Malaysia is geographically a smaller country. Hence this factor contributed heavily in its favour and helped in resurrecting the economy very soon.

The point to be considered now is that although Malaysia did not undergo a IMF/WB directed structural adjustment programme, it still made certain policy changes similar to Indonesia and Thailand. There was a macroeconomic management programme with similar policy adjustments as those directed by the BWIs. These included the fiscal and monetary contraction, control of interest rates, permitting depreciation of the currency by not intervening in the market, privatisation of public sector enterprises, and active export promotion through fiscal and monetary incentives, reduction in tariff rates and all such measures for making the economy liberal and open.

The first reason why Malaysia decided to adopt such a liberalization policy was the fact that the look east policy of 1981 (heavy industrialization, ISI) did not succeed. In the face of a recession, sagging exports and a current account deficit, there seemed very little option but to liberalize, privatise and globalise.

A second and very important reason why Malaysia made macroeconomic adjustments was on the advice of the WB. The WB offered its advice to Malaysia (even though Malaysia did not take a SAL) to make macroeconomic adjustments namely – fiscal controls and tax reforms to reduce its deficit, trade and industrial sector reforms to increase FDI and finally adopt a policy of privatisation to increase efficiency.

Finally since the entire region (barring the socialist countries) had adopted an open economic policy to adjust to the post oil shock period, therefore, Malaysia too followed suit with a competitive liberalization programme.

Table 4.M.1

Basic Economic and Social Indicators of Development in Malaysia

	1981-85 (Average)	1986	1987	1988	1989	1990	1991	1992	1993	1994	1995	1996	1997
GDP Growth %	5.13	1.20	5.40	8.90	8.70	9.80	8.60	7.80	8.30	9.20	9.50	8.60	7.00
Per Capita GDP %	-	-1.50	2.70	6.30	6.10	7.30	6.10	3.30	5.00	6.50	6.40	6.10	5.10
M2/GDP %	0.59	0.59	0.60	0.64	0.68	0.71	0.73	0.78	0.81	0.89	0.93	0.91	1.06
Trade Deficit % of GDP	7.69	-	-	-	-	-	-84.50	-106.00	-4.00	-48.00	-106.00	-12.50	120.00
Budget Deficit % of GDP	-10.50	-14.10	-8.90	-4.30	-3.30	-3.00	-2.00	-0.80	-0.20	2.40	0.30	-0.70	1.60
Current A/c % of GDP	-9.20	-0.40	-0.30	5.20	-0.80	-2.10	-8.80	-3.80	-4.80	-7.80	-10.00	-4.90	-5.80
Pvt. Cons. % of GDP	0.49	0.49	0.50	0.50	0.50	0.52	0.49	0.51	0.53	0.50	0.51	0.46	0.45
Govt. Cons. % of GDP	0.18	0.15	0.16	0.16	0.14	0.14	0.16	0.14	0.13	0.12	0.11	0.11	0.11
GFCF % of GDP	34.40	27.60	28.50	29.10	29.30	32.40	34.01	34.91	35.04	38.17	40.00	42.24	46.00
Govt. expen. % of GDP	-	37.70	30.50	28.50	30.10	29.50	28.50	27.70	24.90	23.70	22.40	22.00	-
Inflation	4.65	0.70	0.90	2.00	2.80	2.60	4.40	4.69	3.59	3.79	4.70	3.80	4.00

Source: IMF International Financial Statistics, WB World Development Report and ADO (various issues)

Table 4.M.2

Exchange rates and Interest rates

	1981-85	1986-90	1991	1992	1993	1994	1995	1996	1997	1998
Exchange rate	2.351	2.643	2.72	2.61	2.70	2.56	2.54	2.53	3.89	3.80
International rate Monetary Market Rate	7.212	4.590	7.83	8.01	6.53	6.53	5.07	6.98	7.61	5.90
Lending rate	10.252	8.060	8.13	9.31	9.05	9.05	7.62	8.89	9.53	10.40
Deposit rate	9.158	5.168	7.18	7.80	6.40	4.94	5.93	7.09	7.98	6.75

Source : IMF, International Financial Statistics

Table 4.M.3

Structure of Manufacturing Exports

Year	Food Beverages & Tobacco	Textiles Apparel & footwear	Electrical Electronics & machinery	Total manufacturing exports as % of total exports*
1981	11	13	52	22
1985	7	11	54	32
1990	5	9	61	56
1991	4	8	63	61
1992	4	8	63	66
1993	3	5	66	71
1994	3	5	67	76
1995	3	5	68	79
1996	3	5	69	79

*(including all others and the 3 mentioned here)

Source: OECD Proceedings "FDI & Recovery in Asia", OECD, France, 1999.

Table 4.M.4

Foreign investment in Malaysia by industry (end December 1996 in %)

	Paid up capital	Fixed assets
Food, Beverages & tobacco	7.0	3.8
Textiles	2.6	1.1
Leather	10.4	11.6
Wood	0.2	0.1
Furniture	3.5	4.5
Paper, publishing	0.6	0.5
Chemicals	0.9	1.1
Oil & Coal	8.1	8.1
Rubber products	4.8	7.7
Plastic	2.9	3.3
Non metallic mineral products	3.2	2.7
Basic metal products	5.7	6.2
Fabricated metal products	5.0	3.5
Machinery	4.0	2.6
Electrical and Electronic products	30.4	34.3
Transport & equipment	3.8	3.2
Scientific equipment	1.7	1.5
Miscellaneous	0.9	1.2

Source : MIDA

Table 4.M.5

Foreign investment by Country Source

	1983 (%)	1986 (%)
Australia	2	2
Chinese Taipei	-	15
Germany	3	3
Hongkong, China	9	3
Japan	16	33
Netherlands	1	4
Singapore	32	18
Switzerland	-	1
UK	18	5
US	6	8
Others	13	10

Source : MIDA

Table 4.M.6

Education indicators in Malaysia

Percentage of cohort reaching * Grade 4				Gross Secondary school enrolment ratio (%)					
(1983)		(1991)		1980		1990		1996	
Female	Male	Female	Male	Female	Male	Female	Male	Female	Male
97.9	98.6	98.6	98.4	45.7	49.7	60.0	55.6	66.1	57.5

*refers to % of children enrolled in primary school in (eg.) 1980 who reached grade 4 in 1983

Source: Key Indicators of Developing Asian & Pacific Countries (various issues)

Development Experience of Thailand

Profile

Thailand, literally means 'land of the free', formerly Siam, a kingdom of South-East Asia bounded by Burma in the north and west, by Laos on the North-East, by Cambodia and the Gulf of Siam, an arm of the South China Sea on the south-east, by Malaysia on the south and by the Bay of Bengal on the south-west. The area is about 513,000 sq. km. a little smaller than France. It can be described as that territory over which the Bangkok Monarchy has been able to maintain its authority. This is because in the early nineteenth century, Bangkok had exercised sovereignty over a larger area that included present day Cambodia and Laos and several Malay Sultanates. However, over the course of the nineteenth century, Siam lost most of these areas to French and British colonial regimes and Siam crystallized within its present borders.

The country can be divided into four regions the cool North, comprising a series of steep mountain ranges incised by steep valleys and rivers; the semi-arid Northeast; the fertile Central Plain, chiefly consisting of the Chao Phraya River Delta; and the densely forested southern isthmus.

Thailand has a ***population*** of 62. mn. Almost half of the population is Thai, with minorities belonging to Lao, Chinese and Malay origin. 99% of the population is ***Buddhist***, while the remainder includes Muslims, Hindus, Sikhs and Christians. There is a heavy rural to urban migration, yet; only 20% of the population live in urban areas, of which half live in and around Bangkok, now the fourteenth largest city in the world.

Thailand is generously endowed with natural resources. About 40% of the total land area is cultivated and some 29% is under forest. Rice remains the staple cash crop, although its dominance has declined in recent years; other major crops include maize, sugar, tapioca, rubber, tobacco, bananas, pineapples and kenalfa (a jute like fibre). Thailand's mineral resources include tin, brown coal, iron and manganese with substantial deposits of sapphires, rubies and other gems. There are also reserves of natural gas and crude oil.

A Historical Retrospective

Various tribes of the Indochinese linguistic stock (mainly Thai speaking people from Southern China, Burma and Northeastern India began to move southwards about the middle of the 6th century A.D. They then occupied the alluvial central plains of the Chao Phraya River. They subjugated the natives and in the course of time penetrated to the tip of the Malay Peninsula before 1160 and as far east as Cambodia before 1284.

It was only in 1350 (14th Century) that Siam as a kingdom was established by a ruler known posthumously as Phra Rama Thiboda[40]. Ayudhya (also spelt as Ayutthya) was the capital city. There were intermittent wars with Cambodia and Burma but notwithstanding the same, the country flourished for the next four centuries. International trade of Siam dates back to this period where it established close commercial relations with various European (Great Britain, France, Portugal and Netherlands) and Asian nations. The Ayudhya monarchy in fact encouraged western traders from the time of the arrival of the Portuguese at the beginning of the sixteenth century to the death of King Narai in 1688[41]. In this year there was a revolution against the French intervention in Thai affairs and the same led to severance of contact with the west until after the fall of the Ayudhya monarchy.

The Burmese launched a full-scale attack on Siam in 1767 and the capital city of Ayudhya was sacked and was completely destroyed. Burmese overlordship was soon terminated and Thai fortunes restored through an uprising led by General Phaya Takh Sin, who proclaimed himself King. A new capital was established at Thouburi near the mouth of the Chao Phraya River.

On the death of King Takh Sin, the crown passed to General Phaya Chakkri (King Ramathibodi or Rama-I, 1782-1809). He was the founder of the present Chakkri dynasty, the royal line that has continued upto the present. In 1782, he shifted the capital of Siam to Bangkok on the opposite bank of the Chao Phraya river. Starting from the period of King Takh Sin, trade and commercial relations with the west was highly suspect, hostile and far between. During this period trade took place mostly with China and Japan.

It was only during the reign of King Mongkut (1851-1868) that commercial relations with the west resumed. King Mongkut signed a treaty with the British at the instance of Sir John Bowring known as the Bowring Treaty in 1855. This treaty opened the way for many such treaties. In these treaties the rules of foreign trade were decided, the fiscal and the trade policy of Siam was curbed (the government's ability to mobilize financial resources were restrained and import duties had to be lowered), state trading and private monopolies were eliminated, extraterritorial rights over legal treatment of foreign nationals were granted.

King Mongkut (Rama IV) was succeeded by his son Chulalongkom (Rama V – 1868-1910). Some of these treaties were re-negotiated during the regime of Rama V so as to eliminate the extraterritorial provisions and financial restrictions. Foreign trade, especially exports of rice, tin and teak grew tenfold in half a century. The process of development continued under Vajirarudh and Prajadipok (Rama VI and VII respectively) though with reduced intensity. Overall a gradual social and technological change did take place since the signing of the Bowring Treaty to the end of absolute monarchy in 1932.

Economic policies during the rien of Chulalongkom

Thailand is unique among the ASEAN3 in the fact that it was never a colony. Some historians allege that a heavy price was paid for the same in the form of giving up suzerainty over large outlying Cambodia, Laos and Malay jurisdictions to pr^ssures from Britain and France. In fact the Bowring Treaty and others are themselves viewed as those that are centralizing and absolutizing rather than modernizing in nature. Contrary to this view is the view that Chulalongkom avoided war with Britain and France and worked towards enabling economic development that is manifest in the export performance of the country. In brief, the economic policies followed during the period are listed below: [42]

1. Promotion of production for export, based entirely on natural resource (agricultural and mining) commodities that were processed (milled or concentrated) only to the first stage that turned them into tradeable goods

2. Reform of manpower institutions (slavery) to encourage greater numbers of scarce Thai labour to put idle cultivable land into rice production.

3. Tax incentives for land settlement and production

4. Public-sector investment in irrigation, communications and rail transit

5. Encouragement of private investment in irrigation canals in the rice delta just north of Bangkok.

6. Promotion of Chinese immigration to provide non-agricultural labour.

7. Encouragement of private business and banking, largely foreign and Chinese owned and managed,

8. Strengthening of public administration,

9. Implementation of all the above within the framework of fiscal and monetary conservatism.

End of Absolute Monarchy, Beginning of a Constitutional Regime

In June 1932, during the reign of King Prajadhipok, a small group of Thai Military and political leaders organized a successful coup against the absolute monarchy prevalent then. The insurgents proclaimed a constitutional regime. Royalist opposition too was overcome by October 1933. In March 1935 King Prajadhipok abdicated in favour of his nephew, Prince Annanda Mahidol (1924-46). Thailand denounced all its treaties with foreign nations and obtained complete autonomy over its internal and external affairs.

Among the more prominent leaders of the revolution were Pridi Phanomyong of the civilian faction and Plaek Phibunsongkram (known as just Phibun) of the army faction. It fell upon Pridi to draft the economic agenda for the country. He was of the opinion that the private enterprise and open economy under the Monarchy had caused the Thais to be persecuted and oppressed and therefore the alternative to this was the adoption of a command economy. At the core of the plan were two proposals – that the government should employ every citizen of Thailand and that the state should own virtually all the means of production. He further proposed that all foreign trade should be routed through the government. In fact he was very much influenced by Fredrich List's ideology of an autarchic government rather than the Smithian ideology of laissez faire.

Pridi's economic programme was termed communist (this world was anathema those days) though Pridi himself preferred to call himself a socialist (a more acceptable term). A factional split arose in the revolutionary group now termed the People's Party due to differences in ideology. Moreover, a counter-revolutionary by the royalists lead by Prince Bawawradet was defeated by Phibun, which now made him stronger. He took control of the government and declared himself Prime Minister in 1938. With this ended Pridi's economic programme that in essence had hardly left any influence on Thailand.

Immediately after taking up the reins he changed the name of the name of the country from Siam to Thailand. Apparently, Siam was a Non-Thai world (possibly Khmer or Chinese). The change of name symbolized the abrogation of the old treaties and declared that the Thailand state warranted a legal status on par with that of the imperial powers of the world[43]. Phibun's economic agenda called for expansion of the government sector and government interventionism in those areas where Chinese enterprise was flourishing. He seeked to eliminate the domestic aliens rather than outright foreigners (Europeans). In fact the act of changing the name of the country from Siam to Thailand was also a pointer in this direction – reclaiming the ethnic Thai control over the economy which was hitherto dominated by the domestic Chinese Phibun openly followed anti-Sino policies – special taxes were introduced that fell only on the Chinese, public enterprises were established to compete with the Chinese, they were not permitted ownership of land, rice farming and taking up a number of other occupations.

Phibun also made an effort to recover the four northern Malay states lost to the British in 1909. For this he took Japanese assistance. But in the very next year, Japan invaded Thailand as the former's request to allow its armies passage through Thailand territory was refused. But Phibun gave into the Japanese request soon (on account of the superiority of the Japanese military). Not just this, he formed an alliance with Japanese and declared ware on the US and Great Britain.

Frequent Change in Leadership

Some Thai leaders, particularly Pridi and the Thai ambassador to the US, Seni Pramoj, looked upon this political move with much scepticism. They organized and developed an intelligence network in Thai to co-operate with the Allied power. Also by mid-1944, since Japan's position in the war became weak, Phibun's policies too were in shambles. Thailand suffered from allied bombing, inflation, severe shortages and corruption against officials.

The fall out of all this was that the government fell and Seni Pramoj became Prime Minister. He persuaded the Americans to treat the declaration of war on the UN as invalid. Thailand also offered 1.5 mn. tons of surplus rice free to the UN. The Thai economy had to be rehabilitated in the post war period. The government imported capital and consumer goods from the US, borrowed 50 mn. rupees from India to buy Indian goods (mainly textiles) and $10 mn. from the US to buy war surplus supplies. In general Thai forex reserves were low.

In the post election period, Khnang Aphaiwong became Prime Minister. But the real power was Pridi Phennomyong who managed to overthrow Khuang in March 1946 and became Prime Minister himself. Later in June the same year, King Ananda Mahidol died under mysterious circumstances; Pridi was suspected of foul play and was forced to step down. Admiral Thamrong succeeded him but in yet another coup in November 1947 was overthrown by Khuang.

Khuang too did not last long. In April 1948, Phibun returned to power and remained there till 1957. This time round efforts were made to improve relations with America. At the end of 1950 an agreement on technical assistance was signed with the US and this was the beginning of the influence on Thai development.

Thai Political Economy (1948-80)

The government of Phibun Songkram established a form of state lead capitalist development strategy. Under this the interests of Chinese and foreign capital were secondary to those of Thai nationals. Foreign investment and manufacturing activity were inhibited by threats of closure, state prompted competition and non-renewal of contracts. In general an ISI development strategy was adopted. However, for fear of protecting the Chinese community, tariffs were not used as a measure of protection, rather, direct participation of the state in production was undertaken. Some of them were fully state owned while others were a partnership between the state and major Thai and Chinese private business enterprises. State monopolies were set up in areas as brewing, paper manufacturing, sugar refining, and gunnysack production[44].

By 1957, severe opposition to the biased development strategy were voiced by the domestic and foreign investors alike and by the World Bank and the Bank of Thailand. A report of the IBRD 1957-58 mission highlighted the declining trade in primary produce, the poor infrastructure and the lack of coordinated planning machinery. These as per the report were the major barriers to the diversification of the economies and the activities of foreign and domestic capital.

With the installation of Field Marshall Sarit as Prime Minister in 1959, there was a change in the development strategy. This also stemmed from the fear that if the recommendations of the IBRD mission were ignored, the American grants and soft loans would be withdrawn. This would affect the long-term growth and development of the economy. In fact as a fall out of this in 1960, the National Economic Development Board was established (NEDB). It was the NEDB, which formulated the First National Development Plan (1961-66) and later the second (1967-71). The plans laid emphasis on the development of infrastructure – transport, irrigation and to a lesser extent health, education and agriculture. The Thai government used a lot of American aid for the development the Northeast since the military bases were established here. American presence here was mainly to suppress the communist movement in the region and with relation to the Vietnam War.

Prime Minister Sarit offered Thailand to be used as a US military base and Bangkok became a rest and recreation centre for US troops. Thailand benefited enormously as US military built roads, communication facilities etc. across the country. There was a monetisation of the Thai economy and expansion of education in this period.

After the death of Sarit in 1963, General Thanon (was the Prime Minister) and General Praphat (Commander-in-chief of Army) took up the leadership. They were considered less dynamic but the economy continued to grow. In 1968, they tried to restore constitutional democracy but failed in the face of opposition from the conservative Thai military and had to revert to autocratic rule. In 1973 the military regime was overthrown and the King withdrew support to Gen. Thanon and Gen. Praphat.

Viewed in totality, the 35 years between 1950-72 was quite eventful. GDP grew at an average rate of 5.2% in the 1950 but accelerated to an average 7.2% during 1960-72. Inflation remained low till the late 1960s and the current account deficit remained at moderate levels but started widening in the early 1970s. The government deficit remained below 2% of GDP over the period 1950-72. Monetary growth was limited to 10-15% annually. From 1963 onwards, the exchange rate was formally linked to the US$ and it remained fixed until the mid 1980s.

Further Political Turmoil and The Two Oil Shocks (1972-79)

The King appointed Sarrya Dharmasakdi as the new Prime Minister in place of General Thanon. The civilian government went on till 1976. But civilian leadership failed and by 1976, a military dominated National Administrative Council seized power in October 1976. Again in 1977 a coup was lead by Admiral Sangad, who offered the premiership to Army General Kriangoak Chamanannd. He remained in power till 1980 but under immense stress and uncertainty. Eventually opposition due to high petroleum prices forced him to quit.

The Army General Prem Tinsulanonda became the Prime Minister after Army General Kriangoak Chamanannd. He was probably one of the longest reigning premiers. During the Prem government, political parties, military and bureaucracy shared power.

In 1988 he resigned following a threat of no confidence. An election was held in 1988 and Chatichar Choonnhavan became the first elected Prime Minister since Seni Pramoj in 1976. Again a coup took place in 1991 when the military took over. Finally since 1992 there has been an elected government in Thailand although the military does have a strong hold in Thailand even today.

By the early 1970s the commitment to ISI was being reassessed especially as the American aid was slowing down and BOP and budget deficits were widening. Hence the Third plan (1971-81) emphasized on both ISI and EOI. Later the Fourth plan (1977-1981) gave EOI a central role. This shift towards EOI was clearly due to pressure from international agencies like the World Bank. On recommendations of the World Bank incentives for export-oriented industries were provided, international trading companies were created for channelising exports, industrial estates and EPZs were established. Yet the industrial strategy was not completely open and liberal since many restrictions still existed.

In the post First Oil Shock period public expenditure was increased. There was an increase in infrastructural investment specially. This resulted in a rise in the fiscal deficit. There was an increase in foreign borrowing too due to a widening current account deficit. However, prices of key inputs like oil were kept below world market levels. Tariffs and other trade barriers were designed to protect domestic industries. This strategy resulted in a rise in the growth. With the efforts made by the Thailand government between 1973-75 and 1974-78 GDP growth rate per annum (average) increased from 6.5% to 9.6%. Inflation dropped form 13.8% to 6.4%. Trade deficit reduced marginally from 5.6% to 5.2%.

However when the economy was confronted with the Second Oil Shock whatever improvements had taken place in between1973-78 started getting washed out. The Third and Fourth Plan with an orientation towards exports had helped exports to become relatively buoyant. But even such buoyant exports could not sustain the onslaught of the Second Oil Shock and the consequent deterioration in the trade balance. During the same time period, when the economy was going through a difficult time, the US bases in Thailand closed down and this caused a decline in service receipts.

As noted earlier, the government was making deliberate efforts to keep prices down. Such an effort misfired and the price structure started looking extremely skewed. The high tariff protection and the steady appreciation of real exchange rates resulted in negative real interest rates. This in turn led to a misallocation of resources and contributed to the already existing imbalances. For eg. the subsidized energy price not only affected the fiscal balance adversely but also discouraged conservatism. In fact further imports of oil became necessary at a time when oil was already expensive.

The only positive event during this phase was the discovery of oil and gas in the Gulf of Thailand towards the end of 1970s that too some extent helped restore confidence in the sagging economy [45]. The other benefit (ironically!) to Thailand came in the form of Vietnam's invasion of Cambodia in the early 1980s. Since Thailand maintained its strong anti-communist stance, it was able to restore the US economic and military aid. This in turn boosted the confidence of the foreign investors.

The economic situation between 1972-79 can be summarised as below:

Effect on Internal balances

1) Gap increased between investment and savings - Since investment increased between 1972-79 (due to increased investment by public enterprises), investment level reached 29% of GDP in 1979 compounded to 20% in 1972. However, savings in public and private sector decreased. The gap between investment and savings was 7% of GDP

2) The expansionary budgetary policy of increased public investment led to fiscal deficit of 7% of GDP on an average between 1979-80 to 1981-82.

3) Rising inflation – As can be seen in the table inflation again increased to 99% in 1979 and by 1980 it increased to 18%.

Effect on external balances

1) Increase in current account deficit –

As mentioned above the Current Account deficit had worsened in 1969-70. Though it had improved between 1973-78, the Second Oil Shock, the increase in inflation rates and the world economic recession caused a deterioration in the trade deficit and consequently the current account deficit too[46] .The current account deficit increased from 4% of GDP in 1976-78 to 7% of GDP in 1980-81. The only silver lining being that despite this adverse situation, Thailand did not reschedule its debt.

2) Increase in debt burden –

To finance the above current account, Thailand borrowed from abroad. The GDP/debt ratio was as high as 25% in 1980. It's debt service ratio increased from 13% in 1976-78 to 17% in 1980. Foreign exchange reserves fell to 4 months worth of import.

All this brought the Thailand economy on the verge of collapse.

Role of World Bank/International Monetary Fund

This is when the IMF/WB stepped in again in a big way. From then onwards to this date these institutions closely supervised Thai economic policy. The Thailand government approached both the IMF and WB for aid. During 1981-83, The Thailand government took loans from the IMF under the following categories:

(1) Purchases under the Compensatory Financing Facility of SDR 186 Million
(2) A buffer stock financing facility of Special Drawing Rights (SDR) 58 Million and
(3) A two-year stand by arrangement of SDR 814.5 million[47].

The two-year stand by arrangement was approved in June 1981 with the general objectives of restructuring demand, reducing the public savings investment gap and limiting the growth of foreign indebtedness. The arrangement included undertaking on monetary and credit policy, fiscal policy and external debt. However, the central government revenue shortfall in the Financial Year 1982 led to an increase in the budgetary deficit, which in turn caused a non-observance of the sub-ceiling on new credit to the government of Thailand. In the circumstances, the initial two years stand by arrangement was replaced with a fourteen month stand by in an amount of SDR 272 million (at that point 100% of quota) which was subsequently increased to SDR 386.6 million under the 1983 general review. Under this new agreement, particular attention was paid to interest and exchange rate policies.

<u>The World Bank recommendations in 1980:</u>

After the conclusion of the agreement with IMF, a group from the World Bank visited Thailand in February 1980 to discuss policies and programs to alleviate the economic problem in Thailand. The World Bank initiated a series of studies of the Thai economy and later in 1980 produced an economic review of Thailand. In essence the World Bank concluded that the Kingdom's economic problems were long term structural ones. The impact of external shocks – oil price rises, fall in commodity prices, the contraction of tourism and markets for manufactured exports – had merely exposed deep seated contradiction of the development process and the failure of previous governments to adjust to changed economic circumstances. To correct the situation, a five-year programme of structural adjustment was agreed with the World Bank, the proposals for which became the broad outline that became the norm during the 1980s[48]. The mission made following specific recommendations[49] –

1. Resource Mobilisation, particularly in the public sectors
2. Monetary policy including measures to maintain high rates of private saving and to manage external debt and the capital account.
3. Energy policy and conservation with particular attention to pricing.
4. Industrial policy and measures to promote industrial exports.
5. Agricultural policy and measures to maintain high rates of growth of agricultural production and exports.

The Thailand government accepted the World Bank's analysis and proposals incorporating them in the Fifth National Plan (1982-86) (See next sub-section). In fact, the implementation of the recommendations was made a condition for the two Structural Adjustment Loans (SAL I and II). SAL I was availed in March 1982 for US$ 150 mn. and SAL II was availed in April 1983 for US$ 175.5 mn.

Before incorporating the suggestions in the Fifth Plan, some 'down payment' had already been made by the Thailand government. This was in the form of certain actions taken in the direction of structural adjustment (See Chart 4.T.I). In the agricultural sector, the government lowered or eliminated export taxes or restrictions on Thailand's major agricultural exports (rice, rubber, maize, cassanna and sugar). Thailand government started the land certification and reclassification programmes. In the industrial sector most of the actions were committee establishment and study initiations. However, an important measure to promote Thai exports was a devaluation of the baht (within the context of the ongoing IMF stand by) by approximately 10% against the US$ in 1981, given the large appreciation of the US$ against other major currencies. Substantial progress was made in the energy sector when the government substantially raised power tariffs and petroleum prices by April 1981 to remove all subsidies.

The Thailand government took these actions before submission of its first Letter of Development Policy (LDP) dated 4 February 1982. Hence this can be considered as down payment by the World Bank for the release of SAL I and II.

Measures Proposed by SAL I:

The major concern of the Thai government when requesting the World Bank to extend the first Structural Adjustment Loan (SAL I) was the rising current account deficits. The measures or actions planned for SAL I are tabulated in Chart 4.T.2. The planned actions for SAL I should be seen as a continuation of the measures or actions taken in the sectors of agriculture, industry and energy and the policy areas of fiscal policy and institutional development prior to submission of LDP for SAL I.

Two more measures in the agricultural sector were added to the actions already taken i.e., the deregulation of livestock marketing and the fertilizer marketing study. Many measures in the industrial sector were new since most measures in this area that had already been taken were committee establishment and study initiation. These new measures were broad-based improvements in the organization and operation of the Customs Department, establishment of export processing zones and more bonded warehouses, general tariff reform, ad hoc arrangements for large scale project evaluation and new studies.

Although many measures in the area of institutional development and development of a medium term fiscal strategy as proposed in the first

LDP were not specific, those in tax policy were specific, for eg. measures of restructuring of personal and corporate incomes taxes.

It is interesting to see that as structural adjustment in Thailand developed over time, the detailed measures shifted from the sectors of agriculture and energy into the sector of industry and the area of tax policy between 1981 and 1982. The focus finally moved to public sector management when submitting the second LDP in 1983.

The proposed measures in SAL I involved formation of many governmental departments and good coordination among them. Therefore, the Thai government, to ensure systematic implementation of the proposed measures, instituted a high level Economic Structural Adjustment Committee, one of whose functions was to undertake regular reviews of progress achieved in co-operation with the World Bank.

Measures Proposed in SAL II

The Thailand government had expected the exports to grow and overcome the current account deficit. However, with the worsening situation in the world economy it had to change its course of action. Some institutional measures were now taken to contain and regulate public finances. Measures introduced (shown in Chart 4.T.3) included reduction in expenditure, intensifying the role of the Fiscal Policy Office (FPO) as a central fiscal planning unit with assistance from the IMF, simplification of tax measures and betterment of tax administration.

Other SAL measures included, exploring the feasibility of exporters and guarantee schemes in the industrial sector, a reduction in fuel price differential, energy conservation measures and the establishment of an Energy Conservation Centre of Thailand (ECCT).

Deterioration of the world economy caused a shift in two targets proposed. Firstly, central government revenue/GDP ratio targeted at 18% in the fiscal year 1986 was dropped to 16%, for the fiscal year 1983,and secondly, the Thailand government imposed a one-year temporary import duty surcharge of 10% of existing duties and the Ministry of Finance was authorised to temporarily increase export duties.

The question that arises now is what were the actual policy measures and changes implemented and what was the effect of the same. The next sub-section explains the same.

Policy Measures Adopted Since Mid-1980s:

Critical to the whole questions of structural adjustment was the Fifth Plan[50]. In fact it has been described as a 'milestone document' in the Thailand's development planning. The key elements of the *Fifth Plan* centred on structural adjustment along the lines suggested by the World Bank. Its objectives were as follows:

- to improve the economic and financial position of the country
- to adjust the economic structure and increase production efficiency
- to adjust the social structure and decentralise social services
- to reduce absolute poverty and accelerate rural development in backward areas
- to coordinate economic development activities with national security management
- to reform economic management and distinction of ownership

The *Sixth Plan* (1987-91) reiterated the commitment to reforms akin to structural adjustment, though not directly by name [51]. Since 1986 and more especially since 1988, a significant number of original recommendations have been implemented. Its objectives were[52]

- To promote economic growth to at least 5% per year in real terms
- Improve the administrative structure of the government and review its role (the private sector was to play a greater role & thereby reduce the burden of the government)

- Increase the mobilisation of domestic saving from both private and public sectors from the target of 18.2% under the previous plan to 23.7%
- Continue the privatisation process and improve the administrative efficiency of the state enterprises (The proportion of their foreign borrowing was also to be reduced)
- Use fiscal and monetary measures to support economic growth & reduce the deficit in the trade and current accounts (an important fiscal measure was to be the restructuring of the taxation system, which was to increase government revenue and to attract foreign investment.

The various policy reforms implemented since the Second Oil Shock included, ***fiscal***, ***monetary and financial***, ***industrial*** and ***trade***, and ***FDI***. They are discussed below.

Fiscal Sector Reforms

There are 4 agencies involved in the fiscal sector operations and policy formulation namely, the Ministry of Finance (MOF), the National Economic and Social Development Board (NESDB), the Bank of Thailand (BOT) and the Budget Bureau. They perform the job of identifying priority areas and public investment projects, estimating their cost and finding the possible resources for financing them. However, the actual implementation of both the fiscal and financial policy is done by the Fiscal Policy Office within the Ministry of Finance[53].

There are two important budgetary laws, which had a significant bearing on the fiscal policy. In 1959 and 1960 the budgetary laws laid down that the planned deficit should not exceed 20% of the planned expenditure, and that the debt service ratio should not exceed 5%[54]. The first was followed meticulously but the second was flouted and this in 1997 became one of the causes of the crisis. However, no restrictions were placed on private sector borrowings.

As part of the broader strategy to narrow the external current account imbalances, the authorities made a number of efforts to reduce the size of the public sector deficit in the early 1980s. These included – a conservative wage policy (government sector wages were not revised between 1982-89), cost of living allowances were payable only to the lowest paid workers, a reduction in capital expenditure was made in successive budgets to the tune of 1% of GDP, and lower investment was made by public enterprises which reduced their finance requirements by over 2% of GDP between 1980-81 and 1984-85.

Efforts were made to increase revenue by increasing the tax base, increase in tax rates, improvement in tax administration and collection, Import duties and excise duties were raised, tax base was broadened in case of income and corporate tax, an exit tax was introduced for residents travelling abroad and so on.

Initially these policies proved inadequate. This was mainly on account of overestimating revenues by an average 1.5% of GDP combined with lack of flexibility in scaling back expenditure. So by 1986-87 further steps were taken to improve the fiscal health. This time round, more conservative revenue estimates were made. Also the tax administration and collection mechanism was spruced up to enable an increase in government revenue.

There was an increase in government revenue even from income tax and corporate tax – which indicated an increase in economic activity. (There was a shift in output from agriculture to industry). In fact the tax collection from this source increased in spite of the downward revision in tax rates and income and corporate taxes. Also on account of an increase in imports induced by a boom in domestic investment, there was an increase in revenue from import duties. These partly offset the decline in export tax revenue. Export duties were eliminated to encourage the same.

Similarly expenditure too was reduced. The major adjustment came from current expenditure, which had been scaled down. This was effected through decrease in government consumption on goods and services and through reduction on interest payments. The latter is a reflection of the reduction in government indebtedness, which in turn got reflected, in a fiscal surplus. Again, as mentioned earlier government

pay scales were not revised between 1982-89, which also enabled a reduction in expenditure. Finally, as a result of reduced capital expenditure and on account of postponing large wasteful capital projects expenditure was further curtailed.
Table 4.T.1 shows that fiscal conservatism helped. The government's expenditure/GDP % came down from 18.63% in 1986 to 14.4 in 1991, then rose marginally to 15.8 in 1995. The government's revenue/GDP % too increased from 15.51% to 20.88% in 1990 but afterwards it fell to 16.4% in 1995. Inflation too came down from 4.9% in 1981-85 to 1.9 in 1986, went up to 6.0% in 1990 and remained at about 5.7% in 1995. Inflation has always been under control in Thailand. The fiscal discipline also ensured a budgetary surplus. The budget deficit during the period 1981-85 of –4.5% turned into a budget surplus of 4.7% in 1991 and remained at 3.0% in 1995.

All this success was not achieved without some casualty. The main casualty of the stabilization programme had been the public investment. The public investment/GDP rates fell from 9.06% in 1985 to 5.18% in 1989. But it may be mentioned here that the same was more than compensated by a rise in private investment to GDP ratio. Yet, by the early 1990s, Thailand started facing severe infrastructural constraints[55].

Thailand's international communications had long been regarded as inadequate particularly with regard to Bangkok – Thonburi Port facilities. By the late 1980s the congestion at the port was giving rise to considerable concern. The opening of Lam Chabang in 1992 to a large extent improved the situation. However, the use of the port is limited due to the lack of dockside facilities. Also progress has been limited with respect to the development of the deep-water ports at Map Ta Phut, Phuket and Songkhla.

In the late 1980s the expansion of the cargo facilities at Duang Muang airport brought considerable relief. But again in the early 1990s this too proved inadequate with the increase in traffic and another airport at Nonng Ngu 30 km. east of Bangkok was constructed.

In terms of domestically oriented infrastructure, the most glaring deficiencies are apparent in the BMR (Bangkok Metropolitan Region). This city required massive investment in roads, water supply, telecom and drainage.

Recognising these problems, the Thailand government came out with proposals for private sector participation in the infrastructure building process. Notable among them are the construction of a light rail system to serve Bangkok area, construction and operation of an elevated highway, expansion of the telenetwork and telecommunication satellite project. Such efforts played a major part in sustaining the Kingdom's export-based growth.

The Seventh and Eight Plans (1992-6 and 1997-2001 respectively) too outlined a number of major projects like highway upgrading and other infrastructural development projects.

The critical factor however here is finance for implementing these projects especially in the light of the currency crisis that engulfed Thailand in July 1997.

As mentioned earlier, Thailand was also facing shortages in skilled labour. During the late 1980s, the reduction and reallocation of government expenditure resulted in a decline in the share of education from 21.1% in 1986 to 16.6% in 1988 (See Table 4.T.3). While there was a gradual re-expansion of the educational budget in 1989 (17.9%) and in 1990 (20.7%), the cut back almost exacerbated the shortages of approximately trained and educated personnel which was manifest in the 1990s. However, it may be mentioned here that with increase in FDI this problem was reduced to a large extent.

Since 1990s a series of private and public educational initiatives have been announced – for eg. The British University Consortium's major campus facility planned for construction in the North at Philsanulok. Also the 8th Plan has placed emphasis on people centred development and the development of education and training.

Another aspect of the shortages of skilled labour is the shift in the structure of the manufacturing sector over the boom period (1986-94) from labour intensive manufacturing to skill intensive production. There seems a unique dichotomy in the economy of Thailand where wage levels are high for labour intensive sector but lack of skilled labour has limited the expansion of the skill intensive manufacturing sector. As compared to this situation, the same in Malaysia is better where more skilled labour is available.

Monetary Policy and Financial Sector Reforms:

The Bank of Thailand (BOT) was established in 1942 under the BOT Act, is the country's central bank and like other central banks forms the core of the Thai financial system. The Thailand financial system including the BOT, 29 Commercial banks (including foreign banks), 3 specialized banks, 94 financial and security companies, government owned or sponsored institutions and a large number of small private and publicly owned institutions.

The BOT's main functions are to act as the banker to the government and financial institutions and as the agent of the government in dealing with the international organizations such as IMF.

The commercial banks account for 70% of the total financial assets. Most of them were originally established by business groups and trading houses to finance their operations. The foreign banks are faced with a lot of restrictions which were over the 1985-95 period eased and accounted for only 5% of banking activity. The banking activity is highly concentrated around 5 large banks that account for two-third of the total bank assets.

The 94 financial and security companies (of which 52 were closed down during the crisis) comprise the second largest group of financial institutions and accounted for 19% of the financial assets in 1994. Their activities cover short-term finance, hire purchase, underwriting and security trade and other investment and advisory services, most of which commercial banks are not permitted to undertake.

The rest of the financial institutions account for about 15% of financial assets. As mentioned above there are 3 specialized banks owned by the government – the Government Savings Bank – this aims at mobilizing primarily household savings through an extensive branch network; the Bank for Agriculture and Agricultural Co-operation (BAAC) – this makes loans to the agricultural sector; and the Government Housing Bank which helps persons of moderate income to buy houses.

Other financial institutions are IFCT (Industrial Finance Corporation of Thailand) which is a privately owned development bank financing mainly through foreign borrowing against government guarantee, and a number of savings and agriculture and agricultural co-operatives, life insurance co-operatives[56].

Conduct of Monetary Policy:

The BOTs Monetary Policy serves several objectives including price stability and economic development. Of these the primary objective is price stability. In general, this objective has been achieved as can be seen from Table 4.T.1, inflation has been in the range of 4 – 6% for the entire time period 1985-96.

The two important instruments of monetary policy in Thailand are open market operations in the repurchase market and to a lesser extent lending by the BOT. In the 1980s, interest rate ceilings were used but this was abolished in June 1992. At times intervention by the BOT in the forex market is also used but changes in reserve ratio requirement have rarely been used. The latter is about 7% and has remained so for 20 years.

The BOT uses open market operations in the repurchase market to inject or absorb liquidity as the situation demands since 1986 with the improvement in Thailand's external position, BOT drained liquidity through purchase of Government bonds since 1987, BOT has introduced its own bonds too.

The other monetary instrument i.e., Central Bank lending is done through a general loan window and a refinancing facility. The former provides short-term loans against government securities as collateral and the latter is meant for providing more financial resources to priority sectors at preferential interest rates.

As far as interest rate ceilings are concerned, they were initially used to import stability to the financial system. In order to have a continued inflow of capital for maintaining the external balance, the BOT increased bank deposits and lending rates by 3% in 1981 from 15% in the previous year. Later it was further revised to 19% and 21%. In fact for the 5-year period lending rates were 18.68%. Gradually, they started to reduce as they came in line with international rates (See Table 4.T.2). In 1990 the ceiling on interest rates were abolished for banks and in 1992 for financial institutions. This was done with a view to allow banks to mobilise more funds from depositors.

There were other reforms – the government relaxed controls on currency exchange. In a series of measures the Thailand government made it easier for Thailand nationals to open foreign currency accounts locally and for Thailand entrepreneurs to remit money abroad. Commercial banks were also permitted to authorise purchases of forex for current account transactions in place of the BOT. All these and other financial liberalization measures gave the private sector banks a boost. Also the banks improved their quality of services through computerization and electronic banking and by increasing the range of services offered.

Financial Market Development

As noted earlier the finance companies and financial security companies hold the largest share of the financial sector assets after commercial banks. It was about 19 % as of 1994. Initially they were regulated under the Act on the Undertaking of Finance Business, Securities Business and Credit Foncier Business implemented in 1979. This was amended in 1992 and the supervision of these companies was now transferred from the BOT

to the Securities & Exchange Commission (SEC). The Stock Exchange of Thailand (SET) was however set up in 1974.
The main objective of establishing SEC was to supervise and regulate the securities industry and the proposed derivatives market, as well as to promote the development of the domestic capital market to trade new financial instruments. The SEC is responsible for the issuance of securities (public offering and private placement), securities trading on the exchange and in the OTC market, securities business (security companies and mutual fund management companies) and information disclosure and preservation of unfair trading practices. This set of reforms boosted growth in the capital market.

Also in 1992, Thailand established the Bangkok International Banking Facilities (BIBF) with the objective of developing Thailand as the regional financial centre for Indochina. The BIBF provides services for trade, investment & finance. The government provided certain privileges such as reduced corporate income tax of 10% compared to the usual 30%, exemption from withholding tax, business tax and stamp duties. These policies enhanced the importance and share of the BIBF in net capital inflows.

Effects of Financial Liberalization:
The abolishing of the ceiling on interest rates in 1992 aimed at increasing domestic saving and long term capital investment.

Also since inflation was low, real interest rates were positive (See Table 3.2) even when interest rates were subject to ceilings. With the reforms the real interest rates further helped in harnessing savings. Table 4.T.1 shows the M2/GDP ratio, which is an indicator of financial deepening (this also indicates that financial liberalization took place), has increased from an average 48.9 in 1981-85 to an average of 64.3 in 1986-90 to 79.5 in 1995. This clearly means that the policies have attracted higher financial savings.

Due to financial sector liberalization the GFCF/GDP % too has increased. From a low 27.8% (average) in 1981-85 it increased to an average of 33.0% during 1988-90. But after 1990 it increased significantly and stood at 42.8%.

The FDI inflows also increased on account of financial liberalization (see sub-section on FDI for details).

The liberalization measures in the stock market/securities market resulted in the SET becoming one of the most dynamic emerging markets during the period 1986-95. Between this period the number of listed companies increased from 98 to 416, while market capitalization increased from US$ 2.9 bn. To US$ 141.5 bn [57] which gives an average of 7209% growth! This has been one of the highest growths in the region.

Exchange rate Management

One of the most important component of Thailand's macroeconomic policy has been the management of the exchange rate. The design and implementation of the exchange rate policy in Thailand rests with the BOT. However, major decisions such as devaluation must be approved by the Ministry of Finance.

Thailand adopted the fixed exchange rate regime by pegging the baht to the US$ between 1960-80. Hence the BOT concentrated on maintaining stability in the exchange rate so as to reduce the risk for traders (importers and exporters) and foreign investors. However, due to appreciation of the US$, the Thailand exports started declining. Hence, to maintain competitiveness, it became necessary to devalue the baht.

There were two successive devaluations, one in 1981 (10%) and again in 1985 (15%). Another major changed occurred in 1985. The peg with the US$ was abandoned in favour of a peg with a basket of currencies – US$, Yen, Mark, Pound Sterling, HK Dollar, Singapore Dollar and Malaysian Ringgit. However, the weight of the US$ was 65% in 1985 which later increased to 85% by 1997.

These measures helped to restore stability of the Thai baht and the country enjoyed BOP surplus since 1985. The level of forex reserves

increased to US$ 35.4.4 bn. in 1995 from 2.1 in 1985 as is evident from Table 3.13. The debt service ratio too reduced to 11.7% in 1995 as compared to 27.5 in 1985.
The exchange rate too remained stable (See Table 4.T.2) over the period 1986-95. However in an effort to maintain this stability, the BOT lost control over the money supplies, where the money supplies would react to the BOP conditions. The regular intervention of the BOT in the forex market to keep the currency stable, increased the gap between foreign interest rates and domestic interest rates over time and this led to an increase in short term capital flows.

To avoid adverse effects of such short term capital flows on the BOT in 1995 imposed certain restrictions. These included – imposing reserve required for the BIBFs out-in business, the minimum amounts of loans made through BIBF was raised from 500000 baht to 2 mn. baht and subsequently to 5 mn. baht, cash reserve required for a non-residence baht account were raised from 2% to 7% , a 7% reserve required for foreign borrowing of financial institutions. These steps helped maintain an artificial stability of the baht vis-à-vis the US$, but at a huge cost, till the Asian currency crisis.

Trade and Industrial Policy Reforms

Thailand was transformed from an agricultural economy to an industrial economy in the last 30 years. This has been possible through the two main instruments of industrial policy – the trade regime and the BOT. Both these policies have favoured outward orientation. Consequently, the policies followed have been export oriented.

Trade regime

As mentioned above, the trade regime was an important arm of industrial policy. Prior to the mid 1950s, the trade regime was extremely protective wherein rice exports were a state monopoly & discouraged by a system of multiple exchange rates and taxes. This was lowered by 1955 but protection for other industrial commodities was not. In the mid 1960s nominal tariffs for finished consumer goods were 25-30% while that on intermediate and capital goods was 15-20%. In the 1970s the protection for finished consumer goods was increased 3.0 – 3.5% while for intermediate and capital goods it remained unchanged. This happened on account of the BOP deficit in 1969. But two years later government lowered tariffs for intermediate and capital goods to reduce costs of industrial production in the aftermath of the First Oil Shock that caused inflation. Again in 1975 due to BOP problems, overall effective rates of production for all industries (except food, beverages and tobacco) increased from 44.2% in 1971 to 90.3% in 1978. However, these rates differed across industries.

But the Thailand government realised that in having such high tariff rates it was encouraging inefficiency in protected industries and causing reallocation of resources from efficient export-oriented industries to less efficient import substitute industries.
Hence from them on the Thailand government made efforts to adopt a policy to promote exports. There were two devaluations (as mentioned in the section on exchange rate management) and tariff rates were rationalised. The tariffs on processed food imports, chemical products, machinery and other intermediate and raw material imports were reduced. Hence the effective protection came down from 28% in 1981 to 26% in 1984.

But persistent budget deficits in the early 1980s made it necessary to increase import tariffs again in 1985. This time round it was 5% on raw material and intermediate products, 10% on textiles and automobiles. The effective production rate again increased to 30% in 1985. Hence although the Thailand government made efforts to reduce industrial protection it was not very successful.

However, the average import tariff rates are moderate in Thailand as compared to those in Indonesia and in South Asia[58] (See Table 4.T.4).

In the 1990s under the leadership of Prime Minister Anand Panyarachun, the government reduced the number of tariff rates from about 60 to just 5. These were 0% for raw materials in short as within the country, 5% for other raw materials, 10% for intermediate products, 20% for finished manufactured products and over 20% for products whose domestic protection was still needed. In fact, in 1992 itself, the government reduced tariff on more than 1000 items within 24 major commodity groups. The rest of the target was met between 1993-1997.

Apart from the above in 1990, the government cut tariffs on capital goods used in manufacturing from 20% to 5%. It followed this in 1991 with large reductions in tariffs on automobiles and computer. In 1992, the government reduced duties on chemicals, textiles, iron, aluminium and glass.

Hence from the above it is clear that an attempt was made since the late 1980s and early 1990s to scale down tariffs.

The NTBs i.e, quantitative restrictions have been modest. In 1986 only 65 products required import licensing. Except for drugs and guns, import-licensing was readily granted. Presently there are bans on only 18 commodities and special licenses are required to import another 30. The Ministry of Commerce imposes and supervises these controls. Commodities under control include those produced in the socialist countries, weapons and strategic firearms, rice and sugar. The controls on rice and sugar are to prevent re-importing after the products have been exported. Export controls are in place on 38 commodities, 16 of which are outright bans. The export controls are meant to ensure domestic supplies for local consumption at low prices. Exports of items such as paper, pesticide, flat iron sheets, polyfiber and cement are regulated to ensure local supplies[59].

Board of Investment (BOI) and Export Promotion Policies:

Whatever restrictions were exercised in the trade regime were more than compensated by the BOIs export promotion measures. As already noted the BOI is the other powerful instrument of the industrial policy of Thailand.

The BOI is a quasi government body established in 1960 to implement tax and promotional incentives to encourage industrial investment and exports. Its main function was to decide which firms would receive promotion privileges. Three categories of industry were defined and their promotion privileges were as follows:

Group A: Capital intensive industries such as chemicals, electrical appliances, automobiles & ship-building industries : full exemption from import duties and business and sales tax on raw materials for 5 years.

Group B: Industries where assembling industries such as transport equipment assembly, electrical appliance assembly and the like : An exemption of 50% of import duties and business and sales tax for 5 years.

Group C: Labour intensive and service industries including food processing, clothing & textiles, hotels and international shipping: An exemption of 1/3rd of import duties and business and sales tax for 5 years.

All three levels were entitled to corporate/income tax holidays upto 5 years.

Since 1986, three more types of firms have qualified for promotional assistance – firms located outside Bangkok, export-oriented firms, firms located in investment promotion zones. These changes correspond to the Fifth and Sixth Plan objectives.

Chart 4.T.5 lists the various incentives provided by the Thai BOI since the mid 1980s.

Since the mid 1980s export promotion, has received a major thrust. The incentives provided by BOI have promoted the creation of an indigenous Thai entrepreneurial class that is dynamic and outward looking[60]. In fact these incentives even compensated for the trade policies anti export bias.

Apart from tax and tariff privileges, exporters were offered duty drawbacks and rebates by the Ministry of Finance. Other export incentives are bonded warehouses and EPZs. The customs department allows large firms engaged exclusively in manufacturing for exports to set up bonded warehouses and import duty free inputs for their export products. Firms located in EPZs are also provided infrastructural support and foreign investors are given freedom to own land, bring in foreign experts and remit foreign exchange abroad.

Export financing is available from the BOT through a concessionary rediscount policy with a maturity period of upto 180 days. The facility is operated through the commercial banks and has been available for short-term credit since 1950s for a variety of exports. So also the Industrial Finance Corporation of Thailand provides equity and loans for the setting up or expansion of industrial enterprises including export projects.

Effects of Policy Measures:

Therefore all these policy measures led to Thailand becoming a classic example of export led growth. During the time period 1986-95, GDP grew at an average rate of 9.9% and export/GDP % rose from 29% to 42% (See Table 3.11). Expressed in dollars, the exports grew at an average annual rate of 22% - in 1985 value of exports was $7185 and this increased to $50912 in 1995.

The composition of Thailand's exports too has changed from agro-based exports to manufactured goods. From the Table 4.T.5 it can be seen that the largest contribution to the growth of exports over the period 1985-95 were SITC 7 and SITC 8 (net effects). Office machinery and electrical machinery together accounted for 25% of the total value of Thailand's exports in 1996.

A more helpful picture is available in Table 4.T.6 which indicates changing composition of the Thailand's exports. The importance of labour and capital intensive have increased and that of land and mineral intensive exports have decreased.

FDI Policy

Thailand is a major destination for FDI inflows ranking 8th among developing countries and 22nd worldwide. The Thailand government has traditionally been liberal towards FDI. However, such policies generally welcomed Greenfield sites. As such FDI was not a priority prior to he 1980s. Foreign investors tended to focus on those sectors where the government promoted import substitution, as a result much of the production was intended for the local market.

Since the 2nd half of the 1980s FDI promotion polices have been openly persued. The widening trade and current account deficits together with the increase in debt service burden induced the implementation of FDI promotion policies especially in export oriented foreign firms.

Policies towards FDI in Thailand are governed by the Alien Business Law (ABL). In general Thailand's laws do not differentiate between domestic and foreign investment with a few exceptions[61]. Table 4.T.7 shows that except for category A, all other areas are open for foreigners. Category B is open for foreigners if promoted by the BOI. Since the BOI actively promotes foreign investment and since in recent years the procedures have been simplified it can be said that category B is practically open for foreigners.

As a general rule foreign equity participation is also governed by the ABL. The investment projects over 1000 mn. baht in agriculture, animal husbandry, fishery, mineral exploration and in service sector initially foreigners may be allowed a majority stake, but within 5 years the Thailand nationals must hold 51% equity. However for manufacturing projects especially those located in certain zones, 100% equity is permitted and so also where at least 80% of total sales are exported.

***Incentives*:** The BOI grants a wide range of incentives and guarantees to investment projects. These incentives do not discriminate between local and foreign investors (See Chart 4.T.5). It offers both tax based incentives (tax holidays or tariff exemptions) and non tax privileges (guarantees, tariff protection, permits & services).

***Policy effects*.**

The policy environment to attract FDI along with sound macroeconomic policies in fiscal and financial sectors did wonders for increasing the FDI inflows into Thailand. Apart from this it seems as if Thailand was in the right place at the right time. This is because Thailand benefited from a massive relocation of production away from Japan, Taiwan and the NIEs as a result of rising labour cost in these economies (flying geese model). Therefore, all put together Thailand's inflows of FDI was substantially large.

After 1987, FDI took off dramatically. The FDI/GDP percent was about 1.7% and it peaked to 2.9% in 1990 (See Table 3.14). The bloodless coup in 1991 and the sharp slowdown in Japanese investment (partly because of difficulties in Thailand and increasing labour costs here) caused a downfall in FDI flows as a % of GDP. However, in absolute terms FDI has been increasing. It has increased from $ 261 mn. in 1986 to $ 1080 mn. in 1988 to $ 1183 mn. in 1995.

Sectoral Distribution: Manufacturing represents the largest sector where FDI is directed. The electronics industry has the highest FDI penetration ratio with it constituting 95% of total investment. In fact electronic products especially – computer parts and integrated circuits which make up 1/3rd of the country's total exports are totally dominated by Multinational Companies. Foreign investors are also active in automotive and metal making industries. Outside manufacturing, Thailand's FDI is directed towards property, particularly hotels[62]. Between 1993-95 this has increased tenfold representing

42% of total inflows in 1995. However, this sector is very volatile and therefore, in the crisis period it fell dramatically.

Sources of FDI

In the 1970s, the US was the main source of FDI accounting for 35% of total flows (See Table 4.T.7). However by 1985-89, Japan overtook the US and accounted for 42% of FDI inflows. Japan's investments, mostly through joint ventures were concentrated in chemicals, electrical machinery and transport equipment. In the 1990s (pre-crisis period) the NIEs constituted 35% of the total FDI inflows. These investment tended to focus on non-industrial sectors especially finance (Hong Kong and Singapore) and on electronic appliances, textiles and chemicals, and property sectors (Taiwan).

During the 1990s portfolio investment and short term capital flows started increasing. In fact short-term capital flows superceded FDI by 1995. Such short-term debts went mainly into the banking sector and from thereon to finance companies. These were invested into non-profitable ventures[63]. Also such flows are highly volatile. This is one of the principal causes of the crisis.

Conclusion

Indonesia and Thailand availed of assistance from the IMF/WB in the early 1980s on account of the financial difficulties faced by them in the wake of the two oil shocks.

The advice of the IMF of a reduction in national spending (fiscal and monetary contraction) along with a devaluation of the currency was readily acceptable to both Indonesia and Thailand where the twin problems of fiscal deficit and BOP deficit (current account) existed. Moreover the ability to combine advice and financial assistance cannot come from private financial markets and for this reason too, the conditionalities attached to IMF loans were readily agreed to by starting in July 1997 came to question the entire achievements of the ASEAN3, the IMF/WB prescriptions for successful economic development and in general, the advocacy of an open liberal economic policy as a sure shot method of achieving 'miracle' status.

Table 4.T.1

Thailand's Social and Economic Indicators

	1981-85 Average	1986	1987	1988	1989	1990	1991	1992	1993	1994	1995	1996	1997
GDP Growth (%) per annum	5.4	4.5	8.4	11.0	10.8	10.0	8.4	7.8	8.3	8.8	8.6	5.5	-0.4
GDP per capita (%)		2.6	7.6	11.0	10.2	8.5	6.0	6.8	7.4	7.3	7.6	4.3	-2.8
Budget deficit/surplus	-4.5	-3.1	-0.7	2.4	3.5	4.9	4.7	2.8	2.1	2.7	3.0	0.9	-0.6
Current Account deficit GDP	-5.1	-4.1	0.2	-1.0	-3.0	-3.7	-7.6	-5.7	-5.1	-5.4	-7.9	-7.9	
Trade deficit/GDP	3.7	15.6	16.8	19.9	21.2	5.6	-11.3	-30.5	3.1	-13.7	-114.3	-19.1	5.5
M2/GDP	48.9	50.1	52.2	56.3	62.1	64.3	72.7	74.9	79.2	78.7	79.5	79.7	89.9
GFCF/GDP	27.8	29.2	31.3	32.8	33.0	35.0	41.4	39.4	40.2	41.0	42.8	42.5	39.5
Population (in mn)		52.51	53.43	54.33	55.21	55.84	56.57	57.29	58.01	58.71	59.40	60.00	60.00
Government expend./ GDP	19.80	18.63	16.85	14.74	14.68	14.86	14.40	15.00	16.00	16.40	15.80	17.80	18.10
Govt. revenue/GDP	11.40	15.51	16.15	17.13	18.33	20.88	18.70	5.80	12.10	17.20	16.40	9.80	-0.60
Inflation	4.9	1.9	2.5	3.8	5.4	6.0	5.7	4.1	3.4	5.2	5.7	5.9	8.0

Source : International Trade Statistics Year books 1996

Pub: UN, New York, 1997

Table 4.T.2

Exchange Rates and Interest Rates

	1981-85 Average	1986	1987	1988	1989	1990	1991	1992	1993	1994	1995	1996	1997
Exchange rate	24.60	26.29	25.72	25.29	25.70	25.58	25.30	25.50	25.50	25.10	25.20	25.60	47.20
Interest rates													
Lending rate	18.68	16.08	13.38	10.71	11.58	12.25	14.42	15.40	12.17	11.17	10.90	13.25	13.40
Deposit rate	12.90	9.75	9.50	9.50	9.50	12.25	13.67	8.80	8.63	8.46	11.58	10.33	10.52

Table 4.T.3

Expenditure on Education % of Total Expenditure

Year	1986-90	1991-93	1995	1996
Exp on Edu	19.08	20.63	21.40	22.00

Table 4.T.4

Import Tariff Protection in Selected Countries

	Average tariff Protection
Bangladesh (1984)	75
India (1979-80)	66
Indonesia (1980)	33
Malaysia (1982)	15
Pakistan (1979)	71
Philippines (1982)	44
Republic of Korea (1982-3)	24
Singapore (1983)	6
Sri Lanka (1983-4)	44
Thailand (1983)	31

Table 4.T.5

Export Performance by SITC 1 - Digit Category, 1985-96

SITC Section	1985	1986	1987	1988	1989	1990	1991	1992	1993	1994	1995	1996
Composition												
0 Food and Live Animals	44.8	43.5	36.3	34.1	33.7	28.2	26.5	25.5	21.4	20.6	19.0	18.6
1 Beverages and Tobacco	0.9	0.7	0.5	0.4	0.3	0.4	0.5	0.5	0.4	0.4	0.3	0.3
2 Crude Matls, excl. Fuels	10.5	8.9	8.9	9.1	7.1	5.7	5.0	4.9	4.4	5.0	5.8	6.0
3 Mineral Fuels, etc.	1.3	0.8	0.7	0.8	0.7	0.8	1.0	1.0	1.1	0.8	0.7	0.9
4 Animal, Vegetable Oil, Fat	0.3	0.1	0.1	0.0	0.0	0.0	0.0	0.0	0.0	0.1	0.0	0.0
5 Chemicals	1.3	1.6	1.6	1.6	1.7	2.0	2.5	2.5	2.8	2.8	3.8	3.0
6 Basic Manufactures	17.5	16.3	16.5	14.4	13.3	13.7	12.7	12.0	12.2	12.1	11.9	10.8
7 Machines, transport Equip.	8.8	10.7	11.9	15.4	16.1	19.8	21.8	24.3	27.7	30.8	31.5	39.7
8 Misc. Manufactured goods	13.8	16.6	22.5	21.5	26.0	28.2	28.8	28.2	28.5	26.9	26.1	19.2
9 Goods not classd. by Kind	0.8	0.7	0.9	0.7	1.0	1.2	1.2	1.1	1.5	0.7	0.9	1.3
Growth												
0 Food and Live Animals	-13.5	21.1	10.5	28.3	24.1	-1.5	15.7	10.2	-4.1	17.2	14.9	6.7
1 Beverages and Tobacco	-15.6	-2.3	6.4	25.2	-0.7	29.9	47.6	27.8	-11.4	9.9	-12.8	28.9
2 Crude Matls, excl. Fuels	-7.7	6.0	12.6	39.7	-2.1	-7.9	8.6	11.1	2.4	38.5	45.8	-1.5
3 Mineral Fuels, etc.	20.0	-23.1	17.7	49.2	19.7	31.6	47.5	13.1	23.2	-11.0	14.9	24.1
4 Animal, Vegetable Oil, Fat	13.9	-59.1	49.6	-42.5	-16.5	1.8	6.8	6.7	18.5	20.0	5.8	-3.3
5 Chemicals	12.9	50.4	35.7	35.0	29.6	34.8	57.9	15.4	26.7	21.1	69.6	-25.0
6 Basic Manufactures	4.9	16.1	33.5	19.4	16.6	18.0	14.0	8.7	15.9	20.8	22.4	-13.0
7 Machines, transport Equip.	24.30	51.20	46.70	77.20	31.50	41.40	35.50	27.90	30.60	35.00	27.80	19.90
8 Misc. Manufactured goods	6.90	49.80	79.30	42.30	39.10	25.20	25.80	12.10	15.40	14.60	21.50	30.20
9 Goods not classd. by Kind	0.00	8.70	73.80	4.20	83.60	36.00	24.20	0.50	62.70	-43.30	55.10	47.10
Total	-3.30	24.50	32.40	36.70	25.60	15.20	23.10	14.60	14.30	21.70	24.70	-4.80

Source :Warr, Peter (2000), Case Study Thailand, in Dilip Das, Asian Exports, OUP,NY.

Table 4.T.6
Composition of Gross Exports by Factor Intensity Selected Years

Year	Land Intensive	Mineral Intensive	Labor Intensive	Capital Intensive	Total
1970	77.4	16.6	1.5	1.2	100
1975	76.3	11.0	7.1	3.4	100
1980	59.5	16.5	11.4	9.7	100
1985	57.1	9.4	18.2	14.6	100
1986	54.5	6.9	20.0	17.9	100
1987	47.6	6.6	24.9	20.0	100
1988	44.5	6.2	24.8	23.7	100
1989	42.2	5.8	25.3	25.7	100
1990	35.5	6.0	26.6	30.6	100
1991	33.1	5.3	27.5	32.9	100
1992	32.1	4.5	26.3	36.1	100
1993	27.4	4.6	26.9	39.6	100
1994	27.2	4.2	24.6	43.3	100
1995	26.1	4.0	24.1	45.0	100
1996	25.9	4.3	16.0	52.4	100

Source: Warr, Peter (2000), Case Study Thailand,in Dilip Das, Asian Exports,OUP,NY.

Table 4.T.7
Share on FDI in Thailand by Principal Investors in % (period average)

	1970-79	1980-84	1985-89	1990-96	1997-98
Japan	30	25	42	26	34
USA	35	26	23	15	19
NIEs	5	19	19	35	27
Others	29	29	16	24	20

Source : OECD, FDI and Recovery,1999.

Chart 4.T.1

Actions Taken Before Submitting LDP for SAL I

	Source or policy area	Action taken
·	AGRICULTURE	
1.	*Land-use policy*	
	(a) Land-use study	The government had prepared, for the Fifth National Economic and Social Development Plan, a study on land-use and development policy and the magnitude and regional distribution of the problem had been identified.
	(b) Land certification	The decision was made to issue 'right to farm' certificates (or 'STK') to farmers who were cultivating soils suitable for agriculture.
	(c) Land reclassification	The government had begun the process of land reclassification with the 1982 fiscal year budget of baht 73 million and had prepared a broad programme for land reclassification aimed at covering the majority of the problem area during the Fifth Plan period.
2.	*Marketing & Pricing Policy*	
	(a) Export restriction on cassava, maize, and sugar	Export quota system for cassava had been eliminated and that for maize had been made more flexible. Ban on sugar exports had been lifted
	(b) Export tax for rubber	Reduced from 25% to 11%
	(c) Rice programmes on price, distribution, and reserve requirement	The efficiency and effectiveness of the rice price support programme had been improved; paddy prices to the farmers increased by about 20-25% over 1981.
		The effectiveness of the cheap rice distribution programme meeting the needs of poverty groups had been improved by limiting quality and eligibility for purchases and by increasing the proportion of cheap rice marketed outside Bangkok from 40% in 1980 to 65% in the first half of 1981.
		In December 1981, rice reserve requirement was halved, resulting in a reduction of its effective burden on rice exports from an estimated 20% down to 10%.

	Source or policy area	Action taken
	INDUSTRY	
1.	Discussions and Seminars	Broad-ranging discussions on industrial development policies had begun between officials of the agencies concerned, industrialists, private bankers and manufacturers. Public seminars were held on (1) rationalisation of industrial protection policies (2) productivity improvement, (3) export promotion, and (4) energy conservation
2.	Committee establishment	Setting up a permanent high level interdepartmental committee to co-ordinate, implement and monitor industrial development
3.	Export Promotion	The dollar value of the baht was reduced in 1981 by about 10% A new export tax drawback Act was approved by Parliament Legislation had been passed to establish an Export Development Fund to provide technical and promotional support for exports.
4.	Reform of the protective structure Subsector study	Arrangement had been made for the World Bank to assist with the study on the electrical goods sector.
5.	Investment Incentives (a) A study	Under the UNDP/IBRD technical assistance arrangement to the Board of Investment (BOI), a comprehensive study had been completed on the system of investment incentives and on the functions and procedures of BOI
	(b) Committee Establishment	A high level committee had been set up to review the existing system of investment incentives, based on the policy recommendations of the above study.

	Source or policy area	Action taken
	ENERGY	
1.	Pricing and tariff	By April 1981, average power tariffs and petroleum prices had been raised by about 120% over the average level in March 1979 to reduce underpricing of energy
2.	Supply -side	Availability of natural gas in the Gulf of Thailand since September 1981 had reduced the dependence on imported oil.
	FISCAL POLICY	
1.	Measures to reduce budget deficits	In fiscal year 1981 and in the budget for fiscal year 1982, the government had started (1) to increase discipline over public spending and (2) to impose selected tax measures and substantially increase public enterprise tariffs.
2.	Short-term fiscal stabilization measures	The government had the Stand-by Agreement with the International Monetary Fund (IMF). Its amount was SDR814.5 million over a two-year period which started in May 1981
3.	Tax policy (a) Tax Administration	AS of January 1982, the Revenue Department had set up five Area Tax Offices in Bangkok. The IMF had provided extensive technical support in the area of tax administration.
	(b) Tax Policy Board	The Board had recently been set up. Its functions were to identify an appropriate long-term tax structure and develop a programme of phased movement towards it.
	INSTITUTIONAL DEVELOPMENT	
1)	Policy analysis and co-ordination	A permanent high-level National Economic Policy Steering Committee was formed in November 1980 under the chairmanship of the Prime Minister and with the NESDB functioning as its secretariat.
2)	Programme formulation, evaluation and implementation	Since March 1980 a consultant firm had been working with the Budget Bureau to improve the national budget system. The first phase of this undertaking was completed in September 1981. The second phase of this project was initiated at the end of 1981 for the conversion of the entire government to full programme budgeting.

1. Source: Sahasakul, Chaipat, et al (1991), '*Thailand*' in Paul Mosley, Jane Harigan and John Toye (eds), 'Aid and Power. The World Bank and Policy Based Lending, Volume 2, Case Studies'

Chart 4.T.2

Specific actions planned for SAL I

	Source or policy area	Planned Actions
	AGRICULTURE	
1.	*Land-use policy*	Work on land certification and reclassification was continued. By March 1982, the Ministry of Finance would prepare a more detailed work programme for land reclassification.
2.	*Marketing and pricing policy*	
	(a) Rice programmes	Further improvements in the procurement and distribution Further reductions in the overall burden of rice taxation.
	(b) Deregulation of livestock marketing	Permitting the establishment of private slaughterhouse facilities for export by April 1982.
	(c) Fertilizer marketing study	Reviewing the public sector programmes for supplying fertiliser to farmers, paying particular attention to pricing issues and distribution mechanisms and objectives.
	INDUSTRY	
1.	Export promotion (a) Customs department	Broad-based improvements, implemented in 1982, in organization of the Customs Department and in procedures for implementing the import tax refund scheme and the new export tax drawback Act. Customs stations would be created at industrial estate locations and in major regional cities.
	(b) Bonded warehouses and export processing zones	Five additional bonded warehouses would be created in 1982. Export processing zones would be set up in Bangkok and Sattahip early in the Fifth Plan period (1982-6).
	(c) Export Development Fund	Details concerning the financing and operations of the Fund would be decided by June 1982.

	Source or policy area	Planned Actions
2.	Reform of the protective structure	
	(a) General tariff reform	During the fiscal year of 1982, tariff rates would be modified so that all imports would be subject to the ratio ranging from 5% to 60%. Exceptions would only be granted in special cases. By mid-1982, further appropriate changes in both tariff and non-tariff restrictions.
	(b) Subsector studies	Plan for automotive industry in 1982; chemical, plastic products, and ceramics in 1983; iron and steel products, machinery and other equipment in 1984.
3.	Investment incentives	
	(a) Board of Investment	By March 1982, the government would formulate a more detailed programme and phasing for the reform of the investment incentives.
	(b) A study	By mid-1982, the Ministry of Finance, in co-operation with the BOI, would initiate a study of the economic and fiscal consequences of the present and proposed incentives.
4.	Large-scale projects	Ad hoc arrangements would be made for reviewing whether large-scale projects met the criterion of economic viability as long as the National Economic and Social Development Board (NESDB) and BOI were not yet in a position to fulfil their functions for all large projects.
	ENERGY	Actions aimed at reducing the demand for largely imported energy and eliminating underpricing of energy.
1.	Pricing	
	(a) A study	A study of the relative price structure of petroleum products.
	(b) Pricing changes	Plan to initiate appropriate changes in the price structure in 1982
2.	Energy strategy formulation	
	(a) Energy studies	Studies on the energy master plan, gas utilisation, domestic non-conventional energy, and energy conservation

	Source or policy area	Planned Actions
	a) Tax measures	Restructuring of personal and corporate income taxes, and a progressive income tax on sales of property Selective increases in import duties on goods now exempted or taxed at low rates. Increases in excise taxes on certain sumptuary items and the change in the excise tax on cement from a specific to an ad valorem base.
	b) Tax administration	By March 1983, the Revenue Department would have set up the total of eight Area Tax offices in Bangkok. By mid-1982, regulatory action required for the Revenue Department to implement a separation of headquarters from operational functions and to organise its headquarters along functional lines would be completed.
2.	Development of a medium-term fiscal strategy	
	a) Integrated fiscal planning	Preparing phased implementation programme for attainment of the expenditure and revenue targets and of the broad fiscal policies identified in the Fifth Five-Year Plan for the entire public sector. Specifically, central government revenues would be raised from 14% to 18% of GDP over the Plan period.
	b) Public enterprises	Establishing realistic financial targets for all major public enterprises and a phased programme for the achievement of these targets. Operational losses in these major public enterprises would be eliminated.
	c) A study	Reviewing the operations and effectiveness of the extra-budgetary funds with the objective of establishing clear performance criteria and a central monitoring system and considering whether they should continue to operate as separate entities.
	INSTITUTIONAL DEVELOPMENT	
1.	Policy analysis and co-ordination	
	(a) In-house capabilities	Strengthening the in-house capabilities of the core agencies (primarily NESDB, Ministry of Finance and Budget Bureau) responsible for economic and fiscal policy analysis and advice.

	Source or policy area	Planned Actions
	b) Outside capabilities	With effect from fiscal year 1983, provision of regular budget resources to permit the greater utilisation of analytical capabilities outside the core agencies in the conduct of key policy studies. The creation of an autonomous economic and social policy research institute early in 1982 to provide research support and consulting services to NESDB and other government agencies.
2.	Programme formulation, evaluation and implementation	Consultants would assist the NESDB to design, test and introduce new planning and programming systems which comprised a three-year rolling investment programming system, a uniform project preparation and investment appraisal system, and a comprehensive programme monitoring and evaluation system.
3.	Personnel Management (a) Studies	The Prime Minister's office would initiate studies of the organization, management and compensation of the civil service during 1982.

Chart 4.T.3

Specific actions planned for SAL II

	Source or policy area	Planned Actions
	PUBLIC SECTOR MANAGEMENT	
1.	*Fiscal Strategy* (a) The revenue side	Strengthening of the link between the new revenue targets and the tax policy and tax administration changes. The target of central government revenue/GDP ratio was dropped from 18% as stated in SAL I to 16% in FY 1986.
	(b) The expenditure side	Improvement of the methods to project central government outlays.
	(c) Public enterprises, extra-budgetary funds, and local government	Medium-term projections would be made for the financial operations of public enterprises. These projections and those for extra-budgetary funds and for local government would then be integrated into an overall financial strategy for the entire public sector.
	(d) Rule of the Fiscal Policy Office (FPO)	With IMF assistance, a programme for broadening and intensifying the role of the FPO of the Ministry of Finance as a central fiscal planning unit.
2.	Medium-term fiscal reform (a) Tax measures	The implementation of a phased programme for simplification of business taxes and excise duties The enactment of selected revisions of the revenue code and customs laws to enhance their scope and impact. The enactment of the new consolidated excise tax law.
	(b) A study	The initiation of a study on the feasibility of introducing value-added taxation on selected items.
	(c) Local finances	The development of an action programme to strengthen local finances by bringing up to date land housing assessment values, local fines and fee structures.
3.	Tax implementation (a) Revenue department	Computerising its operations and further decentralisation on the basis of evaluation of experience gained from the area offices already established.
	(b) The Customs department	Rationalising import/export forms and documents to eliminate unnecessary papers. Decentralising and reorganising this Department to facilitate trade flow
	(*c*) The Excise Department	To be reorganised during 1983, based on IMF proposals and following the enactment of the new excise laws, to eliminate overlaps in several departments and enhance efficiency.
	(d) Tax Training Institute	Its creation for tax, excise and customs specialists.

	Source or policy area	Planned Actions
	(e) Tax Rulings Committee	In October 1982, a high-level Committee for Tax Rulings was established to help solve assessment and tax liability problems and to formulate a tax arrears policy. Its establishment aimed towards a fairer tax system.
4.	State enterprises (SEs)	
	(a) Commercially-oriented Ses	No new SEs competing with the private sector would be set up in the future. Existing SEs would have to stand on their own feet or be liquidated . In 1983, the government would formulate an action programme to implement this policy
	(b) Public utilities Ses	In 1983, the government would determine which SEs it would be willing to assist financially, and to what extent.
	(c) Other Ses	Would have to earn appropriate returns on assets by the end of the Fifth Plan.
	(d) Ses incurring considerable losses	The government would assess and project forward the overall magnitude of the losses. The government would develop, with World Bank assistance, a firm medium-term plan to reduce these losses gradually over 1983-6 through rate increases and efficiency improvements. With respect to the latter, the new policy directions were (i) each major SE would be subjected to a comprehensive programme of efficiency-enhancing measures, (ii) salary structures would be reviewed to attract capable managers, (iii) technical efficiency would be improved by better maintenance, modernisation of accounting and billing systems, and (iv) operations would be decentralised and management by objectives (including programme budgeting) would be introduced.
	(e) A study	To introduce the new policy directions, regarding the efficiency improvements , on a more systematic and permanent basis, particularly in the major enterprises.
	Foreign debt	
5.	(a) Three-year rolling plan	The formulation of a three-year rolling plan for planning, evaluation and monitoring of the government's external borrowing programme, in conjunction with the formulation of the three year (1984-6) fiscal strategy discussed under (1) above.
	(b) Data base and analysis	An improvement in the external debt data base and analysis.
	(c) Co-ordination	Improvement in the co-ordinating mechanism for external resources mobilisation which had been put into operation by the Committee on External Debt Policy in June 1982.
	(d) Reduction in the ceiling on public external borrowing	From US$ 2,400 million to US$ 2,060 million per year, a reduction of approximately 14%.

	Source or policy area	Planned Actions
	INSTITUTIONAL DEVELOPMENT	
1.	Continuation of SAL I	
	(a) Assistance of a consultant team	The design and implementation of new project proposal and rolling investment systems. Monitoring and evaluation systems to meet the needs of central core and line agencies.
	(b) A programme budget system	Had been designed and would be implemented in FY 1984. This system would be linked with the planning systems.
	(c) A report on accounting System	A comprehensive report on necessary changes in the governmental accounting system would be completed in 1983.
	(d) Improvement in systems for provincial financial reporting	Based on recommendations, it was implemented
	(e) Auditing	New procedures and standards for performance auditing had been designed by the office of the Auditor General. A study on the introduction of comprehensive auditing would be undertaken.
	(f) Staff training programme	Would be formulated during 1983 in all of the central management functions
2	New Actions: (a) Studies	A broad study on the organization, compensation and personnel administration of the civil service. The study would also identify weaknesses of the governmental machinery in departmental reorganisation procedures and processes. A reorganisation study for a realignment of several of the NESDB functions. A study of the staffing needs and arrangements for NESDB and of selected ministerial planning units.
	(b) Policy analysis and formulation	Encountering difficulties in establishing an independent research/development institute, the government enhanced the NESDB's capacity to co-ordinate and manage the conduct of policy research.
	INDUSTRY	
1.	Continuation of SAL I	
	(a) Export promotion	Reduction of the bias against exporting vis-à-vis import substitution. Establishment of export processing zones in industrial estates.

	Source or policy area	Planned Actions
	(b) Reform of the protective structure	Overall reduction and greater uniformity of effective protection through general and/or subsectoral actions. Arrangements with UNIDO to implement a programme of restructuring feasibility studies, per subsector. A study on the textile industry was added. Expanding the scope of subsector studies to include the nature and extent of incentives to be granted by the BOI. Implementation of appropriate non-tariff reform policies in the subsectors under review
	(c) Investment incentives	Plan for the reform of BOI activities started to be implemented. A study on the fiscal and investment consequences of the revised investment promotion structure was initiated.
	(d) Large-scale projects	Ad hoc arrangements had been put in place to undertake comprehensive economic and technical evaluations. The NESDB short-listed a number of consulting firms and invited proposals for in-depth technical and economic reviews of the remaining large industrial projects.
2.	New actions	
	(a) Export credit and guarantee schemes	Exploring its feasibility in order to provide the financial needs of new exporters especially of non-traditional manufactured items.
	(b) A study	Recommendations on the ways in which NESDB's capacity to undertake preliminary evaluations of proposed major investments could be strengthened.
	ENERGY	
1.	Continuation of SAL I	
	(a) Studies	On energy pricing, conservation and strategy formulation became available around September 1983.
	(b) Implementation	Based on findings in the above studies
2.	New actions	
	(a) Reduction in fuel price differential	Appropriate steps to gradually moderate the large price differential between gasoline and diesel fuel prices.
	(b) Reduction in energy consumption	Formulating policies and implementing measures
	(c) Strengthening NEA's ability	To prepare, maintain and update the medium-term energy strategy
	(d) Establishment of the Energy Conservationn Centre of Thailand (ECCT)	Providing limited technical and technology assistance to industries for energy conservation.
	(e) Transport energy conservation studies	Two studies on energy policies and on road-user taxation had been completed. An action programme would then be prepared to implement appropriate recommendations on transport energy conservation.
	Source or policy area	Planned Actions

	AGRICULTURE	
1.	Continuation of SAL I	
	(a) Land-use policy	Issuance of 'right-to-farm' (STK) certificates in forest reserve areas. The certificates were legally limited to 15 rai per family but landholdings of up to 50 rai would be recognised. However, land rights for areas in excess of 50 rai per family occupying forest reserves would not be recognised. During the implementation of the land reclassification programme in each forest reserve area, the government would ascertain (1) the extent and location of excess land in holdings over 50 rai and (2) encroachment in areas determined to be unsuitable for sustained-yield agriculture.
	b) Marketing and pricing policy	No increase in the taxation of agricultural exports beyond the levels in March 1983. The Rice Policy Committee would conduct an evaluation of the 1982-3 rice price support programme and project measures to improve it. A new committee had been established to review the whole marketing infrastructure and to develop an agricultural trade information system.
2.	New actions	
	(a) Land Bank study	Aimed at the feasibility and desirability of establishing a Land Bank. The study would be carried out under the supervision of the National Rural Development Committee's Land Policy Subcommittee. The Land Bank would enable transfer of land covered by STKs and leases and thereby improve access to credit by STK certificate holders. It would also function as the financial arm of the government's land tenure and land reform policies.
	(b) Water resource development and management (i) Studies (ii) Staff and institutional support	 On organisational, legal, development potential and information needs would be initiated. Would be strengthened.

Chart 4.T.4
Incentives of the Thai Board of Investment since mid-1980s

1.	Guarantees • Against nationalization • Against competition of new state enterprises • Against state monopolization of the sale of products similar to those produced by promoted person. • Against price controls • Permission to export • Against imports by government agencies or state enterprises with taxes exempted
2.	Protection Measures (subject to justifications and needs) • Imposition of surcharge on foreign products at a rate not exceeding 50 per cent of the CIF value for a period not more than 1 year at a time. • Import ban on competitive products • Authority by the Chairman to order any assisting actions or tax relief measures for the benefit of promoted projects
3.	Permissions • To bring in foreign nationals to undertake investment feasibility studies • To bring in foreign technicians and experts to work under promoted projects • To own land for carrying out promoted activities • To take or remit abroad foreign currency
4.	Tax Incentives • Exemption of business taxes on imported machinery • 50 per cent import duty reduction on machinery which is subject to import duty greater than or equal to 10 per cent • Reduction of import duties and business taxes of up to 90 per cent on imported raw materials and components • Exemption of corporate income taxes 3 to 8 years with permission to carry forward losses and deduct them as expenses for upto 5 years • Exemption of up to 5 years on withholding tax on goodwill, royalties or fees remitted abroad • Exclusion from taxable income of dividends derived from promoted enterprises during the income tax holiday.
5.	Additional Incentives for Export Enterprises • Exemption of import duties and business taxes on imported raw materials and components • Exemption of import duties and business taxes on re-exported items • Exemption of export duties and business taxes • Allowance to deduct from taxable corporate income the amount over the previous years, excluding costs of insurance and transportation.

Source : Thailand Board of Investment

References of Chapter 4

1. Islam, Iyanatul, and Anis Choudhary (1995), '*Asia Pacific Economies: a Survey*' p 209.
2. Mishra, Veena (1995), '*Indonesia: Adjustment in the 1980's*' in Pradeep Agarwal, Subhir Gokaran et al (eds) 'Economic Restructuring in East Asia and India', New Delhi, Macmillan (I), p 104.
3. Simatupang, Batara (1996), '*Economic Transformation and Liberalization in Indonesia*', New Delhi, Segment.
4. Payer, Chery (1974), '*The Debt Trap: The IMF and the Third World*', New York, Monthly Review Press, p 80.
5. Mishra, Veena (1995), '*Indonesia: Adjustment in the 1980's*', in Pradeep Agarwal, Subhir Gokaran et al (eds) 'Economic Restructuring in East Asia and India', New Delhi, Macmillan (I), p 105.
6. Azis, Iwan (1994), '*Indonesia*', in Williamson, John (ed) 'The Political Economy of Policy Reform', Washington D.C, Institute of International Economics, p 387.
7. Robinson, Richard (1986), '*Indonesia. The Rise of Capital*', Australia, Allen and Unwin, p 376.
8. Bevan, David, Paul Collier et al (1999), '*The Political Economy of Poverty Equity and Growth*: *Nigeria and Indonesia*', Oxford University Press, p 267.
9. Robinson, Richard (1986), '*Indonesia. The Rise of Capital*', Australia, Allen and Unwin, p 381.
10. Kappagoda, Nihal (1995), '*Multilateral Development Banks Volume 2: The Asian Development Banks*', UK, International Technical Publication, p 49.
11. Ibid, p 52.
12. Prawino, Radius (1998), '*Indonesia's Struggle for Economic Development. Pragmatism in Action*', Kuala Lumpur, Oxford University Press, p 222.
13. Ibid, p 224.
14. Wardhana, Ali, (1998) '*Economic Reform in Indonesia*', in Henry.S. Rowen (ed), 'Behind East Asian Growth. The Political and Social Foundations of Prosperity', New York, Routledge, p 128.

15. Prawino, Radius (1998), '*Indonesia's Struggle for Economic Development. Pragmatism in Action*', Kuala Lumpur, Oxford University Press, p 240.
16. Nasution, Anwar (2000), '*Reforms of the Financial Sector in Indonesia (1983-91)*', in Robert Ash (ed), 'The Economies of Asia (1950-98)', London, Routledge, p 240.
17. Ibid.
18. Ariff, Mohammed and Ahmed M. Khalid (2000), '*Liberalization, Growth and the Asian Financial Crisis. Lessons for Developing and Transitional Economies of Asia*', USA, Edward Elgar Publishing Inc, p 164.
19. Wardhana, Ali, (1998) '*Economic Reform in Indonesia*', in Henry.S. Rowen (ed), 'Behind East Asian Growth. The Political and Social Foundations of Prosperity', New York, Routledge, p 135.
20. Simatupang, Batara (1996), '*Economic Transformation and Liberalization in Indonesia*', New Delhi, Segment.
21. Wardhana, Ali, (1998) '*Economic Reform in Indonesia*', in Henry.S. Rowen (ed), 'Behind East Asian Growth. The Political and Social Foundations of Prosperity', New York, Routledge, p 129.
22. Mishra, Veena (1995), '*Indonesia: Adjustment in the 1980's*', in Pradeep Agarwal, Subhir Gokaran et al (eds) 'Economic Restructuring in East Asia and India', New Delhi, Macmillan (I), p 112.
23. Bhattacharya, Amar and Mari Pangestu (1997), '*Indonesia: Development Transformation and the Role of Public Policy*' in Danny Leipziger, (ed) (1997), 'Lessons From East Asia', USA, The University of Michigan Press, p 410.
24. OECD (1999), *OECD Proceedings, FDI and recovery in Asia*, OECD, France, p 69.
25. Ross-Larson, Bruce (1980), '*Social and Political Setting*', in Kevin Young, William Bussink and Parvez Hassan (eds), 'Malaysia: Growth and Equity in a Multi Racial Society', Baltimore, John Hopkins University Press, p 11-12.
26. Islam, Iyanatul, and Anis Choudhary (1995), '*Asia Pacific Economies: A Survey*' p 224.
27. Ibid.
28. Salleh, Ismail Mohammed and Dhevan Meyananthan (1997), '*Malaysia, Growth, Equity and Structural Transformation*',

in Danny Leipziger, (ed) (1997), 'Lessons From East Asia', USA, The University of Michigan Press, p 290.

29. Jomo K.S and Chris Edwards (1993), '*Malaysian Industrialization in Historical Perspective*', in Jomo K.S (ed), 'Industrialising Malaysia', New York, Routledge, p 26-27.
30. Ibid, p 27.
31. Lim, Imran and Helen Nesadurai (1997), '*Managing the Malaysian Industrial Economy*', in Seiichi Masuyama et al (eds), 'Industrial Policies in East Asia', Singapore, ISEAS, p 186.
32. Ariff and Senudram M (1987), '*Trade and Financing Strategies a Case Study of Malaysia*' Working Paper No. 21, London, Overseas Development Institute.
33. Salleh, Ismail Mohammed and Dhevan Meyananthan (1997), '*Malaysia, Growth, Equity and Structural Transformation*', in Danny Leipziger, (ed) (1997), 'Lessons From East Asia', USA, The University of Michigan Press, p 293.
34. UNIDO (1991), '*Industrial Development Review Series, Malaysia*', UK, Basil Blackwell Ltd, p 7.
35. Ariff, Mohammed et al (2000), '*Liberalisation, Growth and the Asian Financial Crisis. Lessons for Developing and Transitional Economies in Asia*', USA, Edward Elgar Publishing Inc., p 88.
36. Yusof, Zainal Aznam (2000), '*Financial Reform in Malaysia*', in Robert Ash and Anne Booth (eds), 'The Economies of Asia 1950-98', London, Routledge, p 265.
37. UNIDO (1991), '*Industrial Development Review Series, Malaysia*', UK, Basil Blackwell Ltd, p 11.
38. Rani, Osman H (1994), '*Malaysia's Economic Performance: An Overview*', in Chai Siow Yue (ed), 'APEC Challenges and Opportunities', Singapore, ISEAS, p 22.
39. OECD (1999), *OECD Proceedings, FDI and recovery in Asia*, OECD, France.
40. Bram, Leon L et al (eds) (1980), '*Funk and Wagnall's New Encyclopaedia*', Volume 23 p 99.
41. Shilcock, T.H, '*Thailand Social and Economic Studies in Development*', p 3.
42. Krongkaew, Medhi (1995), '*Thailand's Industrialisation and its Consequences*', London, Macmillan Press ltd.

43. Warr, Peter and Bhanupong Nidhiprabha (1996), '*Thailand's Macroeconomic Miracle. Stable Adjustment and sustained Growth*,, Kuala Lumpur, Oxford University Press, p 9.
44. Dixon, Chris (1991), '*Southeast Asia in the World Economy. A Regional Geography*', Britain, Cambridge University Press, p 173.
45. Islam, Iyanatul, and Anis Choudhary (1995), '*Asia Pacific Economies: A Survey*', p 254.
46. Guillovet, Allian (1990), '*Booming Economies of Southeast Asia*', Singapore, Longman Publication, p 115-116.
47. Sahasakul, Chaipat, et al (1991), '*Thailand'* in Paul Mosley, Jane Harigan and John Toye (eds), 'Aid and Power.The World Bank and Policy Based Lending, Volume 2, Case Studies', p 79.
48. Dixon, Chris (1999), '*The Thai Economy, Uneven Development and* Internationalisation', London, Routledge, p 114.
49. Sahasakul, Chaipat, et al (1991), '*Thailand'* in Paul Mosley, Jane Harigan and John Toye (eds), 'Aid and Power. The World Bank and Policy Based Lending, Volume 2, Case Studies', p 80.
50. Dixon, Chris (1999), '*The Thai Economy, Uneven Development and Internationalisation'*, London, Routledge, p 117.
51. Ibid, 120.
52. Warr, Peter and Bhanupong Nidhiprabha (1996), '*Thailand's Macroeconomic Miracle. Stable Adjustment and sustained Growth*,, Kuala Lumpur, Oxford University Press, p 74.
53. Ariff, Mohammed et al (2000), '*Liberalisation, Growth and the Asian Financial Crisis. Lessons for Developing and Transitional Economies in Asia*', USA, Edward Elgar Publishing Inc., p 196-197.
54. Robinson, David, Yangho Byeon and Ranjit Teta ((1991), '*Thailand*: *Adjusting to Success, Current Policy Issues'*, Washington DC, IMF.
55. Kunal Sen (1995), '*Thailand: Stabilization With Growth'*, in Pradeep Agarwal, Subhir Gokaran et al (eds) 'Economic Restructuring in East Asia and India', New Delhi, Macmillan (I), p 139-140.
56. Chaiyasoot, Naris (2000), '*Industrialization, Financial Reform and Monetary Policy'*, in Robert Ash and Anne Booth (eds), 'The Economies of Asia 1950-98', London, Routledge, p 207.

57. Ariff, Mohammed et al (2000), '*Liberalisation, Growth and the Asian Financial Crisis. Lessons for Developing and Transitional Economies in Asia*', USA, Edward Elgar Publishing Inc., p 207.
58. Suphachalasia Suphat (1995), '*Export Led Industrialisation*', in Medhi Krongkaew, 'Thailand's Industrialisation and its Consequences', London, Macmillan Press ltd, p 75.
59. Warr, Peter (2000), '*Case Study: Thailand*', in Dilip Das (ed), 'Asian Exports', New York, Oxford University Press, p 350.
60. Kunal Sen (1995), '*Thailand: Stabilization With Growth*', in Pradeep Agarwal, Subhir Gokaran et al (eds) 'Economic Restructuring in East Asia and India', New Delhi, Macmillan (I), p 147.
61. Christensen, Scott R, David Dollar et al (1997), *Thailand the Institutional and Political Underpinnings of Growth'* in Danny Leipziger, (ed) (1997), 'Lessons From East Asia', USA, The University of Michigan Press, p 362.
62. OECD (1999), *OECD Proceedings, FDI and recovery in Asia*, OECD, France.
63. Ariff, Mohammed et al (2000), '*Liberalisation, Growth and the Asian Financial Crisis. Lessons for Developing and Transitional Economies in Asia*', USA, Edward Elgar Publishing Inc., p 218.

Chapter 5

Asian Currency Crisis

The preceding chapter has emphasized the remarkable success of the Southeast Asian economies of Indonesia, Malaysia and Thailand in the decade from the mid 1980s to the mid 1990s. The image of success, measured by indicators such as GNP, manufacturing capacity and export performance had gained wide publicity worldwide and the decade 1986-95 was termed as the boom period. These three economies, it was argued had displayed strong economic performance – low budget deficits, low public debt/GNP ratios, single digit inflation rates, high savings and investment rate and so on. The international community thronged to invest in this region and hence FDI inflows were one of the largest, this in turn aided the economies and propelled them into becoming HPAEs.

However, since 1995, there was a slow down in the economy. First signs of the end of the miracle could be seen by 1996 when growth rate of GDP and exports started to decline. At the conclusion of *The East Asian Miracle: Economic Growth and Public Policy (WB, 1993)* exports were identified as a key element helping them achieve high growth rates. Ironically, within a few years of the WB study, export growth started declining. In retrospect, these two indicators viz. decline in the GDP growth rate and the export growth rate could be termed as the early signs of vulnerability of these economies, ending in a financial crash.

The very factors, which brought about a boom, now became a bane for the ASEAN3. The rising inflows (shift from FDI to Short-Term), increasing investment (unfortunately in unproductive areas) and the policy choices (as directed by the IMF-WB) helped to maintain high rate of growth initially. However, these factors among others themselves were responsible for causing a crisis.

Types of Economic Crises

The financial crisis that erupted in East Asia in July 1997 was the latest in a series of such episodes that have been experienced by economies in various regions, the world over and at different points in history. In the 19th century, two severe crises can be mentioned. The Baring Crisis of 1890, which is said to bear an uncanny resemblance to the Mexican crisis of 1994-95 [1]; and the U.S, exchange rate crisis of 1894-96 which was said to be caused by a speculative attack on the US $ [2].

In the 20th century the sterling and French Franc crisis took place in the 1960s. The breakdown of the Bretton Woods system threw a whole lot of currencies into the throes of crisis in the 1970s (dates of currency crisis starting from the 1970s is shown in Chart 5.1). In the 1980s there was a debt crisis in the post Second oil shock period. In the 1990s, the year 1992-93 saw a currency crisis in Europe due to the European Monetary Exchange Rate Mechanism and the Latin American crisis known as the tequila crisis in 1994-95. However, the one that has made all other crisis look small in stature and has elicited voluminous literature the world over is the Asian Currency Crisis since July 1997.

The occurrence and the frequency of the economic crisis in the last century seem ironical considering the fact that international financial institutions such as the IMF were established primarily in response to various crises. These modern institutions and practices such as lender of the last resort, deposit insurance, prudential and regulatory standards etc., were established and evolved to avoid crisis.[3]

The occurrence of the Asian Crisis has prompted a discussion on the different types of economic crisis and their comparison.

Foreign Exchange Currency Crisis:

This generally takes place when there is a speculative attack on the exchange value of the currency and the central bank attempts to maintain the flexible rate (dirty float) at an unsustainable level. In its attempt to maintain the exchange rate the central bank either expends large volumes of international reserves or it may sharply raise interest rates. In case it resorts to the former, the central banks ability to defend the currency is limited to the extent of the forex reserves. On the other hand if it resorts to the latter (also termed as sterilization), domestic bonds are sold at generous interest rates to discourage reversal of foreign exchange. Such a rise in the interest rate has a negative effect on fiscal deficit. However, if the speculative attack continues, the authorities will not able to support the exchange rate and the same plummets.

The modus operendi of the speculators is as follows: They target countries with large fiscal and monetary deficits. They start by borrowing in domestic currency, and then convert it into foreign currency. This reduces the level of international reserves. In other words they 'short' the currency. Such a 'shorting' operation hence has its origin in weak fiscal performance of the state and liquidity creation by monetary authority (known as the standard flow deficit mechanism[4]). Polak first introduced the standard flow deficit mechanism in 1957 that became the basis for the IMF adjustment programme (See Annexure A). The solution to such a crisis is adoption of a tight fiscal and monetary policy. In the previous Chapter, it has been seen that the IMF's solution to a crisis in mid 1980s in Thailand and Indonesia was fiscal and monetary tightening. Such a policy suggestion made sense then as the fiscal deficit was very large and needed to be pruned down.

However, in the case of the 1997 currency crisis Thailand was targeted due to its large current account deficit. The current account deficit was 8.1% of GDP in the year before the crisis. The Thai government tried to defend the baht by expending its foreign exchange resources. In fact when the monetary authorities devalued the baht in July 1997, the international reserves had shrunk to about $1.4 bn from the previously reported level of $ 31 bn. Hence, the fact that the crisis resulted from an unsustainable peg cannot be ruled out in the Asian case. Yet, this was not the only type of crisis that occurred.

Foreign Debt Crisis:

A foreign debt crisis occurs when a country cannot service its foreign debt whether it is sovereign or private [5]. In other words, there is a loss of confidence on the part of the lenders on the borrowers ability to repay the debt obligation. There are three sub types:

1. When there are perceived doubts about the government's inability/ unwillingness to repay debts, a large scale outflow of capital takes place leading to a depreciation in the currency. Also if the debts are designated in domestic currency, they are converted into forex and drained out. A fear that a large domestic currency debt may be financed by monetization leading to inflation and subsequent devaluation triggers off the conversion to foreign currency and the drain on official reserves.

   In Latin America (1994-95) the outflow of capital was caused by the doubts that these governments will not be able to repay their debts. Hence, even though their currencies were not overvalued, a crisis occurred.

2. Sometimes currencies may be attacked on the perception that in future the government debts may increase as the government will be forced to follow an expansionary policy. Such expectations stem from the fact that there currently exists unemployment and slow growth, and to rectify the situation, government's expenditure will increase. This type of explanation best fits the European Exchange Rate Mechanism Crisis of 1992.

3. A third type is a private debt induced currency crisis. The private sector may be unable or unwilling to service its external debt obligations. This, among others, is also the type of crisis that occurred in Southeast Asia [6]. The best example is that of Indonesia. 50% of Indonesia's total external debt was private of which 79% was directly borrowed by the Indonesian Corporations instead of through the banking system. The financial sector's role is to undertake maturity and currency transformation. But in Indonesia, the resources would not have been enough if there were excessive withdrawals due to a panic. Also, the international reserves too would have been insufficient to cover short-term obligation. This knowledge resulted in a run on the currency. In Thailand and

Malaysia (to a lesser extent) it was the banks that had borrowed heavily and lent leniently.

According to Krugman "The Asian Currency crisis had little to do with monetary issues or fiscal issues. It was related to the role of financial intermediaries (the moral hazard associated with such intermediaries when they are poorly regulated) and the prices of real assets such as capital and land. The Asian story is not brought on by fiscal deficit (as explained in foreign exchange crisis) or by macroeconomic temptation (the Latin American case). It was derived from sudden losses of confidence in the overvalued financial system".

Banking Crisis:

This type of crisis refers to a situation wherein actual or potential bank runs or failures induce banks to suspend the internal convertibility of their liabilities or which compels the government to intervene to prevent the same by extending assistance on a large scale. This is similar to private debt crisis.

This type of crisis generally occurs due to the twin liberalization of the domestic financial system and liberalization of the external financial flows. When the confidence in the banking (domestic) system is lost, there is an unwillingness of domestic investors to keep their savings in the domestic financial system. Since external financial flows are liberalized, financial assets will flow out of the country in response to such a domestic banking crisis, provoking a currency crisis. The Southeast Asian's crisis contained elements of this type of crisis too.

Crises of all types have therefore certain common origins; build up of unsustainable economic balances, misalignment in asset prices or exchange rates often in the context of financial sector distortions and structural rigidities. A crisis may be triggered off by a loss of confidence in currency or banking system or an inability to pay debts. In Southeast Asia what began as a currency crisis metasized into banking and debt crisis[7].

Chronology of Crisis is Southeast Asia.

Although, the build up to the crisis had deep-rooted causes, the immediate causes that triggered off the crisis could be said to have started from February 1997.

On February 11, 1997, government decided to go in for budget cuts of about 2% of GDP i.e. to the tune of $2 bn. Such reduction was to be achieved through cuts in military outlays and delay of non-essential projects. This exercise was undertaken to help reduce the current account deficit that was around 8% of GDP in 1996. The deficit in turn had grown so much due to weak export performance and appreciation of the baht against non-dollar currencies.

At the end of February, 1997 the country's largest financial company, was on the verge of insolvency. This prompted the government to announce the suspensions of trading in banking and other financial companies stocks on March 3. The trading however resumed the next day. Also a set of measures to prevent the collapse of financial companies amid economic slow down and high domestic interest rates were announced. These included increased provisions for bad debts and raising of the capital base. A new financial entity was also created to bail out 10 financial companies.

On May 14, 1997 the government of Singapore and Thailand announced that the commercial banks of the two countries had jointly intervened in Singapore Foreign exchange market to support the Thai baht and to prevent monetary instability to spread to other Asian nations. This was the first time that an admission was made publicly although the baht was being defended for the last 4 years. On July 2, 1997 the central bank of Thailand announced it had abandoned the baht's peg to the US dollar and decided to float the currency. Infact by this time 10% of its reserves were already lost in an effort to maintain the peg. The announcement brought about a depreciation of the baht from 24.5 to 29 baht to the dollar. The rise in exchange rate was expected to lead to bankruptcies of private companies. These companies had borrowed heavily in terms of the US dollar but were earning in the Thai baht. The financial companies that had provided credit to real estate developers during the real estate boom were the ones to be most affected.

Immediately, after the Thai Government announcement of July 2, the Bank of Japan pledged that it would intervene in currency markets to help stabilize the baht if requested, but it was not.

The Thai announcement sent ripples around the East Asian developing countries particularly Indonesia, Malaysia, Philippines and Korea. The monetary authorities responded by either intervening in foreign exchange markets or raising short-term interest rates. But this could be done only for a limited period and there ensued a domino effect. Following is a chronological account of events from the July 2 announcement of Thailand.

(See next page)

THE BAHT CURRENCY CRISIS TRIGGERS A CONTAGION

Date	Country	What happened
1997	Thailand	After four years of defending the weakening baht, the Bank of Thailand announced free float of the baht. Baht loses 10% of its pre-float value
July 2	Philippines	IMF grants US$ 1000 millions emergency grant after peso fails outside a widened band to defend the basket peg. IMF warns Thailand to cut its spending, requests it to take a loan from the IMF.
July (undated)		The trade economist Bhagwati condemns free trade in money.
July 24	Malaysia	Malaysian ringgit comes under speculative attack. The famous Mahathir's attack on speculators such as George Soros begins.

August 11	Thailand	IMF, led by Japan's pressure, pledges US$ 16 billion to Thailand as rescue package.
	Indonesia	Indonesia's rupiah under attack. Bank Indonesia's attempt to contain the troubles proves unsuccessful.
	Asia	Asian stock markets plunge in unison: Manila 9.3%. 4.5% in Jakarta, etc.
September 4	Philippines	Philippine peso falls to the lowest level before central bank intervenes to maintain basket peg.
	Malaysia	Malaysia spends US$ 20 billion to prop up the share market.
October 8	Indonesia	Indonesia considers asking IMF for an emergency bailout.
October 27	USA	New York share market loses 7.2% in value.
October 23-8	Hong Kong	Hong Kong share market declines by nearly 25% in value.
November 3	Japan	Japan's Sanyo Securities files for bankruptcy.
	Korea	South Korea begins talk with IMF for tens of billions in emergency aid after Japan turns down Korean request.
November 8	Japan	Japan's third financial house to apply for closure: the seventh largest Yamaichi

		Securities.
November 20	Korea	Korean stock market plunges with a loss of 7.2%
November 24	Japan	Tokyo City Bank, a regional bank, closes.
November 25	Korea	Korea agrees to IMF conditions for restructuring assistance of $55 billion.
December 3	Malaysia	Malaysia imposes tough reforms including budget cuts
December 22	Korea	Korean won plunges further
December 25		IMF and lender nations move to finance US$ 10 billion loan to Korea
1998 January 12	Hong Kong	Peregrine of Hong Kong files for liquidation from share market loss
January 17	Indonesia	Indonesian president fires the central bank governor.
May 21		Indonesia's President Suharto resigns after a wave of bloody riots.
August 11-27	World	Stock markets plunge around the world in expectation of interest rate rises in the USA.
August 20	(Internet)	Paul Krugman supports temporary imposition of fixed exchange rate as the desperate Plan B for a troubled world.
September 1	Malaysian	Malaysia announces going

		back to a fixed rate (RM 3.8 = US$1) from October 1998. All free market troubled world.
September 27	Japan	A major leasing company in Japan files for bankruptcy.
October 2	USA	The Long-term Hedge Fund is reported to have lost US$5 billion. The Federal Reserve mounts a rescue by putting together a consortium to rescue the Long-Term Hedge Fund
October 17	USA	The Fed announces interest rate cuts, and the share market rebounds. Two more cuts follow by November 20.
December 1998	Asia	Most currencies that had overshot (baht, rupiah, peso, ringgit and won) recovered about halfway from their worst declines. The rupiah gained the most from its low of some Rp 20,000 to Rp 7600=us$1.

Source: Internet publications of Asian Economies Reports, 1997-1998

The above events may be summarized as follows. The contagion from the baht crisis spread quickly to Philippines, Malaysia, Korea and Indonesia. In Indonesia, the situation became worse due to political instability and the end of a 34-year rule by Suharto. The currency depreciation in terms of US$ was about 56% in Thailand, 40% in Malaysia, 76% in Indonesia (See Table 5.19). The contagion affected their current level of imports – it had to be reduced and also borrowing became necessary to redress the damages to the financial system and meet trading commitments. Thailand and Indonesia took recourse to a largesse offered by the IMF (and with it the conditionalities), but Malaysia decided to ride the crisis with its own resources. The share market of neighboring countries declined, as institutional rates were about to go up a year after the onset of the crisis. This led to a few spectacular bankruptcies of banks, large securities and leasing companies.

Factors Responsible for the Crisis.

Signs of Vulnerability

Retrospectively, it can be argued that the booming economies of Southeast Asia did not pay much notice to certain early signs of vulnerability that snowballed into a crisis after the Thai baht came under a speculative attack in July 1997. What were these early signs? They were – slow down in the GDP growth rate, slack export performance (both since 1995-96), an appreciation in the real exchange rate, excessive expansion in domestic credit (M2) to reserves expansion, stock price declines and deterioration in terms of trade resulting to current account deficit.

The GDP growth rates had peaked to 8.9% in 1994 in Thailand and to 8.2% and 9.5% in 1995 in Indonesia and Malaysia respectively as can be seen in Table 5.1. By 1996, the growth rates had declined to 5.5% in Thailand, 8.0% in Indonesia and 8.6% in Malaysia. The important aspect here is not that these economies were growing less fast than the OECD but that the gap was closing, reducing the attraction of the region to investors and lenders who had been caught on a wave of mass optimism during the periods of high growth [8].

There was also a slowing down observed in exports after peaking in 1994-95. There was a dramatic drop in 1996 indicating that the end of the boom had been reached. Table 5.1 shows that growth of exports in US$ was 26.2% in 1995 in Thai and dropped to -0.8% in the next year. The same was 13.4% in Indonesia in 1995 and fell to 9.7% in 1996. The drop in the case of Malaysia was more dramatic: the growth of exports in US$ was 25.8% in 1995 and the same fell to 6.0% in

1996. Export growth seemed to determine whether countries would soar or sink[9].

A study conducted by the IMF staff published in *World Economic Outlook, May 1998, IMF, Washington, December, 1998* has assessed the vulnerability of six Asian economies (Indonesia, Korea, Malaysia, Philippines, Singapore and Thailand) to crisis, in the pre crisis period. An **index of macroeconomic vulnerability** was constructed. The index was constructed using, ***the appreciation of the real exchange rate, the growth of domestic credit and the growth of unbacked domestic banking sector liabilities*** (the ratio of M2 to international reserves). The index showed that beginning in early 1997, ***vulnerability increased*** in almost all of the East Asian economies especially Thailand and Malaysia and to a lesser extent in Indonesia. There was a sustained build-up in macroeconomic imbalances (current account deficit) lead to a pressure on the forex market leading to a currency crisis.

Grancarlo Corsetti, Poaolo Pesenti and Nuriel Roubini [10] conducted another study. Here a **crisis index** which was ***a weighted average of the percentage rate of exchange rate depreciation relative to the US dollar and the percentage rate of change in foreign reserves between the end of December 1996 and end of December 1997*** was constructed. A speculative attack against a currency is signaled by a sharp depreciation of the exchange rate or a contraction in forex reserves to help prevent the same. Quite obviously the results showed the crisis index to be – ***38.3 for Indonesia***, **- 38.8 for Malaysia** and ***–47.8 for Thailand***. This study has hypothesized that both financial and real sector imbalances have caused the crisis and these countries displayed vulnerability in the pre-crisis period. Due to weakness in the banking system the Non-performing loans were high and there was a lending boom directed towards non-tradable sector. Also a sizable current account deficit and a significant real appreciation of the currency was a worrisome signal. In general, the results suggested that structural imbalances (current account deficit, currency appreciation, non-performing loans and a lending boom) created a vulnerable situation and made a speculative attack possible .The results of this study are presented in Table 5.20.

There cannot be just one cause for the Asian crisis. Its dynamics were rooted in a number of factors; some of them overlapping and inextricably inter linked.

Chart 5.2 indicates the same, and a discussion on the causes of the crisis will make it adequately clear.

Causes of the crisis

Financial Sector Liberalization

The ASEAN 3 had embarked upon ambitious policies of financial deregulation in the late 1980s and the process was intensified during the 1990s. They were: reduction of barriers to entry for banks and non-banking financial institutions, deregulation of interest rates, relaxation of directed credit requirements, promotion of new financial markets and instruments and liberalization of the external dimension of the financial sector. With small variation, in all countries liberalization of the financial sector from the external point of view meant the creation of conditions for large and easy movement of capital. Local citizens and non-resident foreign entities were allowed to open accounts with commercial banks either in national or foreign currencies; banks were permitted to extend credit in foreign currencies in the domestic market, non-banking private sector corporations, as well as financial institutions were allowed to borrow. Also foreigners could now own shares listed by national companies on domestic stock exchanges, the sale of securities on international stock and bond markets by national companies was allowed and sale of domestic monetary instruments such as Central Bank Bills and Treasury Bills was permissible to non-residents. Finally, the establishment of offshore banks permitted them to borrow abroad and lend domestically.

The extensive liberalization of the financial sector was consistent with the policy goal of providing a large supply of low cost funds to national financial institutions and the domestic corporate sector to encourage exports and assist growth. Such policies of financial liberalization brought in many benefits in the form of greater financial resource mobilization for domestic investment and economic growth to the ASEAN 3 as discussed in the preceding Chapter. But they also increased risk. The case of the Thai financial deregulation will explain the same.

Thailand adopted a programme of financial liberalization in an effort to attract investment funds from global capital markets. Some of these measures undertaken were: removing ceilings on various kinds of savings and time deposits, reducing constraints on the management of portfolio investment, relaxing rules on capital requirement applying to commercial banks and other financial institutions[11]. In 1990 it effectively dismantled the system of forex controls by accepting the IMF's Article VIII that call for removal of all controls on forex transactions in the current account. In 1993 the Bangkok International Banking Facilities (BIBF) were created to increase the flow of funds needed to sustain economic growth. Forty-two licenses were granted to Thai and foreign commercial Banks allowing them to engage in foreign exchange activities.

The above policy of liberalization coupled with the policy of high interest rates led to problems. High interest rates were maintained to limit aggregate dividend and keep inflation low (Tight monetary policy suggested by IMF-WB). But these high interest rates made it cheaper for Thailand (BIBF license holders) to borrow foreign loans at a cheaper cost and lend them in the form of foreign currency to local borrowers. The spread in local deposit rates and the Libor rate was high in Thailand and Indonesia. (Information relating to this is presented in Table 5.2) This spread provided an opportunity for local agents to borrow abroad and lend locally. This way they made a clean profit by relending the dollars to local customers at lower rates than those of baht loans, because the interest rates on the dollar loans were 4-6 % lower than the baht loans [12]. In 1995 the Bank of Thailand tried to slow down the overheated economy by further raising interest rates. But this caused foreign borrowing to increase more rapidly. These were mainly short-term loans and most were not hedged against currency fluctuations. Quite obviously a situation like this makes the economy vulnerable to a speculative attack. Hence it was the very same measures of financial liberalization, which, helped the economy during the boom period, caused a doom too.

Table 5.3 shows that the conservative monetary policy in Thailand was not able to control rising credit flows which rose faster than M2 during the 1990s. Also Table 5.4 shows that even though a conservative monetary policy was followed the ratio of domestic credit to GDP rose. In Thailand this ratio increased from 84 to 130 between 1990 and 1996.

The case of Indonesia was similar. Indonesia too maintained high interest rates on account of a conservative monetary policy. Such a policy was the main instrument of stabilization (for inflation control). But these high interest rates proved to be a bane in the face of a relatively open capital account. The spread in the libor rates and the domestic interest rates (Table 5.2) encouraged the corporations and banks to directly borrow abroad. Most of these loans were unhedged. This was a risky strategy that initially fetched high dividends, but when the Thai baht was attacked, the Indonesian economy became vulnerable to a currency attack. Thus the private external borrowing boom following a financial and capital account liberalization coupled with high local interest rates made the Indonesian economy susceptible to a speculative attack.

In Malaysia also the incompatible trio of an open capital account for the free inflow of both short and long term funds, a domestic monetary policy with interest rates marginally higher than the libor rates, and a more or less defacto peg of the ringgit to the US dollar caused a vulnerable situation. A vulnerable situation in itself may not cause a crisis, it needs a disturbance or a trigger, which came in the form of the speculative attack on the Thailand baht. The announcement of the Thai government to float the baht triggered off a contagion in the region affecting Malaysia too.

The crisis countries had long pursued conservative macro economic policies as suggested by the IMF-WB. When the capital inflows increased on account of financial liberalization (another suggestion of

IMF-WB), the countries faced new challenges of tougher decisions often outside the purview of macro economic policy. The crisis countries unfortunately tried to use monetary policy to sterilize inflows. But attempt to tighten credit only encouraged the same, especially under relatively fixed exchange rates. The exchange rate policy was designed in the first place to encourage exports (IMF-WB directed) so that cross border traders and, investors and borrowers can carry on their activities smoothly. These policy choices helped growth for a while, but gradually as inflows increased, it encouraged unhedged positions.

There is an important lesson to be learnt from the financial liberalization that took place in Southeast Asia. Financial liberalization should be accompanied by viable foreign exchange policies, resilient domestic financial system, a financially prudent corporate sector and an effective framework of international coordination in order to minimize the risks of currency crisis[13].

Large Capital Inflows and the Changing Pattern of Inflows

Since the mid 1980s the Southeast Asian economies have experienced a surge in capital inflows. There were number of factors responsible for such huge inflows

(i) The weak growth in Japan and Europe led to a decline in attractive investment opportunities in relation to available domestic savings. The slow down led to accommodating monetary policies with low interest rates. All this resulted into situation where domestic investors in Japan and Europe started to look for lucrative investment opportunities abroad.

(ii) Financial liberalization in the late 1980s early 1990s in the ASEAN3 opened up new investment opportunities, which the industrial countries were looking for. The returns on investment in the ASEAN3 economies were expected to be attractive as labour was cheap there.

(iii) Finally in the ASEAN3 the interest rates were quite high (tight monetary policy of IMF).At the same time the exchange rates were pegged. This created a sense of security among those holding debt instruments, that they could earn relatively high rates of return without any exchange risk

(iv) Finally international investors often follow a herd pattern wherein investors follow each others investment decisions. Economic fundamentals do not really operate in this situation.

The composition of the inflows started to vary over a period of time. Initially, (mid1980s) the major part of the inflows constituted FDI. This was quite in tune with the policy reforms undertaken by the ASEAN3. They had made the investment climate conducive to FDI inflows especially to promote the export sector.

FDI flows were being replaced by portfolio investment and short- term banking flows in the early 1990s. Having liberalized FDI flows in the 1980s, in the early 1990s, the ASEAN3 started concentrating on liberalization of financial capital flows. In fact the reduction in FDI flows prompted these economies to diversify their sources of foreign capital inflows. Hence, they adopted liberal equity market policies, allowing free entry and exit without much restrictions on repatriation of income and capital. They also shifted to a more flexible policy with respect to foreign banks entry into the domestic market. Such a commitment to capital inflows liberalization and financial market opening, particularly in banking enabled large entry of portfolio investment and short-term capital.

On a cumulative basis, during 1987-96, Thailand received private inflows of US$ 75 bn, Indonesia US$ 68 bn and Malaysia US$ 68bn. Table 5.5 gives a clear picture of capital inflows in terms of percentage of GDP and their changing pattern. It can be seen that the proportion of portfolio investment began to increase in relative terms vis-à-vis FDI over the years. The ratio of portfolio to FDI inflows for Thailand was very low upto 1992 but it increased suddenly in 1993 to 3.01 from 0.43 of the previous year. In subsequent years it remained more than 1.5 through 1994-96. The proportion of inflows in the category others that included short terms inflows to the banking sector remained very high in the total inflows. It varied between 0.53 to 0.74 during 1989-96. Thus about two thirds of the private capital flowed into banking sector and other related activities.

Portfolio to FDI inflow ratio became very high after 1993 in Indonesia. The proportion of others in the total was also high. Only Malaysia stands out as a distinct case as there was a net outflow of portfolio investment from Malaysia, barring a few years. Therefore, disproportionate portfolio investment has not really contributed to the crisis in Malaysia as in Indonesia and Thailand.

Also due to an increase in institutionalization of savings in the developed countries and due to lack of profitable investment opportunities there, emerging market securities were purchased to diversify there portfolio.

It may be noted here that such inflows were largely private inflows and unhedged (short term). During the boom period since the currencies were relatively stable there was no inherent danger for the investors. But since 1995-96 there was a gradual decline in the level of forex reserves relative to stock of portfolio and short term funds. This situation made portfolio and short term funds volatile. The moment there was a speculative attack, such investors started withdrawing their funds (Chart 5.2) and there erupted a crisis. The withdrawal of funds not only caused a depreciation of the currency but also a decline in the share market.

A mention may also be made of the role of credit flows in meeting the liquidity needs of the private sector, which is apparent from the rising leverage ratio of the corporate sector. The pace of financial innovation created a situation where finance became dissociated from real spheres of activities and got diverted to high profit high risk speculative activity. Table 5.6 shows that the mean value of foreign debt to equity ratio of corporates ranged between 1.88 and 2.36 in the ASEAN3 economies in 1996. Moreover, short-term debt to total debt was in the range of 0.54 to 0.64 (mean value) for 1996. Such highly leveraged corporate structure left the economies in a very weak position and added to the financial crisis.

In short, the capital inflows were quite large in the ASEAN3 since the mid 1980s. However, the composition of such inflows shifted from a more stable FDI to less stable portfolio and further to volatile short-term investment by 1997. At the time of the speculative attack on the currency such a situation made the economies vulnerable.

Financial Sector Weaknesses and Imbalances

There is no doubt that the weaknesses in the financial sector was an important factor contributing to vulnerability in the Southeast Asian economies. Insufficient capital adequacy ratios, inadequate legal lending limits on single borrowers or groups of related borrowers, inadequate asset classification system and poor provisioning for possible losses, poor disclosure and transparency of bank operation and the lack of provision for an exit policy for troubled institutions all contributed to financial fragility.

Apart from poor supervision and regulatory controls, there was also the problem of connected lending [14]. This implies lending to bank directors, managers and their related businesses. Again, due to crony capitalism, there was the danger of concentration of credit risk and lack of prudent credit decisions. Finally, there was excessive ownership of and/or government involvement in banks. Banks often became the quasi-fiscal agents of governments, providing an oblique mechanism for channeling government assistance (off budget) to ailing industries 15.

The Graph 5.A illustrates weakness in the financial system as of 1997 in Indonesia, Malaysia and Thailand

On account of external liberalization, the domestic banks could easily borrow from international banks. Therefore, these banks were flushed with funds. Again, on account of domestic liberalization, there was increased competition among banks and non-banking financial institutions. In the absence of effective supervision and control, certain imbalances developed in the banking sector. In other words financial liberalization coupled with a poorly regulated banking sector created a vulnerable situation.

The imbalances created were as follows:

- the foreign liabilities of the banks in relation to their assets increased tremendously. The foreign liabilities of commercial banks in the crisis hit countries (including Philippines and Korea) increased by about 12% per year while foreign assets increased by 7% per year. By contrast in the unaffected Asian countries, banking sectors foreign liability and assets increased at the same rate and the net foreign debt position remained virtually unchanged[16].

- much of the collateral that the banking sector accepted for loans were real estate and equities, assets whose prices contained a large bubble element.

- the maturity structure was mismatched as banks borrowed for short-term a period and lent for long-term period.

- a currency mismatch also emerged as banks borrowed in foreign currency and lent in domestic.

In such a situation, the financial sector was extremely vulnerable. A sudden exodus of capital would lead to depreciation of the currency and increase the banks foreign liabilities (as debts were contracted in foreign currency). Also capital reversal would lead to deflation of equity and real estate prices an this would in turn diminish the value of banks collaterals. Finally, the maturity mismatch would wreak havoc on the banks balance sheets. This is exactly what happened in Southeast Asia when the net private capital flows reversed.

The entire build up to the crisis on account of the financial sector weakness is explained below in detail with facts and figures.

Since there were not enough controls and regulations over the financial system, the financial institutions started to lend indiscriminately. The financial institutions did not bother to screen borrowers and projects in their rush to lend and earn. Moreover, in the initial years, returns on lending were profitable, but in the later years, it became less so. The Graph 5.B shows the profitability through the return on average equity for banks during 1991 and 1995 and the same corroborates the above fact.

However, with the passage of time there were two noticeable changes in the nature of credit allotment of the financial sector. Firstly, there was an increase in credit to the private sector. There was an increase in credit to private sector from 46.9% (of total credit) to 55.8 % between 1990 and 1996 in Indonesia. The same increased from 71.4% to 129.5% in Malaysia and 83.1% to 138.8 % in Thailand during the same time period.

The second change was that by 1996 a large proportion of this credit was directed towards the real estate and equities sector. Table 5.7 shows that the share of bank lending to the property sector was 25-30% in Indonesia and 30-40% in Malaysia and Thailand.

The figures mentioned above were no cause for alarm (although cause for concern surely) till the time that there was no slow down in the economy. When the growth in export sector started to decline and when an effort was made by the governments to defend the exchange rate through high interest rates. This created a pressure on the market. This brought about a fall in property prices and share prices. This in turn had an adverse effect on the banks lending portfolio. Property markets in all the three economies lost value by 30-60%.
As the assets pledged against loans depreciated in value, the banks non-performing loans (NPL) increased tremendously. Table 5.8 shows the estimates of peak and actual NPLs of Banks. Although there are variations across studies, the shares of NPL/TL are in the range of 15-35% for all the three economies. What needs to be noted here is that these proportions stood at less than 5% in Malaysia and Thailand and at 9% in Indonesia in 1996[17].

The overall effect of the NPLs and the general weakness of the banking sector can be better evaluated by examining the revision in the rating of the financial strength of the banking system as documented from the IMF sources in Table 5.11. Indonesia's rating has moved from D to E, Malaysia's from C+ to D and Thailand s rating was revised from C + to E +.

The financial institutions could not recover defaulted loans on account of weakness in legal systems, particularly in bankruptcy laws and cumbersome procedures for their enforcement. These institutions hence found it difficult to repay their own obligations. There was both a maturity mismatch as well as a currency mismatch. The same is explained below.

Table 5.3 shows that the ratio of foreign liabilities to GDP. The same increased from 8.6% in 1991 to 10.9% in 1994, came down to 8.5% in 1996, but rose sharply to 27.7% in 1997 in Indonesia. Similarly in Malaysia too there was a sharp rise between 1995 and 1997 from 6.5% to 18.5%. In Thailand, it is observed that the ratio of foreign liabilities to GDP increased from 20.3% in 1994 to 23.3 % in 1996. But there is a reduction to 15% by 1997. This is because the international lenders became wary of Thai banks and doubted their ability to repay debts and hence had started reducing credit. Also they wanted to retrieve their existing loans.

As mentioned earlier a large part of the debt was short term. The total stock of debt owed to private creditors (Table 5.10) was US $ 28.4 bn in 1992 and this increased to a staggering $58.7 bn in mid 1997 in Indonesia. Of this the short-term debt was about 60% (average) for the period 1992-97. Malaysia's total private debt was only US$ 8.5 bn in 1992, but this increased to US$ 28.8% bn in mid 1997. The percentage of private short term debt to total private debt increased from 48.1% to 56.4% for the same time period. Thailand's position was closer to that of Indonesia. The total private debt increased from US$ 23.0 bn to US$ 69.4 bn between 1992 and mid 1997. For the entire period the percentage of short- term debt to total debt was 68% (average). Such high level of short term debt became unsustainable as the loans were taken from international banks for a short-term period but lent for long term projects (maturity mismatch).

A currency mismatch also existed as most of these loans were contracted in foreign currency, but lent in domestic currency. Investments were made in non-tradables such as land, buildings and infrastructure which generate local currency, vis-à-vis this, repayment had to be made in foreign currency. The ratio of short-term debt to international reserves was very high (Table 5.11). It stood at 1.70 for Indonesia, 0.61 for Malaysia and 1.45 for Thailand in June 1997.

Even prior to the speculative attack on the Thai baht some of international creditors had started to refuse the rolling over of short-term credit or convert them into long-term loans. However, when the speculative attack took place, there was a snowballing effect. The creditors immediately started to withdraw their loans and as a result there was a massive outflow. Here too a herd mentality is applicable where one withdrawal results in hundreds of such withdrawal for e.g. in Thailand, overnight the forex reserves fell drastically. These governments tried to increase interest rates in order to retain deposits/attract more, but the strategy boomeranged. Many banks and non-banking financial institutions were thrown into the throes of bankruptcy/or forced to close down.

The questions that arise are: (i) why did such indebtedness not affect the economy adversely prior to the crisis? and, (ii) why were private creditors willing to lend such large amounts of short- term debts? The answer to the first question is, that while the going was good there was no problem. In other words, as explained in Chapter 4, the high EDT / GDP ratio was not a cause for alarm since export earnings were rising. The high XGS/GDP ratio offset the high EDT/GDP ratio. But gradually as export growth started to decline, and current account deficit began to widen, and that is when problems arose. Such problems started only since 1995.

The answer to the second question lies in the implicit guarantees offered by the governments of the debtor countries and by international financial institutions like IMF. There is a tacit understanding given to the international creditors for the non-guaranteed private loans, that in the event of bankruptcy/debt crisis, the governments or the IMF will bail out the financial institution (domestic) and the private creditors will receive their pound of flesh. Infact, this was the signal given out by the IMF in the past. In the post second oil shock period, developing countries had contracted large amounts of debts from private international banks. When servicing/repayment of such debts became difficult, the IMF stepped in by giving a softer loan option to repay the existing loans and the WB gave a loan for structural adjustment thereafter. Such bailouts came by to Thailand and Indonesia even in the post Asian crisis period as anticipated.

To sum up, premature financial deregulation and capital account convertibility greatly facilitated external borrowing in the form of bank loans with increasingly short maturity structure. This situation coupled with inadequate financial supervision and poor risk assessment, allowed domestic banks to lend indiscriminately. The end result was that the financial institutions found themselves with various imbalances making the economy vulnerable.

External Sector Developments (*Current account deficit, rising real exchange rates and export slow down)*

The ASEAN3 did not display vulnerability in the fiscal deficit, but since 1990s a growing current account deficit was evident, especially in Malaysia and Thailand. The current account deficit to GDP averaged 6.4% in both Malaysia and Thailand during 1991-95 and 2.3% in Indonesia. In 1996 it was about 8 % in Thailand, 5% in Malaysia and 3.3% in Indonesia (See Table 5.1). Such deficits were not viewed with skepticism in the early 1990s as the foreign borrowings were mainly used for an increase in investment rather than consumption. In other words the economies were building the capacity to service those debts[18]. Also since the exports were growing there would be adequate foreign exchange earnings for the repayment of the debts. But, in the couple of years prior to the crisis, the situation started to alter. The large current account deficit could not be sustained on account of a number of reasons as discussed below.

Firstly, the quality of investment had started to deteriorate even though the quantity was large. The investment ratios of 30-40% of GDP are not so attractive when corporate governance is very poor, when so much of private investment is directed towards either speculative activities (e.g. real estate) or in such industries where overcapacity was likely to be a problem over the medium period (electronics industry), and when too much public investment is directed towards either over ambitious infrastructure projects or inefficient government monopolies[19]

Secondly, the large current account deficit was also on account of the rising real effective exchange rate (REER). Before discussing the REER, it would be worthwhile to look at the exchange rate regime of the Southeast Asian countries. Thailand had adopted a currency basket system, Indonesia had adopted a crawling peg against the US$ and Malaysia had adopted a managed float.

Table 5.12 shows the estimated weights of the US$, Japanese Yen and other basket currencies calculated by Fankel and Wei (1994). They regressed each Asian currency (vis-à-vis the Swiss franc) on the US$ (vis-à-vis the Swiss franc) and the yen (vis-à-vis the Swiss franc) for various sub-periods in 1979-92 using weekly data. They came to the conclusion that the US$ had an overwhelming weight in all currencies in all periods except the ringgit that had a co-efficient of 0.7 with the US$ which was relatively low. In other words, relatively speaking Malaysia was the only one of the ASEAN3 economies that had a genuine basket system. The other two had a defacto peg to the US$. The weight of the US$ in the basket peg in the case of Thailand was 80%.

Having noted the above, it follows that any changes in the exchange rate of the US$ will affect exchange rate of Thailand and Indonesia to a larger extent and that of Malaysia to a smaller extent. Therefore, when the US$ appreciated against the Yen in the mid nineties, the currencies of the ASEAN3 recorded an appreciation in REERs. Table 5.13 shows the appreciation in REERs relative to the trend as captured by 1987-97 average. By this measure, at the end of June 1997, the Thailand baht stood at 7% above its long-term average; the corresponding figures for the Indonesian rupiah and the Malaysian ringgit were 4% and 9% respectively. Table 5.14 also shows appreciation of REERs for 1990-96 period.

By itself such appreciation in the REER is not very high. Especially when it is compared to the 30% appreciation in the Mexican Peso in 1994, the real appreciation in the ASEAN3 currencies seems very modest. However, when real appreciation occurs along with large current account imbalances, it becomes a source of increased vulnerability. (See Table 5.13 for a comparative picture).

One of the reasons for the defacto peg with US $ was that a large part of their exports were directed to the US. But Table 5.15 will stand testimony that Japan and the other Asian countries were also important export destinations. This implies that a change in the exchange rate of the Japanese Yen or that of the currencies in the region, will also have an impact on exports of the Southeast Asia countries. As the dollar/yen exchange rate moved from 85 in June 1995 to 127 in April 1997 each of the pegged currencies appreciated sharply against the yen. For e.g. each 100 yen of Thailand exports to Japan brought in 29 baht in early 1995, but only 20 baht by early 1997. There were some benefits, (imports from Japan became cheaper) but at the same time, exports became less competitive.

It would be meaningful to present here the results of a study conducted by Kakotoshi Ito[20]. This study has examined the relationship between export volume (dependent variable) and Asian Countries (ASEAN3 + Philippines) REER vis-à-vis US$, REER of Yen vis-à-vis US$, real GDP growth rate of US, real GDP growth rate of Japan, weighted GDP growth rate of the ASEAN 4(includes Philippines), country specific variable for Indonesia, namely the real oil price (all these are independent variables) for 1971-96.
The following are the results:

For Indonesia, the most important factor seems to be oil.1 percentage point increase in oil price from the preceding year increases Indonesia's export volume by more than 0.4 percentage points and this is statistically very significant. The Yen/Dollar rate is also statistically significant. Yen depreciation is not good for Indonesia's exports: a 1 percentage point depreciation of the yen reduces Indonesia's exports by 0.8 percentage point.

For Thailand, exports increase when the baht depreciates, the yen appreciates, or the ASEAN4 growth rate increases. 1 percentage point depreciation of the baht increases exports by 0.8 percentage points, 1 percentage point appreciation of yen increases the exports by 1 percentage point, 1 percentage point increase in other ASEAN4 countries accelerates Thai exports by 1 percentage point However, since the baht had appreciated, the yen had depreciated and the growth rate of the ASEAN4 had declined, the exports decreased and the Thai economy was hit badly. .

For Malaysia its own exchange rate or that of the yen does not significantly affect exports. However, ASEAN4 growth rate is very important: a 1-percentage point increase in average ASEAN4 growth rate (excluding Malaysia's own) accelerates export growth by 3 percentage points.

Thus, the fact that Indonesia and Thailand's currency was pegged to the US$ on one hand and on the other since US$ appreciated and the yen depreciated, there were adverse effects on the REER of Indonesia and Thailand and consequently on their exports. This means that for Indonesia and Thailand we can explain the decline in exports on account of appreciation in US$, depreciation in yen and slow down in growth rate of ASEAN4. For Malaysia it is mainly due to the last reason, as the other two are not affecting it significantly.

The third reason for the widening of the current account deficit was the export deceleration. Table 5.1 shows that growth of total exports declined from 12.1%, 20.3% and 19.6% during 1990-95 to 9.7, 5.8 and -1.3% for Indonesia, Malaysia and Thailand respectively . Table 5.13 shows the slowdown in manufactured exports growth rate. In Thailand it grew at 23% in 1995 and was almost flat at 0.5% in the next year. The picture is less dismal in Malaysia and Indonesia but not promising either. The growth of manufacturing, exports reduced in Indonesia and Malaysia from 13.4% and 20.3% to 9.7% and 6.5% respectively between 1995-1996. Three reason for the export deceleration is already discussed above i.e., the defacto peg with the US$, the depreciation of the Japanese yen and the decline in growth rate of the ASEAN4 economies. However, there are other reasons for the export deceleration. The worldwide computer related recession in 1996, the emergence of China as a competition for goods exported from the ASEAN3 economies and rapid growth in wages during the early 1990s.

The export slow down in 1996 can be attributed to the glut in world markets to some of the Asian export products, the glut itself driven by Asia's rapid export growth during the previous decade[21]. Too many countries were all trying to export the same products flooding the market for manufactured goods. World prices for manufactured products rose slightly in the early 1990s, but then fell by 3% in 1996 and 8 % in 1997[22]. Prices were especially weak in some markets such as for semiconductors, integrated circuits and computers. World prices for semiconductors rose by about 50% between 1992 and 1995, but the same plummeted 20% between 1995 and 1997. Exports of semiconductors increased by more than 30% in 1993, 1994 and 1995 in Malaysia. But in 1996 it decelerated to 6%. In Thailand computers accounted for more than 90% of total machinery exports. Since the export structure had a large component of electronic products and their accessories, countries like Thailand and Malaysia suffered a set back on account of a recession in world prices.

The loss in competitiveness of exports can also be attributed partly to the emergence of China as an exporter of related goods. Exports from PRC by value shot up in 1994-95. However, here too in 1996, the export growth rate fell. But the point to be noted is that the export items that suffered were textiles and apparels [23]. Exports of electronic and telecommunication equipments did not decrease in 1996. It my be further noted that in the earlier period Thailand's competitiveness in textiles and apparels had reduced due to the depreciation of the Chinese Yuan. In other word China's exports of textiles and apparels had increased earlier due to the depreciation in its currency.

Lastly, export competitiveness was also eroded on account of rapid growth in wages in the ASEAN3 economies. Complete and comparable data on wages is not available, but Table 5.17 shows hourly labour cost in apparel manufacturing between 1990 and 1995. Wage rates in Indonesia, Malaysia and Thailand grew 12% per year or more, with that in Malaysia recording the fastest growth of 23% per year. By contrast wages in China were lower.

Thus, when large current account deficits, deteriorating quality of investment, appreciation in real exchange rate and a slow down in export rate are all put together it is not difficult to see how the external sector developments contributed to the vulnerability of the ASEAN3 economies.

Contagion:

The flying geese hypothesis discussed in Chapter 3 suggests that the ASEAN3 economies in tandem with the NIE's and Japan 'took off' and experienced a boom. This indicates that during the boom period too there was an element of contagion. During periods of turbulence, the contagion factor is bound to be more pronounced. Generally speaking, a crisis spreads from a large country to a smaller one[24]. However, in the case of the Asian currency crisis, it was the other way round as it originated from Thailand a relatively smaller country and spread to the entire region (East Asia).

The driving force behind the contagion does not seem to be bilateral relationship with Thailand or investment in Thailand. Table 5.18 shows the exports of the region to Thailand. It clearly shows that, given the size of Thailand, these bilateral relationships are simply too small to generate the extent of disturbance that was caused to Indonesia (in the case of Malaysia a higher possibility exists).

Hence, one has to look for deeper and more profound causes. One hypothesis termed the "wake up call" hypothesis suggests that Thailand acted as a wake-up call for international investors to re-assess the credit worthiness of Asian borrowers. Earlier in this Chapter a mention has been made of a herd behavior. The above is a variation of the same. The investors now took stock of the similarities in weakness - excess credit growth, the ratio of short- tem debt to international reserves, ratio of broad money to reserves, the ratio of external debt to GDP, the banking systems risk weighted capital ratio and the share of NPLs in the banks portfolio. They found much similarity in such fundamental weakness (See sub-section on financial weakness) and the same created an alarm. Investors in Malaysia and Indonesia (and rest of East Asia) too decided to withdraw their capital and hence contributed to the financial turmoil to spread in the whole region.

The question that arises is why did market signals not produce adequate warning to the creditors prior to the crisis?

It is a fact that creditors suffer from the problem of asymmetric information and do not have accurate knowledge of credit worthiness of borrowers. Such asymmetric information leads to adverse selection and moral hazard [25]. The former occurs before the transaction. It may happen that those parties who are most likely to produce an undesirable (adverse) outcome are those most likely to be selected to receive loans. The latter occurs after the transaction. Lenders run the risk (hazard) that the borrowers have the incentive to engage in activities that are not desirable (moral) from the lender's point of view.

Chart 5.3 gives a bird's eye view of how the contagion factor was responsible for the spread of the crisis from Thailand to Indonesia, Malaysia, Philippines and Korea and not to Singapore, Hong Kong or Taiwan.

Apart from the problem of asymmetric information, the implicit guarantee of the governments of the creditor country and the IMF provided the courage to creditors. They believed that in case of any trouble they would be bailed out.

Another hypothesis to the Contagion theory is related to the competitive dynamics of devaluation. When one country in a region undergoes a depreciation of its currency, the countries that have not devalued - experience deterioration in competitiveness. This is turn makes their currencies more susceptible to speculative attacks. This theory also explains why the emerging economies in East Asia came under pressure after the depreciation of the Thailand baht .

Conclusion

Propelled by the external and financial sector liberalization, a large volume of private capital flowed into the ASEAN3. A large component of this was short- term banking inflows, attracted by pegged exchange rates, difference in domestic interest rates and libor rates, and implicit government and IMF bail out guarantees. On the one hand there were large inflows and on the other weaknesses in the financial sector. The borrowing financial institutions and corporates lent/invested domestically in an indiscriminate manner often in excessively risky projects and asset bubbles. Such a financially fragile economy faced yet another onslaught in the form of an export slow down.

All these factors culminated into a situation where the share market and property market prices started to fall. A scare spread among investors. The Thai economy particularly, became a sitting duck for speculators and was attacked. The contagion spread within days to the other countries in the region. What started, as a currency crisis became a full-fledged financial crisis as all the weaknesses were exposed in the post speculative attack period. Many of the East Asian currencies fell like dominos one after the other and the crisis continued for over a year since the first speculative attack as once the Pandora's box was opened, more and more surprises (bad) came out.

However, it was the sharp *slow down in exports* giving rise to a rapid deterioration in the current account and *liberalization of the capital account* not accompanied by prudent regulations in the related sector that were the villains of the piece. The other elements were essentially accomplices.

Table 5.1

Data on Macroeconomic Funddamentals, East Asian Countries, 1994-98

	Indonesia					Malaysia					Thailand				
	1994	1995	1996	1997	1998	1994	1995	1996	1997	1998	1994	1995	1996	1997	1998
Real GDP Growth (in %)	7.5	8.2	8.0	5.0	-17.0	9.2	9.5	8.6	7.8	2.5	8.9	8.7	5.5	-0.4	-3.1
CPI Inflation Rate	8.5	9.4	7.9	6.6	39.1	3.7	3.4	3.5	2.7	5.1	5.1	5.8	5.9	5.6	10.1
Money Supply Growth	20.0	27.2	27.2	23.2	17.7	14.7	24.0	20.9	22.6	16.1	12.9	17.0	12.6	16.5	15.4
Saving/GDP	29.2	29.0	28.8	27.3	29.2	32.7	33.5	36.7	37.0	36	34.9	34.3	33.1	31.8	32.6
Fiscal Balance/GDP	0.0	0.8	1.4	2.0	3.2	2.5	3.8	4.2	1.6	3.2	2.0	2.6	1.6	-0.4	3.5
Current Acct. Balance/GDP	-1.7	-3.3	-3.3	-2.6	1.9	-7.8	-10.0	-4.9	-4.8	-0.5	-5.6	-7.9	-7.9	-2.2	3.9
Growth of Exports in US$	8.8	13.4	9.7	7.3	-2.1	24.7	25.8	6.0	0.8	-12.9	19.8	26.2	-0.8	4.4	3.3
External Debt/GDP	61.0	61.5	56.7	58.8	49.2	40.4	39.3	40.1	40.2	40.3	45.8	49.7	49.3	49.7	47.5
Short-term/External Debt	61.8	61.9	61.7	58.7	54	48.8.	47.2	50.3	56.4	48.4	71	69.4	65.2	63.7	53.6
Official Reserves (US$ billion)	12.1	13.7	18.3	16.6	15.5	25.4	23.8	27.0	21.7	20.4	29.3	36.0	37.7	26.2	28.6
in months of imports	4.5	4.0	5.1	4.8	7.7	5.1	3.7	4.1	3.3	3.7	6.5	6.1	6.2	5.0	7.9

Various Sources

TABLE 5.2

INCENTIVE FOR FOREIGN BORROWING (1992-96)

COUNTRY	SPREAD OF INTERNATIONAL RATE AND LABOUR	AUG ANNUAL APPRECIATION	EXCHANGE RATE VOLALIBITY *
Indonesia	11.5	-3.8	0.7
Malaysia	1.6	1.2	2.6
Thailand	4	-0.3	1.2

* S.D. ON BASIS OF % DEVIATION OF REGRESSION ON A TIME TREND

SOURCE: WORLD BANK, GLOBAL EXCONOMIC PROSPECTS 1998-99, Page: 68

TABLE 5.3

CREDIT MONEY AND FOREIGN LIABILITIES

S.No.		1990	1991	1992	1993	1994	1995	1996	
	Indonesia								
1	Annual growth in domestic Cr.	58.3	18.9	14.1	21.0	22.9	25.2	26.3	-
2	Annual growth in M2	44.2	17.5	20.2	20.2	20.0	27.6	28.8	-
3	Credit to Private Sector as % of GDP	46.9	46.2	45.5	48.9	51.9	53.7	55.8	-
4	Foreign Liabialities of Business as								
	% of GDP	11.0	8.6	10.3	10.9	10.9	9.6	8.5	
	Malaysia								
1	Annual growth in domestic Cr.	18.0	18.5	29.2	26.6	14.8	29.5	30.5	-
2	Annual growth inM2	12.8	14.5	19.1	22.1	14.7	24.0	20.9	-
3	Credit to Pvt. Sector as % of GDP	11.4	77.0	111.4	113.3	115.0	129.5	135.4	-
4	Foreign Liabilities of Business as								
	% of GDP	7.3	9.0	13.0	19.5	8.8	6.5	-18.5	
	Thailand								
1	Annual Growth in dometic a	26.8	15.5	18.0	22.7	26.9	23.1	14.0	-
2	Annual growth in M2	26.7	19.8	15.6	18.4	12.9	17.0	12.6	-
3	Cr. to Pvt Sector as % of GDP	83.1	89.1	98.6	111.2	128.4	138.8	100.0	
4	Foreign Liabilities of Business as % of GDP	6.4	6.0	6.9	11.7	20.3	24.3	23.3	

TABLE 5.4

RATIO BETWEEN GROWTH RATES OF G TO GDP

Country	1990	1996
Indonesia	45	55
Malaysia	80	136
Thailand	84	130

TABLE 5.5

CAPITAL INFLOWS IN THE SE ASIAN COUNTRIES (1989-96)

Country	1989	1990	1991	1992	1993	1994	1995	1996
Thailand								
FDI	2.46	2.82	2.02	1.91	1.46	0.95	1.25	1.28
Portfolio*	2.06	-0.04	-0.08	9.83	4.4	1.73	2.46	1.97
Others**	5.12	8.07	9.67	5.85	5.44	6.86	11.7	6.52
Total	9.64	10.85	11.61	8.59	11.3	9.54	15.41	9.77
Portfolio/FDI	0.83	-0.014	-0.039	0.43	3.01	1.82	1.97	1.54
Others/Total	0.53	0.74	0.83	0.68	0.48	0.72	0.76	0.67
Indonesia								
FDI	0.96	1.51	1.86	1.94	1.76	1.77	3.28	3.25
Portfolio*	-0.24	-0.13	-0.02	-0.1	1.59	3.26	3.09	4.5
Others**	3.24	4.83	5.3	4.84	1.91	-1.29	1.92	1.94
Total	3.96	6.21	7.14	6.68	5.26	3.74	8.29	9.69
Portfolio/FDI	-0.25	-0.08	0.01	-0.05	0.9	1.84	0.94	1.24
Others/Total	0.82	0.78	0.74	0.72	0.36	-0.34	0.23	0.25
Malaysia								
FDI	4.4	5.44	8.23	9.16	8.19	5.84	4.8	3.8
Portfolio	-0.28	-0.6	0.35	-1.98	-1.16	-2.22	-0.51	-0.63
Others	-0.68	-0.21	1.02	5.63	12.17	-2.59	3.78	4.87
Total	3.44	4.63	9.6	12.31	19.2	1.03	8.07	8.07
Portfolio/FDI	-0.06	-0.11	0.04	-0.21	-0.14	-0.38	-0.1	-
Others/Total	-0.19	-0.04	0.1	0.45	0.63	-2.51	0.47	-

TABLE 5.6

SELECTED INDICATORS OF CORPORATE FINANCING (1996)

Country	Debt to Equity Ratio		Ratio of Short Term Debt to Total Debt	
	Mean	Median	Mean	Median
Indonesia	1.88	1.83	0.54	0.57
Malaysia	1.18	0.90	0.64	0.70
Thailand	2.36	1.85	0.63	0.67

SOURCE: BANK FOR INTERNATIONAL SETTLEMENT (1997)

TABLE 5.7

Country	To property Sector (1997 end)
Indonesia	25 - 30%
Malaysia	30 - 40%
Thailand	30 - 40%

TABLE 5.8

ESTIMATES OF ACTUAL & PEAK NON-PERFORMING BANK LOANS IN THE SOUTH EAST ASIAN ECONOMIES

	THAILAND	INDONESIA	MALAYSIA
Jardine Flemming (1997)			
PNPL/TL	19.3	16.8	15.6
PNPL/GDP	20.0	10.8	22.9
Ramos (1998) Golman Sacks			
ANPL/TL	18.0	9.0	6.0
PNPL/TL	>25.0	>25.0	12.0 - 25.0
PNPL/GDP	40.0	16.0	17.0
Jen (1998) Morgan Stanley			
ANPL/TL	18.0	12.5	6.0
Peregrine (1997) including			
Financial Companies			
ANPL/TL	36.0	15.0	15.0
Erchweiler (1998) JP Morgan			
APNL/TL	17.5	11.0	7.5
BIS (1997) Official Estimates			
ANPL/TL	7.7	8.8	3.9

PNPL: PEAK NON-PERFORMING LOANS

ANPL: ACTUAL NON-PERFORMING LOAND

TL : TOTAL LOANS

TABLE 5.9

FINANCIAL STRENGTH RATING

COUNTRY	MID 1996	END 1996	MID 1997	END 199	End 1998
Indonesia	D	D	D	D	E
Malaysia	C +	C/C +	C/C +	D +	D
Thailand	C +	C +	C +	D	E +

NOTE: A: HIGHEST RATING
E: LOWEST RATING

Table 5.10

STOCK OF DEBT OWED TO FOREIGN PRIVATE CREDITORS 1992-1997 INDICATING MATURITY MISMATCH

	1992		1993		1994		1995		1996		1997 (Mid)	
Country	Total Debt	Short Term Debt	Total Debt	Short Term Debt	Total Debt	Short Term Debt	Total Debt	Short Term Debt	Total Debt	Short Term Debt	Total Debt	Short Term Debt
Indonesia	28.4	60.5	30.5	61.7	34.2	61.8	44.5	61.9	55.5	61.7	58.7	59.0
Malaysia	8.5	48.1	13.0	56.8	13.5	48.8	16.8	47.2	22.2	50.3	28.8	56.4
Thailand	23.0	69.0	29.6	72.1	43.4	71.0	62.8	69.4	70.1	65.2	69.4	65.7

SOURCE: BIS, THE MATURITY, SECTORAL & NATIONALITY DESTINATION OF INTERNATIONAL BANK LENDING, VARIOUS ISSUES

NOTE: SHORT TERM DEBT IMPLIES UPTO AND INCLUDING 1 YEAR MATURITY

TABLE 5.11

CURRENCY MISMATCHES IN 1997

Country	Short Term Debt	International Reserves	Debt-reserve Ratio	Short Term Debt/Total Debt
	($ bn)	($ bn)	(%)	(%)
Indonesia	34.66	20.34	1.70	24%
Malaysia	16.27	26.59	0.61	39%
Thailand	45.57	31.36	1.45	46%

TABLE 5.12

ASIAN EXCHANGE RATE BASKETS 1979-92

Currency	Constant	US $	YEN	R2/DW
MALASIAN RINGGIT	- 0.0003	0.78 a	0.07 a	0.79
	(0.0003)	(0.02)	(0.02)	2.19
INDONESIA'S RUPIAH	- 0.0018 b	0.95a	0.16a	0.44
	(0.0007)	(0.05)	(0.07)	2.04
THAILAND'S BAHT	- 0.0004	0.91a	0.05c	0.75
	(0.0003)	(0.02)	(0.03)	2.24

Note: Standard error in parenthesis

a: STATISTICALLY SIGNIFICANT AT 99% LEVEL

b: STATISTICALLY SIGNIFICANT AT 95% LEVEL

c: STATISTICALLY SIGNIFICANT AT 85% LEVEL

TABLE 5.13

EXTERNAL SECTOR PROBLEMS

	REER Over Valuation (Versus June 1987 to May 1997 Average)	Current A/c balance (% of GDP		Merchandise Exports (annual % growth)	
	June 1997	1995	1996	1995	1996
Indonesia	4.2	3.3	3.3	13.4	9.7
Malaysia	9.3	10.0	4.9	20.3	6.5
Thailand	6.7	7.9	7.9	23.1	0.5

TABLE 5.14

REAL EFFECTIVE EXCHANGE RATE 1990-96
(BASE 1990 AUG, END OF YEAR, HIGHER VALUES MEAN APPRECIATION)

Country	1990	1991	1992	1993	1994	1995	1996
Indonesia	97.40	99.60	100.80	103.80	101.00	100.50	105.10
Malaysia	97.00	96.9-	109.70	111.00	107.10	107.00	111.80
Thailand	102.20	99.00	99.70	101.90	98.30	101.70	107.60

SOURCE: CORSETTI, PESENTI, ROUBINI (1998)

TABLE 5.15

EXPORTS BY DESTINATION & IMPORTS BY ORIGIN, 1996
(values in percent)

Country	World Exports	Exports To			World Imports	Imports From		
	US$ mn	US	Japan	Asia	US $mn	US	Japan	Asia
Indonesia	49.814	16.0	27.8	25.4	42.292	10.3	23.6	27.7
Malaysia	78.246	18.2	13.4	46.8	78.422	15.5	24.5	34.6
Thailand	55.789	18	16.8	36.8	73.484	12.6	27.8	28.2

TABLE 5.16

Southeast Asian Export Growth in %

Country	Total Exports (US $)	
	1990-95	1996
Indonesia	12.1	9.7
Malaysia	20.3	5.8
Thailand	19.6	-1.3

Source: IFS, IMF and UN Trade Database

TABLE 5.17

Hourly Labour Costs in Apparel Manufacture (in US $)

Country	1990	1993	1995
Indonesia	0.16	0.28	0.33
Malaysia	0.56	0.77	1.59
Thailand	0.63	0.71	1.11

Source: Apparel Hourly Labour Cost, Werner International Inc., NY 1996

TABLE 5.18

Bilateral Trade Shares With Thailand, 1996

Countries	Exports To Thailand (as a % of Total)
SOUTH KOREA	2.0
INDONESIA	1.8
MALAYSIA	4.1
PHILIPPINES	3.8
SINGAPORE	5.7
TAIWAN	3.1
HONG KONG	1.0

TABLE 5.19
Currency Depreciation (Currency Units Per US$)

Dates	Indonesia (Rupiah)	Malaysia (Ringgit)	Thailand (Baht)
(Avg for month)			
1-Jun-96	2333	2.5	25.4
4-Jun-97	2428	2.52	24.7
30-Jul-97	2575	2.63	31.7
15-Oct-97	3575	3.15	37
28-Jan-98	11800	4.36	53.7
22-Apr-98	7950	3.77	3.93

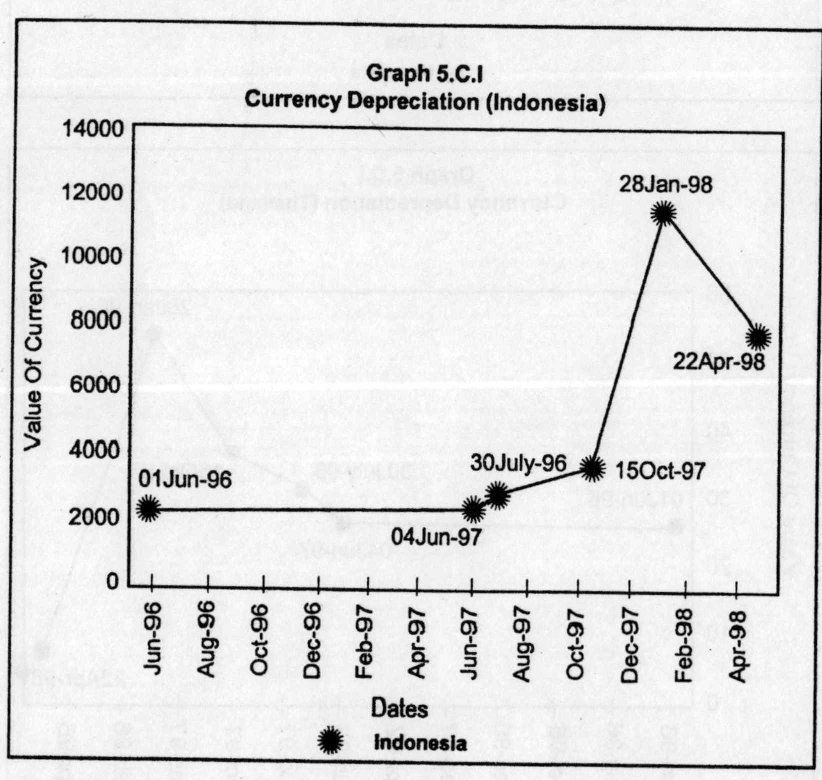

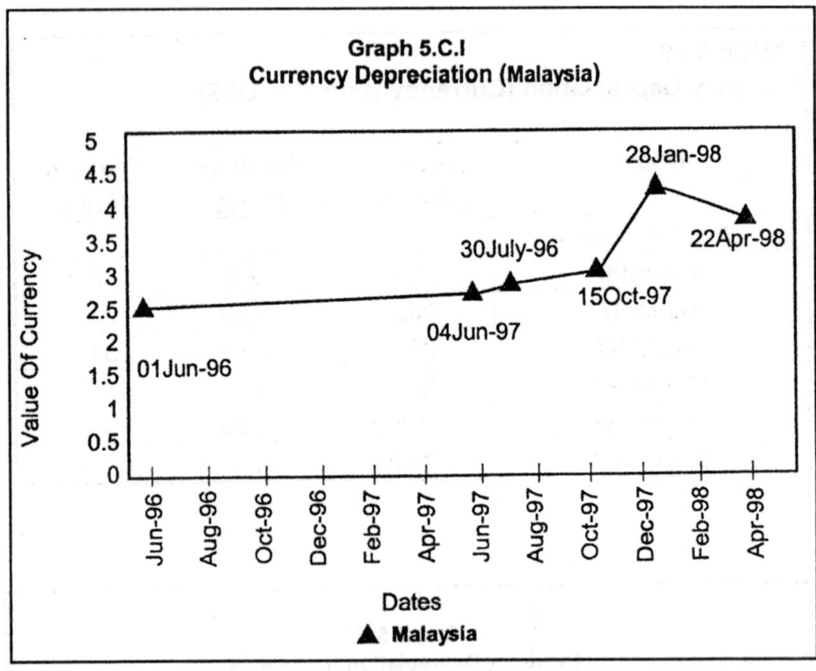
Graph 5.C.I
Currency Depreciation (Malaysia)
Value Of Currency
5
4.5
4
3.5
3
2.5
2
1.5
1
0.5
0
01Jun-96
04Jun-97
30July-96
15Oct-97
28Jan-98
22Apr-98
Jun-96
Aug-96
Oct-96
Dec-96
Feb-97
Apr-97
Jun-97
Aug-97
Oct-97
Dec-97
Feb-98
Apr-98
Dates
Malaysia

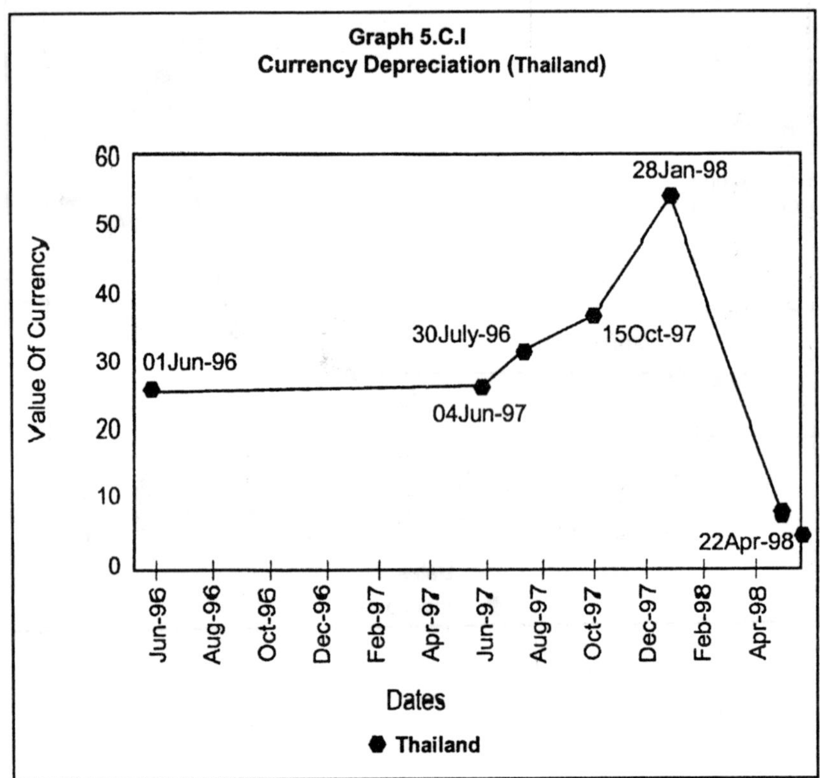
Graph 5.C.I
Currency Depreciation (Thailand)
Value Of Currency
60
50
40
30
20
10
0
01Jun-96
04Jun-97
30July-96
15Oct-97
28Jan-98
22Apr-98
Jun-96
Aug-96
Oct-96
Dec-96
Feb-97
Apr-97
Jun-97
Aug-97
Oct-97
Dec-97
Feb-98
Apr-98
Dates
Thailand

Table 5.20

Country	Crisis Index (IND)	Real Appreciation (RER)	Current Account (CA)	Lending Boom (LB)	Non-Performing Loans	Reserves adequacy (M2/RES)	Reserves adequacy (M1/RES)	Reserves adequacy (STD/RES)
Argentina	4.9	38.6	-1.9	16.5	9.4	351.0	108.2	147.8
Brazil	-0.5	75.8	-2.0	-26.3	5.8	345.9	66.8	78.3
Chile	-1.4	37.5	-1.7	24.1	1.0	188.2	41.9	53.3
China	7.6	4.9	0.8	6.9	14.0	828.9	334.0	26.7
Colombia	-9.1	26.6	-5	35.0	4.6	209.4	104.3	73.9
Crech Rep.	-19.5	50.7	-4.4	22.7	12.0	356.9	139.5	42.9
Hong Kong	5.7	31.8	-1.6	25.5	3.4	411.9	34.2	20.0
Hungry	-1.6	-38.8	-6.5	-56.5	3.2	167.1	83.3	52.3
India	5.7	-29.1	-1.2	-2.3	17.3	860.0	296.5	37.2
Indonesia	-38.3	17.5	-2.9	9.6	12.9	614.8	114.3	188.9
Jordan	9.8	6.1	-4.5	1.4	6.0	437.8	141.4	33.9
Korea	-38.6	11.1	-2.5	11.2	8.4	665.4	147.6	217.0
Malaysia	-38.8	19.9	-6.4	31.1	9.9	364.8	115.6	45.3
Mexico	10.9	8.9	-2.7	-10.9	12.5	444.8	129.3	142.9
Pakistan	11.4	-2.0	-5.3	-3.7	17.5	3369.9	1822.8	399.0
Peru	0.7	-20.4	-6.2	177.2	5.1	123.6	32.4	61.6
Phillippines	-29.8	38.9	-4.6	150.8	14.0	465.6	91.8	849.3
Poland	3.5	30.0	0.9	38.5	6.0	262.3	95.9	14.2
Singapore	-15.7	4.7	16.5	16.7	4.0	103.5	25.0	20.0
Sri Lanka	-1	17.7	-5.7	28.4	5.0	236.4	72.9	26.8
Taiwan	-11.4	-7.0	2.9	43.4	3.9	575.1	141.0	22.8
Thailand	-47.8	20.0	-7.2	58.0	13.3	380.5	43.3	121.5
Turkey	4.3	-16.1	-0.1	43.2	0.8	302.6	48.9	76.0
Venezuela	4.9	2.2	6.8	-51.5	3.8	102.4	58.5	28.2

Chart 5.1

Currency Crisis Staring Dates

Country	Currency Crisis	Country	Currency Crisis
Argentina	Jun-75	Malaysia	Jul-75
	February 1981*		August 1997*
	Jul-82		
	September 1986*	Mexico	Sep-76
	Apr-89		February 1982*
	Feb-90		December 1982*
			December 1994*
Bolivia	Nov-82		
	Novemeber 1983	Norway	Jun-73
	Sep-85		Feb-78
			May 1986*
Brazil	Feb-83		Dec-92
	November 1986*		
	Jul-89	Peru	Jun-76
	Nov-90		Oct-87
	Oct-91		
		The Phillippines	Feb-70
Chile	Dec-71		October 1983*
	Aug-72		Jun-84
	Oct-73		July 1997*
	Dec-73		
	Jan-76	South Korea	Jun-71
	Augut 1982		Dec-74
	Sep-84		Jan-80
			Oct-97
Columbia	March 1983*		
	February 19885	Spain	Feb-76
			July 1977*
			Dec-82
Crech Republic	May-97		Feb-86
			Sep-92
Denmark	May-71		May-93
	Jun-73		
	Nov-79	Sweden	Augut 1977
	Aug-93		Sep-81
			Oct-82
			Nov-92
Egypt	Jan-79		
	August 19889	Thailand	November 1978*
	Jun-90		Jul-81
			Nov-84

Country	Currency Crisis	Country	Currency Crisis
Finland	Jun-73		July 1997*
	Oct-82		
	November 1991*	Turkey	Aug-70
	September 1992*		Jan-80
			March 1994*
Greece	May-76		
	November 1990	Uruguay	December 1971*
	Jul-84		October 1982*
Indonesia	Nov-78	Venezuela	Feb- 84
	Apr-83		Dec-86
	Sep-86		Mar-89
	Aug-97		May-1994*
			Dec-95
Israel	Nov-74		
	Nov-77		
	Oct-1983*		
	Jul-84		

Chart 5.2
The Process Leading to The Crisis

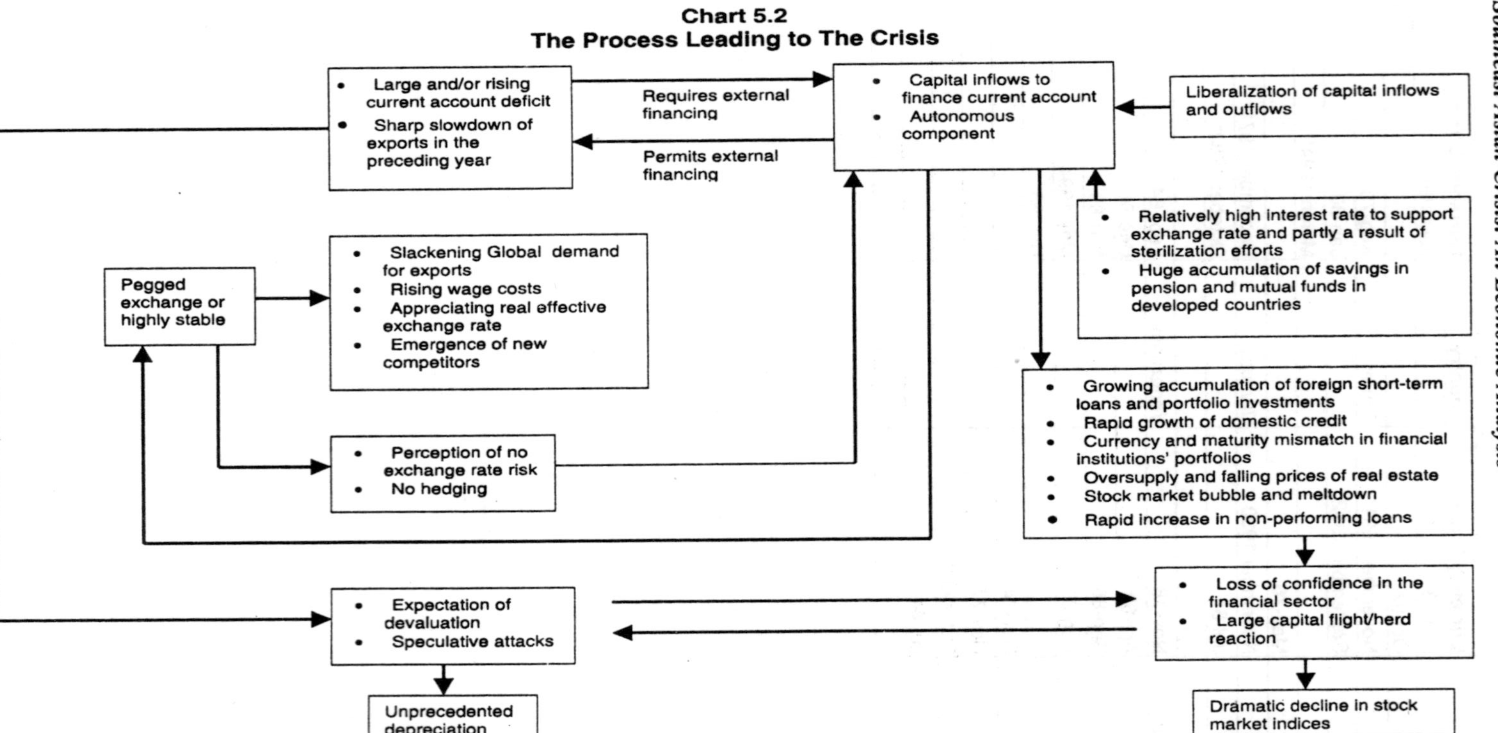

Source: Islam, Azizul (1999), Dynamics of Asian Economic Crisis and Selected Policy Implications in Barry Herman (ed), Global Financial Turmoil and reform : A United Nations Perspective, Washington DC, UN University Press.

CHART 5.3

Financial Flows, Financial Crisis, Financial Policy Needs

Contagion Factors Perceived in Selected Asian Economic in 1997

Country	Some similar domestic policy issues as in Thailand	Some international factors in common with Thailand
Hong Kong Special Administrative		
Region of China	No	Yes
Indonesia	Yes	Yes
Malaysia	Yes	Yes
Philippines	Yes	Yes
Republic of Korea	Yes	No
Singapore	No	Yes
Taiwan Province of China	No	Yes

SOURCE: BARRY HERMAN & KRISHNAN SHARMA, UN UNIV, 98

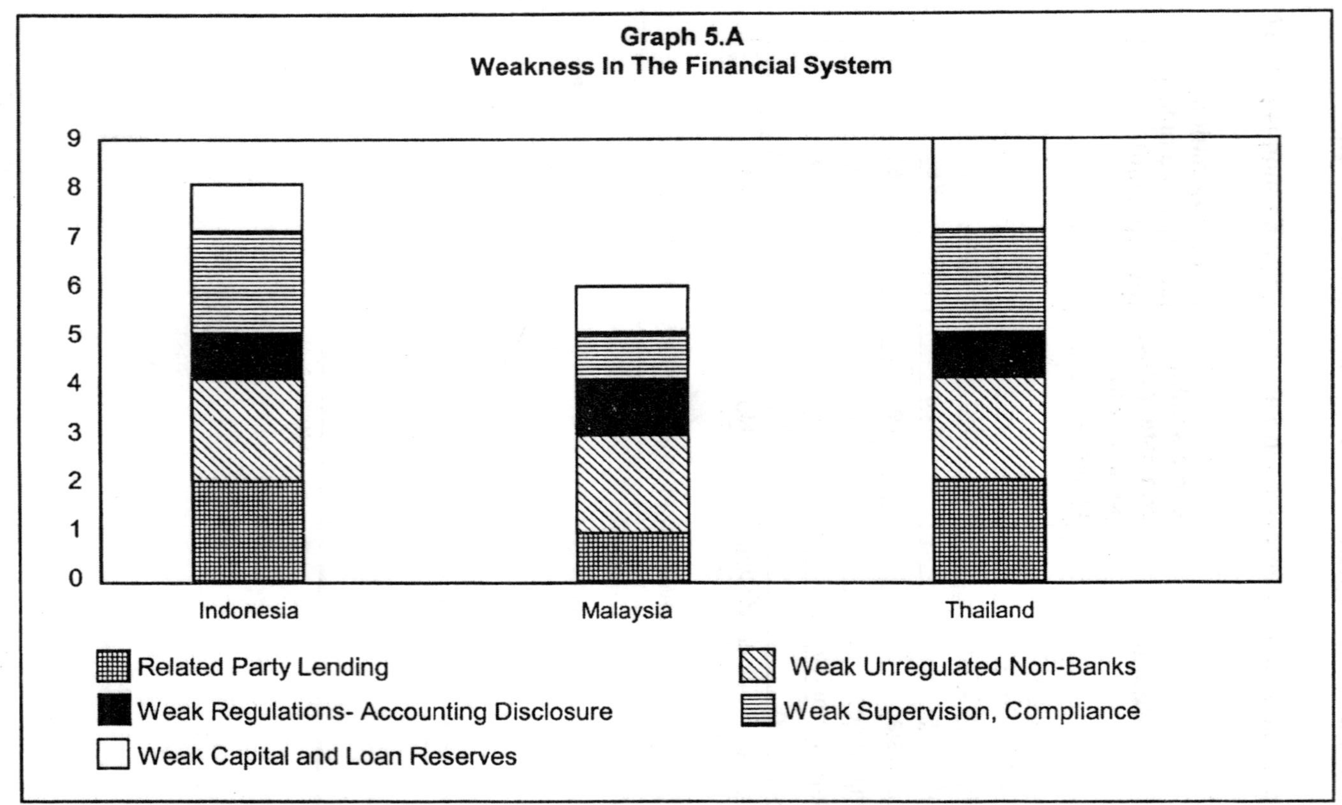
Graph 5.A
Weakness In The Financial System
9
8
7
6
5
4
3
2
1
0
Indonesia
Malaysia
Thailand
Related Party Lending
Weak Regulations- Accounting Disclosure
Weak Capital and Loan Reserves
Weak Unregulated Non-Banks
Weak Supervision, Compliance

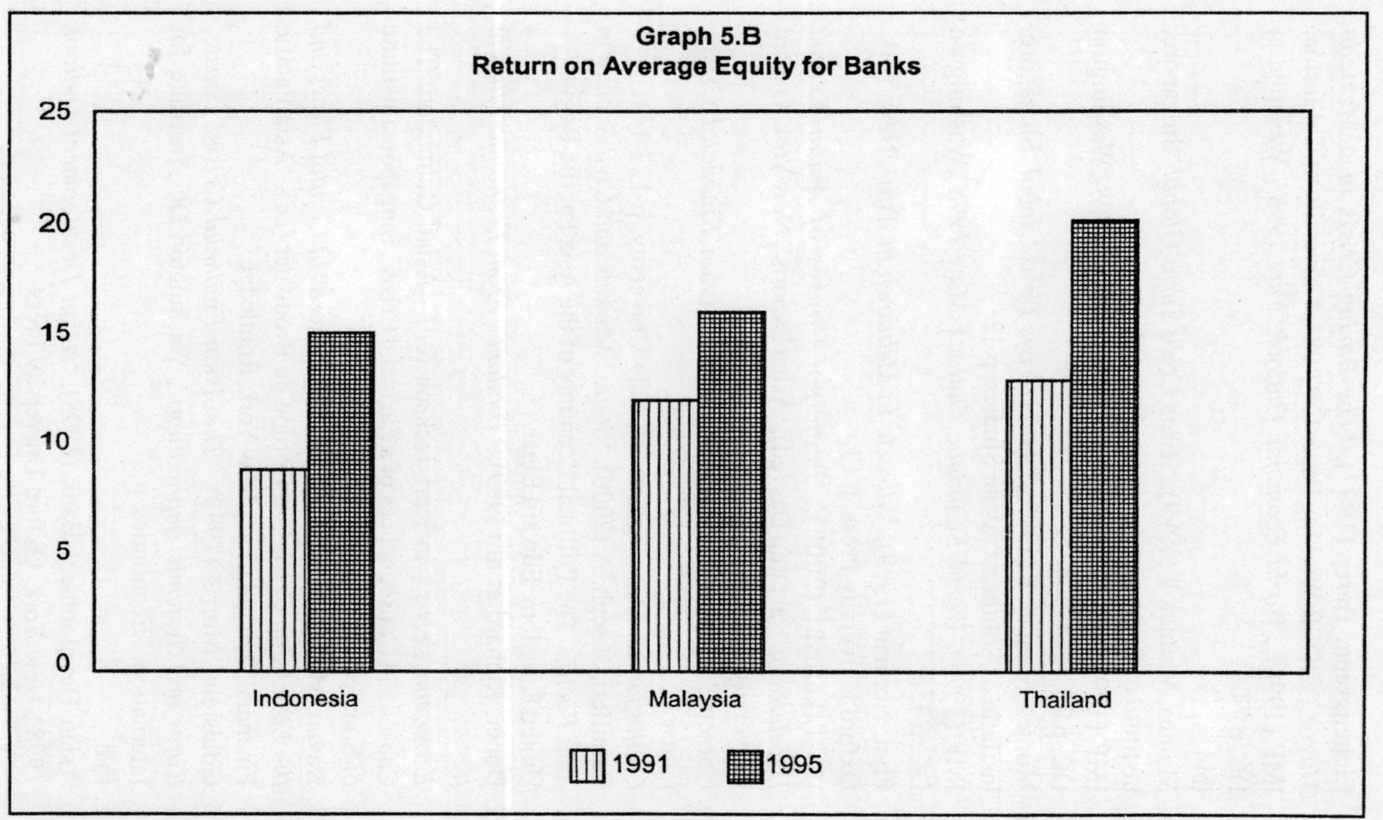

Graph 5.B
Return on Average Equity for Banks

References of Chapter 5

1. Eichengreen, Barry (1997), '*The Baring Crisis in a Mexican Mirror*', CIDER Working Paper C 97-084, University of California.
2. IMF (1998), '*World Economic Outlook, May 1998*', Washington DC, p 74.
3. Ibid.
4. Montes, Manuel. F (1999), '*Asian Crisis Turns Global*' Singapore, Institute of Southeast Asian Studies, p 9.
5. IMF (1998),'*World Economic Outlook May, 1998*',Washington DC, p 75.
6. Montes, Manuel. F (1999), '*Asian Crisis Turns Global*' Singapore, Institute of Southeast Asian Studies, p 12.
7. IMF (1998),'*World Economic Outlook May, 1998*',Washington DC, p 75.
8. Flyn, Norman (1999), '*Miracle to Meltdown in Asia*', New York, Oxford University Press, p 13.
9. Ito Takatoshi (2000), '*Principal Causes of Asian Export Deceleration*', in Dilip Das (ed), 'Asian Exports', New York, Oxford University Press, p 75.
10. Corsetti, Giancarlo et al (2000), '*The Asian Financial Crisis. Causes,*
Contagion and Consequences', Yale University, p 127-141.
11. Camilleri, Joseph. A (2000), '*States, Markets and Civil Society in Asia Pacific*. The Political Economy of the Asia Pacific Region', United Kingdom, Edward Elgar.
12. Doner, Richard et al (1999), '*Thailand: From Economic Miracle to*
Economic Crisis', in Karl Jackson (ed), 'Asian Contagion. The Causes and Consequences of a Financial Crisis', Singapore, Institute of Southeast Asian Studies.
13. Kawai, Masahiro (1999), '*Evolving Patterns of Capital Flows and the East Asian Crisis*', in Gordon de Brouwner (ed), 'Asia Pacific Financial Deregulation', New York, Routledge.
14. Goldstein, Morris (1998), '*The Asian Financial Crisis. Causes, Cures and Systemic Implications*', Washington DC, Institute for International Economics, p 37.
15. Ibid.
16. Asian Development Bank (1998), '*Asian Development Outlook 1998*', New York, Oxford University Press.

17. Islam, Azizul (1999), '*The Dynamics of Asian Economic Crisis and Selected Policy Implications'*, in Barry Herman (ed), 'Global Financial Turmoil and Reform. A UN Perspective', New York, United Nations University Press, p 55.
18. Goldstein, Morris (1998), '*The Asian Financial Crisis. Causes, Cures and Systemic Implications'*, Washington DC, Institute for International Economics, p 14.
19. Ibid.
20. Ito Takatoshi (2000), '*Principal Causes of Asian Export Deceleration'*, in Dilip Das (ed), 'Asian Exports', New York, Oxford University Press, p 109.
21. Hussain, Mumtaz and Steven Radelet (1999), *'Exports and Asia's Recovery'*, in 'Asia Competitiveness Report 1999' World Economic Forum, p 44.
22. Ibid.
23. IMF (1998), '*World Economic Outlook, May 1998'*, Washington DC.
24. Goldstein, Morris (1998), '*The Asian Financial Crisis. Causes, Cures and Systemic Implications'*, Washington DC, Institute for International Economics, p 17.
25. Asian Development Bank (1998), '*Asian Development Outlook 1998'*, New York, Oxford University Press.

Chapter 6

Crisis Management and Call for a NIFO

In the previous chapter, a number of factors that were responsible for the crisis in Southeast Asia were discussed. Various solutions were evolved to overcome the crisis. Indonesia and Thailand considered that the immediate recourse to the problem was approaching the IMF for a rescue package. Malaysia's Prime Minister Dr. Mahathir Mohamed decided on a more autocentric methodology to deal with the crisis without taking recourse to the IMF rescue package. Accordingly, strategies to combat the crisis, have been directed by the Fund through its conditionalities in Indonesia and Thailand. As against that in Malaysia, the policy measures have been self-directed and radical.

According to Krugman, neither of them really worked. He opines "the truth is that an observer without an axe to grind would probably conclude that none of the policies adopted either on or in defiance of the IMF's advice made much difference either way. Budget policies, interest rate policies, banking reform – whatever countries tried, just all the capital that could flee, did. And when there was no more money to run, the natural recuperative powers of the economies finally began to prevail. At best, the money doctors who purported to offer cures provided a helpful bedside manner; at worst there were like medieval physicians who prescribed bleeding as a remedy for all ills"[1].

Measures Adopted To Address The Issue Of Economic Crisis

In providing support to Thailand and Indonesia, the IMF was discharging the responsibilities prescribed in its Articles of Agreement. The IMF's Articles of Agreement call for the IMF to "give confidence to Members by making the general resources of the Fund temporarily available to them under adequate safeguards, thus providing them with an opportunity to correct maladjustments in their BOP without resorting to measures destructive of national and international prosperity". The transactions of Thailand and Indonesia with the Fund are presented in Charts 6.2 and 6.3.

Methodology of Loan Sanctioned and Disbursement

For countries seeking IMF assistance, adoption of a reform programme that restores macro economic stability and lays the foundation for sustainable growth is an indispensable element of the cooperative character of the IMF[2]. In fact, the premises on which the IMF Executive Board decides whether to support the country or not as well as the amount of support, is on the countries' BOP position and the strength of the countries' reform programme.

Just as any financial institution, which offers loan puts forward certain conditions, so does the IMF. In the case of the IMF, although it is the IMF staff that actually draws out the reform programme, the ownership of the reform programme always rests with the country itself. The borrowing country draws out the Letter of Intent wherein economic reform and policy intentions are stated. The country sets out on the task of executing and implementing such reforms. The IMF provides the financial resources and some technical expertise and endorsement.

The loans are not provided in one go. It is always in instalments. The disbursement of subsequent tranche's depends on the implementation of reform programme and the IMF's assessment of the same.

Conceptually, there is nothing odd about the lender imposing conditions on the borrower[3]. Banks the world over, impose restrictions on the use of the money they lend to households and companies. They also make suggestions regarding the methods to improve the borrower's repaying capacity. The same holds good at the macro level were a country's government as to agree to certain conditionalities before being sanctioned a loan from the IMF/WB.

However, the extent to which a borrower accepts or agrees to the conditionalities imposed upon the lender will depend upon the urgency of the borrower. In the case of the two Southeast Asian countries seeking IMF assistance, the need was very high. They were in urgent need of resources to put their house in order.

Framework of the IMF Supported Reform Programme

In the absence of more palatable alternatives, particularly in the critical months immediately following the financial meltdown, the worst hit economies turned to the IMF for assistance. In return, the IMF exacted a heavy price[4]. The outflow of forex had to be stopped and short-term debts had to be rolled over and rescheduled. There was little option for the crisis stricken countries. Since both these countries had long been acting on the IMF/WB guidelines of – export oriented industrialization, financial liberalization, increased privatisation and maintaining low budget deficit as well as tight money policies, the new reformed package was just an extension of the same. In fact, it sought to accelerate the twin processes of financial deregulation and trade liberalization.

The IMF supported programmes in Thailand and Indonesia revolved around three areas – monetary and exchange rate policy, fiscal policy and financial restructuring[5].

Fiscal Policy

While the IMF realized that the fiscal policy was not the cause of the crisis, adjustment and balance therein was necessary to support adjustment, even though this may result in an adverse effect on demand. Such an assessment was the basis for fiscal adjustments recommended in Thailand and Indonesia. The extent of fiscal adjustments depended on the extent of the current account deficit. The basic idea here is that current account deficit was to be brought down through reduced usage of forex. This in turn can be achieved either through reduced public sector or private sector activity. The formed seemed a better option and hence the IMF insisted on austerity in the budget.

Monetary and Exchange Rate Policy

The forex market stabilization is the primary task of monetary policy. Interest rates are set so as to restore confidence in holding the local currency. Consideration is given to both the net domestic assets of the banking system and net foreign assets, components of the monetary aggregates, the latter being captured in the programme by setting a floor on net international reserves.

The interest rates are kept high to reduce currency market instability. The reversal of capital flows itself pushes up interest rates and this is endorsed by raising official rates. Therefore, it is necessary to make it attractive to hold the local currency. Once confidence is restored, interest rates returns to normal levels. The argument against a low interest rate is that it would help local currency to fuel the exchange rate weakness and result in inflation. Forex market instability and inflation can cause a breakdown in the external trading arrangement. Thus, in short till the currency stabilizes, interest rates are kept high, later they are cut when currencies appreciate.

Financial Sector

Restructuring the financial sector is at the centre of reform efforts. The following steps were taken in designing these reforms[6].

1. Assess the true state of the various financial institutions – which are solvent but suffering liquidity problems and which are insolvent? This assessment guides decisions about suspending or curtailing the operations of particular institutions.
2. Develop rehabilitation plans for solvent institutions, recognising that public funding may be required. Public funding should be forthcoming only when two criteria's are met: Owners have their equity reduced, perhaps to zero, and management is changed. Institutions must provide plans for building up capital to acceptable levels.
3. Build a more effective financial sector infrastructure - This means improving supervision and prudential standards, ensuring

banks meet capital requirement, ensuring adequate provisions for bad loans, limiting related party lending, publishing comprehensive and timely financial information and ensuring that insolvent institutions are dealt with promptly.

Thailand's Reform Programme

The announcement of the Central Bank of Thailand to abandon the baht's peg to the US $ on July 2, 1997 sent ripples around Southeast Asia particularly Indonesia, Malaysia and Philippines. The immediate reaction of the monetary authorities was to intervene in the forex markets and/or by raising short-term interest rates. By the end of July, exchange rates seemed to stabilize but there was great scepticism regarding the course of economic policy in Thailand in particular and the forex markets future development in general.

There seemed some respite to the uncertainty when on July 29, the Thai government and the IMF announced that a discussion on a comprehensive economic rehabilitation plan was being undertaken. On August 5, the government of Thailand announced a comprehensive reform package designed in conjunction with the IMF[7]. The package included – the suspension of the operation of 42 ailing financial companies, a pledge to maintain foreign reserves of atleast $ 23 bn and a promise to achieve a balanced budget, as a contribution to which the Value Added Tax was increased from 7 to 10% as of August 16, and cuts were pledged in the next years' budget along with price increases in public utilities. The current account deficit was to be reduced from 8% of GDP in 1996 to 5% in 1997 and 3% in 1998.

The IMF and a group of countries in Asia and the Pacific led by Japan and including Australia, along with ADB and WB made a commitment of a ***loan package amounting to $ 17.2 bn on August 20, 1997***. This loan was to be made available in the form of medium term loans with 3 – 5 years maturity over a 3-year period. In addition to the above, the Japanese commercial banks agreed to roll over about 80% of their short-term loans to Thai enterprises. The roll over of these loans was crucial as these banks held about 50% of the country's $ 89 bn in total foreign debt, as well as a substantial portion of the short- term debt. Chart 6.1 summarises the chronological highlights of financial assistance to Thailand.

Following the economic crisis, there was a political crisis in Thailand. Prime Minister Chavalit Yongchaiyudt and had to step down due to a loss of public confidence in November 1997. His government was replaced by one headed by Prime Minister Chuan Leekpai. The new government carried no baggage of having to defend itself against blame for the crisis[8]. However, there was considerably debate as to what the most appropriate reform package would be. The government felt bound to implement the IMF package and to announce publicly its commitment. Within Thailand it was widely criticised and behind the scenes the government too lobbied to have it modified[9]. The first six months of the crisis were filled with finger pointing. By early 1998, Thailand was addressing structural challenges of economic and financial reform.

The IMF packaging was essentially similar in structure to that proposed in Latin America previously. ***Highlights from Letters of Intent and Financial Sector Restructuring for Economic Recovery (FRER) package are given below***.

Fiscal Reforms in Thailand

In the financial year 1997-98, consolidated public sector deficit was targeted at 1% of GDP. This was however, increased to 3% subsequently. Fiscal deficit was to be kept under control through raising VAT from 7% to 10%, increasing fuel and luxury taxes and sharply reducing government spending. Massive cuts in operative budget and further cuts in investments on infrastructure were to be effected[10].

Monetary Reforms adopted in Thailand

he monetary authority vacillated in their approaches to monetary and exchange rate policies[11]. At times the Central Bank credit increased, acting as lenders of last resort and paying off depositors, occasionally trying to lower interest rates by selling their own and borrowed international reserves to limit outflows on the exchange rate. At such times, obviously the Central Bank was trying to support weak financial institutions. At other times, Central Bank credit was tightened to limit depreciation and outflows and to rebuild reserves.

In Thailand in the first half of 1997, the Central Bank increased its credit to failing non-banks by about 66%. A similar amount of credit was provided for the rest of the year. Infact had international reserves not fallen, monetary base would have doubled. The money base rose only by 16% inspite of massive increase in the Central Bank credit. The money market interest rates rose sharply (10.5% to 12.5% p.a.) despite the large increase in Central Bank credit. However, by 1998, the Central Bank reduced its net credit and exchange rate began to appreciate and interest rates declined.

Commitments were made through Letters of Intent to maintain reserve money growth at about 6.5% during 1998. The government decided to allocate credit to the priority non-bank corporate sector, especially exporters, agricultural producers and small borrowers. Foreign reserves were to be maintained at $ 23 bn.

As far as the external targets were concerned, current account adjustments proceeded faster than expected. There was a surplus in the current account by early 1998. Hence, the large capital outflows that caused the crisis were now offset by inflows. By end 1998, the Bank of Thailand's outstanding forward and swap obligations were expected to unwind to about US$ 9 bn. Also there was roll over of short-term credit lines by Japanese Banks that helped evolve a favourable capital account.

Financial Sector Reforms undertaken in Thailand

a) Asset Disposal of Closed Financial Companies: The Bank of Thailand temporarily suspended operations of 16 and 42 financial companies on June 27 and August 5, 1997 respectively. In October, the government announced new laws governing the regulation and supervision of financial institutions. They included – amendment to and increases in Bank of Thailand supervision of financial institutions, establishment of Financial Sector Restructuring Authority (FSRA) and the Asset Management Corporation. The FSRA closed

56 of the 58 suspended financial companies on December 8, 1997 and a programme for their asset disposal was worked out.

b) To strengthen the financial system, the Thai authority took over four medium sized commercial banks, two small commercial banks and a number of financial companies. The basic idea here was to strengthen the financial system by restructuring and recapitalising and ultimately privatise them.

Financial institutions were to be encouraged to set up capitalise and fund private asset management corporations. Capital support facilities were provided to financial institutions that were viable so as to recapitalise them and help them resume normal but prudent lending. Capital adequacy ratios were set so that lending remained within prudential limits.

Strict rules on loan classification and provisioning came into effect on December 31, 1997 and were gradually upgraded by the end of the year 2000. Both domestic and foreign private investment was encouraged into domestic financial sector. Also the liabilities of the Financial Institutions Development Fund were restructured into government guaranteed bonds with medium and long-term maturities and lower interest rates. The imputed interest costs of financial sector restructuring were to be incorporated into the Central Government budget.

An independent commission was appointed to consider ways and means to restructure the Bank of Thailand. A legal regulatory and institutional framework was set-up for the supervision of financial institutions. Finally, a self financed and limited deposit insurance scheme was to eventually replace the present general guarantee. All these measures were taken on the financial sector front. Chart 6.5 summarises the financial restructuring measures agreed upon with the IMF.

The economic policies and measures proposed by Thailand were similar to the liberalization policies that were launched by the Bank of Thailand since 1990. The only difference was the speed, coverage and intensity of the reform process.

Reforms in Indonesia

As an immediate response to the crisis the Indonesian government on August 31 1997, limited forward foreign exchange selling against the rupiah by domestic banks to non-resident customers to $ 5 million per customer. It also limited outstanding position in the forward exchange market to about $ 5 million per bank. These decisions were aimed at limiting speculative activities. However, they caused a backlash in stock and forex markets where such measures were considered as a possible reversal of 'market friendly economic policies'[12].

The tune of responses changed by the first week of September. On September 3, the Government of Indonesia announced new economic policies to reform the domestic financial sector and attract inflows of external capital to the country. These included the elimination of the 49% limit on foreign purchases of new initial public offerings and measures to foster the merger or liquidation of insolvent banks. The government cut back on large infrastructural projects inorder to improve budgetary balance and contain the current account deficit.

As a reward for this first round of reforms, on October 31, the IMF announced a special international rescue package for Indonesia. Chart 6.1 gives a chronological account of the ***financial assistance to Indonesia***. It consisted of a first line of financing of the order of ***$ 23 bn and*** an additional second line of defence of about ***$ 14 bn***. Break-up of the sources of the loans is presented in Table 6.1.

The policies dictated by the IMF were similar to those imposed in Thailand: Tight monetary policy (including high interest rate to attract foreign investment); closing of unviable financial institutions; trade liberalization (including tariff reduction in specific industries); investment liberalization and privatisation of public enterprises.

The announcement of the first IMF package brought about an immediate strengthening of the rupiah in the first few days of November. By December, the rupiah began to slide again. There were two reasons for the same. Firstly, despite a package of US$ 35 – 40 bn being announced a mere US$ 3 bn was actually released. Secondly, the speculation about the ill health of President Suharto was rife and he not attending two international summits on health grounds fanned it. Moreover, there was no clear indication of who the successor would be. Thirdly, the IMF package insisted on fiscal and monetary austerity, and structural reforms that were very difficult to implement for political reasons at a time when the social impact of the crisis was being manifest in widespread unemployment and poverty.

In ***January 1998, the IMF drew up a new $ 43 bn*** package tied to even more restrictive requirements, including the lifting of subsidies and the ending of state support for a range of strategic industries[13]. The President on March 1, openly stated in the Parliament that the IMF's austerity measures were not working and that a more appropriate set of reforms had to be implemented. In April 1998, yet another agreement was produced in the wake of widespread riots and unrest in the country. This time there was a relaxation of some of its previous conditions and an agreement on indefinite delay in the lifting of food and fuel subsidies. It was also agreed upon to release more funds.

Despite the agreed programme and the likelihood expanded international financial assistance the economic situation worsened after April 1998[14]. The increasingly desperate need to restructure sizeable unhedged private foreign borrowings, the growing fragility of the financial system due to poor regulatory and legal foundations, an apparent reluctance by the government to implement policies agreed upon with the IMF, an ageing leader with no clear successor and spectacular wealth accumulation through 'KKN' (the Indonesia acronym for corruption, cronyism and nepotism); and social unrest [14]all contributed to the same. By May 1998 on account of the increase in public and student unrest the President Suharto resigned and appointed Habibie in his place.

The social and political disturbances had huge ramifications on the economy. The GDP declined by 10 – 12% (negative growth) in 1998, and inflation increased by about 80%. The exchange rate collapsed from Rp 2500 to the US$ to Rp 8000 in May 1998 and further to Rp 16000 by mid June 1998. Interest rates were as high as 60%, imports fell by 20% and export growth slowed down.

In June, the April Agreement was yet again modified although the basic framework remained the same. ***The major reforms undertaken through the April and June Agreements were as under*:**

Fiscal Reforms in Indonesia

A central feature of the April and June programme was the limitation of the budget deficit to a level that could be offset by additional foreign financing. With the deepening of the crisis, the pressure on the budget and fiscal management increased. In fact, the exchange rate depreciation, falling tax revenues, decline in oil prices and high cost of bank restructuring brought about a rise in the fiscal deficit. Over and above all this, a social safety net had to be provided on account of the impact the crisis had on unemployment and poverty. The decline in oil prices were to reduce the government revenue by about 2% of GDP i.e. government revenue as percentage of GDP reduced from 16.2% in 1997-98 to 14.1% in 1998-99. To make up for this, the government raised funds by divesting shares in twelve state companies. This increased revenue by about 1.6% of GDP. The increase in expenditure of social safety net programme like provision of food, fuel, electricity, medicine and expenditure on labour intensive works targeted at the poor was to be financed by postponing major infrastructure projects and external financing as well assistance from the United Nations World Food Programme.

Monetary Reforms Introduced in Indonesia

In tune with the IMF's requirements a tight monetary policy was adopted. This was considered necessary to stabilize exchange rates and reduce inflation. However, short-term interest rates rose to over 50% by mid 1998 and this crippled the already stressed corporate sector[15]. The monetary programme also concentrated on reduction of the bank credit that had grown rapidly. For this purpose limits on net domestic assets (NDA) were placed. Limits were also placed on net international reserves (a minimum amount was agreed upon). The base money and NDA was by and large held constant during the second half of 1998 to curtail the fall of the rupiah and check inflation.

During the initial period of the crisis, the Central Bank had sharply increased the domestic credit, largely to support weak financial institutions (and their depositors) when foreign credits and deposits were withdrawn and borrowers suspended debt service. There was an increase in base money (largest in Indonesia in the region), that was offset by reserve losses. The depreciation was also the sharpest in Indonesia. Later, after a period of reduced outflows and tighter domestic credit the exchange rate appreciated and interest rate fell. To enhance the effectiveness of monetary management Bank Indonesia switched over from a system in which interest rate on Central Bank paper (SBIs) were set administratively, to an auction system for these instruments[16]. This system became the main method of conducting open market operations.

Financial Sector Reforms in Indonesia

Since the crisis had hit the banking sector adversely, it seems only natural that top priority was accorded to the evolving of a comprehensive solution to restructure it. This was essential as the performance of the corporate sector depends on the performance of the banking sector.

As in the case of Thailand, weak banks were recapitalised, merged or effectively closed down. Portfolio reviews by international accounting firms were used as criteria for the same. However, a commitment was made to guarantee all depositors and creditors.

The Indonesia's Bank Restructuring Agency (IBRA) that became operational in February 1998 took up the responsibility of overseeing a large number of banks and imposing tight prudential restrictions and other limitations on them[17]. In early March, new standards for loan classifications and loan loss provisioning were adopted. In early April, the IBRA took control of several banks and terminated operations of some of the smaller ones according to a well-defined and uniformly applied criterion. An asset management company was established to recover whatever possible from the assets of closed or supervised institutions.

The IBRA concluded reviews of about 50 banks by July 1998 and progress was made in the task of restructuring troubled banks and resolving their stock of bad debts. The problem of scarcity of imports and pre-shipment export finance was also looked into. This was of particular importance, as otherwise the non-oil export earnings would be adversely affected. Bank Indonesia established a collateral facility with 10 foreign banks to ensure that country risk is not a barrier to the confirmation of loans and credits. The WB also provided a technical assistance to the Bank of Indonesia to facilitate trade financing for developing schemes that will support renewed provision of pre-shipment trade finance by Indonesian banks. Chart 6.5 summarises the financial restructuring measures agreed upon with the Fund.

The government of Indonesia and Bank Indonesia with the assistance of ADB also reviewed the portfolios of the three largest private banks and several other banks too. The basic idea here was to help establish their financial credentials and assist them to regain access to trade facilities and interbank lines. Bank Indonesia and the Ministry of Finance provided a two-tier capital, generally in the form of subordinated loans as well as entered into discussions with foreign banks for possible investments in Indonesia's banking sector.

Reforms in Malaysia

As mentioned in Chapter 4 has never undergone any structural reform programme of the IMF-WB combined. In the post Asian crisis period too Malaysia did not approach the IMF for official support.

Justification for not approaching the IMF

Two important reasons can be found. The first reason why Malaysia did not seek IMF assistance was that the IMF would have forced the government to commit to a reform programme with severe repercussions on the native community by closing down many of the bumiputra owned companies and institutions. It may be noted here that the Prime Minister Mahathir is looked upon as a crusader for the native bumiputeras. To quote Mahathir "I thought that resorting IMF would not be good for the economy in the first place and would weaken our position to the point were we would lose control over our economy and also our policies"[18].

A second and equally important reason for not approaching the IMF is that even prior to the crisis Malaysia was less vulnerable than its Southeast Asian neighbours (See Chart 6.6). External and short-term debts were relatively lower; this reflected that there were more controls on short- term borrowings. The banks too were in better shape, with a lowest reported share of non-performing assets and among the highest capital adequacy ratios among the crisis countries.

Notwithstanding the fact that Malaysia refrained from seeking IMF assistance, some of the measures implemented to combat the crisis were similar to those in Thailand and Indonesia while others were radical and unique.

Non Acceptance of a Crisis Situation in Malaysia

The initial response of the Malaysian government to the outbreak of the currency crisis was one of denial[19]. The Malaysian policy makers considered the crisis to be a passing phenomena and squarely blamed the currency speculators to have caused the same. Prime Minister Mahathir at the IMF and WB meeting in Hong Kong on September 20, 1997 remarked that currency trading was unnecessary, unproductive and immoral. He squarely blamed the likes of George Soros, American financier for indulging in speculative activities and trying to destabilize the economy. He called for international cooperation to tame speculators ("ferocious beasts") and to control the activities of hedge funds.

As a punishment to the speculators initiatives were taken to intervene directly in the share market. On August 27, the Kuala Lumpur Stock Exchange (KLSE) banned short selling of 100 blue chip stocks.

This implies selling of shares not yet owned with the intention of buying them later at a cheaper price to enable completion of the deal at a profit. Other restrictions included – rules to discourage selling of stocks, sellers were required to deliver physical share certificates to their brokers before selling, and settlement period was reduced from 5 to 2 days. On September 3, the Prime Minister unveiled a plan to use funds from the Employees Provident Fund to prop up share crisis by buying stocks from Malaysian shareholders, but not foreigners, at a premium to prevailing prices.

Unfortunately, these moves did not work well. There was a massive sell off of stocks on KLSE inspite of the above controls. Moreover, the government's intervention in the stock markets was seen as an inability on the part of the BNM to manage the crisis.

However, Mahathir's unorthodox policy was immediately changed when the proof came in that it was not working. On September 4, the ban on short selling was withdrawn. In September many grandiose projects – the huge uncontroversial Bakun Dam, a new airport and part of new administrative capital amounting to US$ 10bn were postponed. In fact apart from the postponement of the infrastructural projects no other major reforms were announced. Probably, the only other ones, which came close enough, was reducing of the current account deficit through selective import duties and a 'buy Malaysia' campaign.

Even on October 17, 1997 when the Budget of 1998 was unveiled no coherent programme of reforms was announced. The forecasted growth rate was unchanged at 7% for 1998 although the economic situation started to deteriorate. The ringgit had lost 25% of its value and yet the government continued to treat the crisis as a passing phenomena. Rather than announce a reform programme, Malaysia made an offer of RM 3.4 bn (US $ 1bn) to Thailand and Indonesia each as part of the IMF sponsored rescue package!

Change in Stance

It was only by December 1997 that the first step to the admission of a crisis and the need to tackle the same was made. The economic scenario looked bleak as total domestic loans stood at 160% of GDP by the end of the year, and M2 increased by over 30% between July and December 1997.

Dr. Mahathir announced the formation of a National Economic Association Council (NEAC) to act as the pivotal body in economic policy making. ***On December 5, 1997 the Deputy Prime Minister and Finance Minister Anwar Ibrahim unveiled a major economic policy statement involving a series of fiscal austerity measures.*** It may be mentioned here that in November that year Michel Camdessus had visited Kuala Lumpur had advised the Prime Minister on fiscal austerity. *Thus, the new policy of fiscal austerity was announced following such advice.*

The new policy abandoned the aggressive high growth policies pursued earlier. ***The key elements of the package were***[20]:

1. Cutting government spending by 18%.
2. Postponing indefinitely all public sector investment projects that were still in the pipeline.
3. Stopping new overseas investment by Malaysian firms.
4. Freezing new share issues and company restructuring.
5. Cutting salaries of government ministers by 10%.

The overall economy growth was now forecast to be a more realistic 4-5% as against the earlier rate of 7%. Earlier the Prime Minister had said that the Vision 2020 plans would be continued. Hence, the September policy announcement was definite change from the initial stance..

The above measures were strikingly similar in character to the IMF sponsored package as far as fiscal policy was concerned. A key missing element was the raising of the domestic interest rates. However, what did not happen in a formal manner, was looked after by the market mechanism. The flow of ringgit funds from the onshore to the offshore market resulted in an increase in domestic interest rates. This contributed to the acceleration of economic contraction and aggravated the difficulties in Malaysia. By February 1998, the interbank one-month rate stood at 12.2% up from 9% in July 1997. The average base-lending rate of commercial banks and financial companies too increased from 10.2% and 12.1% to 13.2% and 15.3% respectively during the same period[21]. The economy contracted by 4.8% in the first half of 1998.

Further Reforms introduced in Malaysia

In August 1998, the NEAC announced another economic agenda, the six objectives of which are[22]:

1. Stabilizing the ringgit, reducing over dependence on the US dollar,increasing external reserves and adopting a balanced interest rate policy.

2. Restoring market confidence by improving transparency and the regulatory environment, assisting industries and companies in trouble, adopting more liberal market based policies, increasing consistency in government policies and improving public relations.

3. Maintaining financial market stability by resolving the NPLs in the banking system, encouraging bank mergers, and establishing an asset management company to take over the NPLs from banking institutions,
recapitalising the banking sector, implementing a credit plan target, strengthening the regulatory framework in the capital market, and developing the private debt securities market:

4. Strengthening the economic fundamentals, in particular investment quality, productivity, price stability, BOPs, fiscal position and monetary policy to avoid unnecessary business failures:

5. Continuing the social economic agenda of poverty amelioration, bumiputra equity ownership, tertiary education, employment opportunities and foreign workers.

6. Revitalising the affected sectors such as manufacturing construction, property, motorcar industry and infrastructure.

Currency Controls imposed in Malaysia

On September 1, 1998 the government imposed a wide range of direct capital and exchange controls (details are presented in Chart 6.7). The main objective of the measures was to regain monetary policy independence by containing speculation on the ringgit through the elimination of the offshore ringgit market and to stabilize the short-term capital flows. The ringgit was effectively withdrawn from the international financial system by declaring all offshore ringgit inconvertible i.e. without value. The ringgit now, was freely convertible only in Malaysia. This was a landmark in the economic history of Southeast Asia, as till then the region had flaunted the advantages of convertibility as well as the lack of exchange controls. The IMF and its supporters disapproved of such unorthodox policies and considered them regressive.

The Malaysian Prime Minister considered this measure as an alternative in the absence of an effective financial architecture that would limit volatility of international capital movements and exchange rates.

In an interview to FEER, June 24, 1999, Mahathir has pointed out "we looked around, we looked at Chile, we looked at China and at a number of other countries which were poorer than us but were not attacked by the currency traders. And we discovered that the difference between them and us is that we allow our currency to be traded, whereas they keep a tight control over their currency ......by preventing currency traders from getting hold of your currency, you can stabilize the economy......... most of our money was in Singapore. What Singapore did was to offer very high interest rates, siphoning off all the money. Banks had no money to lend. And people were of course attracted by the high interest rates or they have a loss of confidence in Malaysia's banks and kept their money with branches of foreign banks in Singapore. There was atleast 32 bn ringgit in Singapore".

Hence, Mahathir thought it to be a master move to impose capital controls and declare all offshore ringgit as longer legal tender if within one month the money is not moved back into Malaysia. With this one move, Mahathir capped all offshore transactions.

The immediate effect of such an announcement was the repatriation of RM 10 bn from offshore banks/foreign exchange markets. Trading of Malaysian stocks and shares on Singapore OTC ceased. The Central Bank of Malaysia could now regain sovereignty over the monetary policy and it pushed the interest rates down. The exchange rate was pegged at RM 3.8 to the US $. The government could inject new liquidity into the economy to reflate it.

Other Exchange Control Measures

The other aspects of the exchange control policy applied to such items as[23]:

1. The external accounts (approval is required for transfer of funds)

2. Authorised depository institutions (for purchases and sales of ringgit financial assets)

3. Trade settlements (all settlements are to be made in foreign currency)

4. Limits on the amount of foreign currencies held by travelers (a maximum of RM 1000 per person); no limit on import of foreign currencies; export of foreign exchange limited to a maximum of RM 10,000.

Financial Reforms brought about in Malaysia

Malaysia imposed controls on portfolio investment and short-term capital that was now required to remain in Malaysia for at least 12 months. This is obviously designed to reduce volatility of hot money and to bring about more orderly trading in the Malaysian stock market.

In October 1998, (in keeping with the August policy objectives), the asset management company, Danaharta, issued RM 15 bn in 10 year zero coupon bonds guaranteed by the government to help purge the NPL's, estimated at 11.4% of total loans, from the banking system.

Danamodal Nasional Bhd. a special purpose vehicle injected RM 16 – to recapitalise banking institutions through the issue of irredeemable, non-cumulative preference shares (INCPS) and Exchangeable Subordinated Capital loans (ESC). In addition, a Corporate Debt Restructuring Committee was to raise RM 5.5 bn to assist 23 troubled Malaysian companies while the Infrastructure Development Corporation was to issue 15 year bonds with a nominal value of RM 10 bn, guaranteed by the government and that by the future income of infrastructure projects.

Review of currency control and financial sector reforms

The exchange controls provided a breathing space to resurrect the financial institutions in Malaysia. Although, such controls ran contrary to orthodoxy and many observers' predicted severe consequences, the results were actually **positive**[24].

1. Interest rate spreads over the US federal funds rates fell. It had risen to over 12% in July 1997 and by January 1999 it was in tune with the US federal funds rate at about 5%. The overall balance of payments continued to strengthen, reflecting a steeper decline in imports than in exports, in view of the real depreciation of the ringgit and weak domestic demand. Net portfolio capital outflows were contained and foreign exchange reserves to increase. It should also be kept in mind that substantial amounts of capital outflows had already taken place prior to the imposition of the controls, and reserves had stabilized. The short term capital account recorded a substantial net outflow of capital overall in1998 (RM 21.7 bn, compared with a net outflow of RM 11.3 bn in 1997 and a net inflow of RM 10.3 bn in 1996), but short term outflows stabilized in the last quarter, following the implementation of the 12 month holding period for portfolio investment effective from September 1998.

2. Forex reserves increased by $ 10 bn between September 1998 and October 1999.

3. Offshore activities, especially in Singapore, dried up reducing the potential pressure from an organised parallel market.

4. The stock market and the capital market reacted positively, rising immediately after the controls were introduced and outperforming Thailand's index.

Also, the overall process of cleaning up the bad loans and recapitalising the banking sector through Danaharta (the Asset Management Company, which is in charge of cleaning up non performing loans of the financial institutions) and Danamodal (the recapitalisation agency) appears to compare favourably with efforts elsewhere in the region, with some positive results already achieved. There is, however, a need to speed up corporate restructuring. Moreover, despite the significant decline in interest rates and the increase in financial sector liquidity, bank lending growth remained subdued, and real GDP contracted by 6.7 percent in 1998, owing to sharp falls in investment and, to a lesser extent, in consumption, compared with the 7.7 percent growth in 1997. Malaysia was able to raise $ 1 bn in European Bond market in May 1999, and was over subscribed three times.

Notwithstanding the above benefits there were initially **adverse external reactions** to the September measures, which was suggestive of the weakening of investor and market confidence in Malaysia. Reflecting this reaction: the stock market initially fell by 13.3%, to its lowest in 1998, but rose subsequently against the background of purchases by state controlled institutional funds, investment by non-resident investors that had their funds blocked in Malaysia and a loss of confidence in the region generally. Several rating agencies downgraded Malaysia's credit and sovereign risk ratings immediately following the measures, citing that the controls threatened Malaysia's relative openness to trade and foreign investment, which was one of the corner stones of its rapid economic development. Malaysia was removed from key investment indices that track emerging country stock markets and that are used as investment benchmarks for funds managers. Malaysia's risk premium in international markets also increased rising the costs of foreign currency funding to Malaysian Corporations and banks. This is because of an increase in sovereign bond yield spreads following the implementation of capital controls.

On the domestic front also some initial confusion prevailed. The BNM met with investors and provided seminars on the new controls and subsequently issued many clarifications and press releases that were later compiled and published in "A Guide to the Exchange Control Rules". Although these efforts helped reduce the confusion among investors it increased the administrative burden of the BNM, of the traders and investors who had to supply necessary documentation and proof to execute their bonafide transactions and the authorised banks who were delegated the responsibility to implement the controls.

Modifications Incorporated in the Financial Sector Reforms

In February 1999, the authorities made modifications to the capital controls. They replaced the outright prohibition of repatriation of portfolio investment for a 12-month holding period with a market-based measure of a system of exit levies, effective from February 15, 1999. The objective of the exit levy system was stated to be to encourage "existing portfolio investors to take a longer view of their investments in Malaysia, and attract new funds into the country, while at the same time discouraging destabilizing short-term flows".

The replacement of the twelve month rule with the graduated levy on the repatriation of principal of investments has been viewed by many market participants as a positive development since it makes it possible to withdraw funds before the end of the twelve month holding period even if at a price. Moreover, the graduated nature of the levy provides some scope for phasing this repatriation as the high rates of the levy may limit the extent to which investors take advantage of the freedom to repatriate. Available evidence suggests that despite the high levy of 30% on early repatriation of investments, some fund managers promptly liquidated part or all of their holdings on the KLSE in the days following the announcement which lead to a sharp fall in the stock prices.

But, after this initial reaction the levy on capital repatriation as contributed to an improvement in the investor confidence. Preliminary data indicate that between the introduction of the levy and mid June 1999, the total inflow of capital through the special external accounts of non-residents amounted to RM 2.9 bn compared with the net inflow of RM 18.5 million as of March 10, 2000. In addition, as a result of the introduction of the exit levy, IFC announced plans to reinclude Malaysian equities in its capital index in November 1999. The rating agencies have also upgraded Malaysia's international credit rating in April 1999 and have cited the changes in the control measures as the reason for it. Capital outflows were only about $ 330 million in the quarter after controls were lifted on September 1, 1999, far less than predicted.

Critical Review of the Role of IMF

In the initial period of the crisis the IMF prescriptions as a cure in Indonesia and Thailand were worse than the disease. The problems that it created in the crisis prone countries is summarised in Chart 1. IMF rescue operations had begun in August 97 in Thailand and by October 97 in Indonesia, but even after one year from the date of the crisis the currencies had not stabilized. Therefore the IMF came under strong criticism from the international community for its role in the Southeast Asian crisis.

The appropriateness of the IMF remedies was questioned. The massive international rescue operations was said to have impeded the freeplay of market forces, serving only to encourage high risk investment and dubious financial transactions i.e. in other words the IMF induces **moral hazard**. This was one of the chief criticisms against the fund. Other critics pointed to the IMF's insistence on budget austerity, high interest rates and reduced government spending saying that such measures would accelerate the economy down turn and **exacerbate social and political tensions**[25]. Opposition to the IMF also stemmed from the view that the IMF was infringing on the sovereignty of nations seeking its support. Finally critics of the IMF considered that the rescue package was **too little**

and too late. This section discusses these and other criticisms levelled against the IMF and how far they are justified.

One of the strongest critics of the IMF was Jeffrey Sachs[26] "At the epicentre of the crisis, we now know, was a remarkable **panic of foreign investors,** created in part by a panic of the IMF itself". He has explained his statement as follows. By mid 1997, there was an estimated $ 274 bn of international banks loans outstanding to Indonesia, Malaysia, Thailand, Korea and Philippines. Of this about $ 175 bn was short term. When these international banks started to sniff trouble in 1996 (due to overvalued currencies, weakening exports and overcapacity) these banks began to reduce their lending. After the speculative attack on the Thai baht, they began to flee. At a time like this the IMF declared that Asia needed drastic financial surgery – immediate and widespread bank closure, astronomical interest rates and drastic fiscal cuts – the investors panicked alongside. Sachs is of the view that such a situation primarily arose on account of IMF's earlier policies of financial liberalization. He says that markets were opened in the wrong way; restrictions were kept on long term capital inflows, while short-term inflows were encouraged. Thus, he claims that poor advice from Washington tended to exacerbate panic and economic contraction. In the case of Indonesia Sachs claims that a virulent banking panic, triggered by the IMF measures brought Indonesia to its knees, more than Suharto's corruption.

As a policy measure Sachs suggested that Asian banks be sold to foreigners (this even the IMF has suggested) after sufficient public funds are injected. This would help recapitalise banks, and since foreign owners would bring high quality management, the banking sector would in future be less vulnerable to panic. Financial supervision should be tightened to prevent the next generation of banks and corporations from borrowing short-term funds in such large amounts from overseas.

Second criticism levelled against the IMF by several observers is that IMF policies have led to foreign control of Asian countries. One of the greatest fears of a country that is forced to seek IMF assistance is that, the policy conditions that come with such loans would spell the **end of that nation's economic sovereignty.**

A photograph widely published of Indonesia's president Suharto signing on to the IMF conditionalities with IMF managing director Michel Camedesus standing over him with folded arms seemed to reinforce this perception.

George Shultz, William E Simon and Walter Writson co-authors of "Who Needs the IMF" in The Wall Street Journal, February 3, 1998 were among the few Americans who strongly condemned the IMF for infringing on the sovereignty of a national state. They are of the opinion that the IMF through its conditionalities is doing just this and taking advantage of a vulnerable economy.

Another outspoken critic of the IMF, Malaysia's Prime Minister Mr. Mahathir Mohamed, warned that powerful nations had been given the opportunity (through the IMF) by the crisis to force open the economy of Southeast Asia further more, so that they (foreigners) could dominate them. He mentioned in particular, that the IMF conditions would include financial policy changes to enable large foreign banks to take over the financial sector.

Such fears are almost a reality in Thailand and Indonesia. As part of its deal with the IMF, Thailand was asked to allow foreign banks to own more equity in the local banking sector. In October 1997, the government had announced it would allow foreign institutions to hold a majority stake in operating financial institutions for upto 10 years, after which any further capital increases would have to be sold to local investors, if the foreign share is more than 49%.

This opened the door for foreign banks to take advantage of the present situation and quickly raise their share of the banking business. The local Thai banks were reeling from overdue loans and many were suffering from a weak capital base. Foreign banks were taking advantage of this vulnerability and were swooping in to take over the local banks.

A third criticism against the Fund is that it is **bailing out foreign banks** as against countries through its rescue package and therefore inducing a **moral hazard**. Also the IMF has been practicing double standards wherein it treats the institutions of local banks and international banks differently. On the one hand the fund insists that local banks and companies should not be aided by the government as it would be against market rules but on the other hand it ensures that the international banks avoid losses by getting the government to guarantee or take over the bank's loans to the private sector. In fact as a result the fund has earned the label of chief debt collector for the foreign banks.

The IMF conditions place top priority on governments repaying banks the foreign debts not only of the public sector but also the private sector. The governments hence have to guarantee and in the event of default by the private sector take over these foreign debts. In normal circumstances, if a bank provides a loan to a company or individual, it takes the risk of suffering losses if the customer cannot pay up. But due to the IMF conditionalities of government guarantee the international banks escape any loss/risk. This is of crucial significance since most of the loans were contracted by the private sector.

While the fund protects international banks, the client government is not supposed to spend public funds to rescue or subsidise the country's ailing banks, financial companies and corporations. Aiding private sector is considered inefficient and against the rules of the free market. In other words, such firms who have made business mistakes should pay for them by declaring themselves bankrupt.

A large portion of the IMF – coordinated loans is normally to be transferred from the IMF to the governments for re-channelling to the international banks to service some private sector loans. In this it appears that the IMF and the creditor countries that have contributed to the rescue package wanted to ensure that international banks and institutions that lent heavily to the troubled Asian countries are paid back in full. No wonder the IMF has portrayed as the chief debt collector on behalf of international banks. As such it seems that the IMF funds to Asia is primarily to bail out foreign banks, paid for by local taxpayers, shareholders and workers[27].

International Banks that have lent excessively and indiscriminately in the form of short-term loans should not be spared nor should rescue funds be used to bail out bankrupt financial establishments and insolvent firms. It should be used to help governments and central banks recreate liquidity in markets that have been bled dry by panic and encourage healthy firms to take over the remaining assets of failed enterprises[28]. Thus the IMF bail out package as such induces moral hazard and permits international banks to lend without fear.

The fourth set of criticism levelled against the fund is that it has been doling out cookie-cutter solutions, whatever is the problem. **The fund has prescribed the standard austerity, belt tightening programmes on the fiscal and monetary front and further structural reforms that required more market liberalization and opening up of capital markets.**

Since the crisis countries did not have serious fiscal imbalances before the crisis and because bank closures can lead to a credit crunch, the IMF's recommendations had made the contraction deeper than it needed to be. Due to this faulty policy mix the rescue packages have not produced a quick turnaround in currency and equity markets.

Evidence in support of this view is not hard to fund. Within a few months of being prescribed, the IMF's medicine had contributed to the doubling of Thailand's and Indonesia's unemployment rates. A preliminary analysis of social indicators in Thailand indicated that the economic downturn had compounded the country's social problems in particular the incidence of suicide and child drug abuse and the members of children in orphanages [29]. Similarly the suspension or closure of financial enterprises had two sets of effects. Firstly due to suspension of certain banks/financial institutions in Thailand and Indonesia there were doubts regarding the financial soundness of the solvent ones too. Investors behaving in a herd fashion started withdrawing deposits from solvent banks. Secondly although the closure of banks may have helped to contain unproductive speculation real estate, it deprived small and medium sized businesses of access to much needed funds. This provoked further bankruptcies and escalated the economic downturn.

Are These Criticisms Justified?

Indonesian Case:

As mentioned in the previous section, the austerity measures imposed on Indonesia between October 1997 and June 1998 worsened the economic situation. President Suharto even announced unwillingness to continue them. But, the IMF threatened withdrawing of aid in the event of not cairying out the conditionalities.

In all fairness to the IMF, the case of Indonesia is not as simple as explained above. The politics and economics of Indonesia were much more deep rooted and needs to be clarified.

Although Indonesia was a prime victim of contagion from bahtulism in the early fall of 1997, it had plenty to atone for on its own[30]. Between July and early October, 1997 a 40% fall in the Indonesia rupiah led to a spate of bankruptcies of financial institutions as foreign debts could not be repaid at the new exchange rates. The crisis revealed that Indonesia's largest corporations and business families had quickly borrowed funds from offshore sources, without listing them as debts. To a public debt of $ 100 bn, one should add a private debt of more than $ 65 bn[31].

By early October Suharto was a prime target for worldwide accusations of crony capitalism. His family and close friends (Sons/daughters/golf partner/social circle) were all found to be involved in some case of corruption/cronyism/money making racket. Just as such information was percolating, Suharto decided not to go ahead with the IMF reform programme. This situation caused the rupiah to slide from 2500 to the dollar to 17000/$. President Suharto kept went back on the first agreement with the IMF. Some of the projects that were agreed to be postponed were re-instated and some banks that were to be closed were started with new names.

One of the policy requirements of the IMF was that cartels and monopolies on some key primary materials like flour, palm oil, plywood etc be dismantled. The abolishing of the cartels caused the prices of palm oil in particular (essential product for the livelihood of Indonesians) to soar. In defiance of the IMF diktats Suharto banned exports on these products. Here Suharto's action seems justified as the socio-economic situation warranted it.

The IMF in turn decided to keep the aid on hold. Suharto did not succumb. He instead appointed Habibie as vice president who was a symbol of a new generation technocratic high spenders, who sought to build national industries from scratch largely with public funds and an infusion of heavy investment (this is not what the IMF desired at the moment). He also was a known pro Islam and anti Christian and anti-Chinese. Suharto was displaying his reluctance to bow down to IMF pressure.

Imposition of a Currency Board

Amidst all the pressure in the economy, Suharto was looking for alternative to the IMF's plans and he came up with the idea of a currency board.

The idea of the currency board was popularised by Steve Hanke[32] and Kurt Schuler. They saw the Indonesian crisis as an opportunity for their monetary experiment. The keenness of Hanke and Schuler to sell their experimental toy was matched by the desperate willingness of the Indonesian President to grasp it. He was looking for an instant solution to the currency turmoil, which would save him from political embarrassment and at the same time provide a convenient way to rescue his empire[33].

According to Schuler, the central bank was responsible for the currency problems and replacing it with currency boards was the panacea. A currency board is a monetary regime where the control of local, currency is fixed once and for all against say, the dollar. The value of the currency is taken out of the hands of the central bank and monetary authorities. With complete exchange rigidity, there were two ways of ensuring the safety of the plan. (a) Back monetary creation and large reserves (b) counter forward speculation against the local currency, which results in indirect monetary creation by an iron will to infinitely raise the interest rates applied to the domestic currency.

Thus the rupiah was fixed at 5000/US $ a rate substantially higher than the then rate (January 1998). This would help Indonesian Companies to refinance themselves and Suharto's entourage to repay their debts. Also the much needed dollar reserve would be procured by the IMF's injection of rescue money.

Compromise Between IMF and Suharto

Even though Suharto seemed to be a hero and even acclaimed by the media as one who could stand up against the IMF, the economic situation was sinking in Indonesia. Finally by April 1998 a third rescue plan was clinched with the IMF. This time round some of the conditionalities (oil palm embargo was lifted by Indonesia, but with 40% tax on exports) were softened, provisions were made for social subsidies etc. By early June 98, IMF also stopped insisting that subsidies be removed on basic foodstuffs. Also in the same month Indonesian indebted firms received a 3-year grace period on the principal (not interest). Indonesia's banks too could spread their interbank repayments over a period of 3 years. An Indonesian Debt Restructuring Agency was set up, guaranteeing the availability of foreign currency and limiting the impact of exchange fluctuations.

The conversion process of the central bank into a currency board was also halted. The IMF had in any case not approved of the idea of the currency board in Indonesia.

The entire episode described above however shows that the ***IMF too realised some of its follies and a new precedent was set.*** The cost of Indonesia's staggering private debt would be shared between the debtors themselves. The foreign banks would have to cross their fingers and wait and the Indonesian state was expected to pitch in.

This was a clear change from the earlier system where the international were left scot free from any risk (with the IMF aid to the crisis country being used to pay them – this time considerably lesser amount was used) and the taxpayers would have to be penalised for the folly of such bankers.

The lesson to be learned from this, is that when the emergency room is full of train crash victims it makes good sense to give top priority to those in mortal danger, leaving those with minor lacerations for later[34]. ***The IMF would have done well to pace down drastically its wish list of reforms and measures for a while.***

Thai Case

In Thailand, too, the initial programme focussed largely on monetary, fiscal and financial sector policies. The three main conditions (evident from the first LOI) were a 1% budget surplus, caps on public sector borrowing and a tight monetary policy. The IMF hoped that in 6 months time there would be a return to stability as had happened in the Latin American case. However, the Thailand case was different since here the government's debt was small and the budget was in surplus for over a decade. The large current account deficit was due to the high level of private sector foreign debt, which had resulted from massive capital inflows.

Thus as the currency floated downwards in Thailand, the private sector debt burden increased (especially of the banking sector). ***The deflationary implications of the IMF package aggravated the problem.***

By November 1997, inspite of the worsening situation, the IMF insisted on the second stage of the programme i.e. financial restructuring and privatization[35]. The August 1997 suspension of 58 financial institutions and subsequent closure in November 1997 of 56 of these sparked a run on many other financial institutions. The restrictive monetary policy deprived many borrowers of access to credit. By the end of the year, the formal credit system had virtually collapsed.

The IMF maintained its strategy with minor concessions in February 1998 on the budget. Infact, it still hoped that the situation would improve with a firm adherence to its prescriptions. It was in the 3rd quarter of 1998 that a fundamental revision was effected. ***This was the first time that the IMF started to show some repentance and admissal of a flaw in its earlier strategy.***

Changes were brought about not only in the macroeconomic programme but also in the legal sector and corporate governance. Social safety net issues were also addressed. An allowance was made for public sector deficit of 3% of GDP in 1997-98 and an additional 1.5% to finance interest costs from the financial bail out and targeted use of the deficit 'to maximise the impact on the real economy and on the social safety net'[36].

In the banking sector too there were changes. Although 2-3 banks were outright purchased by foreigners, henceforth the state would have an increased role. In August 1998, the government took over 6 of the 15 commercial banks, merged 4 of them with state institutions and reserved 2 for a later date.

It is clear from the above discussion that the IMF has had a major role in exacerbating the situation. But it cannot be solely blamed for it. Governments of the individual countries should also accept blame.

The fund has indulged in a lot of rethinking about its programmes in Asia. Some of the IMF reports released after the Fund came under severe attack for its policies have tried to justify why it included certain reforms in the early crisis period. It also admits to have mishandled them and that corrective measures were taken subsequently. The next section discusses in detail the various suggestions made for a change in the international financial architecture and the changes executed subsequently by the IMF in its perception towards the needs of developing countries.

Call for a New International Economic Order

When the Bretton Woods Institutions completed 50 years in 1994, discussions were conducted on the viability of the present international financial architecture as manifest by the IMF and WB. At that time it was emphasized that the IMF and WB had become similar institutions, particularly because the role of the IMF had grown from a short-term financing for exceptional needs to a longer-term development financing institution[37].

In the early 1990s there was a surge of private capital flows to developing countries and it was thought that the IMF would now become merely a consulting body. But the Mexican crisis and then the Asian crisis saw the IMF still at the centre of the stage[38]. However, the IMF was chastened, challenged and castigated[39] for its role in the latter as discussed in Section II. As a consequence there was a renewal for a rethinking on a reform in the international financial architecture.

It was argued that the IMF was created to assist in adjustments of current account imbalances in a world with fixed exchange rate and widespread capital account restrictions. The WB was given the responsibility for capital transfers on the presumption that government programmes were needed to compensate for a sub-optional volume of development lending. The conditions under which these institutions were founded are no longer in existence. Hence, it was opined that it is time to develop the institutions and managements that are more in tune with current requirements.

Calls for the abolition of the IMF/change in the IMF strategy to deal with the crisis came from a variety of neoliberal economists and think tanks. Some of these are discussed below. **The Task Force's Reform Package**[40] had made recommendations for improving the financial architecture.
Recommendation 1: greater rewards for countries that join the "Good Housekeeping Club". The aim here is to improve the incentives for emerging economies to undertake greater crisis prevention efforts by forging a closer link between implementation of crisis prevention

measures and the terms of emergency financial assistance from private capital markets and from the IMF.

Recommendation 2: Open capital markets, yes, but guard against "too much of a good thing". The objective here is to moderate the boom bust cycle in private capital flows and to tilt the composition toward less crisis-prone flows, while still preserving most of the benefits of grater market access. Here it is proposed that a country should impose penalties/taxes on short-term inflows so as to discourage the same. Also the IMF must step up its surveillance over countries public debt management.

Recommendation 3: The private sector promoting fair burden sharing and market discipline. The objective here is to include the timeliness ad orderliness of debt rescheduling and reduce the moral hazard for private lenders associated with national and international financial rescue packages. It is suggested that to reduce moral hazard at the national level, the IMF should advice emerging economies to adopt a "structured early intervention and resolution approach to deposit insurance reform in the banking system, and reward countries that do so in line with recommendation 1. To reduce moral hazard at international level, the IMF should make it known that it will provide emergency financial assistance only when there is a good prospect of the recipient country's achieving "BOP viability" in the medium term and that such viability requires a sustainable debt servicing profile.

The other recommendations include - abandoning of a pegged exchanged rate regime, reforming the lending policy whereby more aid may be made out in case of systemic crisis (multi-country) and less in case of a single country crisis and refocus the IMF and the WB's so as to make their mandates are more compatible with the needs of today's global economy.

Hence, the task force does not recommend the abolition of the IMF It is of the opinion that the IMF must definitely stay. It suggests that it must change some of its lending policies so that the problem of moral hazard is reduced. Moreover, the Fund should be more vigilant and farsighted to perceive/predict coming danger and make efforts to forestall the same.

Azizul Islam[41] has warned that although speculative activities can be useful in correcting imbalances between national (or regional) markets, thus promoting global efficiency in the long run, but in the short run it imposes unacceptable high costs. Thus he suggests the creation of a World Financial Order (WFO) by the Committee for Development Planning (CDP) of the United Nations. The CDP is an independent body of experts constituted by the Secretary-General of the United Nations. Its members are chosen from a large cross-section of both developed and developing countries. The proposed WFO should monitor the implementation of sound international principles and practices for accounting, payments and settlements, banking supervision, security market supervision, insurance supervision and supervision of financial conglomerates.

In addition, it should formulate acceptable forms of international regulation for short-term capital movements to complement national measures, as well as formulate and apply international guidelines for short term lending and borrowing by private creditors and borrowers. The WFO should also play an important institutional role in the formulation of an international debt strategy. In the event of a crisis, it could bring the investors and borrowers together so that they share the responsibility for debt relief, for rescheduling debts or for delaying claims on repayments.

Azizal Islam also advocates the establishment of an Asian Fund. According to him this could reduce the probability of a crisis, or mitigate its adverse impact. The Asian Fund would provide liquidity additional to that provided by the IMF. He opines that the very existence of this liquidity would help improve market sentiment. The Asian Fund should be designed to be quick disbursing in nature.

It may be noted here that the creation of an Asian Fund could further increase the moral hazard problem created by the IMF unless it is controlled through high and varying interest rates with the volume and frequency of drawing. In this way countries can be discouraged from borrowing indiscriminately with the hope that if things go wrong;

the Asian Fund is at bay. Another problem that the AF could throw up is that it may dilute the conditionalities agreed upon with the IMF. However, making the AFs assistance contingent to the IMF's conditionalities can easily rectify this.

Barry Eichengreen[42] has sorted through the controversies surrounding the IMF's response to the crisis and offers suggestions for how it might go about its business differently in the future.

The first suggestion he makes is with regard to the exchange rate policy. He opines that in a world of high capital mobility there are two options; currency boards (discussed earlier in this chapter) and more flexible rate. For the adoption of a currency board certain conditions have to be fulfilled. Firstly, the country must conform to the monetary and financial conditions prevailing in the rest of the world. Secondly, the country that adopts this system eliminates all scope for the domestic authorities to act as lender of the last resort (Therefore alternative arrangements have to be made for putting controls on commercial banks, say nationalization). Thirdly, since the exchange rate is fixed, adjustments to a macroeconomic disturbance have to be made through flexible labour market arrangements. This implies that there could be a persistent high unemployment.

Thus, it is only countries in which investors harbour exceptional distrust of discretionary monetary policy, where the domestic economy is sufficiently flexible to adapt to whatever monetary and financial conditions are implied by a fixed exchange rate, and where there is a deep rooted public support for the policy however painful its consequences, can sustain the currency board option. Thus, this option does not seem to be viable.

Given the demanding preconditions for establishing a currency board, the other choice is a more flexible exchange rate policy. This way banks and firms will have an incentive to hedge their foreign exposures and will acquire insurance against the negative financial effects of unexpected large currency fluctuations. Eichengreen opines that the IMF must push its members to adopt more flexible exchange rates and to harmonise prudential regulation with exchange rate policy.

The second suggestion of Eichengreen revolves around the monetary and fiscal policies. Here he opines that the IMF must avoid giving 'one-size-fits-all' advice but modify the same according to the situation.

The next suggestion is that the IMF should not be too intrusive in countries' internal affairs. For instance Eichengreen has questioned the demand of the IMF to break up its clove monopoly or scale back its national car programme in Indonesia. Such intervention borders on infringing upon the sovereignty of the country and should be avoided.

Eichengreen also offers suggestions for preventing banking crisis in future. He asserts that since the IMF cannot realistically regulate banking practices in its 182 member countries, it should in unison with the national governments encourage public and private sectors of these countries to adopt international standards for 'minimally acceptable practice'. In other words, although national practices may differ, they must meet minimal standards if greater financial stability is to be attained.

The IMF has been an ardent advocate of the capital account liberalization. Although there are many benefits of the capital flows that ensue as a result of such liberalization, there are some risks attached as is evident from the Asian crisis. Hence, according to Eichengreen, the IMF must not just advocate capital account liberalization but also advise prudent regulation of the capital account as a guardian against financial crisis in the future.

Morris Goldstein[43] has remarked that "there is nothing like a crisis to motivate a rethink of the adequacy of the existing crisis prevention/management architecture". Goldstein has provided a set of suggestions known as Halifax II reforms for the improvement of the existing financial architecture.

They revolve around the following 5 issues.

1. *Reducing moral hazard and making private debt rescheduling more orderly and more flexible* For this he suggests that :-

(a) in future the governments should not expect blanket guarantee they issue to their creditors to be honoured through an IMF rescue package. This should be made adequately clear.

(b) emerging economies should adopt a system of deposit insurance that is incentive compatible and that sets out a maximum on the payout in case of failure of banks.

(c) the scope and duration of the official safety net should be limited i.e. the countries receiving official rescue packages should not extend protection to financial companies and merchant banks

(d) more order and flexibility should be brought about in rescheduling private external debt. Eichengreen's suggestion of a standing steering committee for bondholders and that which includes sharing clauses and majority voting clauses in debt instruments seems agreeable to Goldstein too. The idea here is to avoid the costs and delays of organising creditors on the spot and to make it more difficult for rogue creditors to block rescheduling efforts.

2. *Strengthening prudential/supervisory standards in emerging economies and improving the incentives for their early adoption.* In September 1997, at the Annual Meeting of the IMF and WB group in Hong Kong, agreement was reached on the Core Principles (Basle Committee on Banking Supervision 1997). Goldstein suggests here that the sample of the agreements on the Core Principles be implemented urgently. The Core Principles urged countries to implement an international banking standard but without setting a deadline. Goldstein suggests that this mistake may be rectified by setting a target date (say 2003). He also suggests that an international agency should evaluate compliance with the Core Principles. An incentive to countries that comply with them could be larger access to IMF and WB loans. Goldstein suggests that the IMF would do better to established strong supervisory and prudential framework first before pushing ahead with a capital account liberalization

agenda. In other words financial stability should precede capital account liberalization. He also opines that countries facing large capital inflows, however, should consider imposing 'Chile-type' taxes on short-term capital inflows.

3. *Improving transparency and disclosure in international financial markets* Goldstein's suggestion regarding this are that all parties would profit from the availability of more comprehensive, more frequent and more timely data on maturity and currency composition of external debt. It may be mentioned here that the BIS publishes such data semi-annually. Goldstein opines that analysts should pay more attention to such data and that BIS should publish it once a month or once in 3 months.

Another area where Goldstein seeks transparency is better data availability on net international reserves, i.e. gross international reserves less related liability (including commitments in the forward exchange market). He has also urged that an internationally acceptable definition on NPL be evolved and data pertaining to the same be published semi-annually.

4. *Making IMF surveillance more effective.* In all fairness to the IMF it may be said that it had warned Thailand to take corrective actions, but the latter had ignored it, resulting in a crisis. But, the IMF had not foreseen anything in Indonesia and Malaysia. Therefore, it is necessary to intensify surveillance especially of the financial sector issues and capital flows. A tiered response can be developed whereby countries that are seriously offcourse could be given stronger warnings. The IMF publishes Article IV country reports on recent economic performance. It could do better by also publishing IMF staff's evaluation of the country's policies and prospects.

5. *Shoring up risk management in global financial institutions.* It is well known now that one of the causes of the Asian crisis is the poor credit evaluation and risk management on the part of the lending banks. Goldstein therefore suggests that global auditors should work with global firms, audit standard bodies and supervisors to achieve an agreed upon approach to financial statement audits and other

information for portraying risk. Also, financial supervisors should agree upon a lead co-ordinator for all global financial institutions, formulate standards for exchanges, clearing houses and settlement systems, including risk management and financial stability, protection of customer assets, funds and positions; and netting, contract enforceability and insolvency.

The **G7 recommendations** for an improved financial artchitecture are similar to that of Eichengreen and Goldstein. Close on the heels of the Asian crisis was one that erupted in Russia. The Russian rouble plummeted to abysmally low levels. This caused the Dow Jones to plunge by 554 points on August 31, its second largest decline in the history of the New York Stock Exchange[44].

The G7 proposal was to install a 90 billion dollar fund "to help protect vulnerable but essentially healthy nations" from currency and stock market speculation. The precautionary fund was to be established under the stewardship of the IMF. The basic idea of the fund is to determine financial turbulence spreading from country to country in a contagion process and to send a clear message to speculators that they may be taking big risks if they (short) sell a nation's currency[45].

The G7 proposals accordingly aimed to reduce uncertainty about countries and financial market through greater transparency and more complete and quicker provision of relevant information. Transparency would be fostered by adoption of codes of good practices for fiscal and monetary policy, principles of sound corporate governance and accounting and new standards of disclosure and transparency of internationally active financial institutions in developed and developing countries. The G7 called upon the IMF to monitor compliance and publish regular transparency reports on individual countries[46].

To address the moral hazard problem they suggested shifting more of the risk to the creditors. Since foreign debt is increasingly in the form of bonds, the private sector should include 'collective action clause' for more orderly debt workouts in bond contracts. This would put bondholders more on par with bank creditors of governments in renegotiating debt servicing and make bonds a little less "risk-free". The IMF had approved of a "lending into arrears" policy and the G7 endorsed the same. The "lending into arrears" policy implies lending to a government in a currency crisis even if it did not yet have an accepted plan for a sovereign debt work out. This was aimed to pressure the creditors to some to an agreement with the debtor, implicitly accepting bigger share of the losses than otherwise[47].

Reform of the Global Financial Architecture undertaken by the IMF

The Mexican peso crisis helped to motivate progress on, interalia, an international data standard (the IMF's Special Data Dissemination Standard - SDDS), an international banking standard (the Core Principles), an Emergency Financing Mechanism in the IMF, and expanding the credit facilities available to the IMF under the New Arrangements to Borrow[48]. Similarly, the Asian crisis too saw a number of changes being effected in the international financial system. As mentioned earlier the Asian financial crisis exposed weaknesses in the international monetary and financial system, underscoring that globalisation entails risks as well as potentially substantial benefits. Over and above this the mechanism to combat the crisis provided by the IMF (atleast in the first 6 months) were lacking on many scores.

Quite naturally the international financial system (read the IMF) was criticised severely for its role in the pre and post crisis. In the pre crisis period it was said to have propagated excessive liberalization with very little surveillance. In the post crisis period it was said to have propagated very stringent fiscal and monetary policies leading to a recession.

The IMF in coordination with many institutions and forums – WB, Financial Stability Forum (FSF) BIS, other Basel based groups, the G20* and the OECD made efforts to evolve a comprehensive response to strengthen the international financial architecture. In addition other standard setting bodies were also involved – The international organization of security commissions (IOSCO), the international associations of insurance supervisors (IAIS), the international accounting standards committee (IASC), the international federation of accounts (IFAC) and the United Nations Commission of International Trade Law (UNCITRAL).

The progress made on key elements of a strengthened financial architecture as of the end of April 2000 is discussed below[49]: -

I. Transparency and Accountability:

Improved provision of information to the markets and the broader public is a central element of the reform of the international financial system. It is also a corner stone of the IMF reforms put in place in the past few years and plan for the future. Transparency on the part of IMF member countries and the IMF itself helps foster better economic performance. It encourages more widespread analysis of their policies by the public; enhances the accountability of policy makers and the credibility of policies; and critically informs financial markets so they can operate in an orderly and efficient manner. The IMF Executive Board has adopted a series of measures aimed at improving the transparency of members' policies and data and act enhancing the IMF's own external communication.

As of April 30, 2000 the Executive Board has agreed to:

1. Make available more information about IMF's surveillance of members through Public Information Notices (PINs) following their country (Article IV) consultations.

2. Make available more information on countries' IMF supported programmes through making available the Letters of Intent and other country programme documents.

3. Carry out internal and external evaluation of IMF practices like the ESAF and publish the same.

4. Continue dialog and consultation with the public, WB, NGO's on IMF activities. For example, the comprehensive review of the Heavily Indebted Poor Countries Initiative (HIPCI) incorporated their views into the enhanced HIPCI announced on September 1999. Key external reports on IMF's policies and operations as well as periodic summaries of the Executive Board's work and a wide range of policy documents are being released.

5. Release more financial information about the IMF – the IMF posts on its web site "Members' Accounts in the IMF" which provide timely information on every member country's financial position with the IMF.

II. Developing Standards, Principals and Guidelines:

Executive Board discussion on strengthening the international financial architecture has stressed the need to develop and implement internationally recognised standards and codes of good practice. Adopting such standards in areas central to economic and financial system stability can contribute to better informed lending and investment decisions, increased accountability of economic policy makers and private sector decision makers and improved economic performance.

Following the development of standards in areas of direct operational concern to the IMF data dissemination, transparency of fiscal, monetary and financial policies, banking supervision – efforts have focussed on disseminating and implementing these standards including by providing technical assistance. Material has been prepared to help countries implement the standards through a manual for the 'Code of Good Practices on Fiscal Transparency' has been available on the IMF web-site since 1998,and the IMF is finalising the supporting document to the 'Code of Good Practices on Transparency in Monetary and Financial Policies', which was adopted by the IMFC in September, 1999.

Other steps to improving standards were:

1. Developing a standard format for disseminating data on official reserves and foreign exchange liquidity based on Special Data Disseminating Standards (SDDS). This helps assessing external vulnerability.

2. A separate SDDS data category for external data statistics was to be introduced to disseminate comprehensive and timely data on a quarterly basis.

3. The General Data Disseminating Systems (GDDS) was to be enhanced with respect to external debt, with public and publicly guaranteed debt and associated debt service schedule in the core data categories of GDDS.

4. To improve the data quality, the IMF staff has introduced a data quality reference site established on the Dissemination Standards Bulletin Board (www.dsbb.imf,org.) to foster a common understanding of data quality, drawing on contributions from the international statistical community.

III. Assessing Standards

The IMF and World Bank have developed an organising framework to assess the observance of standards in cooperation with national authorities and other international bodies. Assessments are prepared using a range of different instruments:

1. The joint IMF-World Bank pilot Financial Sector Assessment Programme that focuses mainly on assessing financial sector vulnerabilities and identifying developmental priorities. This involves assessing financial sector standards in compliance with the Code of Good Practices on Transparency in Monetary and Financial Policies.

2. Adherence to standards on data dissemination and fiscal transparency in compliance with the Code of Good Practices on Fiscal Transparency.

3. The World Banking cooperation with the other bodies is experimenting with assessment in areas of corporate governance and accounting and its developing methods for conducting assessments for the same.

V. *External Vulnerability and Capital Flows:*

Countries can benefit substantially from capital account liberalization if liberalization is properly sequenced and managed. IMF surveillance aims to assess risks and vulnerability at both national and international level. Timely frequent and high quality data are critical for an effective assessment. As a result much effort is being focussed on how to improve data quality and reporting and the use of vulnerability indicators in conjunction with standard economic analysis.

Work to develop better methods for evaluating external vulnerability has advanced on several fronts in the IMF, WB and other international institutions. They are:

1. The IMF and WB are collaborating on series of papers on external debt management. They have undertaken work on debt and reserve related indicators of external vulnerability, which considers the analytical usefulness of various indicators and the scope for the derivation of simple benchmarks in order to gauge countries' ability to withstand external shocks. Also in preparation is a study on sound practices in sovereign debt management.

2. With the IMF support systems for high frequency monitoring of external liabilities of domestic banking system have been established in a number of countries to detect emerging signs of vulnerability and help in crisis management.

3. The IMF has initiated a project to identify statistical data, referred to as macro prudential indicators, needed to support the evaluation of financial systems and to develop strategies to compile the data's and encourage their dissemination to the public.

4. The IMF has also joined in efforts to develop early warning systems for external crisis – i.e. formulation of formal models that estimates the probability of crisis from a compact set of variables – to improve surveillance.

V. *Capital Account Liberalization and Capital Controls*:
In several discussions during the financial year 2000 Executive Board underlined the substantial benefit of Capital Account Liberalization but stress the need to manage and sequence liberalization carefully to minimise risks.

In September 1999, Directors agreed that there was no single approach to securing the benefits of international capital flows while limiting risks. Based on a series of country studies, the following tentative observations were made.

1. Capital controls cannot substitute for sound macro economic policies, although they may provide a breathing space for corrective action. Countries with serious macro economic imbalances and no credible prospects for correction in the short run have regularly been unable to address large-scale capital outflows by just using capital controls. In fact in some countries controls have reduced the pressure on the authorities to introduce much needed reforms.

2. Capital controls tend to be distortionary, impede desirable transactions, dampen financial market development and adversely affect investors confidence and access to international capital markets. Thus, the possible benefits of controls have to be weighed carefully against their costs.

3. Building effective regulatory and supervisory institutions for financial markets may take a long time. But there is no substitute for the same.

VI. *Exchange Rate Regimes:*
The Executive Board Directors drew the following conclusions:

1. No single exchange rate regime is suitable for all countries or in all circumstances. Whatever exchange rate regime is adopted, its consistency with underlying macro economic policy is essential.

2. The existing system of flexible exchange rates among the three major currencies is likely to continue.

3. In recent years, several emerging market countries have adopted a flexible exchange rate regime but with this a supporting macro economic policy system should be adopted.

4. Large exchange rate swings in small or medium sized open economies may have significant economic costs, it may also be appropriate to use the domestic monetary policy or intervention to limit swings.

5. The IMF should not provide large-scale assistance to countries intervening heavily to support an exchange rate peg, if this peg is inconsistent with underlying policies. In some cases it should offer an advice on a suitable exit strategy.

Thus from the above it is clear that the IMF has paid heed to the criticism levelled against it and has also looked into the suggestions offered for improvement. It has made a lot of effort at correcting its shortcomings and to strengthen the international financial architecture. This is definitely a change from the earlier rigid stance of dictating policy options. The IMF is now looking at preventive measures rather only at cures. In other words steps for avoiding a crisis are being suggested to member nations than to combat a crisis after it has occurred. It remains to be seen how the member nations will cooperate with the IMF in adopting the prudential reform measures, as it is this that will decide the fate of future developments. Also as the IMF has a renewed stance towards foreign banks/ investors wherein they are asked to pay for their mistakes, they will be more careful while making lending decisions. The IMF will no loner be available to bail out these banks/investors in the event of incorrect lending decisions.

Present Scenario of the ASEAN 3

The financial crisis that began in Asia in 1997 was particularly alarming because it struck hardest at some of the largest and fastest developing countries. It threatened to reverse the years of economic and social progress made by the ASEAN3. However, by 1999, signs of recovery could be seen. Also preliminary estimates for 2000 show that all have returned to positive growth.

Indonesia

The crisis in Indonesia has bottomed out and signs of recovery are appearing after nearly two years of financial of economic turmoil . Infact by the year 2000 the situation was far better and most economic indicators showed positive changes.

GDP recorded a marginal growth of 0.8 % in 1999 (this is a revised estimate as against the – 0.1% as per earlier reports), and a modest growth of 4.8% in 2000 (See Table 6.2). Such developments were a welcome change after the recession in 1998, when GDP had contracted by 13.1%. The initial reaction to the IMF suggested reform policy had been adverse. However, after certain changes in the policy measures were effected, confidence returned and the economies started to look up.

The inflation rate as reflected by the consumer price index registered a rise of only 3.7%, considerably lower than the 20.5% for 1999. It may be noted here that the 20.5% rise in 1999 was much lower than the 58.4 % rise in 1998. The falling food prices, the appreciation of the rupiah from Rp. 9,000 to the US$ at the beginning of 1999 to 7200/US $ towards the end of 1999 and the tight monetary policy all helped bringing about this decline in the inflation rate.

The price increases in 2000 was larger than targeted especially during the second half of 2000 when renewed weakness in the rupiah led to an upward inflationary pressure. In addition higher fuel costs, resulting from the governments program of reducing subsidies also led to price increases in this period. The government was compelled to increase prices of oil as the world over the same had risen. Yet, inspite of the increase in GDP and the rise in oil prices, inflation could be contained at 3.7%.

Indonesia has a relatively flexible labour market and even during the financial crisis, on an annual basis, the number of people reported working increased. Changes in aggregate economic activity, even severe changes, are reflected in real wage rates rather than in aggregate employment. Thus, preliminary estimates for 2000 suggest that modest GDP growth encouraged only a small increase in aggregate employment - up roughly 2 percent from 1999.

In 2000, for the framing of the domestic policies the Indonesian parliament sponsored a national debate that led to the adoption of a medium term development strategy. The strategy set out five broad national objecives[50].

I) Ensuring national cohesion and social stability,
II) Achieving good governance and rule of law
III) Accelerating economic recovery and strengthening the foundation of sustained growth.
IV) A strengthening regional autonomy rural and urban development and structural poverty programmes
V) Developing the social sectors and human welfare;

The focus on improving good governance is a result of the crisis since in many respects the weakest link in Indonesia's past development strategy was governance. The governments strategy includes an anti corruption programme, administrative and fiscal decentralization improved public financial management, civil service reforms, dismasting state monopolies of further deregulating trade, finance, industry and investment. The government also attached high priority to market based economic decision-making rather than a politically determined one.

Indonesia's fiscal deficit was within manageable limits prior to the crisis. However in the aftermath of the crisis, measures to simulate domestic demand, large expenditures to recapitalise the banking systems and the effect of the recession in 2000 on tax receipts saw an increase in the fiscal deficit and public debt. (See Table 6.3). The nominal balance increased from – 1.6 in 1999 to – 3.2 in 2000. The public debt increased from 105.7% of GDP to 106.9% of GDP. Since, govt's liability were high interest payments constituted a large proportion of the GDP, the same increasing form 3.8% to 5.7%.

As far as the external sector was concerned, the Current account showed a surplus of 4.1% of GDP in 1999. This surplus was possible mainly due to low imports and near doubling of oil process in 1999. (Indonesia is a net exported of oil). Although the natural resource based exports increased, that of manufactured exports remained sluggish. In the first half of 2000 also, exports increased and the oil exports was an important contributor to the increase in GDP. Imports were low mainly on account of lack of widespread investment spending therefore, the current account showed a surplus of 7.2% of GDP.

By the second half of 2000, due to a worldwide recession, there was a slower growth of exports especially that of electronics. This development led to a fall in the Nasdaq index and the same further led to an outflow of portfolio equity investment. Terex reserves however have improved and were about $ 27 bn. (worth 6 months of imports) at the end of 1999 and increased in 41 bn at the end of 2000 (7.6 months of imports).

Malaysia

The Malaysian economy achieved a robust recovery in 1999 with real GDP expanding by 5.8% after contracting by 7.5% in 1998. During 2000 it grew at the rate of 8.5% (See Table 6.2). The economic recovery was mainly on account of buoyant export growth, increased private consumption and a recovery in gross fixed investment.

Consumer price inflation decreased steadily from 5.3% in 1998, to 2.7% in 1999 to just 1.5% in 2000. Inflation was low inspite of the higher energy prices in the fourth quarter of 2000. Inflation was under control mainly on account of lower food prices, minimal imported inflation, stable exchange rate and excess capacity in some sectors of the economy.

The continuing recovery led to a decline in the unemployment rate to 2.9 percent of the labour force in 2000, from 3.0 percent in 1999[51]. Reflecting a higher level of economic activity, the number of job vacancies in 2000 increased by 14 percent relative to 1999, whereas the number of workers retrenched declined by 32.4 percent. Although real wages increased by an estimated 12.9 percent during the year, this was more than offset by an increase in real labour productivity of 22.7 percent.

The govt. followed expansionary fiscal and monetary policies in 1999 and 2000 to consolidate the recovery. Infact reflationary measures were initiated since mid 1998 itself. As a result, the fiscal deficit increased form 1.9% of GNP in 1998 to 4.9% in 1999. The fiscal default was estimated at 5.5% of GDP in 2000. Such counter cyclical measures benefited the social sector. Allocation for the health and education were also increased.

With inflation under control the government continued its accommodative monetary policy stance of low interest rates and a fixed exchange rate regime. All monetary aggregates (M_1, M_2 and M_3) expanded reflecting stronger economic activity. The total loans outstanding in the banking system at the end of 2000 amounted to RM 453 bn, an increase of 5.2% relative to the end of 1999 level RM 429.7 bn. During the year of 2000 substantial progress was made in merging the country's domestic banks to achieve a more effective and competitive banking system. Bank Negara Malaysia had in 1999 itself announced a merger program for the banking system in July 1999, aiming at consolidating the existing banks and financial institutions under six financial groups.

As mentioned above there was an increase in exports, hence the external sector too looked up. In 1998 a trade surplus was brought about by import compression but the trade surplus in 1999, was brought about by stronger and robust US demand for Malaysia's electronic goods. Additionally, since the exchange rate of the ringgit was fixed vis a vis the US $ (exchange controls), exports were boosted. The current account surplus was 15.9% of GDP in 1999.
However, the slower export growth especially in electronics in the second half of 2000 caused the current account surplus to reduce to 9.2% of GDP (See Table 6.2). As compared to Thailand and Indonesia, Malaysia was affected to a greater extent by the fall in demand for electronics as the same is a large proportion of Malaysia's exports. Yet, another factor that has contributed to a fall in the current account surplus is the fact that imports have outpaced exports . The

Malaysian economy is very dependent on trade related service imports and the outflows of profits and dividend from an improving economy has contributed to the decrease in the current account surplus.

In the capital account, a net outflow of short-term capital totalled $ 5.8 bn. Portfolio investment amounting to $ 1.8 bn was repatriated between September 1 and October 15, 1999 after the 12-month holding period for portfolio expired on September 1,1999. The net inflow of long-term capital increased from $ 2.2 bn in 1998 to about $ 3.0 bn in 1999.

The net international reserves increased from $ 2.6 bn at the end of 1998 to 30.9 bn or six myths imports at the end of 1999. The external debt position too remained manageable in 1999. The debt service ratio declined to 6.2% in 1999 from 6.6% in 1998. The ratio of short-term debt to foreign exchange reserves declined to 23% in 1999 from 32% in 1998. A noteworthy development in 1999 was Malaysia's re-entry in 3 bench mark equity indexes: the International Finance Corporation and the Dow Jones Global Indexes (both effective Nov. 1999) and the Morgan Slanley Capital Group of Indexes[52].

Thailand

Like in the case of Indonesia and Malaysia, there were signs of recovery seen in the Thai economy too. After an unprecedented real GDP contraction of 10.4% in 1998. The economy started showing signs of recovery in the beginning of 1999. Real GDP growth in 1999 was about 4.0%. The growth in GDP was on account of increased consumption, higher capacity utilization in the manufacturing sub sector and encouragement from several government's stimulus packages.

The economic crisis had resulted in high unemployment. In 1999 unemployment including the seasonally inactive labour force reached 1.9 mn persons, 5.9 % of total labour force. Underemployment also increased significantly. Even though employment was boosted through public employment programme unemployment level remained high. However, by 2000 the situation improved to some extent. In 2000 the unemployment rate decreased to 3.2% (1.1 mn persons).

Inflation was contained at 0.3% in 1999 (See Table 6.2) following a year of relatively high inflation of 8.1% in 1998. This was largely because of lower prices for food and agricultural commodities. In 2000 however, consumer price inflation increased by 1.6%, largely because of rising world oil prices and depreciation of the baht against most major currencies. The core inflation rate, which is the 12-month increase in consumer prices excluding food and energy, remained relatively low at 0.7 % well within the Bank of Thailand's inflation target range of 0-3.5 % for 2000-02.[52]

As mentioned in Section II, initially on the IMF's recommendation a tight fiscal policy was followed. Later succumbing to pressures from the social sector, an expansionary fiscal policy was followed both in Indonesia and Thailand. The government maintained an expansionary fiscal stance to boost domestic demand, provide liquidity and establish a social safety net for minimizing the impact of the financial crisis on the poor. In 1999, the government launched two economic stimulus packages with expenditures of 53 mm baht in March and 100 mn baht in August 1999. The March package was aimed at stimulating private consumtion and the August package focused on tax and tariff measures, equity investment funds, measures to improve the recovery of the real estate sector, and financing for small and medium enterprises. In August and October 2000 also the govt. launched two economic packages. The August package focused on supporting rural and community development and the October package aimed at strengthening the economic and social foundation for long term sustainable growth.

The monetary policy was also eased out. But, in spite of the same the growth rate of money supply continued to be slow in 1999. The increase in M_2 was 2.3% compared with 9.5% at the end of 1998. Interest rates declined, the interbank rate stood at 1.2%, prime rate (minimum lending) at 8.25 – 8.50% and deposit rate at 4.00-4.25 %. The credit crunch was expected with the local banks concern regarding the high levels of non-performing loans and tightened loan loss provisioning requirement. NPLs were as high as 38.5% in December 1999.

By 2000 there were some more improvements in the financial sector. M2 increased by 3.6%. With increased liquidity interest rates remained at the low levels mentioned above. Commercial banks continued their cautions lending stance. The growth in commercial bank credit to the private. sector declined by 10.2% at the end of 2000. NPLs too declined further to 18.0% of total loans in December 2000.

The external sector was buoyant from 1999 up to mid 2000. The export earnings in US $ terms increased by 7.4% while imports grew at a higher rate of 17.7%. The same were 19.6% and 31.3% respectively in 2000. The current account balance was at a surplus of $ 11.2 bn in 1999, but dropped to $ 10 bn in 2000. An international reserve increased to $ 38.8 bn (8.7 months of imports) in Dec. 1999 and was a comfortable $ 32.7 bn at the end of 2000. This was equivalent to two times the short term debt or provided about six months of import coverage.

Despite increased FDI inflows the net capital movements registered a deficit of $ 8.2 bn, reflecting large private capital outflows as commercial banks continued to repay their external debts. Consequently, external debt stood at $ 75.6 bn at the end of 1999, down from $ 86.2 bn at the end of 1998. It came down further to $ 81.3 bn by November 2000. The maturity profile showed a shift towards a long-term period. Short term declined from 27% in 1998 to 19% in 1999to 18% of total debt in 2000 .

Thus all the three economics have definitely improved in their economic health since they were devastated by the crisis. In all the economies for a year and half since the out break of the crisis the situation (both political and economic) deteriorated. But with a change in policy stance there was on improvement as shown by the economic indicators. Of course, it will take a few years more for these economics to bounce back to their growth levels of the pre crisis period.

Table 6.1

Packages of Official Support for Crisis Countries (Breakdown of Sources)
(bn of US $)

	Indonesia	**Thailand**
Total	38.1[a]	17.2
(as a % of 1997 GDP)	18.0	12.0
IMF	10.1	4.0
WB	4.5	1.5
ADB	3.5	1.2
Others (largely Japan)	20.0[b]	10.5[c]
Date of Approval	5.11.97	20.8.97

a: augmented by $ 42 bn (including debt rescheduling and new funds) in June 1998/in June 1998
b: second line of defence in Indonesia includes $ 5 bn of its own resources.
c. Japanese funding disbursed parallel to IMF loans.

Table 6.2

Growth, Inflation and Current Account Balances

Country	Real GDP			Consumer Prices			Current Account Balance		
	Annual % change			Annual % change			as % of GDP		
	1993-98	1999	2000	1993-98	1999	2000	1993-98	1999	2000
Indonesia	3.2	0.8*	4.8	15.4	20.5	3.7	-1.8	4.1	7.2
Malaysia	6.3	5.8	8.5	3.7	2.7	1.5	-3.4	15.9	9.2
Thailand	3.2	4.2	4.3	5.6	0.3	1.5	-3.6	10.2	7.6

Source: BIS, 71st Annual Report, 1st April 2000-31st March 2001

* revised estimate

Table 6.3

Fiscal Balance and Public Debt

Country	Nominal Balance			Interest Payments			Public Debt		
	as % of GDP			as % of GDP			as % of GDP		
	1996	1999	2000	1996	1999	2000	1996	1999	2000
Indonesia	1.1	-1.6	-3.2	2.0	3.8	5.7	27.3	105.7	106.9
Malaysia	0.7	-3.2	-5.8	2.7	2.6	2.7	35.3	37.3	37.0
Thailand	0.7	-2.6	-2.2	0.2	1.2	1.2	16.3	42.4	54.4

Chart 6.1

Chronological Highlights of Financial Assistance to Thailand & Indonesia

Dates	Indonesia
5 Nov. 1997	Stand by Credit approved
15-Jan-98	Memorandum of Economics & Financial Policies on
	additional measures
10-Apr-98	Supplementary Memorandum of Economics &
	Financial Policies on additional measures (copy
	attached)
	First review of stand by arrangement
25-Jun-98	Second supplementary MEFP between Indonesia &
	IMF
7-Jun-99	5th review of IMFs EFF and approval of US$ 450 bn
Jan. 20, 2000	Memorandum of Economics and Financial Policies
17-May-00	Letter of Intent on MEFP of Jan 20, 2000
July 31. 2000	Letter of Indent on additional measures
	Thailand
20-Aug-97	Financial support approved
25 Nov. 1997	Letter of Intent on additional measures
8-Dec-97	First review of the stand by arrangement
24-Feb-98	Letter of Intent on additional measures
4-Mar-98	Third review of the stand by arrangement

Chart 6.2a

Indonesia: Transactions with the Fund

from January 01, 1984 To January 31, 2002

(in SDRs)

Year	General Resources Account			Structural Adjustment Facility/Trust Fund Enhanced Structural Adjustment Facility/Poverty Reduction and Growth Facility					
	GRA			SAF/PRGF/TF			Total		
	Purchases		Charges Paid	Loans		Interest Paid	Purchases and Loans		Charges and Interest Paid
	Disbursements	Repurchases		Disbursements	Repayments		Disbursements	Repayments	
2002	275,240,000	91,728,000	0	0	0	0	275,240,000	91,728,000	0
2001	309,650,000	1,375,920,000	369,498,855	0	0	0	309,650,000	1,375,920,000	369,498,855
2000	851,150,000	0	398,846,600	0	0	0	851,150,000	0	398,846.600
1999	1.011.000.000	0	267.539.445	0	0	0	1,011,000,000	0	267,539,445
1998	4,254,348,000	0	133,963.634	0	0	0	4,254,348,000	0	133,963,634
1997	2,201,472,000	0	0	0	0	0	2,201,472,000	0	0
1992	0	115,725,000	3,483,910	0	0	0	0	115,725,000	3,483,910
1991	0	231,450,000	22,770,767	0	0	0	0	231,450,000	22,770,767
1990	0	115,725,000	43,374,701	0	0	0	0	115,725,000	43,374,701
1989	0	0	39.938.336	0	0	0	0	0	39,938.336
1988	0	41,962,259	30,602,157	0	0	0	0	41,962,259	30,602,157
1987	462,900,000	0	16,778,898	0	0	0	462,900,000	0	16,778,898
1986	0	0	3,206,764	0	0	0	0	0	3,206,764
1985	0	379,500,000	19,179,361	0	0	0	0	379,500,000	19,179,361
1984	0	3,637,741	28,853,985	0	0	0	0	3,637,741	28,853,985

Chart 6.2b

Indonesia: Financial Position in the Fund

As of January 31, 2002

I. Membership Status: Joined: February 21, 1967; Article VIII

II. General Resources Account:	**SDR Million**	**%Quota**
Quota	2,079.30	100.00
Fund holdings of currency	9,369.03	450.59
Reserve position in Fund	145.48	7.00
Holdings Exchange Rate		

III. SDR Department:	**SDR Million**	**%Allocation**
Net cumulative allocation	238.96	100.00
Holdings	12.26	5.13

IV. Outstanding Purchases and Loans:	**SDR Million**	**%Quota**
Stand-by arrangements	2,201.47	105.88
Extended arrangements	5,233.74	251.71

V. Latest Financial Arrangements:

Type	Approval Date	Expiration Date	Amount Approved (SDR Million)	Amount Drawn (SDR Million)
EFF	Feb 04, 2000	Dec 31, 2003	3,638.00	1,436.04
EFF	Aug 25, 1998	Feb 04, 2000	5,383.10	3,797.70
Stand-by	Nov 05, 1997	Aug 25, 1998	8,338.24	3,669.12

VI. Projected Obligations to Fund Under the Repurchase Expectations Assumptions [1]

	Forthcoming				
	2002	2003	2004	2005	2006
Principal	1,742.80	979.30	678.10	774.80	923.90
Charges/Interest	192.80	151.30	130.00	110.00	87.20
Total	1,935.60	1,130.60	808.10	884.80	1,011.10

[1] Disbursements made after November 28, 2000 --with the exception of disbursements of emergency assistance and loans from the Poverty Reduction and Growth Facility-- are expected to be repaid on the expectations schedule. Countries may request the IMF Executive Board to make repayments according to the obligations schedule if their external payments position is not strong enough to meet the repayment expectations without undue hardship or risk. Please note : Repayments under the Supplemental Reserve Facility are scheduled to be repaid on the expectations schedule

Chart 6.3a

Malaysia: Transactions with the Fund

from January 01, 1984 To January 31, 2002

(in SDRs)

Year	General Resources Account			Structural Adjustment Facility/Trust Fund Enhanced Structural Adjustment Facility/Poverty Reduction and Growth Facility					
	GRA			SAF/PRGF/TF			Total		
	Purchases		Charges Paid	Loans		Interest Paid	Purchases and Loans		Charges and Interest Paid
	Disbursements	Repurchases		Disbursements	Repayments		Disbursements	Repayments	
1986	0	107,210,733	2,837,142	0	0	0	0	107,210,733	2,837,142
1985	0	155,646,081	16,212,882	0	0	0	0	155,646,081	16,212,882
1984	0	52,220,883	19,914,449	0	0	0	0	52,220,883	19,914,449

Chart 6.3b

Malaysia: Financial Position in the Fund

As of January 31, 2002

I. Membership Status: Joined: March 07, 1958; Article VIII

II. General Resources Account:	**SDR Million**	**%Quota**
Quota	1,486.60	100.00
Fund holdings of currency	878.45	59.09
Reserve position in Fund	608.16	40.91
Holdings Exchange Rate		

III. SDR Department:	**SDR Million**	**%Allocation**
Net cumulative allocation	139.05	100.00
Holdings	99.58	71.62

IV. Outstanding Purchases and Loans: None

V. Latest Financial Arrangements: None

VI. Projected Obligations to Fund: None

Chart 6.4a

Thailand: Transactions with the Fund from January 01, 1984 To January 31, 2002

(in SDRs)

Year	General Resources Account			Structural Adjustment Facility/Trust Fund Enhanced Structural Adjustment Facility/Poverty Reduction and Growth Facility					
	GRA			TF			Total		
	Purchases		Charges Paid	Loans		Interest Paid	Purchases and Loans		Charges and Interest Paid
	Disbursements	Repurchases		Disbursements	Repayments		Disbursements	Repayments	
2001	0	1,012,500,000	97,186,733	0	0	0	0	1,012,500,000	97,186,733
2000	0	150,000,000	127,406,361	0	0	0	0	150,000,000	127,406,361
1999	200,000,000	0	94,186,157	0	0	0	200,000,000	0	94,186,157
1998	500,000,000	0	89,207,423	0	0	0	500,000,000	0	89,207,423
1997	1.800,000,000	0	10,533,042	0	0	0	1,800,000,000	0	10,533,042
1991	0	0	0	0	505,955	617	0	505,955	617
1990	0	202,867,787	12,629,347	0	4,073,600	7,753	0	206,941,387	12,637,100
1989	0	271,390,850	36,477,810	0	13,266,000	48,756	0	284,656,850	36,526,566
1988	0	171,118,960	43,113,000	0	22,337,113	130,610	0	193,456,073	43,243,610
1987	0	162,528,445	51,841,785	0	26,089,112	250,292	0	188,617,557	52,092,077
1986	110,000,000	230,845,188	65,106,671	0	26,089,112	380,657	110,000,000	256,934,300	65,487,328
1985	335,000,000	213,475,757	70,848,768	0	22,015,512	505,981	335,000,000	235,491,269	71,354,749
1984	0	59,333,170	68,480,490	0	12,823,112	595,542	0	72,156,282	69,076,032

Chart 6.4b

Thailand: Financial Position in the Fund

As of January 31, 2002

I. Membership Status: Joined: May 03, 1949; Article VIII

II. General Resources Account:	**SDR Million**	**%Quota**
Quota	1,081.90	100.00
Fund holdings of currency	2,419.39	223.62
Reserve position in Fund	0.02	0.00
Holdings Exchange Rate		

III. SDR Department:	**SDR Million**	**%Allocation**
Net cumulative allocation	84.65	100.00
Holdings	4.19	4.95

IV. Outstanding Purchases and Loans:	**SDR Million**	**%Quota**
Stand-by arrangements	1,337.50	123.63

V. Latest Financial Arrangements:

Type	Approval Date	Expiration Date	Amount Approved (SDR Million)	Amount Drawn (SDR Million)
Stand-by	Aug 20, 1997	Jun 19, 2000	2,900.00	2,500.00
Stand-by	Jun 14, 1985	Dec 31, 1986	400.00	260.00
Stand-by	Nov 17, 1982	Dec 31, 1983	271.50	271.50

VI. Projected Obligations to Fund
Under the Repurchase Expectations Assumptions [1]

		Forthcoming			
	2002	2003	2004	2005	2006
Principal	1,050.00	237.50	50.00		
Charges/Interest	29.30	7.70	2.50	1.80	1.80
Total	1,079.30	245.20	52.50	1.80	1.80

[1] Disbursements made after November 28, 2000 --with the exception of disbursements of emergency assistance and loans from the Poverty Reduction and Growth Facility-- are expected to be repaid on the expectations schedule. Countries may request the IMF Executive Board to make repayments according to the obligations schedule if their external payments position is not strong enough to meet the repayment expectations without undue hardship or risk. Please note: Repayments under the Supplemental Reserve Facility are scheduled to be repaid on the expectations schedule

Chart 6.5

Financial Restructuring Measures Agreed upon with IMF

Thailand		Indonesia	
Measures	**Dates**	**Measures**	**Dates**
Suspension of 58 insolvent finance Companies	Aug-97	Closure of 16 insolvent banks; conditional liquidity support to others	Nov-97
Tightened loan classification and bank licensing rules	Nov-97	Placement of weak regional development banks under B1 supervision	Dec-97
Guidelines for assessment of owners, board members and managers of financial institutions	Dec-97	Establishment of Indonesia Bank Restructuring Agency (IBRA): external guarantees to all creditors and depositors of all locally incorported banks; compensation of small depositors of closed banks	Jan-98
Amendment of bankruptcy laws, stronger loan classification and provisioning rules to meet international standards by 2000.	Mar-98	Transfer of 54 week banks to IBRA; new loan classification and provisioning rules based on international standards	Feb-98
Preparation of restructuring and privatization plan for intervened banks, review of banking supervision laws.	Jun-98	Merger of two state-owned banks; legislation enabling state bank privitazation and removing limits on private ownership of banks; establishment of new asset resolution entity.	Aug-98
Memoranda of understanding with financial institutions on implementing stricter loan classifiction and provisioning rules	Aug-Spt-98	Portfolio, systems and financial review of IBRA and major non-IBRA banks by internationally recognized audit firms	Aug-98
Revision of Bankof Thailand laws; completion of amendments to foreclosure laws.	Oct-98	Preparation of restructuring plan for IBRA banks	Oct-98
Completion of disposal of assets of 56 (of 58 suspended) finance companies; new prudential regulations; stronger rules governing disclosure, auditing, and accounting practices; new deposit insurance scheme	Dec-98	introduction of deposit-insurance scheme	nd
Development of plans for privatizing institutions undergoing state intervention	nd		

Sources: Thailand's Letters of Indent to the IMF (25 November 1997 and 24 February 1998); Indonesia's Letters of

Intent to the IMF (15 Jan 1998 and 10 APR 1998)
nd = no date specified

Chart 6.6

Key Economic Variable of East Asian Economies

	Indonesia	Korea	Thailand	Philippines	Malaysia	Japan	China	Taiwan
Exchange Rate	Crawling Peg	Managed Float	Peg	Managed Float	Managed Float	Freely Floating	Peg	Managed Float
Significant accumulation of short-term foreign debt in relation to foreign exchange reserver	Yes	Yes	No	No	No	No	No	No
Significant real exchange rate appreciation 1996	Parial	No	Yes	Yes	Yes	No	No	No
Capital account liberalisation	Yes	Partial	Yes	Yes	Yes	Yes	No	Partial
Indequate prudential regulation	Yes	Yes	Yes	Partial	Partial	Yes	Yes	Partial
Current account deficit 1996	Moderate	Moderate	Large	Moderate	Moderate	No	No	No

Source:Gregory W Noble, "The Asian Financial Crisis & the Architechture of Global Finance"; Cambridge University Press, UK 2000

Chart 6.7

IMF Prescription/East Asian Dilemma

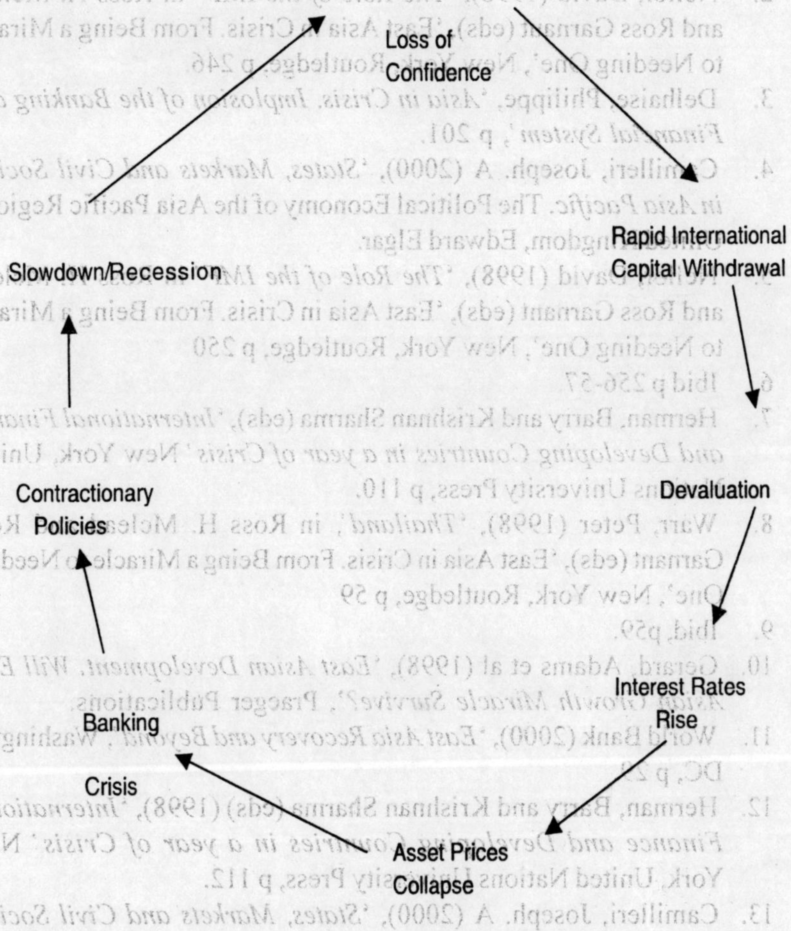

Loss of Confidence

Rapid International Capital Withdrawal

Devaluation

Interest Rates Rise

Asset Prices Collapse

Banking Crisis

Contractionary Policies

Slowdown/Recession

Source: Jomo K.S (ed), 'Tiger's in Trouble',Hong Kong,HK University Press.

References for Chapter 6

1. Krugman,Paul (1999) 'What Happened to Asia?', Time Asia.
2. Nellor, David (1998), '*The Role of the IMF*' in Ross H. Mclead and Ross Garnaut (eds), 'East Asia in Crisis. From Being a Miracle to Needing One', New York, Routledge, p 246.
3. Delhaise, Philippe, '*Asia in Crisis. Implosion of the Banking and Financial System*', p 201.
4. Camilleri, Joseph. A (2000), '*States, Markets and Civil Society in Asia Pacific*. The Political Economy of the Asia Pacific Region', United Kingdom, Edward Elgar.
5. Nellor, David (1998), '*The Role of the IMF*' in Ross H. Mclead and Ross Garnant (eds), 'East Asia in Crisis. From Being a Miracle to Needing One', New York, Routledge, p 250
6. Ibid p 256-57.
7. Herman, Barry and Krishnan Sharma (eds), '*International Finance and Developing Countries in a year of Crisis*' New York, United Nations University Press, p 110.
8. Warr, Peter (1998), '*Thailand*', in Ross H. Mclead and Ross Garnant (eds), 'East Asia in Crisis. From Being a Miracle to Needing One', New York, Routledge, p 59
9. Ibid, p59.
10. Gerard, Adams et al (1998), '*East Asian Development. Will East Asian Growth Miracle Survive?*', Praeger Publications.
11. World Bank (2000), '*East Asia Recovery and Beyond*', Washington DC, p 29.
12. Herman, Barry and Krishnan Sharma (eds) (1998), '*International Finance and Developing Countries in a year of Crisis*' New York, United Nations University Press, p 112.
13. Camilleri, Joseph. A (2000), '*States, Markets and Civil Society in Asia Pacific*. The Political Economy of the Asia Pacific Region', United Kingdom, Edward Elgar.
14. Harvie, Charles (2000), '*Indonesia: The Road from Economic and Social Collapse*', in Tran Van Hoa (ed), 'The Asian Crisis. The Cures, Their Effectiveness and the Prospects After', Great Britain, Macmillan Press, p 121.
15. Ibid, 125
16. Ibid,126

17. Nellor, David (1998), '*The Role of the IMF*' in Ross H. Mclead and Ross Garnant (eds), 'East Asia in Crisis. From Being a Miracle to Needing One', New York, Routledge, p 250
18. Far Eastern economic Review, *Mahathir Interview*, June 24, 1999.
19. Athukorala, Prema-Chandra (1998), '*Malaysia*', in Ross H. Mclead and Ross Garnant (eds), 'East Asia in Crisis. From Being a Miracle to Needing One', New York, Routledge, p 95.
20. Ibid, 97.
21. Ibid.
22. Cheong, Ong Hong (1999), '*Evolution of the Malaysian Financial System Beyond the Financial Crisis*', in Seiichi Masuyama (ed), 'East Asia's Financial System. Evolution and Crisis', Singapore, Institute of Southeast Asian Studies', p 159.
23. Huynth, Frank Hiep (2000), '*Malaysia: Current Problems and Prospects to 2010*', in Tran Van Hoa (ed), 'The Asian Crisis. The Cures, Their Effectiveness and the Prospects After', Great Britain, Macmillan Press, p 147.
24. World Bank (2000), '*East Asia Recovery and Beyond*', Washington DC, p 34.
25. Camilleri, Joseph. A (2000), '*States, Markets and Civil Society in Asia Pacific*. The Political Economy of the Asia Pacific Region', United Kingdom, Edward Elgar.
26. Economic Survey, February 25, 1999.
27. Martin Khor, Director of Third World Network on the Internet.
28. Godement, Francois (1999), '*The Downsizing of Asia*', New York, Routledge.
29. Camilleri, Joseph. A (2000), '*States, Markets and Civil Society in Asia Pacific*. The Political Economy of the Asia Pacific Region', United Kingdom, Edward Elgar.
30. Godement, Francois (1999), '*The Downsizing of Asia*', New York, Routledge, p82.
31. Ibid.
32. Hanke Steve, and Kurt Schuler (1994), '*Currency Boards for Developing Countries: A Handbook*', San Francisco, International Centre for Economic Growth Press.
33. Ghosh, D.N (1998), '*Currency Boards: Missionaries and Converts*', Economic and Political Weekly, March 7, p 498.

34. Mclead, Ross (1998), '*Indonesia*', in Ross H. Mclead and Ross Garnant (eds), 'East Asia in Crisis. From Being a Miracle to Needing One', New York, Routledge, p 47.
35. Phongpaichit, Pasuk and Chris Baker (2001), '*Thailand's Crisis. Neo Liberal Agenda and Local Reaction*', in Hajoon Chang et al (eds), 'Financial Liberalization and the Asian Crisis', Great Britain, Palgrave, p 89.
36. Ibid, 96.
37. Monti, Paola (2001), '*Financial Crisis and Reforms*', in B.N.Ghosh, 'Global Financial Crisis and Reforms. Causes and Caveats', New York, Routledge.
38. Ibid.
39. Eichengreen, Barry (2000), '*The IMF in the Wake of the Asian Crisis*' in Gregory Noble et al (eds), 'The Asian Financial Crisis', UK, Cambridge University Press, p 170.
40. Task Force (1998), '*Safeguarding Prosperity in a Global Financial System. The Future International Financial Architecture*', Institute For International Economics.
41. Islam, Azizul (1999), '*The Dynamics of Asian Economic Crisis and Selected Policy Implications*', in Barry Herman (ed), 'Global Financial Turmoil and Reform. A UN Perspective', New York, United Nations University Press.
42. Eichengreen, Barry (2000), '*The IMF in the Wake of the Asian Crisis*' in Gregory Noble et al (eds), 'The Asian Financial Crisis', UK, Cambridge University Press.
43. Goldstein, Morris (1998), '*The Asian Financial Crisis. Causes, Cures and Systemic Implications*', Washington DC, Institute for International Economics.
44. Choussudovsky, Michel (1998), '*G-7 Solution to Global Financial Crisis. A Marshal Plan For Creditors and Speculators*', Mumbai, Economic and Political Weekly, December 26, p 3309.
45. Sanger, David (1998), '*Wealthy Nations Back Plan to Speed Help to the Weak*', New York Times, October 31.
46. Herman, Barry and Barbara Stallings (1999), '*International Finance and the Developing Countries: Liberalisation, Crisis and the Reform Agenda*', in Barry Herman (ed), 'Global Financial Turmoil and Reform. A UN Perspective', New York, United Nations University Press, p 19.
47. Ibid, 19-20.

48. Goldstein, Morris (1998), '*The Asian Financial Crisis. Causes, Cures and Systemic Implications*', Washington DC, Institute for International Economics, p 45.
49. IMF (2000), '*IMF annual Report 2000*', Washington DC, p 37-47.
50. ADB (2000), Annual Report,1999,ADB Publications, Manila, Philippines.
51. IMF (2000), '*IMF annual Report 2000*', Washington DC, p 37-47.
52. ADB (1999), Annual Report,1999,ADB Publications, Manila, Philippines.

Chapter 7

Lessons For India

The development experience of Southeast Asia has certain lessons to offer that India and other developing nations cannot afford to ignore or overlook. The South Asian countries looked upon the Southeast Asian economic performance with envy till 1997 and had been prompted to emulate the same. However, in the post 1997 period there is a barely concealed sense of relief among South Asian policy makers and technocrats that their economies escaped the contagion and experienced no major turbulence. Notwithstanding the above, India and other such economies need to prepare themselves for the future and gear up to new challenges that liberalization and globalisation have thrown up.

The Indian Economic Scenario Since 1991

In the post independence era, India decisively followed an inward looking policy with a major role for the state. The growth rate termed as the Hindu growth rate was a pathetic 3.6 percent per annum during the 1950s, 3.1 percent per annum during the 1960s and 3.6 percent per annum during the 1970s. The 1980s saw an improvement in the same (5.7 percent per annum), but accompanied by large fiscal and current account deficits. These deficits reached unsustainable proportions by 1991 resulting in a major balance of payment crisis. This time round there was a change in the policy stance that the Indian policy makers adopted. The same was more in line with the international trend of being more liberal, open and pro-market. India adopted a New Economic Policy (NEP) wherein the industrial, trade, fiscal and monetary policies underwent a metamorphosis. As mentioned earlier all these policies became more open and liberal.

The GDP growth rate had plummeted to 0.8 percent in 1991. With the adoption of the NEP and assisted by a relatively stable political climate it rose to 5.3 percent by 1992 and averaged to around 7 percent between 1994-1996. The GDP growth rate was lower at 5.0 percent in 1997. This was mainly on account of the recession experienced worldwide.

The inflation rate was a matter of concern, which was as high as 13.1 percent in 1991. However, this was brought down gradually to 9.4 percent by 1996 and further to 8.3 percent by 1997. The fiscal deficit was 8.3 percent in 1990 and it was brought down to 5.2 percent by 1996. But, fiscal profligacy seems to have reasserted itself, as by 1997-1998, the fiscal deficit was 6.1 percent. The fiscal deficit (although cause for concern) is not alarming as care has been taken not to spill the same into a current account deficit via external borrowings as happened in 1990 [1].

The current account deficit in 1990 had increased to 3.2 percent but, ever since efforts have been made to keep it low at modest levels. By 1997-1998, ratio of current account deficits to GDP was 1.7 percent. The other external sector macro variables have also been favourable Export growth rate was about 15 percent between 1993-1995. However, since 1996 export growth has slowed down mainly due to lower export prices. The increase in net investible receipts helped in keeping current account deficit in control.

Why India Escaped the Crisis:

Joshi and Little (1994) identified four crisis episodes in India between the mid 1960s and early 1990s. All of them were balance of payment crisis (BOP) accompanied by inflation[2]. The first three (1965-1967, 1975-1976 and 1979-1981) were caused primarily due to adverse unanticipated exogenous shocks. The 1965-1967 period was affected by two bad harvests and unanticipated foreign aid problems; the second and third crisis was related to the two oil shocks. The fourth crisis was mainly policy induced though even this was triggered by an exogenous shock (the oil price hike due to the Gulf conflict). All these bop crisis resulted mainly on account of the inward looking policy followed by India. This policy not only discouraged non-essential imports but it also ensured that exports could not grow [3]. Thus India was beset with problems of low external reserves on the one hand and restricted capacity to finance any unexpected increase in imports or their prices on the other hand. In other words the economy was vulnerable to shocks whether domestic (drought) or foreign (oil price hike) resulting in a BOP crisis.

However, since 1991 with the change in the policy stance and the satisfactory growth rates that India had achieved when compared to historical standards it was less susceptible to a BOP crisis. The outward oriented policy reforms had to some extent cushioned the impact of external shocks. The question that remains to be answered is that although India was, by 1997 less vulnerable to a BOP crisis, was it also less vulnerable to a currency crisis? By virtue of the nature of the policies followed prior to 1991, India never experienced a currency crisis. But in the post 1991 period has India's vulnerability increased? Also it is essential to know why India escaped the crisis. These questions can be answered after examining for India the macroeconomic parameters that contributed to the crisis in Southeast Asia. The major contributors to the crisis in Southeast Asia were the high current account deficit, a pegged exchange rate arrangement, increasing inflow of portfolio investment vis-à-vis FDI, high short-term debt, financial sector weakness and decline in exports.

In India the *current account deficit* was less than about 2 percent of GDP over the period 1991-1998. As compared to the 8 percent in Indonesia and 10 percent in Malaysia, during 1995 and about 5 percent during 1990-1996 in Thailand, India's current account deficit is very modest. So at least as far as current account deficit is concerned, it was maintained within safe levels and kept India away from the crisis. However, it may be mentioned here that the ratio of current account deficit to GDP is low in India due to industrial recession, which had caused a slow down in non-oil imports. Moreover, in India consumer goods still constitute a part of the negative list.

Another important factor that insulated India from a currency crisis in 1997 was the fact that although the current account has been liberalised, the goal of *capital account convertibility* had not yet been achieved. The Tarapore Committee appointed to examine the issue of convertibility had recommended the same in May 1997 and that it be achieved in a phased manner over a three-year period. (The Asian crisis however put off this programme indefinitely.) Due to restrictions in the capital account large-scale capital transfers in short periods cannot take place in India. For example the Foreign Institutional Investors (FII) have invested more than 9 billion as portfolio investment in India, but these investments are not allowed to be hedged. Debt investments total less than a billion dollars and have only recently been allowed to be hedged. External corporate borrowings are controlled by the Ministry of Finance. Out flows by domestic residents are also not allowed – indeed any illegal foreign exchange transaction is considered a criminal offence[4].

The foreign exchange market operates only on the basis of the current account transactions with a number of small players and a few big players. The latter includes The State Bank of India, which is 55 percent owned by the Government of India. With hardly any players and foreign exchange dealers not being allowed to speculate even for a microsecond, the central bank is in complete control. Thus India was unlikely to be affected by the currency crisis in Southeast Asia.

This is exactly opposite to what prevailed in Southeast Asian countries particularly in Thailand and Indonesia. These countries pegged their currencies to the US dollar and liberalised their capital account. Banks could borrow freely abroad at a lower rate and lend in the home market at a higher rate, thus creating a currency arbitrage gains. Due to the *free-floating currency* and the control on capital accounts the same was not possible in India. Hence even the kind of currency switching that took place in Southeast Asia, with domestic residents dumping their own currency in a wild scramble for foreign currencies, was far less likely[5].

The insulation provided by the absence of full capital account convertibility is not always an insurance against a currency crisis. This is because capital controls are never completely effective and currency black markets always run parallel to controls. Moreover, the maturity profile of foreign debt is an important factor adding to vulnerability. If there is an excessive portfolio dependence on short-term debt or if portfolio investment is increasing, they can contribute to vulnerability.

The Table 7.2 shows that *portfolio to FDI* ratio was rather high at 6.25 in 1993-1994. But since then it has decreased and stood at 0.57 for 1997-1998. It may be mentioned here that this ratio was very high in Indonesia and Thailand. Since in the pre-crisis period this ratio was low in India it therefore helped India escape the crisis. India needs to be watchful of this indicator and has therefore to be careful that portfolio inflows do not increase excessively in proportion to FDI as the portfolio investments are volatile and can be reversed.

In fact, the Southeast Asian crisis itself could have caused the portfolio investment to move away from the crisis countries towards India. However, this unfortunately did not really happen as the stock market was down. Examining the share prices in dollars from December 1997 to June 1998, Indian stock industries lost out to several other clear winners among the emerging markets (China, Greece and Portugal) [6]. In fact, a vicious cycle operates here – portfolio investment is not forthcoming unless stock markets revive and the revival itself depends on increased portfolio investment. Table 7.3 stands testimony to the fact that even after the Asian crisis the FPI did not increase significantly in India, on the contrary the same has declined.

As mentioned earlier the other factor that can cause volatility is the quantity of short-term debt. As discussed in chapter five, the ratio of short-term debt to foreign exchange reserves (FER) was very high in Thailand and Indonesia. For India this ratio was less than 25 percent from 1993-1994 onwards and was well within safe limits through 1991-1998. Hence, due to the low short-term debt to FER ratio, India did not run the risk, of being destabilized by a speculative attack on the currency.

However, complacency in the above matter is definitely not right if one looks a little more deeply rather than just superficially. This is because in India, the large component of the foreign exchange reserves is the NRI deposits that constitute a volatile source. In 1997 the break up of the foreign exchange reserves were as follows: short-term debt was US$ 7.5 billion, FPI was about US$ 6.7 billion and NRI deposits were about US$ 10 billion. In other words about US$ 24 billion constituted volatile capital inflow out of the total stock of US$ 26 billion foreign exchange. Looked at in this light one can say that India narrowly missed undergoing a currency crisis and therefore must be vigilant in the future. However, as mentioned earlier due to the foreign exchange restrictions, transfers are not easy and therefore, till such restrictions are in place India's position is relatively safe.

Table 7.2 also shows that the debt service payments as a percentage of current receipts was 26.2 percent in 1994-1995 and this has decline to 24.3 percent in 1995-1996 and further to 19.5 percent in 1997-1998. Thus India does not face risk from this area.

As far as the *financial sector* is concerned there is a lot of improvement as a result of the reforms since 1991. According to the Reserve Bank of India there has been a reduction in gross non-performing assets (NPAs) as a proportion of advances to about 18 percent in 1996-1997. As is now well recognized rapid growth of credit to the private sector tends to lower the quality of bank loan portfolios, as more credit goes to poor quality projects and creditors, and actual NPAs may increase without being immediately brought to light. But the growth of bank credit to the private sector did not increase; in fact, it fell in 1996-1997 to 8.9 percent from 17.7 percent in the previous year.

The external liabilities of banks were at 2.8 percent of GDP in 1996-1997 and for non-bank private sector it was higher at 8.5 percent of GDP. The bank borrowings abroad though low, constituted US$ 10.1 billion i.e. 37.2 percent of foreign exchange reserves as of June 1998.

The Indian banks needs to be vigilant regarding the NPA and their external borrowing so that they do not have to undergo the kind of problems that occurred in Thailand and Indonesia due to a weak financial system.

As far as the share of goods *exports* in the total GDP of India is concerned, it has been very modest as India has never really been an export-oriented economy. This ratio was about 6.7 percent in 1991-1992 and peaked to 8-9 percent in 1995-1996 and declined marginally to 8.3 percent in 1998-1999 (Table 7.2). It is worth noting that growth rate of exports has declined from about 20 percent to about 2 percent between 1995-1996 and 1998-1999. Thus, although, as mentioned above India is not following an export-led growth like Southeast Asia, yet a continued decline in export does not portend well for the economy as a whole [7].

Impact of the Crisis

Although India managed to escape the crisis that hit the Southeast Asian countries, there was some impact felt of the same. Throughout the South Asian region despite growing worries particularly among exporters about the likely impact of the Asian currency depreciations on their competitiveness – the general response has been a cautious watchfulness, belied by occasional screaming headlines in the financial press with central banks closely monitoring developments in the currency markets and attempting to ensure that there is no sudden collapse in their currencies. The impact of the crisis was felt to some extent on the *Indian currency*, on the *stock market, exports* as well as on *capital inflows.* In fact the same will even have a bearing on the economic policies and reforms for the future.

Impact on Exchange Rate and Stock Index

One of the most visible reactions of the Southeast Asian crisis was a brief speculative attack on the currency. Dr Bimal Jalan's first statement on taking over as the RBI Governor regarding the Southeast Asian economic crisis and its possible fall out was "We will not go the Southeast Asian way as the economic fundamentals of our country is very strong."[8] These comments made in August 1997 unfortunately pushed the rupee down briefly, but it staged a quick recovery. Later in the year in December 1997, despite the RBI intervention the rupee slipped below Rs.40 to the US$ from Rs.35 mid year. In January 1998 the RBI implemented a series of measures to support the rupee including an interest surcharge of 30 percent on import finance, and a domestic interest rate increase, which stabilised the currency (see Table 7.4) .In other words the Indian Rupee which had been stable from much before January 1997 remained so till July 1997, at around Rs.35 per US$. But it fell by about 1.3 percent between July and October 1997 and by about 10 percent between July and December 1997.

The stock price index, which had increased between April 1997 and July 1997, started sliding after July 1997. It went down by 11.7 percent during July-October 1997. The decline over July-December 1997 was by as much as 15 percent. It may be mentioned here that though there was a fall in the stock markets as a fall out of the Asian crisis, the Indian Stock Market was going nowhere for the past seven years prior to the crisis (See Table 7.5). This was the case even after economic reforms were effected in 1991. It may also be mentioned that such reforms resulted in over regulation of the stock market in India. As part of its economic reforms the Government had set up the Securities and Exchange Board of India (SEBI) in 1993. Although this brought some good it also brought a lot of bad. For example some rules were anti-market and anti-performance. The largest mutual fund i.e. the Unit Trust of India is allowed to guarantee returns on an absolute basis. This is definitely anti-market.

Impact on Trade and Investment

The impact of the Asian crisis on trade and investment can ascertained in three ways, the direct negative impact on South Asian trade and investment due to the economic recession in the crisis affected economies; the competitive impact of devaluations by those countries in international markets and the indirect effects that arise from the impact on the global economy.

The direct effect on trade will be significant as 7.4 percent of India's exports and 6.6 percent of India's imports is linked to Southeast Asia (See table 7.6). Table 7.8 shows that India's exports to Thailand grew at high rates during 1993-1996. The rate of growth was as high as 52 percent in 1993-1994 and in two subsequent years it was 14 percent and 24 percent respectively. However, exports to Thailand had slowed down subsequently and the growth was 0.33 percent in 1996-1997 and became -19.33 percent in 1997-1998. The negative impact of the Southeast Asian crisis is even more obvious in the case of Indonesia and Malaysia as is evident from table 7.8. India's exports to Indonesia had a positive growth rate during 1993-1996 but the decline set in 1996-1997. Although the decline was a modest 5 percent initially it increased to a phenomenal 52 percent in 1998-1999. However, it may be mentioned here that the decline in India's exports was not solely on account of the Asian crisis since the decline had started even prior to the crisis. The crisis only aggravated the situation.

Since India competes globally with these countries in a range of products the enhanced competitiveness of the Southeast Asian exports (on account of the currency depreciation there) has affected the manufactured exports of India. The Indian rupee too depreciated in value, but not to the extent of the baht, the rupiah or the ringgit. In fact since 1998-99 imports into India from these economies have increased as these countries are offering very competitive prices and are pushing their products with fervour through various campaigns (See Table 7.8). Imports from Thailand have increased from 23.87 percent to 31.43 percent from 1997-98 to 1998-99. Similarly imports from Malaysia have increased from 18.52 percent to 50.78 percent for the same time period. A mention may be made here that not withstanding the economic and political turmoil in the Southeast Asian countries their exports had started looking up in 1998-99 as mentioned in Chapter six. It is only in the second half of the year 2000 that exports have declined and that too due to a worldwide recession. Hence the devaluation that occurred in Southeast Asia has given their exports a competitive edge over Indian exports.

Finally, the Southeast Asian crisis has had an adverse effect on the world economy on the whole. There has been a sharp decline in world real GDP growth rate from 3.2 percent in 1997 to 1.8 percent in 1999[9]. A slow down in the world GDP is manifest in the contraction of trade worldwide and this has created a negative impact on the exports of India. In other words to the extent that the global economy is negatively affected by the Asian crisis, the Indian economy is also affected. The slow down in the Indian exports is an indication of this negative impact.

As far as FDI is concerned, in principle there should be a decrease of investor funds from the crisis-affected economies to India. This has proved true in practice as well. During 1991-97 South Korea had emerged as the third largest source of FDI in India at 5 percent after USA and UK at 26 percent and 6.7 percent respectively. Combined FDI from the ASEAN5 amounted to nearly 6 percent of total FDI during 1994-97. As these economies are putting their house in order, the FDI to India has naturally decreased in the post crisis period. For example as can be seen from table 7.7 although FDI from Thailand to India was US$ 259 million in 1997, it reduced to US$ 3.45 million in 1998. A similar story is seen in the case of Indonesia and Malaysia too.

It may be mentioned here that the decline in FDI to India had other reasons too. A crucial factor that affects FDI flows to a country is the attitude towards foreign investment. The Dhabol fiasco and the 1998-99 budget with no specific measures to attract FDI have in large measures contributed to a fall in FDI. In fact foreign investors dissatisfaction with the recent Indian policies is reflected in the international credit agency, Moodys, pushing India into the special grade category by lowering its rating to Ba2 in June 1998; Standard & Poor lowered India's rating from BB+ to BB in October 1998[10].

Outlook for the Future:

The development experience of Southeast Asia has many important lessons to offer for the future development of India. As has been mentioned earlier till the 1970s the growth rate in India was between 3 percent to 3.5 percent per annum. It is only after liberalization and opening of the economy to some extent occurred since 1985 and with a great impetus since 1991 that growth rates started reaching 7 percent. The Southeast Asian economies with their open and liberal policies reached much higher levels of growth rates at an earlier point of time. This gives out a clear signal that liberalization has led to higher growth rates. Similarly, even the savings rate and investment in India has been low. For example savings rate was 25-26 percent while the same is 35-40 percent in the Southeast Asian countries. It would do well for India to spruce up its savings rates and investment rate so that the virtuous circle of high saving leading to high investment, which in turn leads to high growth can come into operation. The financial sector *per se* has not been able to mobilise/tap the available resources so as to push up the savings rate. Neither has the financial sector been able to tap the latent entrepreneurial talent to its optimal level so as to increase the investment rates.

India's budget deficit has been very high compared to Southeast Asian economies where budget surpluses are observed. It is an established fact that a low deficit results in lower inflation rates and higher growth. As discussed in Chapters 3 and 4, this has been a major factor in enhancing growth in Southeast Asia. So India should learn from the development experiences of these economies that it is worth the while to have low fiscal deficits, low inflation and high growth. In India the contrary is seen, high deficits, high inflation and relatively lower growth. However it may be mentioned here that there is a visible change towards a lower fiscal deficit in recent years.

Yet another worthwhile lesson India can learn from the pre crisis development experience is that export led growth is definitely beneficial. It may be noted here that it was quality goods along with competitive prices is what assisted the Southeast Asian region in enhancing their exports. Also they have been able to meet delivery schedules. To improve upon the quality, technology upgradation is necessary and to meet delivery schedules, a more professional attitude must be adopted.

The Asian crisis is a part of the development experience of the Southeast Asian economies and accordingly India can draw many inferences from the same so as to avoid such a situation in the future. The big lesson of the East Asian crisis and its aftermath for India and South Asia is the importance of following a path of fundamental and sustained reform, while paying due attention to their proper sequencing and timing[11]. Indian policy makers have to be continuously alert and appropriate adjustment have to be made at the right time. Any delay can prove costly. Deregulation need not be equated to a *laissez faire* system. Along with openness and liberalization of the economy there must exist a supervisory and regulatory role for the Government.

Symptoms of financial ailments do exist in India and hence India must exercise caution in this area. Financial and real sector liberalization must be preceded by and continuously supported by a sound financial structure. Thus a sound financial system and sound banking practices are *sine qua non* .In fact, the Asian financial crisis has sent this message worldwide and now a country's ability to attract investment from abroad depends on whether the banking standards practiced match up to international standards. As mentioned in the previous Chapter the Basle Core Principles have laid down 25 basic principles for adopting an effective supervision system and these may therefore be integrated into the financial system. At the micro level the banks and other financial institutions must be prudent in their lending activities and be able to assess the risk factor objectively. The currency and maturity mismatches that was an important contributor to the crisis should definitely be avoided. The borrowing and lending decisions must be made accordingly. The RBI has indicated from time to tome that it will not allow too much short-term cross border transactions.

The next lesson to be remembered by India is to keep the current account deficit under control. In fact a large current account deficit often encourages large borrowing especially for a short-term period. Moreover in India's case particularly since the exports cannot sustain a large deficit, the same must be constantly monitored. It must not be overlooked that a deceleration in exports among others was a primary cause of the crisis. Also the quantity of India's foreign exchange has to be adequate to support the current account deficit. As has been seen in the previous section exports have declined owing to various reasons and it follows that the level of forex will also be low. Hence India must be vigilant about this indicator.

The other important inference that India must draw from the Southeast Asian development experience is relating to the timing of capital account convertibility (CAC). India is certainly likely to heed the message from the East Asian crisis: that caution is needed in moving to capital account convertibility[12]. In the post crisis period it has been decided to postpone the CAC to a later time as against by the year 2000 as had been suggested by the Tarapore Committee Report. However this does not mean that India must never adopt a free capital account. The integration of the foreign exchange market and the money market require more sustainable foreign exchange reserves backed by a high growth rate of exports, and a strong financial sector. A premature freeing of the capital account can result in speculative and destabilising capital inflows. Hence till India's position is more secure it would do good to postpone the CAC, else it will have to pay with a currency crisis. However the sole objective of policy making cannot be avoiding of a crisis. As mentioned earlier it should just be sequenced properly to avoid costly turbulence.

Finally when India does adopt CAC, it must also simultaneously adopt a prudent exchange rate policy. As discussed in Chapter 5 a pegged exchange rate and a free capital account are incompatible. Thus it is better to have a free-floating exchange rate policy, whenever CAC is adopted. This can bring down the chances of a currency crisis risk.

A survey conducted by Surendra Yadav and P.K. Jain[13] to get an idea of the perception of Indian corporates on issues relating to the Southeast Asian crisis and the lessons to be learnt from it, is presented below:

- About 76 percent of the respondent felt that the biggest lesson to be learnt from the crisis is that India must increase its exports.

- The next important lesson was with regard to encouraging FDI inflows wherein 71 percent considered this necessary. Although they do not think that portfolio investment inflows should be discouraged altogether, they consider it important that the proportion of FDI to portfolio ratio should not become skewed.

- 68 percent of them felt that external commercial borrowings must be monitored continuously

- 53 percent of the respondents said that capital account convertibility should be deferred to at least a period of five years.

- 50 percent of the respondents considered a decrease in short term borrowings as very important, and

- 37 percent of the respondents emphasised the need to curtail speculation and currency arbitrage operations.

Conclusion:

There are a lot of positive and negative fall out of the development experience of Southeast Asia. India can learn a lot from both these. The savings and investment rate should be increase by mobilising the latent resources. It can concentrate on increasing exports and improving their quality as well as keeping to delivery schedules. The financial and real sector liberalization should be preceded by strong economic fundamentals and a mature financial sector. Finally CAC can be put off for the present.

Table 7.1

Key Economic Variables for India

	Average 1985-89	1990	1991	1992	1993	1994	1995	1996
GDP Growth (%)	6.1	5.4	0.8	5.3	6.2	7.8	7	7.5
CPI Inflation Rate (%)	7.8	13.7	13.1	8	8.6	9.5	10.1	9.4
Current Account Deficit as % of GDP	-2.2	-3.2	-0.4	-1.8	-0.5	-1.1	-1.8	-1
Fiscal Deficit as % of GDP	-8.4	-8.3	-5.9	-5.7	-7.4	-6.1	-5.4	-5.2
Total Debt as % of Exports	286.6	320.1	316	336	290.6	253.8	201.2	170.8
Total Debt as % of GNP	22.3	27.8	32.1	33.7	36.4	34.2	28.2	25.6
Short term Debt as % of Total Debt	10.4	10.2	8.3	7	3.9	4.2	5.4	7.5

Table 7.2

External Sector Indicators for India 1991-98

Sr.No.	Indicator	1991-92	1992-93	1993-94	1994-95	1995-96	1996-97	1997-98
1	Current Account Balance (percentage of GDP)	-0.3	-1.70	-0.4	-1	-1.6	-1.1	-1.6
2	Portfolio to FDI ratio	0.03	0.77	6.25	2.94	1.29	1.23	0.57
3	Goods Exported (percentage of GDP)	6.7	7.1	8.1	8.1	8.9	8.6	8.3
4	Growth of Exports (percentage)	-1.14	3.3	21.16	18.39	20.31	5.63	2.1
5	Short term Debt to Forex ratio (percentage)	76.7	64.5	18.8	16.9	23.2	25.5	17.2
6	Debt Service Payment as percentage of current receipts	30.2	27.5	25.6	26.2	24.5	21.2	19.5
7	Short term Debts as percentageof total debt	NA	NA	3.9	4.3	5.4	7.2	5.3

Source: Ministry of Finanace, Economic Survey 1998-99,Government of India, New Delhi, 1999,p 76-77

Table 7.3

Foreign Inflows ($ US bn)

	1990-91	1993-94	1994-95	1995-96	1996-97	1997-98	1998-99
FDI	0.1	0.6	1.3	2.14	2.82	3.55	2.46
Portfolio In	0.09	3.6	3.58	2.74	3.3	1.83	-0.06

Table 7.4
Exchange Rate and Sensex

	Jan-97	Apr-97	Jul-97	Oct-97	Dec-97
Exchange Rate	35.87	35.82	35.7	36.17	40.85
Sensex	NA	3841	4306	3803	3659

Table 7.5
Stock Market Index in US $

	1991	1992	1993	1994	1995	1996	1997a	1997	1998
Stock Market Index	116.6	142.3	166.6	177.5	125.4	121.9	168.3	134	108.1

Note: All figures are as of end December except 1997a which is June 30 1997 and 1998 which is June 30 1998
Source: O(x)us Research and Investments Database

Table 7.6
Direction of Trade,1995 (Share of Total Trade %)

	South Asia	Japan	China	NE Asia	SE Asia
Exports from India to	5	7	0.9	8.1	7.4
Exports by India to	0.5	6.5	2.4	3.9	6.6

Source: IMF Direction of Trade Statistics Year Book (1996-97)

Reference for Chapter 7

1. Bhalla, A.S and D.M. Nachane (2000), 'The Economic Impact of the Asian Crisis on India and China', in Gregory W. Noble and John Ravenhill (eds), 'The Asian Financial Crisis and the Architecture of Global Finance', UK, Cambridge University Press, p 240.
2. Jayasuria, Sisira (1998), 'India', in Ross Mclead et al (eds), 'East Asia in Crisis', London/New York, Routledge, p 133.
3. Ibid, p 134.
4. Bhalla, Surjit S (1999), 'Domestic Follies Investment Crisis: East Asian Lessons for India', in Karl D Jackson (ed), 'Asian Contagion: The Causes and Consequences of a Financial Crisis', Singapore, ISEAS, p 133.
5. Jayasuria, Sisira (1998), 'India', in Ross Mclead et al (eds), 'East Asia in Crisis', London/New York, Routledge, p 135.
6. Bhalla, A.S and D.M. Nachane (2000), 'The Economic Impact of the Asian Crisis on India and China', in Gregory W. Noble and John Ravenhill (eds), 'The Asian Financial Crisis and the Architecture of Global Finance', UK, Cambridge University Press, p 245.
7. Yadav, Surendra and P.K.Jain (2000), 'Economic Crisis in Southeast Asia', Delhi, Hindustan Publishing Corporation, p 86.
8. Sen Sunanda (1997), 'Southeast Asian Economic Turmoil: Implications for India', Analyst, p 37.
9. Yadav, Surendra and P.K.Jain (2000), 'Economic Crisis in Southeast Asia', Delhi, Hindustan Publishing Corporation.
10. Bhalla, A.S and D.M. Nachane (2000), 'The Economic Impact of the Asian Crisis on India and China', in Gregory W. Noble and John Ravenhill (eds), 'The Asian Financial Crisis and the Architecture of Global Finance', UK, Cambridge University Press, p 246.
11. Jayasuria, Sisira (1998), 'India', in Ross Mclead et al (eds), 'East Asia in Crisis', London/New York, Routledge, p 139.
12. Speech by Joseph Stiglitz in New Delhi on 19 May 1998,Business Line (20, May 1998).
13. Yadav, Surendra and P.K.Jain (2000), 'Economic Crisis in Southeast Asia', Delhi, Hindustan Publishing Corporation, p 97.

Chapter 8

Conclusions and Suggestions

The development experience of the Southeast Asian economies has been eventful and offers a panorama of lessons for other developing countries. From being 'miracle economies' in the early nineties they turned into 'debacle economies' by the end of the decade. While they rode the boom their economies were lauded and accolades were showered on them by none less than the international financial community. But once a crisis emerged they were criticised and their policy framework considered avoidable like the plague. The international financial institutions that praised their policies and had recommended the same to the rest of the developing world were also attacked and accused of making false claims.

The following are the conclusions that can be drawn on the basis of the analysis of the development experience of the ASEAN3. The suggestions wherever possible are incorporated after the respective conclusion.

- The Southeast Asian economies followed open and liberal economic policies since the mid 1980s.Such policies included, the maintenance of macroeconomic stability through low inflation and low budgetary deficit; giving the export sector a boost through appropriate policy measures; raising the savings and investment through an intensive exercise in resource mobilisation; the creation of a favourable environment for attracting FDI; and the pursuance of an industrial policy that increased the value addition to industry. The interplay of all these factors had a favourable effect on the GDP growth, which increased at an unprecedented rate much to the envy of the rest of the developing world.

- The WB and the IMF had advocated such policies both directly and indirectly. Directly they did so through the conditionalities they laid down when Indonesia and Thailand approached them for SAL/SAP.in the early 1980s. Malaysia did not require financial assistance but sought policy advice. Indirectly, these institutions advocated the economic policies followed by the ASEAN3 as 'growth creating' and being the panacea to all the economic ailments that developing countries suffered from. Such recommendation reassured the Southeast Asian economies that they are indeed on the right path.

- The achievements of the Southeast Asian economies during the decade of the mid 1980s to the mid 1990s was proof to the developing world that open and liberal economic policies are necessary for high growth. The endorsement of the same by the international financial community strengthened the belief.

- The foreign investors in Southeast Asia too were reassured of the profitability of their investment. They also reveled in the fact that in the event of any change in the situation, the IMF would come to the rescue of Southeast Asia as it had in the case of Mexico previously. In other words the IMF created the problem of moral hazard bailing out foreign investors in the event of an adversity.

- In the euphoria accompanying the miraculous growth of Southeast Asia the first signs of vulnerability that were emerging by 1995 were not taken much cognisance of. These were: (a) the burgeoning current account deficit due to the pegging of their currency to the US dollar that was appreciating, and, the decline in exports following a worldwide recession (b) changing composition of capital inflows wherein the more stable FDI was being replaced by the less stable portfolio investment and the volatile short-term inflows.

- In these economies the capital account was fully convertible. This along with other favourable policy measures caused an increase in the inflows. To sterilize the increase in inflows these economies used a tight money policy. Robert Mundell in his famous theory on the use of an appropriate policy mix has warned that a tight money policy becomes incompatible with a fixed (pegged) exchange rate regime. The pegged exchange rate regime and tight money policy increased inflows especially in the form of short-term investment.

- The financial sector exhibited weakness. There were currency mismatches and maturity mismatches. The banks had borrowed in foreign currency but had lent in domestic currency creating a currency mismatch. Again, the borrowing was for a short-term period while the lending was for a long-term period suggesting a maturity mismatch. Much of the collateral that the banking sector accepted for loans were real estate and equities whose prices are known to contained a large bubble element. When the growth in export sector started to decline an effort was made by the governments to defend the exchange rate through high interest rates. This created a pressure on the market and brought about a fall in property and share prices. This in turn had an adverse effect on the banks lending portfolio.

- These problems made the economies vulnerable and a speculative attack on their currencies ensued. All the weaknesses in the economy were exposed and what began as a currency crisis turned into a financial crisis.

- Financial liberalization that occurred after 1980 appears to play a significant role in explaining the high probability of crisis in the 1990s. In other words not only in Southeast Asia but also in other countries, a private lending boom caused by liberalisation precedes a financial crisis.

- The solutions offered by the IMF were inadequate to overcome the new problems thrown up by liberalisation since the 1990s. The IMF suggested standard austerity measures in the fiscal and monetary regime and further opening of the financial and trade sectors to combat the crisis. The contractionary measures suggested were not appropriate as in these countries the internal balances were well within manageable limits. These measures proved to exacerbate the crisis.
- The IMF was not solely to blame for the worsening of the economic situation. The political problems, corruption and capital cronyism were equally responsible. Market mechanism once initiated should not be interrupted through nepotism. Contracts should not be based on contacts. The emerging structure of markets should

be supervised and analysed so that an oligarchy structure of markets does not emerge.

- The IMF received severe criticism for its handling of the crisis from the international community. Giving in to these pressures and in the face of the worsening economic situation it retracted some of its oft- treaded paths. The fiscal and monetary austerity was reduced and allowances were made for a social safety net to soften the socio-economic impact of the crisis. This brought about an improvement in the economic scenario in these countries.

- The IMF must avoid giving blanket solutions to all economic problems. The situation must be assessed and solutions should be offered to befit the same. A fiscal and monetary austerity advise when these balances are within controllable limits can lead to widespread social unrest due to increase in unemployment, poverty and income inequality. Moreover there are certain problems unique to each nation, ' here are differences in their populations, geographical location and political climate and hence one standard solution cannot help in all the countries.

- The IMF was also accused of inducing a moral hazard problem by bailing out the foreign banks through the financial package it offered to the crisis prone countries. International investors had lent indiscriminately to these countries following tacit guarantees offered by the governments of these countries, which in turn were reassured of a financial package from the IMF.
- The developing countries must be prudent while undertaking structural adjustment and accruing high debts for the same. They should not treat the IMF as a lender of last resort. Indigenous efforts should be made to mobilise resources.

- Financial and real sector liberalization must be preceded by and continuously supported by a sound financial structure. Thus a sound financial system and sound banking practices are *sine qua non.* The Asian financial crisis has sent this message worldwide that now a country's ability to attract investment from abroad depends on whether the banking standards practiced match up to international standards or not.

- India was not affected by the contagion following the Asian economic crisis because the vulnerabily exhibited by the Southeast Asian economies prior to the crisis were not present in India. This however should not make the Indian economy too complacent or too cautious. The thin line separating caution and prudence must be firmly drawn.

- The big lesson of the Asian crisis and its aftermath for India and other developing countries is the importance of following a path of fundamental and sustained reform, while paying due attention to their proper sequencing and timing. The timing of capital account convertibility (CAC) should be postponed till the economy is fully matured.

- The sole objective of policy making cannot be avoiding of a crisis. In other words the crisis should not deter the developing countries from undertaking a liberalisation programme. The development experience of the Southeast Asian economies should indicate the steps to be taken and those to be avoided in order to achieve sustained growth.

- Following the Asian crisis the IMF has made efforts to strengthen the financial architecture. These include developing standards, principals and guidelines to improve the financial sector, increasing the transparency in the operation of the IMF vis-a-vis the developing countries.

- The developing countries must cooperate in implementing the prudential norms, maintaining capital adequacy ratios and supervisory standards in the financial sector. However, the IMF should not infringe on the sovereignty of the member-nations in policy making.

- The policy measures offered by the IMF along with a loan should enable the member-nations to generate resources to repay the loans rather than increase the indebtedness of these countries. The programme of structural adjustment should be so designed that the borrowing country should be able to pay back the loans without painful consequences.

Thus the Southeast Asian development experience and the role of the international financial institutions in the pre and post crisis period should not be ignored. They have rich lessons to offer to the developing countries and the international community in dealing with the former's problems. The policy options of the developing countries for the future should reflect the inferences drawn from the Southeast Asian experience and should be better prepared for the challenges thrown by liberalisation and globalisation.

Annexure A

Genesis of Structural Adjustment Loans

The ***International Monetary Fund*** began as a multilateral institution, which administered the global international monetary system. It presided over a specific system of rules relating to fixed exchange rate regimes, explicitly containing the macroeconomic policies of member governments.

Today the Fund has diversified and provides assistance for developing countries with underdeveloped policy making capability. It does so in 3 stages – it offers detailed advice on macroeconomic policy, second it provides lending to countries with adjustment difficulties, subject to conditionalities and thirdly during a debt crisis it is drawn into the management of the debt crisis. The IMF is the world's premier institution for research about, and analysis of macroeconomic policy, and for the provision of advice on macroeconomic adjustment policies. [1]

Most developing countries like Indonesia and Thailand found it convenient to avail a loan from the IMF during economic difficulties since –

(a) The international institution provides advice out of research done which national governments cannot afford,
(b) The financial resources are otherwise not available with these countries
(c) The fund not only provides financial resources and advice but also works in cohesion with the country to overcome its difficulties.

Traditionally the IMF's financial support was sought by countries facing imbalances in their external account and wish to tide over this difficulty. To correct a fundamental disequilibrium (a term coined by IMF itself to indicate a disequilibrium in the balance of payment for 5 years consecutively) the IMF made certain prescriptions along with financial assistance. These generally included devaluation to encourage exports and discourage imports, and fiscal and monetary tightening to bring about macroeconomic stability. The conditionalities have been a part of the IMF right from the initial days, but had not been rigorously enforced then. The entire application to macroeconomic management by the IMF was from the demand side.

The World Bank began as an institution for funnelling capital to the global periphery in the face of liquidity constrained capital markets[2]. It conducts research on development economics and on microeconomic development. In this it complements the IMF's advice on macroeconomics. The Bank generally funds infrasturctural projects like transport, power, irrigation etc. and participates in these projects right from the design, origin and their implementation. The Bank also advises on trade liberalization, mobilization of savings, pension schemes and designs of taxation, designs of foreign investment schemes and privatisation of inefficient state enterprises.

The argument as to why countries like Indonesia and Thailand seek Bank lending is similar to that in the case of the Fund. The Bank has the ability to monitor loans and projects and has a large research staff to provide development-improving strategies. Moreover, it is generally the experience that in the absence of Bank surveillance it may lead to an anti-development bias or alternatively rent seeking.

The member-nations approach the WB for long-term financial support. It assesses the viability of a project in terms of its capacity of repaying the loan with interest and offers loans on the basis of guarantees provided by the government. Hence, the WBs concerns are micro-project based lending. It urges the governments to get the prices right, to make the private sector the main player in the economic scenario and reduce the role of the state in the economy to the minimum.

However, both twins work in tandem with each other. This became more evident especially since 1986.These institutions worked then together with the borrowing countries to produce what is called the ***Policy Framework Paper*** (PFP) that forms the basis of their support programme. Polak has humourously quoted 'you twist their right arm and we will twist their left arm' to describe the strategy of the IMF-WB combine vis-à-vis the borrowing country. Though these two agencies normally deny operating cross conditionality, the manner of formulation and implementation of PFP suggests otherwise [3]. Moreover, generally it is seen that the stabilization package under the IMF umbrella is succeeded by the structural adjustment programme.

The World Bank introduced the ***StructuralAdjustment Programme*** (SAP) as a loan package in 1980 and IMF began offering ***Structural Adjustment Lending*** (SAL) from 1986. However, to understand the genesis of the same, a small flash back to the 1970s is needed. The 1970s saw two oil shocks on account of steep rise in oil prices. The LDCs, which were exporting oil benefited from the same while the non-OPEC LDCs, faced a severe BOP crisis. The only source of mitigation was the special IMF facility set up for compensatory and contingency purposes.

The OPEC nations flush with petro-dollars in the post first oil-shock period recycled them back to the West, more specifically to private international banks there. These international banks induced and offered high cost loans to LDCs in Africa and Latin America mainly. Since these loans were granted with minimum questions and less paper work, they were very popular.

However, the international banks started to realise that the excessive lending to LDCs were highly risky and they started to adopt a conservative attitude towards lending. During the same time period, there was a slump in the world demand for agricultural exports and their prices. Hence the LDCs were faced with a dual problem of having to repay debts and suffer disequilibrium in the BOP. Moreover during 1982 the Monetarist approach became popular (Regan-Thatcher regime) and hence interest rates went up on account of tighter monetary control. So higher interest rates accentuated the debt burden.

Mexico in August 1982 was first to declare bankruptcy and the debt crisis followed. At this time the IMF stepped in with loans tied to stabilization and structural conditionalities.

Model of the IMF Stabilisation Programme:

The stabilization programme of IMF and its conditionalities are based on a **Monetarist Approach** as given by **Milton Friedman and Polak**[4].

According to *Friedman* in the long run, society's resources determine growth of output and employment. The price level is simply the rate at which money can be exchanged for this output. Since the behaviour of prices over time is determined by the growth in the money stock relative to the growth in output, total spending and the rate of inflation are uniquely dependent on money supply. What is necessary as per this view is a long-term monetarist policy. Friedman true to his form suggests that fiscal solutions alone, without a monetary policy, will not work.

In the IMF stabilization programme based on *Polak's* model, heavy reliance is placed on the familiar quantity theory identity – National Income or output = Money Supply x Velocity of circulation of money

Here money supply is defined as domestic credit plus foreign exchange reserves. The balance of payment (BOP) consists of the balance of trade plus capital imports. Capital imports are independent of money stock and money incomes but the trade balance depends on income, through the propensity to import and not on expenditure. National income is determined by money stock, which depends on either domestic credit creation or forex reserves.

Therefore, if money supply is held constant, any growth in domestic credit will be offset by a reduction in forex reserves and this in turn will result in BOP deficit. This is because an increase in domestic credit raises the money stock and therefore money income, which leads to an increase in imports thereby reducing the international reserves and BOP deficit. In future rounds the deficit leads to a decrease in the money stock and hence money income, until the initial equilibrium is restored. ***The main point that emerges here is that BOP deficit can be corrected by controlling domestic credit expansion.***

Another aspect of the programme based on Polak's model is that there is perfect arbitrage in the international price level or exchange rate. In this situation, imbalances between aggregate demand and aggregate supply arises when the domestic rate of absorption is too high in relation to its income and wrong macroeconomic policies are being pursued. Where domestic prices are out of line with international prices, the overall competitiveness of the economy is reduced as also the efficiency of the allocative process. In this situation, adjustment of the exchange rate or devaluation becomes a remedy.

Model for World Bank Conditionalities:

The conditionalities imposed by the World Bank aim principally at reorienting the incentive structure in line with a market economy[5]. The three main components of World Bank conditionalities seek to achieve liberalization, privatisation and globalisation – the LPG Model.

***Liberalization*:** The central idea here is that economic management should be the job of the market. Interaction of demand and supply forces is what should determine prices of commodities, labour, capital, land or foreign exchange. When demand and supply forces are allowed to interact freely, there automatically results an optimal allocation and efficiency, thereby avoiding unnecessary social costs.

Thus state intervention in the form of controls, subsidies, selective protection – all of which could distort prices should be done away with. Also, certain controls (like licensing) lead to rent seeking and corruption. Doing away with such controls enables smooth working of the economy.

***Privatisation*:** As per this economic philosophy, public sector operation should be restricted to only natural monopolies and strategic industries. Therefore, if public sector operates outside this region, they should be phased out/trimmed down or passed on to the private sector. Privatisation of public enterprises would serve a dual purpose – improve their efficiency and secondly bring in resources for reducing the fiscal deficit.

***Globalisation*:** The rationale here is that more trade is better for all parties concerned. Therefore, all efforts must be made for allowing free flow of capital goods and services. In other words, tariffs, controls and restrictions should be dispensed with. Here, the Heckscher-Ohlin trade theory forms the basis. A country should specialize in and export such goods in which it has a comparative advantage, given its factor endowments. With such exports, it can pay for whatever imports it requires, rather than produce them indigenously. Most LDCs therefore should initially concentrate on labour intensive products such as food products and textiles as here they have a comparative advantage given large labour resources.

Washington Consensus (WC)

The conditionalities imposed by the IMF-WB are derived from the WC. John Williamson has coined this term. He chose to use such a term for two reasons – firstly, because the headquarters of both IMF and the WB is in Washington and secondly, because Washington is the capital of USA that has played a major role in the formulation of the WC.

The WC is a list of 11 elements focussed on macroeconomic stability, financial sector liberalization, privatisation and trade liberalization. The same are listed below[6]:

1. The most fundamental lesson is that long periods of the application of inwardly oriented import substitution industrialization

are harmful, even in countries, such as Brazil, or India, with very large domestic markets. A separation from the world market produces an inappropriate price structure, which generates misleading signals for the allocation of resources and as a result, misinvestment. Governments are sometimes tempted and sometimes forced to manipulate the internal price structure to the advantage of influential groups. The result is an overall economic loss. The world market does not provide simply "competition" which might stimulate innovation and development; it also provides the only reliable and effective guide to the appropriate distribution of scarce resources (and a much better one than could be given by any government planner). In addition, the turning of the internal terms of trade to the disadvantage of agriculture contributes to the growth of rural poverty and to the generation of extreme disparities of income and wealth. The consequences are socially and politically destabilising.

2. Links with the capital market affect the course of development. Industrialization or development that proceeds through a series of abrupt stops and starts as a result of changing conditions on international capital markets can carry harmful economic and political consequences. But capital movements are an essential part of the development process. There is a need to ensure that there are no substantial misallocations that might produce an abrupt reversal of confidence and a capital outflow. Again, the economically optimal outcome is best produced by letting a price system respond to market conditions. A code for capital liberalization might be a desirable successor to the existing IMF code, which requires a movement to current account convertibility (under Article VIII of the Articles).

3. There are times when it appears that the markets do not necessarily always "know best" (through governments acting on their own usually "know even less"). Major failures of coordination between countries can produce dramatic shifts in the pattern of capital movement. Steady and coordinated policies are required for capital allocation to be made in accordance with the appropriate judgment by the market of long-term development potential. States have to help the markets know best by pursuing consistent policies, through time as well as among countries.

4. The public sector is a major player in capital markets. It appears to offer potential investors the greatest security. But in an uncertain world such security has its disadvantages. State borrowing may be less appropriate as a means of facilitating market judgments than borrowing and investing through corporations and individuals. There are, then, a much larger number of judgments being made about the economic future, and there is scope for some to be right (succeed) and for others to fail. States may feel the temptation to steer against the judgment of the markets and then, if such steering does not prove effective, to impose capital controls. These controls are rarely watertight and have not, on the whole, been effective instruments in stopping or reversing capital flight.

5. In addition, large fiscal imbalances can be very destabilizing and contribute to a mismatch of national savings and investment. Balance of payments problems are often a consequence of excessive monetary creation for the purpose of financing fiscal deficits. But fiscal problems are often highly intractable, and can only be dealt with effectively within a wider framework of general structural reform.

6. Over-valued exchange rates, which are often presented as an effective way of subsidizing basic or necessary imports, or as an effective way of fighting inflation, and which are frequently supported by powerful and influential lobbies and interest groups, represent the equivalent of a tax on exports and frequently harm long-term development prospects.

7. Flexible exchange rates are not undesirable, and indeed often represent an ideal way of accommodating external shocks. On the other hand, highly volatile exchange rates, which are often the result of the pursuit of inconsistent policies, have a damaging effect on economic performance and are likely to intensify calls for the adoption of protectionism.

8. Monetary policy is best set by authorities which are as independent as possible of both the government (and associated

political pressures) and the financial and banking sector (and associated day-to-day market pressures). It may be desirable to anchor the autonomy of the central bank through legal provisions.

9. The process of economic growth everywhere – including in developing countries – can be profoundly affected by an inappropriate policy mix in the major industrial economies.

10. There is no separate economic truth that applies to developed or to developing countries.

11. It is necessary to ensure soundness of banking systems through strong prudential regulation and supervision, improved coordination, better assessment of credit risk, stringent capital requirements, timely disclosure of bank's financial conditions, action to prevent money laundering and improved management of banks (added in September 1996).

References

1. Vines, David (1999), '*Global Economic Institutions from the Southeast Asian Perspective*', in Colin Barlow (ed), 'Institutions and Economic Change in Southeast Asia', New York, Edward Elgar Publication Limited, p 151.
2. Ibid, p 155.
3. Dasgupta, Biplab (1998), '*Structural Adjustment, Global Trade and the New Political Economy of Development*', New Delhi, Vistar Publications, p 74.
4. Ibid.
5. Ibid.
6. James Harold, (1996), '*IMF and the International Order Since 1945*' in Uzan, Marc (ed), 'The Financial System Under Stress. An Architecture for the New World Order' London, Routledge, p 43.
7. Fernandez Jilberto, Alex, and Andre Mommen (1996), '*Liberalization in the Developing World. Institutional and Economic Changes in Latin America Africa and Asia*' London, Routledge, p 5.
8. Dasgupta, Biplab (1998), '*Structural Adjustment, Global Trade and the New Political Economy of Development*', New Delhi, Vistar Publications.

Annexure B

Empirical findings on crisis

Kaminsky and Reinhart in 1996 examined 71 BOP (debt) crisis and 25 banking crisis during the period 1970-95 (Pre Asian crisis period). They found that only 3 banking crisis were associated with 25 BOP crises during 1970-79. Sharply contrasting this situation is the one during 1980-95 when 22 banking crisis co- incided with 46 BOP crisis. ***In their view, financial liberalization that occurred after 1980 appears to play a significant role in explaining the high probability of a banking crisis preceded by a private lending boom.***

Another study conduced for the World Economic Outlook, May 1998, IMF, Washington; December 1998 also gives similar results. Here a group of 50 countries – 22 industrial and 31 developing – were taken to identify currency and banking crisis for the period 1975-97. An index of forex market pressure was constructed as a weighted average of monthly exchange rate changes and reserve changes. Occasions when the values of the index exceeded the threshold of 1.5 times the pooled standard deviation of the calculated index plus the pooled mean of the index, were classified as crisis. On the basis of this 158 currency crises and 54 banking crisis took place for all these countries. However, the point to be noted here is that the numbers of currency crisis were high in the mid 1970s and in the mid 1980s. In contrast, between 1987-97, the banking crises were more prevalent. Therefore, here too it suggested that ***the financial sector liberalization since the early1980s is associated with the high incidence of banking crisis***.

Chart 5.1 shows the starting dates of banking crisis since the 1980s and provides adequate evidence of the increase in incidence of the same.

The Southeast Asian economies liberalized their economies (domestic and external) on the suggestion of the IMF. One of the propositions of the WC suggests that countries should encourage current account convertibility and make careful progress towards inclined freedom of capital movements through efforts to promote stability and financial soundness. Another proposition also suggests that the countries should ensure the soundness of the banking system through strong prudential regulation and supervision, improved co-ordination, better assessment of credit risk, stringent capital requirement, timely disclosure of banks' financial conditions, action to prevent money laundering and improved management of banks. With hindsight it may be said that even though it was warned that financial liberalization and capital liberalization should be accompanied by a sound banking system, such warnings were ignored.

Bibliography

1. Akrasanee Narongchai et al (1991), *Thailand's Export led Growth: Retrospect and Prospects*, Bangkok, Thailand Development Research Institute (TDRI).

2. Ammar, Siamwall et al (1998), *Responding to the Thai Economic Crisis*, Bangkok, TDRI.

3. Amsden, Alice, (1989*), Asia's Next Gaint*, New York, Oxford University Press.

4. Ariff, Mohamed (1994), *External Trade*, in Jomo K.S., Malaysia's Economy in the Nineties, Kuala Lumpur, Pelanduk Publications.

5. Ariff, Mohamed et al (1998), *Malaysian Economic Outlook, 1998-99*, First Quarter 1998 Update, Kuala Lumpur, The Malaysian Institute of Economic Research.

6. Asian Development Bank, *Key Indicators of Developing Asian and Pacific Countries*, Hongkong, OUP, Various Issues.

7. Balasa, B. (1978), *Exports and Economic Growth Further Evidence*, Journal of Development Economics.

8. Bank Negara Malaysia (1997*), Annual Report 1997*.

9. Bank Negara Malaysia (1998), *Monthly Statistical Bulletin Various Issues.*

10. Bhattacharya et al (1988) *Trade and Industrial Policies in the Developing countries of East Asia.* World Bank discussion papers No. 27, Washington DC, World Bank.

11. Cady, John (1964), *Southeast Asia its Historical Development*, USA Mc Graw Hill.

12. Casserley, Dominic et al (1999), *Banking in Asia. The End of Entitlement,* Singapore, John Wiley and Sons (Asia)

13. Chng, Nancy (1977), *Questioning Development in Southeast Asia*, Singapore, Select Books Ltd.

14. Christie, Clive (1966*), A Modern History of Southeast Asia*, London, Taurus Academic Studies, IB Taurus Publication.

15. Cole, David. C, (1992), *Financial Development in Indonesia,* in Anne Booth, The Oil Boom and After, Singapore OUP.

16. Crone, Donald (1998), *Southeast Asia: A Year When High Ambition was Challenged,* Southeast Asian Affairs, Singapore, Institute of Southeast Asian Studies.

17. Dollar, David, (1992), *Outward Oriented Economies Really do Grow More Rapidly: Evidence from 95 LDC's*, 1976-85.

18. Encarnation, Dennis (1997), *Foreign Direct Investment. The Key to Asia's Economic Growth?* The Brookings Review.

19. Field, Graham, (1995), *Economic Growth and Political Change in Asia*, Great Britain, Macmillan Press.

20. Gan, W.B. (1987), *Macroeconomic Policy, Real Exchange Rate and International Competitiveness: The Malaysian Experience During the 1980's*, Kuala Lumpur, University of Malaya.

21. Goldstein, M. and Turner, P (1996), *Banking Crisis in Emerging Countries: Origin and Policy Options*, Basle, BIS.

22. Government of Malaysia (1993), *Mid-Term Review of Sixth Malaysia Plan, 1991-95*, Kuala Lumpur, PNMB.

23. Guillouet, Alain, *Booming Economies of Southeast Asia*, Singapore, Longman Singapore Publishers.

24. Gupta, Satyadev et al (1997), *Globalisation, Growth and Sustainability*, Massachussets, Kluwer Academic Publication.

25. Hill, Hall (1990), *Foreign Investment and East Asian Economic Development*, Asian Pacific Economic Literature.

26. Hill, Hall (1992), *Manufacturing Industry,* in Anne Booth, The Oil Boom and After, Singapore, OUP.

27. IBRD (1978), *Thailand: Towards a Development Strategy of Full Participation (* Report No. 2059-TH), Washington DC.

28. International Monetary Fund, Various Issues of *Direction of Trade Statistics,* Washington DC.

29. International Monetary Fund, Various Issues of *International Financial Statistics,* Washington DC.

30. Jayasuriya, K. (1998), *Authoritarian Liberalism, Governance and the Emergence of the Regulatory State in Post Crisis East Asia*, in Robinson et al (eds)

31. Jomo, K. S. (1990), *Growth and Structural Change in the Malaysian Economy*, London, Macmillan.

32. Jomo, K. S. (1997), *Southeast Asia's Misunderstood Miracle*, Boulder, West View Press.

33. Kruegger, A. (1978), *Liberalisation Attempts and Consequences, Cambridge*, Ballinger Publishing Company.

34. Krugman, P. (1989), *Differences in Income Elasticities in Real Exchange Rates*, European Economic Review.

35. Lateef, Sarwar, (1995), *The Evolving Role of The World Bank. Helping Meet the Challenge of Development,* Washington DC, WB.

36. Leipziger, D.M. and V. Thomas (1994), *Roots of East Asia's Success*, in Finance and Development, 31, IMF.

37. Letter of Development Policy (1982) No. MF.0304/4460, RE: Thailand Structural Adjustment Loan, from Mr. Sommai Hoontrakool, Minister of Finanace to Mr. A.W. Clausen, President of the World Bank, dated 4 Feb.

38. Letter of Development Policy (1982) No. MF.0304/4460, RE: Thailand Structural Adjustment Loan, from Mr. Sommai Hoontrakool, Minister of Finanace to Mr. A.W. Clausen, President of the World Bank, dated 7 Mar.

39. Loan Agreement (Structural Adjustment Loan) Between Kingdom of Thailand and IBRD, Loan No. 2097 TH, dated 15 Mar 1982.

40. Loan Agreement (Structural Adjustment Loan) Between Kingdom of Thailand and IBRD, Loan No. 2256 TH, dated 27 Apr 1983.

41. McLeod, R. (1994), *Indonesia Assessment 1994*, Singapore, ISEAS.

42. Ministry of Finance (1996), *Economic Report 1995-96*, Government of Malaysia.

43. Mohamed, Mahathir (1991), *Malaysia: The Way Forward*, Kuala Lumpur Centre for Economic Research, Malaysian Business Council.

44. Muscat, Robert. J (1994), *The Fifth Tiger. A Study of Thai Development Policy*, United Nations University Press.

45. Nagraj, S. and K.H. Lee (eds) (1991), *The Malaysian Economy Beyond 1990: International and Domestic Perspectives*, Kuala Lumpur, Malaysian Economic Association.

46. Nasution, Anwar (1983), *Financial Institutions and Policies in Indonesia,* Singapore, ISEAS.

47. Nasution, Anwar (1990), *Recent Deregulation of the Banking Sector in Indonesia,* in Jacques Pelkmans, Singapore, ISEAS.

48. Nelson J.M. (ed) (1990), *Economic Crisis and Policy Choice: The Politics of Adjustment in the Third World*, Princeton, Princeton University Press.

49. Nipon, Paoponsakorn et al (1997), *Thailand's Development Experience from the Economic System Perspective, in East Asian Development Experience: Economic System Approach and its Applicability,* Toru Yangihara, Tokyo, Institute of Developing Economies.

50. OECD, (1998*), Financial Market Trends*.

51. Page, J. (1994), *The East Asian Miracle: Building a Basis of Growth,* in Finance and Development, 31, IMF.

52. Parker, Stephen, (1998), *Southeast Asia's Struggle Through Crisis*, The Brookings Review.

53. Phongpaichit, P. and Baker, C. (1995), *Thailand: Economy and Politics,* Kuala Lumpur, Oxford University Press.

54. Phongpaichit, P. and Baker, C. (1998), *Thailand's Boom and Bust*, Chiang Mai, Silkworm Books.

55. Phongpaichit, P. and Baker, C. (1998), *The Political Economy of the Thai Crisis,* Journal of the Asia Pacific Economy, Volume 4 No. 1, Feb.

56. Radlet, Steven and Jeffrey Sachs (1998), *The East Asian Financial Crisis: Diagnosis, Remedies, Prospects*. Harvard Institute for International Development, 20 April.

57. Robinson, R. et al (eds) (1998), *From Miracle to Melt Down: The End of Asian Capitalism?* London, Routledge.

58. Schlosstein, Steven (1991), *The Dynamic Emergence of Indonesia, Thailand and Malaysia*, Chicago, Contemporary Books.

59. Stigletz, Joseph (1998), *The Role of International Financial Institutions in the Current Global Economy*, Addressed to the Chicago Council on Foreign Relations, 27 Feb.

60. The Economist (1998), Why Did East Asia Crash, Jan 10.

61. UN International Trade Database.

62. UNIDO, (1985), *Medium and Long Term Industrial Master Plan (1986-95), Executive Highlights*.

63. Uzan Marc, (1996), *The Financial System Under Stress. An Architecture for the New World Order*, London, Routledge.

64. Vatikiotis , Michael (1998), *Anatomy of Crisis*, Far Eastern Economic Review (May 21)

65. Vatikiotis, M. (1998), *No Safety Net*, Far Eastern Economic Review, 8 Oct 1998.

66. Warr, Peter (1992), *Exchange Rate Policy, Petroleum Prices, and the Balance of Payments,* in Anne Booth, The Oil Boom and After, Singapore OUP.

67. Watsaya, Limthammahisom (1997b), ASEAN at 30: *The End of the Economic Miracle?,* Bangkok Bank Monthly Review (Oct)

68. Wolf, Martin (1998), *Why Banks are Dangerous*, Financial Times 6 Jan.

69. World Bank (1992), *World Development Report* 1992, Washington DC.

70. Yokoyama, H. (ed) (1990), Malaysian Economic Policy and Political Change, Tokyo, Institute of Developing Economies.